NELSON

AT

NAPLES

NELSON
AT
NAPLES

Revolution and Retribution in 1799

JONATHAN NORTH

AMBERLEY

He who has any experience of mankind, will be cautious to whom he dedicates. I am under no apprehensions of that nature, when I inscribe this book to Evgenia and Alexander. And thank you Boswell.

First published 2018

Amberley Publishing
The Hill, Stroud
Gloucestershire, GL5 4EP

www.amberley-books.com

British Library Cataloguing in Publication Data.
A catalogue record for this book is available from the British Library.

ISBN 978 1 4456 7937 2 (hardback)
ISBN 978 1 4456 7938 9 (ebook)

Typesetting and Origination by Amberley Publishing.
Printed in the UK.

Contents

List of Maps and Illustrations   7

Preface   13

Overture   15

1   Rulers and Ruled: Naples and the Neapolitans   17

2   Revolutions: Naples in the 1790s   35

3   Rome: War and Defeat in 1798   43

4   Rebellion: Anarchy in the Capital   52

5   Republic: New Rulers   63

6   Ruffo: Royalists and Renegades   77

7   Reconquest: The Republic in Peril   87

8   Restoration: Naples Recaptured   102

9   Rancour: Nelson's Arrival   131

10   Retribution: Betrayal of the Republicans   155

11   Revenge: Consequences of Revolt   176

12   Rewards: Loyalty Repaid   200

13   The Controversy   207

Annex: The Capitulation   232

Bibliography   235

Endnotes   242

Index   282

List of Maps and Illustrations

The Kingdom of Naples in the 1790s
The Gulf of Naples
The city of Naples in 1800
Sketch of the siege of St Elmo

Plates are author's collection unless otherwise noted.

1   Portrait of Admiral Nelson in 1799
2   Nelson in 1800, a miniature
3   Emma Hamilton in 1800, a miniature
4   Emma Hamilton at Naples
5   Sir William Hamilton in happier times
6   King Ferdinand IV of Naples and Queen Maria Carolina
7   Giovanni Acton, the Neapolitan statesman, in his youth (Anne S. K. Brown Military Collection) and (7b) in later life
8   Cardinal Fabrizio Ruffo, commander of the Army of the Holy Faith
9   A view of Naples in 1800
10 The royal palace in Naples
11 The Uovo fort
12 The Nuovo fort
13 The St Elmo fort
14 General Championnet's army storms Naples in January 1799.
15 Championnet creates the Neapolitan republic.
16 Francesco Conforti, the republic's Minister of the Interior
17 Domenico Cirillo, botanist and president of the legislative commission
18 Pasquale Baffi, republican and professor of Greek, executed by the counter-revolution.

19 Ferdinando Pignatelli, an officer in the republic's army, was captured when St Elmo surrendered.
20 Francesco Mario Pagano, author of the republic's constitution
21 A Calabrian marksman (ASKB Military Collection)
22 Captain Edward Foote
23 Thomas Troubridge, Nelson's faithful subordinate (ASKB Military Collection)
24 Count Giuseppe di Thurn (ASKB Military Collection)
25 Charles Lock, a Nelson critic
26 Ruffo's Army enters Naples
27 St Anthony guides Ruffo's army into Naples
28 The siege of St Elmo by the royalists (British Library, London, UK © British Library Board. All Rights Reserved/Bridgeman Images)
29 The *Foudroyant* in the Nay of Naples (British Library, London, UK © British Library Board. All Rights Reserved/Bridgeman Images)
30 The tree of liberty is cut down as the British look on. (Private Collection, Photo © Bonhams, London, UK/Bridgeman Images)
31 Cognoscenti, a satirical print of Nelson and the Hamiltons

The Kingdom of Naples in the 1790s

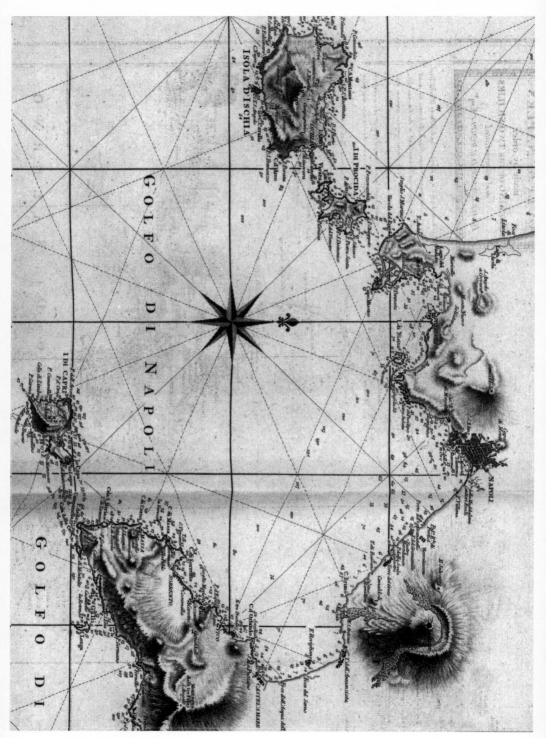

The Gulf of Naples

The city of Naples in 1800

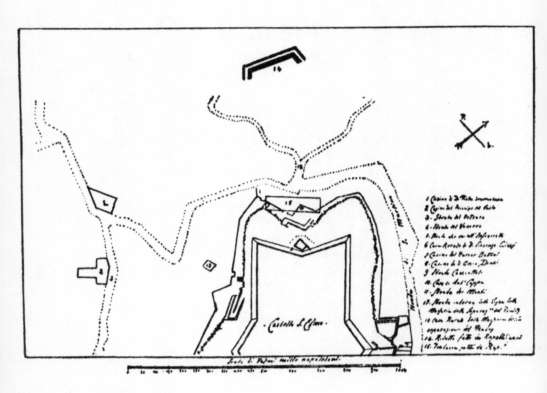

Rough sketch of the siege of St Elmo

Preface

Empires collapse, kingdoms fall, but republics are not immune from bloody ruin. Such was the case in Naples in 1799. During the wars that followed in the wake of the French Revolution, the armies of the French republic turned on Britain's last ally in Italy, the kingdom of Naples. The French chased out the Bourbon royal family and enabled the establishment of a brief republic in January 1799. It lasted six months before a counter-revolution led by a militant cleric, Cardinal Ruffo, overran the provinces and trapped the republicans in their capital. As the final battle began that June, those loyal to the republic sought shelter from the mob and retreated into the city's forts. Ruffo, keen to see the city spared further destruction, authorised an honourable surrender that granted the republicans safe transport into exile in France. The capitulation was signed and sealed. Shortly afterwards Horatio Nelson's fleet sailed into the bay. Bolstered by the support of Sir William and Lady Hamilton, and with the Bourbons now declaring that there would be no treating with rebels, Nelson declared that he would not permit the terms of surrender to be carried out. Then, apparently, he relented. As the republicans embarked for France Nelson struck, violating the treaty of surrender and seizing the would-be exiles in their transports. Hundreds of Neapolitans, having trusted to the inviolability of treaties, now found themselves delivered up to merciless victors and their vindictive courts.

Nelson's early biographer, Southey, would have it that the episode was 'a deplorable transaction, a stain on the memory of Nelson and upon the honour of England'. The question as to whether it was Nelson who might have put the perfidy into perfidious Albion continued to trouble the Victorians, who mostly sidestepped the charge by blaming Emma Hamilton, but events have posed a headache to Nelson's biographers ever since.

The aim of this book is to tell the wider story behind those events, and to attempt a sifting of the evidence both for and against Nelson's conduct that summer. This has involved examining material form a disparate range of sources, scattered from Syracuse to Monmouth and from St Petersburg to Naples. My view, after having looked at as much of the material as possible, is that Nelson did indeed commit a crime at Naples and was guilty of betraying the prisoners. Nelson should take the blame for such double-dealing, although Sir William Hamilton proved a reliable accomplice and Lady Emma a willing support. I have tried to concentrate on the drama but have devoted the last chapter to the controversy, setting out my reasoning and citing the evidence as appropriate. But more evidence, and the entire context and background to the events of June 1799, is found scattered through the book itself.

The project has consumed much time, and translating the material, drawn from half a dozen European languages, has also been demanding. Most translations, unless otherwise noted, are my own. I have made use of archival material but also tried to indicate where it is available in secondary sources so that those interested can more easily refer to the wider context.

I could not have achieved this task on my own. I would like to thank Carlo Knight for sending material on the Hamiltons in Naples, and I also owe a great deal to Steven H. Smith for providing me with countless texts (particularly on Russian involvement). Thanks must also go to James Cheevers at the US Naval Academy for access to the Zabriskie Collection; Barbara Orciuoli and staff at the Archivio di Stato di Napoli; Peter Harrington at the ASKB Military Collection at Brown University Library; staff at the Beinecke Rare Book and Manuscript Library at Yale; the National Library of Scotland; the National Maritime Museum; the British Library; the Warburg Institute; the London Library and the Archives of the Russian Fleet in St Petersburg (with thanks to Olga Chetverikova for translating Russian material). I would also like to thank Roy and Lesley Adkins for commenting on a draft of the last chapter. The participants at the Napoleon Series forum, in particular Eman Vovsi, Susan Howard and Tom Holmberg, have also provided considerable assistance over the years, as did the anonymous people who make the Bibliothèque Nationale de France's Gallica digital repository of rare texts possible.

In addition, I would like to thank Shaun Barrington, Nicola Embery and Jonathan Jackson at Amberley Publishing for coaxing the manuscript into life. Those who commented on that manuscript and who provided advice also deserve gratitude. However, I retain responsibility for any errors or lapses in continuity.

The process of research, translation and writing has been one which has lasted many years, something which has caused a physical and mental absence from family life. And for that I owe the greatest debt to Evgenia and Alexander for their forbearance.

Overture

On the afternoon of Thursday 29 August 1799 Nicola Fiani sat listening to the crowd roar as four of his fellow prisoners were put to death beneath his cell windows. After last rites, administered by Father Eustachio Dentice of the white-cloaked clergy of the Confraternity of the Bianchi della Giustizia, he too was then blindfolded and escorted out of the gates of the medieval Carmine fort on the edge of Naples. Surrounded by a troop of cavalrymen he was dragged along to the main market place, the Mercato, jostled at every step by an angry crowd. As he climbed the steps of the gallows, the mob jeered. His retort, 'I scoff at you, and your king' was almost lost as the masses howled back in derision.

The hangman, rejoicing in the name of Tommaso Paradiso, placed the noose around Fiani's neck and, to delighted cheers, pushed him into oblivion. The prisoner's body was left dangling whilst Paradiso removed the more expensive items of clothing in order to sell them. As he did so, the crowd surged forward. The mob's blood was up, their appetite for death unquenched despite this being the second month of such morbid spectacles, and mere riot had left them wanting. One of the confraternity present on the scaffold recorded what happened next as the crowd broke through the weak cordon of soldiers:

His body was left hanging, as he was not a Neapolitan, so that it could be buried the following day. However on that day the populace began by slashing at the body, shooting at it and swinging on it; they stripped it and then, with knives, began to cut it to pieces, so that only bones remained, and the populace went off, carrying bits of flesh on their knives, and were shouting and selling the flesh, saying 'who wishes to see the flesh and liver of a Jacobin', and were carrying the flesh around on the point of a pike and it so happened that they fried and ate the man's liver.[1]

15

Another witness, the conscientious diarist and doctor, Diomede Marinelli, confirms the account in his own shocked manner:

> I'll tell the truth, though it is unbelievable. Today a hanged man was left to hang. The people flung themselves on it leaving just the bones. He was cut to shreds by the carnivorous mob. He was roasted and eaten. His liver was cut out and cooked, and eaten in that same market place by those vile Sanfedistas. One of the mob who refused to eat was murdered.

The day after Nicola Fiani's execution, his brother, Onofrio, in prison with a broken arm and himself awaiting trial, was disturbed by the entry of a German soldier called Sebastian Gusler. The northerner threw down a bundle of torn rags, saying 'take these, they are what is left of your brother, he was killed at the Mercato yesterday'.[2]

Nicola Fiani's progress to the scaffold began ten years before, when the Bastille fell and revolutionary ideas swept into Italy. Fiani was an early adherent to the principles of liberty and equality and he, with many other sympathisers in Naples, hoped that reason and enlightenment would now triumph where ignorance and superstition still reigned. For a brief moment it seemed as though they might, the radicals seizing power and making a republic in January 1799. But the century of the philosophers, and the decade of hope, was destined to end with the year of the hangman.

Counter-revolution would triumph at Naples and Nicola Fiani, who had only played a small, undistinguished part in the Neapolitan republic, was on the losing side. When the royalists, with an army led by a cardinal and supported by Admiral Nelson and his fleet, swept back into Naples in June 1799, Fiani, with those still true to the republic, had surrendered on condition that they be allowed to go into exile in France. They evacuated their forts trusting to that capitulation. But Nelson, waiting for them to troop out, then dishonourably reneged on the treaty of surrender and eagerly handed them over to their Bourbon executioners. Fiani and his companions were betrayed by Nelson, and went to their deaths because Nelson tricked them. It was an act of duplicity which shocked Europe and cast a long shadow over Nelson's reputation.

This is the story of Fiani and his companions, and of Nelson and the forces of reaction, in that age of revolution and year of tragedy. It was a remarkable time, and such great events inevitably called for a remarkable cast of people. Some of them would finish swaying from the gallows, whilst, for others, their reputations alone would be left kicking in the wind, either to be honoured or to be torn to shreds by history.

1

Rulers and Ruled: Naples and the Neapolitans

Metternich would dismiss Italy as being 'nothing more than a geographic expression', a tangle of states weak enough to be derided by Europe's witty statesmen. This situation had endured for hundreds of years and, at the time of Metternich's birth in 1773, the peninsula was still being divided by the machinations of France, Spain and Austria. The north was kept fragmented and only in the south was there a relatively homogenous state. This was Naples, its two kingdoms, the island kingdom of Sicily (rather quaintly called Sicily this side of the lighthouse) and the mainland kingdom of Naples extending to the north of the eponymous city (Sicily beyond the lighthouse), united, rather like Scotland and England, under a shared monarch, in a sizable realm.

It was also a realm strategically placed to dominate the central Mediterranean, and those essential trade routes which crisscrossed the sea. This made the kingdom interesting to larger powers that were sensitive to the interconnection of trade and geopolitics, and their interest was in keeping Naples weak. For many decades, the Neapolitans had by and large obliged and if Italy was indeed a geographic expression, the kingdom of Naples was something of a disappointed sigh. The state's territories were ancient but the kingdom had only recently emerged from centuries of Spanish, and decades of Austrian, rule, and since independence it was, by common consent, poor and increasingly badly managed. Lack of money and incompetence did not, however, prevent the monarchy from harbouring some delusions of grandeur and, in an affectation of regional power status, the king also ruled half of Elba (as well as Piombino, Santo Stefano, Orbetello, Talamone and Porto Ercole on the Tuscan coast), had pretensions to Malta and, more in hope than in deed, also claimed to be King of Jerusalem.

The apparent stagnation of late 18th Century Naples was unfortunate as the kingdom had got off to an auspicious start when Charles (son of the King of Spain) had wrested it from the Austrians in June 1734 and steered an independent course, preventing the kingdom from resuming its status as a Spanish colony and granting it wide autonomy. Independence was ratified when, in 1759, Charles inherited the kingdom of Spain, renounced Naples and had the kingdom presented to his youngest son, the eight-year-old Ferdinand of Bourbon. This so-called Pragmatic Sanction simplified matters for Spain but heralded a period of mismanagement for Naples, made worse by the fact that Ferdinand was quite ill-suited to rule. Perhaps this is understandable. This dynastic development was, after all, accidental. Charles's oldest son, the Infante Felipe, who would normally have assumed the crown, was epileptic and, in the language of the time, had an 'incurable imbecility of the mind'. He was excluded from the succession in 1759 and bundled away to live out the remaining 18 years of his life in the backrooms of various Neapolitan palaces, spending his days eating, drinking and pursuing chambermaids. Smallpox killed him in 1777.[1]

So it was through dynastic and genetic chance that Naples and Sicily were now unified in the young person of Ferdinand IV of Naples (or Ferdinand III of Sicily). Ferdinand's father established a regency for his progeny, selecting Bernardo Tanucci, a Tuscan lawyer, to govern Naples and manage his son, and the Bishop of Avellana to act as the boy's conscience. Unfortunately, when it came to actually educating the new monarch, the boisterous Ferdinand was given the Prince of San Nicandro as a governor, a man avid for pursuing game, but less distinguished in the pursuit of knowledge. Ferdinand could not quite escape the slur that he too had an imbecility of the mind and the royal intellect was neither stretched by the constant talk of hunting and shooting, nor troubled by irksome duties of state. Duties which loyal Tanucci was happy to shoulder.

One duty could not be escaped. Marriage. Here, too, ubiquitous smallpox played a part in selecting his partner. It was hoped that Ferdinand would marry a spare Austrian princess. The redoubtable Empress Maria Teresa of Austria, staying true to the maxim *bella gerant alii, tu felix Austria nube* (let others wage war: you, happy Austria, marry), thought Archduchess Maria Johanna would suit. Tragically, she died of smallpox in December 1762. Maria Josepha was next to be offered up and was actually engaged to Ferdinand when she too was struck down by the same disease in October 1767. A final attempt led to agreement that Ferdinand would wed Maria Carolina. The pair married by proxy in April 1768, Maria Carolina was 15, Ferdinand a very young 17. The Austrian princess, torn from her favourite sister, Marie Antoinette, destined to be

France's most infamous queen, travelled to Naples that May to begin life as joint sovereign of Naples. Her mother, hinting at the imminent culture shock, gave her young daughter some parting advice:

> Do not be always talking about our country, or drawing comparisons between our customs and theirs. There is good and bad to be found in every country. In your heart and in the uprightness of your mind be a German; in all that is not important, though in nothing that is wrong, you must appear to be Neapolitan.

The queen would experience some cultural malaise but an altogether greater shock awaited her in the form of her new husband. Among a slew of disappointments, she thought her new husband crass and ugly.[2] Maria Carolina's brother, and Ferdinand's new brother-in-law, Joseph of Austria, sided defensively with his sister. He was critical of Ferdinand, laughing into his silk handkerchief, that

> His head is relatively small, surmounted by a forest of coffee-coloured hair, which he never powders, a nose which begins in his forehead and gradually swells in a straight line as far as his mouth, which is very large with a jutting lower lip, filled with fairly good but irregular teeth. The rest of his features, his low brow, pig's eyes, flat cheeks and long neck, are not remarkable.[3]

This distinctive and distinctively Bourbon face masked a childish personality:

> There was an unpolished simplicity, or rather a rude nature, in his manner, attitudes, deportment and conversation, which pleased for a double reason: on account of its own intrinsic claim to be liked, and as being rarely found on a throne, where we naturally expect disguise, artifice, and habits of concealment. ... He always reminded me of a rustic, elevated by fortune or accident, to a crown.[4]

Neither time nor age would alter Ferdinand's simplicity. In 1779 a visitor, Nathaniel Wraxall, heard from the British representative at the court Sir William Hamilton:

> No European Sovereign, without exception, said Sir William, has been so ill educated as the King of Naples. He is not even master of any language, except Italian, without making a painful effort; and his ordinary Italian is a Neapolitan dialect, such as the lowest of his

subjects, the Lazzaroni, speak in their intercourse with each other. It is true that he understands French, and converses in it when indispensable; but he rarely reads any French author, and still more rarely attempts to write in that language. All the correspondence that takes place between him and his Father, the King of Spain, is carried on in the common Neapolitan jargon. They write very frequently and largely to each other; but seldom does this intercourse embrace political subjects; their letters, of which I have seen numbers, being filled with accounts of the great quantity and variety of the game respectively killed by them, in which the great ambition of each Prince is to exceed the other.[5]

Ferdinand's simplicity masked a tendency to be cruel and vindictive if he didn't get his way. In 1800 Paget, who replaced Hamilton as ambassador, would write:

The King, whose real character has from circumstances shown itself during and since the revolution more than at any former period, is timid and bigoted and, as is often the case in the same disposition, cruel and revengeful.

Although many more deficiencies were apparent to the courtiers of Europe these did not prevent Ferdinand from being popular on the streets of Naples. Wraxall set down Hamilton's opinion that 'Ferdinand is greatly beloved by his people, who know, and who do justice, to his good intentions. He is even far more popular than the queen.'

This would not be difficult as the new queen failed to charm her expectant kingdom, and its king. It was clear that the couple were mismatched. Ferdinand, everything the queen wasn't, hated the ritual of court and was frustrated by etiquette and driven to tantrums should state business intrude on his pastimes. He let his favourite dogs foul the marbled floors of the palace at Caserta and delighted in butchering the animals he shot. There were plenty of them, for he shunned politics in favour of shooting deer and boar at point-blank range. Indeed, it seemed as though Ferdinand spent much of his time in pursuit of small, fugitive animals,[6] whilst in order to keep the state operative, his wife, Maria Carolina, would spend much of her life attempting to manage her large, fugitive husband.

Fortunately, she had a vast appetite for work, was intelligent and, much to the annoyance of her husband, bookish and fond of intellectual pursuits. At least her friends, the British, were a little in awe of this daughter of Maria Teresa:

The Queen of Naples, who was not quite twenty-seven years old at this time [1779], seemed much better fitted to represent the Majesty of the Throne, and to do the honours of a Court. Though not possessing beauty of face, nor loveliness of person, yet she was not absolutely deficient in either; and if her figure may not be esteemed too large, still it wanted neither grace, dignity, nor even attractions.[7]

Ferdinand, who seems to have suffered from an inferiority complex before the imperious Austrian clan, was soon at odds with his wife, known as Charlotte to her family, and complained repeatedly in his letters to his father in Spain that she was using temper and tantrums to force him to act against his will. For example in November 1776 he told his father that he was 'being persecuting to death by my wife' and that from now on he would be writing from the casino at San Leucio as she was insisting on seeing all his letters. Her adage that 'In order to make one's people happy ... unfortunately one has to frequently act like a despot and, when one does, one is not loved'[8] seems to have been applied domestically as well as in politics.

This attitude was unfortunate as Naples was not accustomed to despotism, and her outsider's frustration at the real failings of the Neapolitan system did little to enamour her to her new subjects. She soon met resistance and, in the face of it, tried to establish her own clique and so implement some of the ideas that her brothers were attempting to introduce in Hapsburg lands. However, this only became possible after the birth of her first son when, as per the agreement in the marriage contract, she was authorised to participate in meetings of the royal council. This auspicious event occurred in January 1775, when Prince Carlo was born. He was to be another victim of smallpox, dying in 1778, but the next in line, Francesco who became the Hereditary Prince on Carlo's death, was such a nonentity that the queen felt obliged to continue at the helm ever after.[9]

This was partly because she was ambitious for her new state, wishing to see it detach from the orbit of Spain and France and reposition itself politically as a satellite of Austria, with or without Ferdinand's consent. The queen outlined her plans to Denon, the French ambassador:

> It might cost me my kingdom, it might cost me every last drop of my blood, but I shall escape from dependency on the house of Bourbon. My brother shall never abandon me and he has told me that he has 40,000 Croats ready to serve under my orders.[10]

As an outsider facing hostility from the Neapolitan elite, she inevitably sought advice from the wider Hapsburg clan, and in the late 1770s, having finally ousted the bloated Tanucci, she asked her modernising brother Leopold, the Grand Duke of Tuscany, to send her some of his reformers.[11] Wanting to make Naples a regional power, the queen thought she needed a naval expert most and asked for one on 28 April 1778. John Francis Edward Acton[12] arrived that August. Acton was remarkably ambitious and would soon effectively monopolise state power and, through force, habit and the queen's close support,[13] dominate the king. The king seems to have suspected there was more to Acton and the queen's relationship than mere politics. Cacault, Denon's replacement as French ambassador, was writing in 1788 that,

> The animosity and scenes between the king and the queen are increasing in violence. The king suspects Monsieur Acton. His Majesty has angrily told the queen that 'I will surprise you when you are together. I will kill both of you and will have the bodies thrown out of the palace windows'.[14]

Acton would never be prime minister in name, as the queen had an aversion to such a title, thinking that to create such a minister 'would be to declare the king stupid, dumb, incapable of doing anything himself'. But through ministerial posts and as secretary of state he dominated the council of state. Sir John, as he was after 1791,[15] was the Neapolitan government and was handsomely rewarded for his pains receiving more than 60,000 Ducats a year, excluding gifts and bonuses.

His pains were considerable, there was much work to do. After all, Naples, weak in effective institutions, dogged by inertia, resembled a forgotten Spanish province rather than the modern, Mediterranean power Acton and the queen imagined it might be.

Acton, a naval man, began with the navy, as Neapolitan trade badly needed protecting and encouraging.[16] The French ship designer, Antoine Imbert, was hired and, from 1783, a series of 74-gun ships began to take shape in the renovated shipyards and arsenals dotted around Naples, particularly Castellammare and Procida. Whilst this was an impressive fleet, the expense was astronomical and finding sufficient officers and men to man the ships was problematic, indeed many officers were lured from abroad.[17]

As Minister of War, Acton's reform of the army followed a similar trajectory, but that institution was blessed by some fifty years of peace, and hollowed out by a complete lack of martial enthusiasm amongst the people. Their aversion was well known, Ferdinand remarking to General Filangeri, who had proposed modernising the uniforms of the troops, 'dress them as you will, they will still run away' (*Vestili come vuoi, fuggiranno sempre*).

Acton's attempts to reform were often superficial, and his race to bankrupt the state resented. His friends blamed factions or the labyrinthine nature of the Neapolitan state, but others, surly towards foreign influence, and especially resenting these Tuscan parvenus, took the view that Acton was simply acting beyond his competencies. This was certainly the case by the 1790s, when even the queen tired of Acton, complaining to one of her ministers, the polished Marquis of Gallo, in March 1797 that:

> Everything is in the hands of Acton, he forgets, prevaricates, confuses finances, plans, requests, justice, laws, war, money, expenses, systems, procedures, diplomacy, correspondence, etc, in short, everything. He can't cope, but won't give anything up, grows desperate, kills himself with work, but achieves nothing, and the Tower of Babel is complete.

The queen was not alone in her frustrations. By then Acton's power, combined with his evident overspending and palpable lack of improvement, weighed like a dead hand upon the state. But he still had allies and amongst them, unsurprisingly, were the British. More particularly that educated knight, the British representative in Naples, William Hamilton. Acton's policy of weaning Naples off the influence of Bourbon Spain and France found enthusiastic support in Britain and Hamilton was all too pleased to serve as the pivot on which their majesties swung towards Austria. The queen would later tell Hamilton *'c'est vous qui a de-Borbonisé le roi et notre cour'* and Hamilton, pleasing to the king and useful to the queen, was ever a court favourite.

Envoy Extraordinary[18] William Hamilton had kissed King George III's hand on 13 July 1764 and was sent off to the Kingdom of the Two Sicilies. Hamilton was a fourth son and so was without his own means, despite being foster brother to the king, but his marriage to the asthmatic Catherine Barlow in 1758 had landed him an income of nearly £8,000 per annum. His appointment to the politically undemanding post at Naples allowed him and his musical wife free rein to indulge their taste for the arts, and Hamilton had money enough for his other passion – collecting.

Before long the well-positioned Hamilton had accumulated an impressive collection of valuable artefacts in his properties in Naples.[19] When not writing scholarly works he hosted similarly minded visitors and acted as an informant,[20] and middleman, for other collectors. He also found time to source vases and decorative pieces for visitors and clients or commissioned James Clark, his assistant, to keep such clients happy, being paid a finder's fee for his expertise. However, in 1782 the entrepreneur of erudition experienced tragedy when his wife Catherine died 'of a violent fever of the putrid kind'. 'The happiest tempered man in the world' was plunged into despair and in November he wrote to his niece, Mary, that,

> I have nothing for it but to drive away thought as much as I can and indeed His Majesty is so good as to assist me greatly in that respect, for he takes me out a shooting every day and says he will do so as long as the shooting season continues, to day above 70 wild boars have fallen ... The Queen of Naples is also very kind to me and often sends for me to pass the evening with her and the Prince Royal. The present distractions and the healing hand of time will, I hope, recover my spirits in some degree, but I must for ever sensibly feel the loss of the most amiable, the most gentle and virtuous companion that ever man was blessed with.[21]

In August 1783 Hamilton travelled to Wales with the embalmed body of his wife and also spent some time in the equally lively company of his nephew Charles Greville. The son of Earl Brooke of Warwick Castle, but not a wealthy man, Greville was a fastidious bachelor, despite his penchant for street girls, and a solemn and serious man. His redeeming feature, in the eyes of his distinguished uncle, was that he too was keen on the acquisition of beautiful works of art. Whilst visiting London Hamilton put his affairs in order, made a will (preferring Charles Greville) and then sold Correggio's *Venus*. During this extended stay he also encountered Greville's own Venus, or Hebe Vestina, Emma Hart, then Greville's mistress, at Edgware Row.

Hart was born in Cheshire in April 1765 and was initially known as Amy Lyon. She moved to London when she was 12, serving as a maid, but had fallen into the hands of Mrs Charlotte Kelly, a procuress, by 1778. Kelly, operating out of Duke Street, ensured that loss of virginity, and the virginity of loss, was over quickly; however, soliciting in Bagnigge Wells proved less interesting for Hart than posing as Hebe Vestina on Dr Graham's magnetic-electrical celestial bed[22] at the notorious Temple of Health. Sir Harry Fetherstonhaugh removed her from that place of worship and took her to Sussex in 1781, but that isolated usage would end in tears, and pregnancy, and the wilful girl, now calling herself Emily Hart, turned to another willing protector, Charles Greville. By mid-1782 Emily, now calling herself Emma, had settled into a house in Edgware Row with her mother, who had appropriated a respectable persona and was known as Mrs Cadogan. All went well until Greville, perhaps thinking 'it is a sad thing if a rich man has no heir to his property',[23] began to plan how he might acquire a substantial marriage settlement and baulked at keeping expensive Emma and Emma's infant daughter. Hamilton arrived at the moment of crisis and Greville gamely offered Emma to his uncle who, despite the charms on offer, initially demurred, concerned he was too old for the youthful model. Indeed, in an honest passage that can only be seen as ironic given the events of 1799, replied 'It would be fine fun for the young English Travellers to endeavour to cuckold the old Gentleman the Ambassador, and whether they succeeded or not would surely give me uneasiness'.[24]

Before long temptation won out over solitude and Hamilton agreed to take Emma off Greville's hands. Emma travelled out to Naples in 1786, staying, with her mother, at the three-storied Villa Sessa. When she realised she had been traded, she lambasted Greville, telling him 'If I was with you, I would murder you and myself boath'[25] but a generous allowance, some £200 a year for clothes alone, and Sir William's solicitude, eased the pain. The barbs of the visiting British aristocrats, who found the match hysterical, were still painful, however. The antiques dealer James Byres, for instance, was not above noting,

> Our friend Sir William is well. He has lately got a piece of modernity from England which I am afraid will fatigue and exhaust him more than all the volcanoes and antiquities in the kingdom of Naples.[26]

Fortunately, Emma was soon diverting some of the politer guests with her artistry, notably her increasingly famous attitudes which, in an age of sense and sensibility, mesmerised select audiences. Goethe described one such performance a year after Emma's arrival:

> an English girl of twenty with a beautiful face and perfect figure. He has had a Greek costume made for her which becomes her extremely. Dressed in this, she lets down her hair and, with a few shawls, gives so much variety to her poses, gestures, expressions, etc., that the spectator can hardly believe his eyes. He sees what thousands of artists would have liked to express realized before him in movements and surprising transformations – standing, kneeling, sitting, reclining, serious, sad, playful, ecstatic, contrite, alluring, threatening, anxious, one pose follows another without a break. She knows how to arrange the folds of her veil to match each mood, and has a hundred ways of turning it into a head-dress.[27]

This present dubious state as Hamilton's mistress was mercifully short, and the couple married in London in 1791, returning to the social whirl of Naples shortly after. Marriage lent Lady Hamilton nobility, gave her a title, and allowed access to the court where an increasingly friendly Maria Carolina welcomed her. Swapping the stews of London for the marble halls of Caserta inevitably went to Emma's head and she was soon declaring 'the queen is like a mother to me', and showing her 'all sorts of kind and affectionate attentions'. Her husband, who should have known that the queen had been an arch-intriguer since she had been an archduchess, and wanted to keep Emma close to keep Britain closer, would write glowingly that 'the queen is quite fond of her and has taken her under his protection'. Thomas Francis Freemantle, sent into Naples on the *Inconstant* in June 1794, also hinted that she also enjoyed the king's favour

> I do not know whether you saw her when she was in England. I confess she is not to my taste, much too large and masculine, and little the manner of a woman of fashion. ... The scandal of the place is that His Majesty has shown some degree of kindness for the lady, but I do not hear of any harm.

Whilst Naples followed the royal lead, and some of the waves of British visitors were 'remarkably civil' to the new lady, most of the Grand Tourists enjoyed indulging themselves in some degree of harm:

> Lord Bristol is full of wit and pleasantry. He is a great admirer of Lady Hamilton, and conjured Sr. W. to allow him to call her Emma. That he should admire her beauty and her wonderful attitudes is not singular, but that he should like her society certainly is, as it is impossible to go beyond her in vulgarity and coarseness.[28]

Even belittling her famous attitudes:

> Just as she was lying down, with her head reclined upon an Etruscan vase to represent a water-nymph, she exclaimed in her provincial dialect: 'Don't be afeard, Sr William, I'll not crack your joug'.[29]

One of the most hostile in attitude was Charles Lock, who, when appointed as consul in Naples in 1799, entertained some hope of replacing Sir William at court. He wrote in June of that year lambasting that 'superficial, grasping and vulgar-minded woman' who wished 'to retain her husband in a situation his age and disinclination render him unfit for'.[30] Lock became an unflinching foe of the Hamiltons and of another visitor to Naples, Nelson.

Nelson, in contrast to Lock, was an early and significant admirer of Lady Hamilton. He visited Naples in September 1793 as the young captain of the *Agamemnon*, and, a little in awe of everyone, wrote home that Sir William and Lady Hamilton had visited his ship and that 'Lady Hamilton has been wonderfully kind and good to Josiah.[31] She is a young woman of amiable manners and who does honour to the station to which she is raised.'[32] Nelson, for all he fell for the Hamiltons, was less impressed with Naples, later writing to Earl of St Vincent 'I am very unwell, and the miserable conduct of this Court is not likely to cool my irritable temper. It is a country of fiddlers and poets, whores and scoundrels.'[33]

There were indeed fiddlers at the glorious San Carlo theatre, and there were certainly tarts in the strada dell'Imbrecciata, but there were also 400,000 other inhabitants in the capital alone. The kingdom boasted some five million people (Italy had 18 million people) and the city of Naples was, by 1789, the third largest in Europe and easily the biggest in Italy. The capital stretched from the burning fields of Pozzuoli to the cool arcades of Portici and was teeming with inhabitants going about their business or idling in the hot languid streets. A French visitor attempted a scientific analysis of who was doing what:

> There were 500,000 people in the city and its suburbs. Included in this were 36,000 priests, monks or clerics, 50,000 servants, 10,000 nobles, 20,000 lawyers or notaries, 6,000 fishermen or sailors, 300 important merchants and 6,000 lesser ones, 20,000 labourers, 2,000 doctors or surgeons, 4,000 employees of the customs, 6,000 soldiers, women and the lazzaroni.

This crude census simplified a reality in which the number of inhabitants was in a constant state of flux, varying according to season, and fortune; more worrying was that the population had doubled since 1707, increasing the burden on authorities already stretched by the existing inhabitants. Most of the newcomers were economic migrants from the rest of the kingdom and they soon found themselves close neighbours to penury, swapping familiar desperation for the uncertainties of life in an enormous and badly-governed metropolis. In addition to overcrowding and unsanitary conditions, with spasmodic cholera epidemics plaguing the city, regular shortages of food, as in 1793, and related sharp rises in prices, hounded this urban population and fuelled discontent and unrest.

For a state which resembled that of a creaking provincial government it proved difficult to prevent such upheavals, or push reforms through a byzantine administration to ameliorate the consequences of misrule. In any case, administration was, at best, a questionable concept in Naples. There was no parliament, and any authority within the capital was rendered hollow by privilege and corruption, the latter safeguarded by confusion as to who was responsible for what. The city itself was divided into five piazze (Porto, Portanova, Capuana, Montagna and Nido) plus the city's piazza del popolo, Montesanto. A complication occurred in 1779 when the city was reformed into 12 quarters but, in a typically Bourbon fudge, this did not entirely sweep away the old system. To complicate matters further most inhabitants identified their district by referring to the parish name and most streets remained unnamed and unnumbered until 1792.

The idea behind these attempts at reform was to improve urban policing. Such drives for law and order were necessary in a society where there was such animosity between all the classes and where the government was absent or, where present, universally held in contempt. Law enforcers had to navigate a complex and overlapping system of justice in which exemption, sanctuary, conflicting jurisdiction and bribery usually ensured that the well-connected evaded punishment, although a less privileged suspect could also do this by simply running off into the network of more than 1,315 intermittently illuminated streets and dark alleyways. The traditional approach to curbing crime had seemingly been taken directly from the Roman maxim of bread and circuses, transcribed into *farina, feste, forca* (flour, festivals and the gallows). Although there were countless processions to celebrate the lives of saints or miracles, the most dramatic manifestation of when flour met festival was in the *cuccagna* which took place on the largo del castello and in which, following a cannon shot fired from the Nuovo fort, a horde fell on a lavishly-prepared mountain of food.[34]

All this meant that the capital was notorious for being disorderly, and crime, noise and beggary competed for the visitors' attention. It was a place of theatricality and of contrasts, where the dirt and squalor of the city was gilded by luxury and ostentation. Where an excess of religion and piety mingled with ubiquitous criminality and brutality, enabling a sharp-eyed Frenchman to remark that, 'the Neapolitan is a superstitious individual with one of his hands clutching a holy relic to his heart and with his other in someone else's pocket'.

There were plenty of holy relics to choose from, and no shortage of clergy to watch over them. Estimates put the number at around 35,000 in the city and 73,000 in the entire kingdom in 1786. There were some 58 holy orders, and the Capuchins alone had 3,600 monks. In Naples itself Gasparo Soderini claimed that there were 43 parishes containing more than 300 religious houses, seven hospitals (staffed by the clergy) three conservatories and numerous pious foundations 'apt rather to put on celebrations than to communicate true religion to the people. This can be proved by the presence of thousands of men such as one could find in deserts, both in terms of their religion and of their use of reason.' This formidable religious and unreasonable system was led by a grand hierarchy, which in 1792 consisted of 110 bishops, 21 archbishops (appointed by the Crown) and 55 absent bishops, mostly in the neighbouring Papal States. Managing this state within a state was initially too much for the young kingdom, although in 1767 the Crown successfully expelled the Jesuits and seized their property.[35] Shortly afterwards the king's ministers moved against the pope's rights over nominations and revenue, again winning this limited struggle by merely promising, in return, to honour the pope with a fixed stipend every year, a pill sweetened by the annual gift of a white horse which was trained to kneel before his Holiness. The Crown was content to leave it at that. The clergy relaxed back into bloated laxity whilst those reformers who had hoped to diminish the power of the bishops, and for the dissolution of surplus monasteries, now found themselves disappointed as the establishment again closed ranks.

Another pampered class consisted of the nobility, whether of the cloak or of the sword. These inhabited the splendid palaces which lined the Via Toledo or Via Pontenuovo, where Dr Cirillo had his botanic library, or in Chiaja along the waterfront. To support this nobility there were, reportedly, 15,000 carriages, and at least 45,000 people received modest wages as domestic servants. Aristocratic prestige was propped up by immense wealth drawn from huge estates or trade as there was little industry to speak of. In contrast, the position of the city's bourgeoisie, its professional and propertied class, was still precarious. The middle class was growing in size and confidence, and the university gilded their ambition with education. Hundreds of the sharp-elbowed would find employment in the law, a huge sector where social advancement could be made by 'men a little less deprived of instruction than the other inhabitants', but applicants easily outstripped opportunities. The 120 doctors who were graduating a year could not find work; the dusty, desiccated bureaucracy was monopolised by elderly functionaries; the army and navy by foreigners, and the kingdom's few secular institutions were skeletal when compared to those of the Church.

These were middle class worries. The ordinary people, the artisans, many living in huge *fondachi*, and the shop workers concentrated around the Mercato and the Pendino, the most densely populated parts of the city (47,225 and 43,637 inhabitants respectively in 1789), were more in fear of being swallowed up by the virulent Neapolitan underclass. This was the infamous *lazzaria*, whose constituent members, the *lazzaroni*, appalled and fascinated visitors in equal measure. They baffled Neapolitans too, and taxed the brains of the reformist elite who pondered why the rural poor were working themselves to death whilst their feckless urban counterparts rejoiced in idleness. There were said to be 50,000 of these wastrels, although this fluctuated as numbers were bloated by new arrivals from the provinces, or those driven out from there by hunger, ambition or injustice. Dupaty, writing in 1785, was of the opinion that 'the majority of the people only work as much as they have to prevent themselves dying of hunger. When a lazzaro has earned sufficient in a few hours to enable him to live for a few days, he lies down, goes out for a walk or bathes. He lives.'[36]

They crammed into the network of Angevin alleyways ensnaring the city centre, lived in crowded tenements in the Porto and S. Carlo all'Arena quarters or glared alarmingly from the infamous Imbrecciata slum in the Vicaria quarter. They thrived off handouts, the ubiquitous Zumford broth, or macaroni, and pestered passers-by for charity or work, clogging the streets, cluttering the squares and loving, not a little, their own servitude. Ferdinand, who played to this particular gallery, was careful to leave these people undisturbed by reform and reformers, and to keep on the good side of the mob's leader, the capo-lazzaro. Indeed, in 1788, he allowed the lazzaroni the privilege of policing themselves, ordering Pasquale de Simone to assume command of a band of 1,200 men given the impossible task of keeping order in this disruptive class.

So the city was heaving, bursting with all kinds of people, a capital of glory and of misery, a centre of power. Some even dubbed it the tyrant of the kingdom, for beyond the suburbs there were few other important centres, and it did indeed tower over the provinces, sucking in all the essential resources like a sponge. The estates north of Naples were happy to comply, for the land was rich and prices were high, and along the Adriatic coast a few ports, such as Bari, Manfredonia and Brindisi, served as conduits between Naples and the Levant when not subjected to the depravations of Barbary raiders. But outside these pockets of wealth the population was sparse, the land unforgiving. The kingdom's bad roads were plagued by its own indigenous pirates, the celebrated brigands of the south, and, in the badlands of Abruzzo and Calabria, poverty induced many to take to the hills for life as an outlaw, preying on travellers and merchants.

The dangers of the road no doubt contributed to the characteristic gulf between the cities and the countryside. It was as though the urban centres and the agrarian heartlands were living apart, perhaps in different centuries and certainly subject to different authorities. For the government's hold was weak and anaemic and, whenever it exerted itself, it merely added to the burden pressing down on the provinces. Even the regime's best friend, Sir William Hamilton, had to admit that there was universal complaint of total want of justice and good government throughout the kingdom of Naples and that the provinces were in the most extreme want and misery so that few, should it come to the trial, would think such a government worth fighting for.

Indeed, for many, the king and his ministers were abstract notions, the obedience of the peasantry, and many in the towns, was to the more immediate presence of the landowner. Occasionally, this was the crown, which acted as landowner in 384 demesnes in 1786,[37] but, more often, it was a noble family that dominated rural life. For example, 1,616 demesnes were in the hands of feudal overlords with just 90 noble families exercising jurisdiction over two million vassals.

Such families enjoyed an absolutist authority and ran a system recognisable to the Normans. They ran the judiciary, selecting and keeping its personnel in dependence, and levied fees for the most routine access to justice. They used the militia (established in 1782), or even the state's soldiers, to put down stirrings of discontent or to punish recalcitrant communities. They excluded individuals from the courts, leaving petitioning the crown as the only, but uncertain, means of redress. In an established injustice, for their avoidance of payment meant the financial burden fell on the poor, the nobility had numerous loopholes through which they could reduce their tax, some escaping with the annual donation of a harnessed horse. In any case, financial impositions on the rich were haphazardly gathered, and it was more common for funding to be granted, or lent, to the crown and all on condition that the nobility's private privileges were confirmed. They controlled production, and the means for production, leasing tools, ovens or mills, and asserting rights over ponds, rivers and woodland. They disputed who had rights to common land, restricted access to pastures or levied charges (*fide*) for grazing rights. They charged tolls on the use of rivers and roads, and there were even dues for the sowing of crops. And then, on top of that, rents and sales taxes were exacted.

Whilst this privileged clique provided the Enlightenment with some of its finest minds, most of the nobility were more inclined to the kind of idleness the lazzaroni might envy, only stirred to activity by gaming or gallantry, or to brief lawyers to protect their indolence. To the majority the notion of reform seemed like a direct threat to their fortunes. Their fortunes were made on the backs of the most impoverished class in Europe: that of the Neapolitan rural labourer. This abusive system ensured the penury of a multitude and created a class where 'it depends entirely on the personal character of the masters whether their poverty is not the least of their grievances'.

The labourers led a short and precarious existence, the successful keeping destitution at bay by scraping by on an income of 15 to 20 *grani* a day, either working on estates, where they were usually subject to short leases, or migrating in search of work. The less fortunate joined the *cafoni*, a rural underclass, dependent on occasional work, and all too often failing to find it. Whatever could be scraped from the land was diminished to nothing by a complex system of tax. Taxes, like the *gabelle*, on food stuffs, were imposed by the municipalities. Then there was the *battaglione*, which taxed income, and the *testatico* a poll tax, paid per occupant. The middle class was largely exempt above a certain threshold and so the chief burden again fell on the poor. Indeed, even in times of hardship the poor still had to pay the *estaglio*, an absolute rent that was due on whatever the land produced, with confiscation of goods imposed should payment be missed.

With so many kept deliberately close to the breadline, a bad harvest, natural disaster or conflict could easily tip the peasantry into disaster. Amateur philanthropy, the Church and a few charitable institutions aside, there was no protection when times were bad. Inevitably, the rural community was easy prey to famine,[38] and apocalyptic catastrophes such as the Calabrian earthquakes, which ruined the region in the 1780s. That disaster was so damaging that much of the south struggled to emerge from the ensuing impoverishment although, in one enlightened case of good fortune, the destroyed town of Castel Monardo was rebuilt nearby and christened as Filadelfia.

The name of the new town hints at a different kind of country. For despite the precarious and brutal economic life of the common man and woman, and the miserable life of the majority of inhabitants, Naples enjoyed the paradoxical status of being a leading centre of intellectual progress. The capital was a beacon of the Enlightenment, its cultural and intellectual life had no parallel in the south of Europe and Enlightenment ideals, whether borrowed from northern counterparts or developed closer to home, found fertile soil beneath Vesuvius.

Although much of the city's cultural life was dominated by pleasure, a Sybarite feast of music, opera,[39] ballet and theatre, more sober pursuits were also flourishing by the mid-1770s. Intellectual debate was being fed by volumes widely circulated by publishers such as Giuseppe Maria Galanti, and intellectuals, by their very nature wishing for innovation and reform, were making confident inroads into public life. The university indulged such tendencies and allowed men of letters such as Gaetano Filangieri and Francesco Mario Pagano to develop their reformist ideas. This long-standing institution was soon augmented by the Royal Academy of Sciences and Arts, the Accademia Ercolanese, the

Royal Military Academy and a network of private schools or academies for gentlemen (such as Carlo Lauberg and Annibale Giordano's Academy for Chemistry and Mathematics in the Vico dei Giganti), all of which contributed to a cerebral clamour for a new ordering of things. When debate was not enough, a network of Masonic lodges allowed the kingdom's ambitious to feel that they were influencing politics from outside the twisted corridors of power.[40] Indeed, these semi-secret clubs were so popular that a temporary ban was introduced in 1775 to curb their enthusiasm.

So it was that Neapolitan lawyers began to discuss streamlining the courts and improving access to justice. Economists discussed improving trade and manufacturing, whilst scientists dreamed of rational improvement to agriculture. Historians and antiquarians recalled the splendours of the past and called for renewal of the Italian present. Whichever path these restless intellectuals chose they agreed that only reform and an improved and modernised Naples would enable the nation to hold its head up amongst the powers of Europe, and perhaps bring happiness to millions.

It seemed as though the philosophers' credo would receive the queen's blessing in the 1770s. She, like her brothers, encouraged the formation and activities of academies, nodding towards promotion of Freemasonry as a driver for change and as a handy instrument to undermine her enemies.[41] However the queen's support, for that of the king never extended to intellectual pursuits, faltered once the Spanish faction, personified by Tanucci, was evidently broken, and that of the pope declared moribund. Indeed, Maria Carolina was soon distancing herself from the forces she'd helped unleash and Acton, never one to tolerate opinions that weren't his own, shared her suspicions. The reformers, flushed from the corridors of power, but offered the consolation of generating ideas without the difficulties of implementing them, were reduced to publishing projects and treatises, to sending in petitions pleading for change.

Few seemed unduly troubled, and chaotic society limped on. Anaemic institutions and unconvincing platitudes were enough to support the existing order through the 1780s, when stagnation ruled. But continuing as before in an age of revolution would be a very different matter.

The rebellion which morphed into a revolution in the kingdom of Louis XVI and Marie Antoinette sent shockwaves through Europe. Europe looked on following that summer of 1789 as the French began to abolish feudalism, the Church lost its privileges, and tithes, and the Rights of Man were fused with the Rights of the Citizen to create a new nation. Reformers took note in that blissful dawn that change could come with or without the approbation of the old order, that revolution could accelerate all the cherished ambitions of the philosophers. The maxims of liberty, equality and fraternity were now being sounded along the frontiers of France and the sounds of revolution were soon reverberating in the streets and squares of neighbouring states.

The old order, meanwhile, girded itself for conflict. In distant, placid Naples, the royal couple and Acton would be the focus for those sheltering from the storm, supported by a loyal clique and bolstered by the Hamiltons loyally firing off royalist broadsides. Nelson would later join these stout defenders of God, King and Country, doing what he could to stem the tide. But, for now, agitation and alarm owned the moment. The age of crisis had arrived.

2

Revolutions: Naples in the 1790s

On 27 July 1789, a merchantman from Marseilles sailed into Naples bringing news that the Bastille had fallen and that there had been a revolution in France. The assault on a fellow monarchy terrified Ferdinand and frightened Maria Carolina, whose beloved sister, Marie Antoinette, was the target of much of the revolutionaries' bile.

The Neapolitan regime's hasty response was to simply ban all news from France. Then it instructed its compliant clergy to denounce the French from every pulpit of the kingdom. Censorship was tightened and bookshops, such as those of Giuseppe Porcelli, were raided for distributing seditious literature. Acton, who had assumed even more powers following the death of the popular Domenico Caracciolo, enthusiastically enforced this state suppression. But this only allowed him to see danger in more quarters, and he was unnerved by the sight, fretting as early as December 1790 that 'a certain Buonarroti, an enemy to the tranquillity of the kingdom, is in Corsica and is translating infamous and seditious books from French into Italian with the intention of sending them in to the king's dominions, to corrupt the masses, and incite trouble.'

The kingdom's secret police placed those were most likely to be susceptible to French influence, or who had already been corrupted by it, under surveillance. Potential traitors apparently included those sporting long trousers as some young gentlemen attending a play at the Teatro Nuovo found to their cost. A repeated government ban on Masonic activity on 3 November 1789 added to the atmosphere of oppression. Inevitably, the harshest measures were reserved for Frenchmen. Matters came to a head in July 1790 when those Frenchmen in Naples, including Michel de Cubières-Palmézeaux, were expelled. In revenge for this pre-emptive strike to disrupt the celebration of the fall of the Bastille, Cubières-Palmézeaux imagined a revolution in which

The people have risen up and beaten down the doors to the arsenal, seizing those weapons which were kept there to oppress them and now bravely brandishing them ready for vengeance. I see the furious Neapolitans charging forwards and throwing themselves against the palace of Chevalier Acton. He is struck by a thousand blows and falls, dying beneath the blades of those seeking to finish him off and who, keen to be the first, dispute for the honour of completing such an easy but indispensable victory. Chevalier Acton is no more and his head, separated from his body, is being carried aloft on a pike. But let us not dwell on the barbarous details.[1]

This fantasy was not to be, at least not yet. The risk of a popular revolt in indolent Naples was still rather low, Sir William Hamilton taking the pragmatic, if rather patronising, view that 'the Neapolitans, provided they can get their bellies filled at a cheap rate, will not, I am sure, trouble their heads with what passes in other countries and great pains are taken to prevent any of the democratic propaganda or their writings finding their way into this kingdom'.[2]

True, there was a handful of troublemakers, excited by the radicalism of the Parisian streets, but they were preaching in what was still an alien tongue to the Neapolitan masses. And those intellectuals who troubled their heads for their fellow citizens, and who still yearned for reform, were better suited to debate than demagogy. All was quiet for now and, although the skies of Naples were now flecked by Gallic clouds, the new decade began lavishly enough. On 19 September 1790, the Neapolitan princess, Maria Theresa, married Francis of Austria, whilst her sister, Maria Louisa Amelia, married the Archduke Ferdinand, Grand Duke of Tuscany. Despite the cost, which was in excess of 1.6 million Ducats, with the queen imitating the largesse of Marie Antoinette by setting aside 290,683 Ducats for her travel expenses alone, the royal couple determined to be at the weddings. They would travel up to Vienna, and then to Frankfurt to see Leopold II crowned Holy Roman Emperor. Those that remained at home were also distracted by pomp when Naples celebrated as the heir to the throne, awkward Francesco, married his thirteen-year-old Austrian cousin Maria Clementina by proxy. The composer Giovanni Paisiello, elevated after his triumph with his opera *Nina*, conducted grand music in the royal chapel.

The music of his celebratory mass had scarcely died away when it was replaced by more martial airs from beyond the Alps. In April 1792, Habsburg Austria, now under Ferdinand and Maria Carolina's son-in-law Francis, and the King of Prussia declared war on France. France responded by storming the Tuileries, where the king and queen were being kept under house arrest, and on 21 September 1792 a republic, one and indivisible, was proclaimed. A well-organised clique of radicals, proclaiming themselves the Society of Jacobins, Friends of Liberty and Equality, consolidated power and these Jacobins, galvanised by Robespierre, mobilised in defence of the new republic. Making it clear that this was to be no war between nations, but one between classes, they brought revolution to Flanders and Italy and sent a marauding fleet under the noble Jacobin freemason Latouche Treville into Naples in December 1792.

This peaceful visit, loathed by some, welcomed by others, marked the point at which, for Naples, revolution hove into view. Now secret but patriotic societies sprang up to prepare for regime change and to better resist Acton's repression. The most important of these clubs flourished under the energetic guidance of Carlo Lauberg, a defrocked priest and graduate of the Royal Military Academy, and was energised by the 'Without Compromise' Masonic lodges established in the late 1780s. Unfortunately, and in a sign of things to come, the club then went the way of most political parties on the cusp of great events, splintering into factions, the most important of which was the radical Romo club (*Repubblica o morte*) under the watchmaker Andrea Vitaliani; and the marginally more moderate Lomo club (*Libertà o morte*) under Rocco Lentini and the mathematical child prodigy Annibale Giordano.

These clubs, codenamed Reomo and Liomo by the Bourbon police, who kept a close eye on any Club Rivoluzionario, were preaching popular revolution on the French model, advocating universal suffrage; liberty in belief and expression of those beliefs; a social system based on the rights of man and the responsibilities of the citizen; meritocracy rather than privilege; respect for property, but regulation of wealth; state control of prices; and centralisation of power with control exerted through a network of municipal democracies. It was the antithesis of life in Bourbon Naples, but one based as much on British or American concepts of personal liberty quite as much as on French equality. The ideals of the Neapolitan revolutionaries were moderate, and would soon seem even more so compared to a France where many colours of revolution, hammered by the pressures of war, had blended into the red of Terror.

There King Louis was tried for treason, found guilty by 693 deputies of the Convention, and guillotined on 21 January 1793. News reached Naples on 9 February and caused consternation. Britain, now also at war with France, promised support to Spain and Naples and they joined the alliance against the regicides of France. As well as fighting a conventional war, the coalition also managed to exploit a counter-revolution in Provence and the British used the opportunity to seize the great Mediterranean port of Toulon. That September they sent Captain Horatio Nelson of the *Agamemnon* to Naples to appeal for a Neapolitan reinforcement of 6,000 men to protect the port. Nelson met with Sir William Hamilton at Palazzo Sessa, and was introduced to Lady Emma Hamilton. The young officer was impressed by such high company but just as pleasing was word that the Neapolitans proved steadfast allies, their rare resolve strengthened by news that Maria Carolina's sister, Marie Antoinette, had been beheaded in Paris. Such unity amongst allies augured well, but Allied operations against Toulon were a disaster. On 14 December, following his morning hunt, Ferdinand heard with horror that the best of his Neapolitan troops had been badly mauled when a young French officer, Napoleon Bonaparte, had forced the hapless allies to flee.

Disaster at Toulon shook the Neapolitan regime. Those sympathetic to the French sensed the change and stirred into action. In February and March 1794, a large-scale Jacobin conspiracy was discovered in Naples. Andrea Vitaliani was accused of having plotted to seize control of the castles and then kill the king and queen, and of having conspired to introduce an Italian version of France's 1793 constitution, which was then printed by Giordano at the cost of '30 or 40 Ducats'. A copy is rumoured to have been placed on the queen's table with the note 'like it or not, this is what must be done'.

The plotters were arrested or scattered, the regime hitting back against the revolutionaries by establishing a grand *Giunta di Inquisizione* to try opponents and hound dissent. Hamilton was relieved and noted that 'I hope in a few days and by a few executions all will be quiet again'. Tommaso Amato, who was arrested for profanity and blasphemy, was indeed executed that May. Vincenzo Vitaliani, Andrea's brother, Emanuele de Deo and Vincenzo Galiani went to the scaffold in October, de Deo being put to death for having rather flamboyantly stabbed a portrait of the king with a table knife during a revolutionary banquet at Posillipo.

Further repression was accompanied by a renewed attempt to keep the war against France as far away as possible. In June 1794, with Vesuvius erupting in bellicose sympathy, the Neapolitans sent a force of 1,686 cavalrymen under General Federici, to northern Italy and also prepared some of their fleet to assist the British off Tuscany. Nelson, delighted to be involved in Neapolitan affairs, wrote to his ally Hamilton about his preference for a commander of the Neapolitan ships: 'Admiral Fortiguerri [sic] is the most of all men unlikely to conciliate the esteem of the English. We all love the captain of the *Tancredi* – Carraghohilli [Caracciolo].'[3]

Allied optimism was short-lived. In 1796 the young hero of Toulon, Napoleon Bonaparte, eyeing the riches of Italy and the bedraggled state of his men, invaded Piedmont and chased out the Austrians. He was so successful that France's armies were soon establishing client states.[4] The exiled Neapolitan radicals, travelling to Milan in the train of the conquering troops, had hoped for a purer kind of revolutionary system, but the French general surprised them with his conservatism, even repackaging the beauties of liberty and equality into the much more banal 'a free people is one that respects people and property' for his Italian audience.

French victory inevitably raised the hopes of the exiled Neapolitan revolutionaries and those who had survived at home. In northern Italy Lauberg published a call for the establishment of a Vesuvian Republic whilst Vitaliani opted for action rather than elegant phrasing and returned to plotting a coup in which the assassination of the king or queen of Naples, by placing barrels of gunpowder below the Portici Palace, would trigger a revolt and French intervention. He just needed money to pay the assassin and then the '40,000 people who had been persecuted by the royal family' would rise up. Spies such as Giuseppe Torelli and Jean-François Borel, kept an eye on republican plans, whilst Acton and Hamilton corresponded nervously about 'Vitagliano [sic] at Genoa, Abamonti at Milan, Salfi and the Pignatellis at Venice'.[5]

It was understandable that that the British were as worried as the Neapolitans. France had started the war against the whole of Europe in 1792 but, by 1798, the First Coalition was reduced to a peevish Britain and an impoverished Portugal. Naples was their only Mediterranean friend, albeit a clandestine one after peace was signed with France that year, and only senile Rome stood between it and revolution. Lord Bristol shared a widespread concern when he told Sir William 'I tremble for Naples if once the monkeys are able to reach Rome'. Troops were indeed soon pouring into that city for General Berthier used an attack on the French embassy on 27 December 1797 as a pretext to intervene. He easily captured Rome from its moribund defenders, and soon established a republic and sent a dispirited pope into exile. As the papal carriage trundled off to Tuscany, all-victorious France began to scheme for the defeat of the last of her remaining enemies. There were rumours of a secretive expedition being prepared in the French Mediterranean ports. Many thought that Naples or Sicily would be the obvious target, and the kingdom lurched into paranoia and nerves, as the diarist Marinelli noted:

In the evening of Tuesday 7 June the king attended the Teatro de' Fiorentini to watch a play and had eight youths arrested on the spot for wearing their hair short like Jacobins. Amongst them was the son of Santorelli.[6]

The British were also fearful that the French would monopolise the Mediterranean, but news of the loading of stores for a longer voyage induced fear that Ireland, then on the cusp of a major rebellion, was the real target.[7] Hedging their bets, the admiralty sent Nelson into the Mediterranean on 2 May. A month later the French fleet, carrying Napoleon's army, eluded Nelson, reached Malta on 10 June, and seized the islands from the Knights of Malta. King Ferdinand, whose dubious claim to the islands was now in ruins, was horrified and hoped Nelson would save Naples by preventing the French from coming closer, telling his wife 'I really hope that the English squadron encounters the French and makes a salad out of that scum'. Such worries only began to recede when word came that the French had sailed away. The queen, using Emma Hamilton as go-between, was tempted to break the treaty with France by supplying Nelson's ships, offering pilots and food as they cruised through the Messina straits. Nelson hoped for more active support, suggesting to Sir William that 'the King of Naples may now have part of the glory in destroying these pests of the human race' but could not stay to hear Neapolitan reluctance as he had to sail off eastwards in pursuit of the mysterious French. Failing to find them and, in dire need of supplies, he then returned to Sicily, arriving off Syracuse that July. Now Nelson's relationship with the Hamiltons and the royal family proved its worth. Lady Hamilton and the queen had arranged matters so that the admiral was treated as a favoured ally. The governor of Syracuse, Giuseppe della Torre, made 'an ostensible opposition' for French consumption, publically denying Nelson the right to enter the port, but doing nothing to prevent the British squadron from sailing in and refreshing itself at the fountains of Arethusa.

Napoleon had greater concerns than this irritating Neapolitan breach of the treaty as he sailed into Aboukir Bay. His army disembarked on Egyptian sand and tramped south to Cairo, beginning a rather quixotic attempt to cut British communication to India, to thereby destroy Britain's economy. The Directory in Paris rejoiced, and basked in the glory of seeing the Mediterranean turned into a French lake. In Naples anxiety at another French triumph manifested itself as anger or despair. The ambassador of the Cisalpine Republic, Giovanni Estore Martinengo Colleoni, was new to the capital and was presented to the court on 27 July 1798. He reported that 'the queen spoke in a warlike tone whilst the king spent the whole time studying my boots'.[8]

However, more encouraging news for Ferdinand and Maria Carolina was on its way. On Sunday 2 September the king had spied a British brig approaching the bay whilst he was munching on his favourite mozzarella. The next day a close friend of Lady Hamilton, Cornelia Knight, saw the ship enter the harbour: 'I also saw plainly that a blue ensign was hoisted ... The vessel was the *Mutine*.'[9]

Captain Thomas Capel disembarked and, accompanied by Sir William Hamilton, was ushered up to the palace so that he could impart his important news. He informed the court that Nelson had found the French fleet at Aboukir, and, in an audacious attack, had destroyed it. The burning decks of the French ships lit up the night sky, and it was clear that a victory had been won that would change the balance of power in the Mediterranean. To cap it all, not only had France's best fleet gone, but Napoleon and France's best army were now stranded in Egypt.

No wonder, then, that the messenger Capel and the new commander of the *Mutine*, the youthful lieutenant William Hoste, were welcome visitors, as Capel informed Nelson:

> I am totally unable to express the joy that appeared in everybody's countenance, and the burst of applause and acclamations we received. The queen and Lady Hamilton both fainted; in short, Sir, they all hail you as the saviour of Europe.[10]

The British officers were escorted through the streets that evening by Lady Emma Hamilton who, incongruously, wore 'a bandeau round her forehead with the words 'Nelson and Victory' emblazoned upon it'. Hoste stayed with the Hamiltons, whilst Capel set off for England accompanied part of the way by a royal courier heading to Vienna.[11] Back in Naples, Nelson fever reigned and the queen was in a kind of ecstasy as she wrote to loyal Emma 'Oh, if I ever had a portrait of the brave Nelson I would have it in my bedroom, my gratitude is engraved on my heart, long live that Brave Nation, that worthy navy'. Sir William Hamilton was also elated, calling the admiral 'our bosom friend' gushing 'you have now completely made yourself, my dear Nelson, *immortal*'.

Then, on 22 September, the immortal but badly damaged Nelson appeared at last. The conquering hero and his band of brothers were hailed with considerable acclaim. Nelson would send Lady Nelson, now a-bed in England, a frank account of his reception. The ending of which might have caused her to sit up in alarm:

> Sir William and Lady Hamilton came out to sea, attended by numerous boats with emblems, &c. They, my most respectable friends, had really been laid up and seriously ill; first from anxiety, and then from joy. It was imprudently told Lady Hamilton in a moment, and the effect was like a shot; she fell apparently dead, and is not yet perfectly recovered from severe bruises. Alongside came my honoured friends: the scene in

the boat was terribly affecting; up flew her ladyship, and exclaiming, 'O God, is it possible?', she fell into my arm more dead than alive.[12]

Ferdinand was more prosaic, noting in his diary 'returned home at nine, changed, took the launch and with the Guard Cavalry went to greet Admiral Nelson', but his phlegm disguised his immense pleasure. His practical spouse recognised, along with the belligerent of Europe, that the loss of the French fleet and the stranding of Bonaparte in Egypt, presented a tremendous opportunity – especially in Italy, where the French seemed suddenly vulnerable to a joint attack by the British, Austrians and Neapolitans. Nelson had realised this early on and less than a week after victory was writing to Hamilton that 'As this [Napoleon's] Army will never return, I hope to hear the Emperor [of Austria] has regained the whole of Italy'.

Exhausted Austria, however, would not listen and Nelson was out of action for the moment as he had been wounded, was suffering from headaches, had been sick with fever, and was still weak. To hasten recovery, the saviour was lodged on the third floor of the Hamiltons' house[13] recuperating before he could be more fully involved in the planning for the coming campaign. The bellicose Hamilton filled the void, promising British support if the Neapolitans took the field against France, even before Austria was ready or willing to fight. His hawkish stance undermined the foreign minister, the Marquis of Gallo who, as cool and smooth as San Leucio's silk, was intriguing to prevent Naples acting without Austria. Hamilton's own campaign to bring about war seemed frustrated by Gallo's dovish charm and, from the comfort of his Neapolitan palazzo, he railed against inaction, reminding everyone in earshot of Plutarch's maxim that 'a state's well-being stems not from so-called prudent advice by timid men, but rather from audacity and action'.[14] It was a call to arms worthy of Nelson himself.

3

Rome: War and Defeat in 1798

The timid men, and the pragmatists, were not yet won over. Before news of the Nile reached Naples, Acton had been telling Nelson that the Neapolitans were ready 'to join in the most sanguine manner with your future undertakings, *as soon as Vienna answers to our repeated and warmest demands*'. After Nelson's victory Acton seems to have been won round to Hamilton's way of thinking, rashly telling Nelson on 28 September that the Neapolitans were determined to declare war, and not wait for the Austrians. Hamilton enthused that Aboukir 'has induced this government to take a decided part and march immediately a part of its army without waiting for a decision of the court of Vienna and take possession of Rome'. This was premature, Gallo and more cautious heads in Naples still demurred and were loath to commit to a ground war against France until the friendly Hapsburg juggernaut began to move. With the Neapolitans blowing hot and cold, it was now that an exasperated Nelson complained to St Vincent about Naples being 'a country of fiddlers and poets, whores and scoundrels'.

Having necessarily put music and poetry aside, Lady Hamilton and Sir William united with Nelson in pushing for action, and the threesome were soon spending their time prodding the court into a war they presented as being easily winnable. It was true that the French hold on the peninsula was precarious. In Rome the Roman republic played host to an embattled French contingent under General Macdonald, a French general whose father was Bonnie Prince Charlie's loyal friend Neil MacEachen (later changed to Macdonald, to placate Gallic ears), but he had his hands full with a rebellion then sweeping the old papal states, a fratricidal war that was clearly being stoked by Neapolitan agents.[1]

The Neapolitan war party, led by the queen, were therefore convinced that now was the time for more overt action. But a state in search of a victory must be in want of *a capable army,* a truth the king and queen painfully acknowledged. The forthcoming attempt to dislodge the French from Rome would be the biggest test of Neapolitan armed forces since the kingdom became independent. Nobody was quite sure they were ready. The Neapolitans had, by common consent, a fraught relationship with military service and the government mostly relied upon foreign officers, an assortment of Swiss, Belgian and Jacobite Scottish and Irish careerists predominating. The situation was more dire when it came to generals who could command the army, as the queen was only too aware:

> We don't have any generals here who have seen action, except for Arezzo [aged 63], who will do. Even he is a walking corpse. It has been 50 years since a shot has been fired in anger in this country, they have no idea what war is.

In an early indication that, with Bonaparte out of Europe, the queen's mind tended towards war and Rome, Maria Carolina wrote to her imperial brother on 12 August 1798 pleading for an Austrian general to set her officer corps straight. She hoped the Austrian emperor would send them Karl Mack von Leiberich, a man who knew what war was but who would soon show that he had less idea as to how to win it.[2]

When it came to filling the expanded ranks of an enlarging army, the authorities were forced to make use of mercenaries of dubious loyalty, mostly Macedonians and Albanians, known as Camiciotti,[3] and of largely unwilling local material. Recruitment was initially voluntary, with bounties of six or 12 Ducats being given to encourage infantry or cavalry recruits to join.[4] These volunteers would be supplemented by levies taking ten out of every thousand inhabitants,[5] a blood tax which led to many attempting to evade such conscription through self-inflicted wounds:

> One young man knocks out teeth from his mouth. Another has a mysterious burn on his arm. Yet another is deaf, or an idiot, or someone debilitated by gout, nor should we forget the one who so badly damages his legs so that they take two months to heal. So it is by using these, and other such ploys, that they were lucky enough to avoid the draft.[6]

With the draft forcing more men into the ranks of the bandits than the army, the authorities resorted to desperate measures and, in July 1798, began combing the prisons and galleys for the physically fit, offering amnesties and thereby raising 13 companies of dubious soldiers.[7] It was still not enough and a new and ambitious levy was proclaimed on 2 September as Gian Carlo Berarducci of Trani noted in his journal:

On 2 September a dispatch arrived here which was sealed and which was marked as urgent and to be read at once, or face punishment. Everyone was worried. It was about conscription and the drafting of men between 16 and 45, now even including family men.

All this was because the court, stuck in the treadmill of ambition, thought great power status lay with fielding an army of 74,000 men. Many of those powers were turning against France, and Ferdinand's diplomats were busy with the complex minuet of ensuring that Naples would not be sending whatever army she could scrape together into the field alone. The Ottoman empire had declared against France (14 September 1798) and the conservative ruler of Russia, Czar Paul, appalled by the seizure of Malta, also despatched a Russian fleet of six ships and seven frigates under Admiral Fedor Fedorovich Ushakov for operations in the Mediterranean. Ushakov reached Constantinople and there created an uneasy combined fleet with the Turks in order to attack Corfu, and perhaps even retake Malta.

This imperial fleet would take time to arrive and so attempts to form an anti-French alliance closer to home were also launched. Not unreasonably Carlo Emanuele IV of Sardinia-Piedmont and the Duke of Tuscany rejected the notion of a *Pax Italica*, preferring to wait for Austria to make the first move. However, Austria kept a low profile, and having recently agreed a defensive alliance with Naples, only acting if Naples was attacked,[8] counselled patience to every power that talked of war. This makes Nelson's declaration, expressed to St Vincent, that 'the Emperor has desired the king of Naples to begin, and he will support him', wishful thinking.[9] Austria was clearly saying the opposite and, indeed, Emperor Francis explicitly stated that his first concern was towards his dynasty and his people, and stressed that his defensive alliance with Naples would only be activated if Naples was attacked, not if it attacked. He then told his parents-in-law that, in any case, Austria could not be ready to wage war before at least the spring of 1799.[10] These warnings impressing upon Naples the need to keep its peace were repeated to Gallo on 21 October.

Austria's one gesture of support, or perhaps a devious ruse to delay the war, was to send General Mack to Naples to assume command of the Neapolitan forces. This dour and unimaginative officer had been summoned to Vienna on 9 September 1798, had left the capital on 20 September, and, with his suite of staff officers in their crisp, white uniforms, reached Caserta on 9 October. The queen urged him to attack at once but Mack knew not all was well with his new command with even the minister of war, Giovanni Battista Manuel y Arriola, tangled in the sinews of war, pleading that the available resources could only sustain a short defensive war. Meanwhile, treacherous, or perhaps realistic, voices were whispering that Acton was in the pay of the English and dragging the country into an unwanted and unaffordable war. Unfortunately, this chorus failed to sway a king besieged by the siren sounds coming from the more belligerent party, led by an ambitious queen and her insistent British friends. Of them, Nelson was stentorian as he cast caution to the winds, lambasting 'the worst of all policy – procrastination'. The admiral's rather reckless push for war was clearly stated in his letter to Lady Hamilton on 3 October:

> I trust that the arrival of General Mack will induce the government not to lose any more of the favourable time which providence has put in their hands; for, if they do, and wait for an attack in this country, instead of carrying the war out of it, it requires no gift of prophecy to pronounce that these kingdoms will be ruined, and the monarchy destroyed.[11]

Nelson had a trusted ally in the recipient's husband, the two continuing to needle for an offensive.[12] They finally seem to have got what they wanted at the council of 11 October. A French émigré, Chastellux, collecting gossip in the marble halls, noted Nelson's presence throughout the court's deliberations:

> The queen still has a little of the fever, but her courage is sufficient and she continues to exert herself. On Thursday [11 October] she went to dine at Belvedere where Nelson was paying court to the king. The following day she left at seven in the morning in order to be at the Capua garrison's manoeuvres that the king wanted General Mack to witness.[13]

It was there at Belvedere that the awful vision of war became real, but no one was quite sure when it would be launched. There was a brief interlude as Nelson set sail to Malta on 15 October, the admiral inspecting Captain Ball and the Portuguese squadron's blockade of the French.[14] However, Nelson left the Hamiltons to steady Neapolitan nerves and to pressure them to set a date. Lady Hamilton fired a few broadsides to sink, once and for all, Gallo's timid faction, using her influence with the queen to urge that war on the French should begin at once. It seems to have worked as Lady Hamilton reported to Nelson on 24 October that

> Mack is gone to the army to prepare all to march immediately. And I flatter myself, I did much. For whilst the passions of the queen [were] up and agitated, I got up, put my left arm like you, spoke the language

of truth to her, painted the drooping situation of this fine country, her friends sacrificed, her husband, children, and herself led to the block; and eternal dishonour to her memory, after once having being active, doing her duty in fighting bravely to the last, to save her country, her religion, from the hands of the rapacious murderers of her sister, and the royal family in France, that she was sure of being lost if they were active, and there was a chance of being saved if they made use now of the day, and struck now while all minds are impressed with the horrors their neighbours are suffering from these robbers.[15]

Sir William seemed as optimistic as his artful wife, telling Nelson that 'the court and ministry here seem in high spirits, and they say the army is the same' and that 60 battalions and 30 squadrons were ready for the march on Rome. However, privately, his actions betrayed his doubts. With permission from Nelson, he packed up some of his collection of antiquities and a first consignment of eight secure trunks of vases was loaded onto the ill-fated *Colossus* bound for Britain.[16]

Nelson himself returned from blockaded Malta on 5 November[17] and was playing billiards with a distracted king on 7 November. Placated by the prospect of war, the admiral was relieved to see the Neapolitans, and their monarchs, on a war footing and felt authorised to offer to 'endeavour to be useful in the movements of their army' as they set off on their crusade.

The king, snookered by his wife's pressure, reluctantly left Caserta to ride at the head of his troops. Farce was a precursor to tragedy as a little more hectoring was then required to get the reluctant monarch out of the security of the San Germano camp. Hamilton, now also present, took centre stage, co-opting the king by declaring, 'we all agreed that the boldest measures were the safest'. Nelson joined them all on the 12th, and told Earl Spencer that he had reviewed 30,000 men, that Mack was happy and that 'as far as my judgement goes in these matters, I agree, that a finer army cannot be.' Nelson felt confident enough to lecture the king, urging him 'to advance, trusting to God for his blessing on a just cause to die with *l'epée à la main*, or remain quiet and be kicked out of your kingdoms.'

Ferdinand, trusting to God rather than anyone with more recent military experience, took his cue from Nelson, drew his sword and ordered the advance. By now, even the hitherto unshakeable queen was also trembling with nervous anticipation:

Yesterday the vanguard left, along with some reserves, and advanced on the frontier. Every step the troops take is a stab to my heart. What will be, will be. We hope heaven blesses us. The king approves of the letter for Vienna prompted by the Grand Duke's letter. This morning he assisted at mass in the camp. A square of 4,000 men was drawn up. I humbly but fervently prayed that God protect our army and grant it victory ... We must not upset the English or break with them, but we must do what we can to get them to help us, subsidies,[18] or, at the very least, a loan. By the saints, Ariola has not provided boots, shoes, warm clothes and cloth, coats, cannon, wagons, etc and leads us to ruin.[19]

On paper all the advantages were with the Neapolitans. The Directory in Paris had assumed, quite wrongly, that they had 33,000 men in central Italy, but the actual figure was closer to 12,000 French and Polish troops around Rome, all destitute and facing a populace in open revolt. But the French had one significant advantage. The talented General Jean Etienne Championnet had just been appointed commander at Rome and he arrived to take charge of his paupers on 18 November. Championnet, unlike Bonaparte, was also something of a radical and he energised his little army, particularly that band of Neapolitan exiles who now hoped to march home and, with French help, transform Naples into a republic. Before they could advance on Naples, however, Naples first came marching on them.

On the evening of 25 November, Colonel Girardon, sitting astride his horse on the slopes of Mount Cavo by the watery crater of Lake Albano, was puzzled to see a single horseman trotting forwards towards his French cavalry outposts. Two days earlier, following a ball given in his honour, Championnet had received word that the Neapolitans were marching across the frontier. Girardon was, then, expecting them but, instead of a hostile force, here was a single horseman, dressed in the white tunic of an Austrian staff officer. The envoy handed over a quaint letter, rich in menace, and Girardon informed his superior:

> Monsieur de Mack has just sent me an envoy in order to invite me to fall back because that general wished to place his army in Frascati. I replied that I had received no orders to do so and that I would resist should he advance against me.[20]

This courtly but absurd exchange sought to underline that Naples had not declared war. The Neapolitans were hoping that France would withdraw or attack, and perhaps then Austria could be persuaded that France was the aggressor, thus triggering the defensive alliance.[21] But, even as this letter was being read, Neapolitan columns were pouring northwards, outflanking Girardon and his comrades and, despite the horrendous weather, pushing for Rome. Mack then thought to strike into Tuscany where his columns would meet the 5,000 troops of General Naselli being transported on Nelson's ships to Livorno.[22] Meanwhile, another force, under Alberto Micheroux, would act as a diversion along the Adriatic coast.

These were sound plans on paper, but hopeless in mud. Relentless rain was making the soldiers' lives a misery as a depressed king, still trying to rein in his fugitive courage, told his queen

> the weather continues to be atrocious and the soldiers suffer as a result, almost all of them have lost their shoes. Mack is in a bad mood, blaming the bad roads which force him to change his plans as it is impossible to carry out those determined upon.[23]

Soon, however, the latent self-pity of a monarch mired in anxiety surfaced and poor Ferdinand was soon writing home

> The position in which we find ourselves is most disagreeable for everyone concerned, but especially so for me as I am responsible for everything that is happening. I'm in despair and everything is in confusion, orders are not carried out, the soldiers are dying of hunger and misery or run off here and there, to such an extent that I can say we no longer have an army ... it will be a miracle if I don't die of grief. Mack wants to advance, forwards, forwards, but with whom and how, I must face the facts as must poor, faithful Acton, who might also die of despair.

The king's piteous correspondence was echoed by voices from the ranks, one soldier writing

> And the rain, as I mentioned, rendered the lives of the infantry and cavalry miserable and morale continued to plummet just as the rain continued to fall. Even the officers who carried orders from the general had to wade across the Melfa river on foot and the water came up to above their knees.[24]

Fortunately for the Neapolitans the first act of their tragedy was nearly over. As the bedraggled Neapolitans approached Rome, Championnet retreated northwards, leaving behind a small garrison under Colonel Francois Valterre in the Sant' Angelo citadel. The Neapolitan vanguard gingerly entered, General Burkhardt and his exhausted troops seeking shelter and food, and camping at the San Pietro piazza, whilst the Roman mob turned on the Jews and the French in the Sant' Angelo fort opened fire.[25] On 29 November, at five in the evening, the King of Naples also entered the chaotic city. He rode through the streets and sought out the comparative calm of the Farnese palace. In gossipy notes, far removed from the self-pity of the week before, he told his wife how unimpressed he was with the Romans and their women:

> The people, especially the peasants, are religious but, as for the other classes they are so corrupt you would not believe it, and there is hardly a lady who is not a whore.

The populace, unaware of such opinions, welcomed their conqueror and the city was illuminated. It was the high point of the campaign. Over in the east, the Neapolitan column under General Alberto Micheroux had been routed by the French whilst north of Rome, at Civita Castellana, the eminently resistible Neapolitans under the Chevalier de Saxe,[26] met the unmovable French and Prince Francesco Pignatelli Strongoli's Neapolitan Jacobins. The royalist Neapolitans again fled, Gaetano Rodinò, carrying the purple standard of the Sannio Regiment, recalling how a single trumpet call had pitched his Neapolitan unit into panic:

> Generals, officers, soldiers, everyone set off in precipitous flight. In order not to slow us down we cast aside artillery, munitions and weapons. Mules and horses were left behind or ran off, and the unarmed soldiers fled, although most of them were barefoot, having lost their shoes when they sank into the mud caused by all the rain.

His regiment's colonel, Leopoldo de Renzis, rode after them, declaring 'our duties as soldiers are over, those as citizens begin'. Mack seemed frozen in indecision whilst Ferdinand again had a crisis of confidence, telling the queen:

> you are right to say that I should not be discouraged, that crisis reveals men's characters, and that, now, courage is necessary in order to overcome and triumph. But you should be in my shoes, locked in a room, receiving bad news again and again.

The news was true, the army was collapsing. Nelson was aghast. Cumulative setbacks seem to have sent him into a depression, which even Lady Hamilton found hard to counter.[27] The admiral was convinced that the defeat stemmed from cowardice, and related that the Neapolitan officers 'seem alarmed at a drawn sword, or a gun, if loaded with shot. Many of them, peaceable heroes, are said to have run away when brought near the enemy.' But he thought that treason had probably also played its part, informing Sir Charles Stuart that:

> Although I could not think the Neapolitans to be a nation of Warriors yet it was not possible to believe that a Kingdom with 30,000 Troops and good looking young men could have been overthrown by 19,000 men without anything which could be called a battle ... I do not flatter myself that all that remains are good men and true.[28]

Few now remained, most had deserted their posts. As had the king. That regal deserter quit his Roman palace on 11 December, travelling with his valet, Vincenzo, and the Duke of Ascoli, to Belvedere. They arrived at dawn on 13 December, the exhausted king telling his wife: 'After 23 hours on roads which were initially terrible and with bad horses, and 32 hours without having anything other than bread and ricotta in my stomach, I am really shaken up.'[29] The queen, after publically praying for salvation at San Lorenzo Maggiore in Naples, travelled up to join her terrified husband and then to bring him into the capital later that evening. There, the king, relieved to be home, 'embraced the children, had supper with my wife, who was most kind, went to bed at eleven thirty' and found sufficient energy to make love to her.

As he was doing so, the French under Championnet were penetrating into Rome. Above them, on the battlements of the San' Angelo castle, where the French garrison had held out throughout the Neapolitan occupation, the Archangel Michael was decorated with the cap of liberty and swathed in a jovial tricolour. The revolution had returned in triumph, and now began to hope for fresh conquests to the south.

4

Rebellion: Anarchy in the Capital

After having established the Roman republicans back on their shaky throne, Championnet marched against Naples on 20 December. But even before the French began their descent on the capital, the royal family had determined on flight. Ferdinand and his queen had returned to a restless capital the week before and called for a council of war with Acton and Gallo for the 14th.[1] There the king broached the decision of evacuating to Sicily to Admiral Bartolomeo Forteguerri but the Neapolitan commander dithered, and so Nelson was asked for help.[2] The queen had already asked Lady Hamilton whether Nelson could evacuate the royal children 'in case of misfortune', and the request was now extended to the entire royal family. Fortunately, Nelson was all too willing to comply having already sworn, with suitable melodrama, that he was 'ready to save the sacred persons of the king and queen'.

The Bourbons would fly quickly, go far and return slowly, but preparations for their departure were to be kept secret. On the morning of the 14th the queen had written to Adélaïde and Victoire Bourbon, the surviving daughters of Louis XV living in exile in Caserta palace, informing them of 'our decision is to cross to Sicily and we would regard having you there with us, and sharing our bread of misery, as a small consolation.'[3] Acton, however, was more concerned with the state treasure than some old princesses, telling Hamilton

You know as well as myself the nature of this mollified [sic] people since ages and ages, and of their being without any caracter [sic], but ready to follow any leader, even against their own advantage. If the Government's cares are useless, we must think of saving the Royal Family and appear as soon as possible in Sicily, with all the possible and imaginable means to rise the spirit of a reasonable defence in that country ... we shall do what we can for a proper and general defence. But must think of quitting Naples in a few days, if the extremity forces to this resolution. Their Majesties confide in the friendship and loyalty of Lord Nelson. His Squadron and the Portuguese, and the King's own Squadron, may execute this cruel but necessary departure. I have been told that Lord Nelson has some transports. Can we begin to send to morrow [*sic*] night money and pretious [*sic*] things on board of them?[4]

This decision was given further impetus when news came on the 15th that the French had conquered the Abruzzo and that a republican government had been established at Civita Ducale. Scapegoats for defeat were sought, and Mack was blamed as was the minister of war, Ariola, who, a few days later, was taken to the Uovo fort and placed under arrest. In such an atmosphere, few could be trusted, and the queen, anxious that treason had followed the king to Naples, wrote in cypher to tell her daughter of her fears:

there are no sailors, they fear for their wives and children, and all is gone or corrupt, the nobility make long faces and hide their money and property and do nothing to help, the magistrates and lawyers have gone into hiding, plots, the military has fled and are infamous poltroons the people are less bad but follow the others, in short there are only traitors with modern principles or vile poltroons without courage or energy, our fate is horrid.[5]

Fortunately the Bourbons had their one-eyed hero to count on.[6] Forteguerri's Neapolitan ships were available[7] but Nelson preyed on the court's fears when he told Captain Ball that 'there are traitors in the Marine. In short all is corrupt'.[8] So the admiral would be entrusted with the most valuable cargoes, and would get to play the role of saviour he so much desired.[9] The queen was ready to entrust her personal treasure to the British, explaining to Lady Hamilton on 16 December that she had 60,000 Ducats and that her jewels and diamonds were to be given to a certain Saverio and then passed to Nelson, the queen's 'liberator and saviour', for safe-keeping. Public money was the next to move, Forteguerri was entrusted to transfer the reserves from the national bank to the Nuovo fort and then oversee its embarkation. There were 445 quintals of coin in small barrels and it was an Olympian task to load it aboard Captain George Johnstone Hope's *Alcmene*,[10] as Acton told Hamilton:

The embarcation [sic] ought to succeed in this very night, but as the money could not be put on board of the Alcmene in the night, for many reasons depending on the bulk, bad chests, etc., etc., it is likely that it shall be postponed for to morrow [sic] night. Count Thurn shall open the little rooms at the Molesillo, and there receive Lord Nelson, or what officers his lordship pleases to send, with the word All goes right and well. In case of the contrary, All is wrong, you may go back, as Lord Nelson has expressed himself to Belmonte.[11]

Whilst the treasure was slow to load, the passengers were allotted their berths. On the 19th, in preparation for the regal exodus, the king made sure that four hunting rifles and six of his hunting dogs were brought down from Caserta. Caracciolo's ship, the *Sannita*, was designated to take 116 royal servants, whilst the *Aretusa*, *Fortuna* corvette and five galeottes also took passengers even though there were insufficient sailors as many of the crews had gone ashore to protect their homes. In an irony of historic proportions the British ensured that the Cardinal Duke of York, the last of the Jacobite Stuarts, got to join the king across the water by offering him quarters on the Neapolitan *Archimede* as it sailed to Sicily. All was going smoothly until news from the palace put a stop to the evacuation. On the 20th a crowd of some 3,000 people gathered beneath the palace windows in an attempt to prevent the royal family from leaving, as the king's diary records:

Acton came, bringing replies from Nelson about plans for departure and, whilst we were discussing them, a crowd gathered before the palace. They were clapping, demanding that we wouldn't abandon them, asking to be armed so they could attack the French and, especially, to hunt down the Jacobin nobles. I went onto the balcony to calm them but seeing that they were trying to climb up, I had Pignatelli go out and have them pushed back, which he did.[12]

The following morning the already tense situation escalated when the crowd, now chanting 'long live the king!' and 'long live the holy faith!', seized a royal courier, Alessandro Ferreri. An eyewitness recorded

A courier from the Viennese court had been sent off to an English ship in the bay. Asking for a small boat to ferry him across, it was noted that he did not speak the Neapolitan language. 'He is a Frenchman!', cried the sailors and, ignoring the man's gestures and signs, beat him a thousand times and dragged him, half dead, through the streets of the city until they arrived beneath the king's windows. He was seized with horror, and covered his face with his hands.[13]

The king's version accords with this account:

> They carried a flag bearing an image of Christ. They fell back to reveal a few
> others dragging a body behind them, shouting he was a Jacobin. I told them
> not to commit such excesses and the mob dispersed, but took the corpse
> with them and gathered again at Santo Spirito, so I sent Pignatelli against
> them to quieten things. The dead man was an emigrant, a good man.

Doctor Marinelli, a Neapolitan professional perturbed by the turn of
events, saw the body there the following morning:

> The body of the unfortunate man was taken to the churchyard of
> S. Spirito and was guarded by soldiers. I myself saw it at three in the
> morning as I was on my way to Galesso to see the Prince of Scilla.[14]

The queen, now that she had loaded her valuables, and haunted by visions
of the guillotine or royal heads on pikes, spurred royal efforts to get away
as soon as possible. A minimalist baggage was allowed those singled out for
salvation, although the Hamiltons won special treatment from friends in high
places and a pessimistic Hamilton had already had James Clark draw up a
list of valuables and had them packed into crates by his *Maestro di Casa*,
Vincenzo Sabatino. Clark says that the first 14 items were packed into crates
on 12th and 13th December. Nine more items were packed on 17 December.
Then 27 more on 18, 19 and 20 December, including the rather cumbersome
marble base from a temple at Delphi. The precious collection was loaded
onboard the *Samuel* and *Jane* transports and young Captain William Hoste
of *La Mutine* took care of other treasures. The houses and some of the
furniture had to be abandoned,[15] however, as were the servants.

On the evening of 21 December, at the appointed time, British boats
from the *Vanguard* and the *Alcmene*'s cutter, under Nelson and Captain
George Hope, arrived at the Neapolitan quay at quarter past eight.
The British officers gave the appointed watchword 'all goes right and
well'. Count Giuseppe di Thurn of the Neapolitan navy had the palace
apartment's doors opened and the royal family came down through a
secret passageway to the Molosiglio.[16] The first to be transported to the
British ships were the king, the hereditary prince and his wife and their
child, Carolina, on the *Alcmene*'s boat, and, on that of the *Vanguard*,
the queen, princes Leopoldo and Alberto with his nurse, three princesses,
Acton, Castelcicala, Belmonte and Thurn. The queen remembered:

> We went down that cursed staircase. I was trembling like a leaf and
> without my virtuous and loyal Mimi I would have collapsed a thousand

times. Through that awful darkness, with six children, a daughter-in-law and an infant at the breast we made it on shivering from cold and with me shivering from despair.

It took half an hour to ferry them over. Then came the enormous number of household staff deemed essential by the court, including, in a slight to Sicilian cuisine, Monsieur Pernet the cook. The Hamiltons were almost the last to arrive, Nelson escorting them through darkness as black as Stockholm tar to his ship. Emma relates the adventure in her embellished account of their escape:

On the 21ˢᵗ, at 10 at night, Lord Nelson, Sir Wm, mother and self went out to pay a visit, sent all our servants away, and ordered them in 2 hours to come with the coach and ordered supper at home. When they were gone we sett off, walked to our boat, and after 2 hours got to the *Vanguard* at twelve o'clock.

With the court stowed safely onboard, it would not wait for late comers. On the 21st Maria Carolina wrote to Francis II of Austria telling him who was saved:

We had our little fleet in the harbour, Lord Nelson himself and a few Portuguese vessels. Our other boats: four ships, frigates, corvettes, xebecs, galleys and 120 gunboats and mortar-launches were to be crewed with sailors on double pay. Nobody wanted to come. The sailors said 'we want to go and see what is happening to our homes'. With so much cowardice, vile behaviour and treason, we had to burn a navy which costs millions so that it would not be captured by an enemy who could use it to come to Sicily. There are 12 of the family including the two old Mesdames de France whom honour and justice oblige us to save.[17]

The truth was that the Mesdames were not onboard but had been informed by royal courier that they should head for Manfredonia and from there follow Gallo to Austria.[18] Instead of the frail French ladies, five of the king's finest horses were loaded onboard the Portuguese *Principe Reale* taking space reserved for the princesses.

Despite the rush, the actual departure of the royal fugitives was postponed until the 22ⁿᵈ because of bad weather and strong contrary winds. Delay gave the city authorities time to send over a delegation and Paggio the *capo lazzaro* and the archbishop came to plead with the royalty not to abandon the kingdom. The king, in a foul mood because 'I barely slept all night out of worry and because of the noise all the people coming on board were making', dismissed the cleric with

> If the people dare to say I have abandoned them, tell them they are at fault for the excesses they have committed and that they should hope to see me return once they have, through obedience and discipline, learnt how to defeat the enemies of God and the nation without destroying the peace of its inhabitants.

The Cisalpine ambassador, Martinengo, heard about this spurning of the delegation, and blamed the British

> All the deputies of the city and of the various orders went onboard to beg the king to return onshore and to remain but they were not given audience and were rudely driven off by Acton and My Lady Hamilton who said that the king did not wish to receive anyone. The deputies insisted upon an audience but Nelson's sentries threatened to open fire if they did not leave. The Austrian ambassador whispered to one of the deputies that they have been chained below by the English.[19]

The following morning, with the gales continuing and the ships still not departing, General Mack used the opportunity to drag his shattered body onboard for one final audience. The queen recorded the meeting:

> Arrangements to burn the boats and so on meant we were in the harbour until Sunday and deputations came out to harangue us, asking us to return but never to talk about arming or defending themselves. Mack came on board on Sunday morning, he was half-dead, weeping, and explaining that all was lost, that treason and cowardice were at their peak and that his only consolation was to see the family on board Nelson's ship and saved. ... Forteguerri came and asked that he might be saved, saying that his life had been threatened and that the conscripts had mutinied. The sailors were leaving their ships and so English and Portuguese seamen had to replace at least 1,500 sailors who left in one night and so that we could save the *Samnite* and *Archimede* without which Nelson would not leave. The Portuguese stayed on in the harbour so that, to my eternal distress, our beautiful navy, which had cost so much, could be burnt.

The capital was being left to its fate, and the population was horrified. A proclamation that the royal family was leaving was met with incredulity and 'the consternation in the city was enormous' when they realised that the king would rather turn rebel to his people by deserting them than staying with them during the coming storm. That evening the winds abated and at sunset the royal fleet of 'the *Vanguard, Sannite* [sic] and *Archimedes* with about 20 sail of vessels' according to Nelson, got underway for Palermo. Admiral Caracciolo of the *Sannita* recalled in his log:

> On the night of the 21st the sovereign and the entire royal family were embarked on the *Vanguard* of Admiral Lord Nelson, from whom I received orders to leave at dawn but a strong and bitterly cold wind prevented this and only eased off on the 22nd. During this time I had brought onboard all those from the noble families and the court who were prepared for embarkation. On the morning of the 23rd we had orders to weigh anchor and as we were short of some 300 sailors we received a reinforcement of 25 English sailors and at 10 we set sail, following on behind other ships and gunboats.[20]

So the royal family turned its back on the lunacy of Naples, and committed itself to the foaming madness of a stormy Mediterranean, Nelson telling his superior that 'it blew harder than I ever experienced since I have been at sea'. The queen's anguished letter confirmed the shock and Nelson's disbelief:

> Antoinette was in her nightshirt, on her knees; Amelia was asking for a confessor for absolution; as was Leopold. As for myself, from all that had happened or was about to happen, I saw death, and hoped for divine eternal forgiveness and was glad it would end whilst with my children. At around two the danger ended and Nelson said that, in thirty years at sea, he had never seen such a wind or storm.

Tragedy struck when Prince Alberto, aged six, died just before the little fleet arrived off Palermo. The royal family was understandably grateful to arrive in their island kingdom on 26 December, and Ferdinand attended the public veneration of Santa Rosalia. Nelson, feted almost as much as the Sicilian saint, was loudly proclaimed honorary citizen of Palermo while a traumatised Maria Carolina sought isolation and quiet so she could mourn her lost infant.

Naples would not find quiet to mourn its loss, the chaos was closing in. The royal family had left Francesco Pignatelli, the Count of Laino, in charge as Vicar General, but he was overwhelmed by the tasks confronting him, and terrified by the prospect of pandemonium. Pignatelli's position was further complicated by a clear signal that he was being abandoned. For the expensive Neapolitan fleet was now consigned to the flames. Maria Carolina had already mentioned the destruction of the ships on 21 December.[21] It was an operation designed to deprive the French of any fruits of victory and had been carefully planned by 'the master of the arsenal and harbour, along with the help of Lord Nelson'.[22] On 24 December the port authorities began loading munitions onto Niza's Portuguese ships, but they also dumped 1,000 quintals of gunpowder into the sea and burnt stores and naval equipment. On 28 December 80 gunboats were destroyed at Posillipo and, ten days later, on 8 January, what remained of the Neapolitan fleet went up in flames. Niza delegated Commodore Donald Campbell, an Englishman in Portuguese service, to supervise the destruction of the bigger ships. The *Tancredi* (74), *Guiscardo* (74), *San Giacchino* (54), the *Pallade* frigate (40), the *Flora* corvette (24), the *Lampreda* schooner and dozens of smaller vessels were consigned to the flames. Over at Castellammare the British voiced concern that the great copper-bottomed *Partenope* (74), completed in August 1786, was also in danger so Forteguerri had Captain Guellichini scuttle it.

The Neapolitans, already 'anxious and miserable', were horrified by this destruction. Giacomo Puccini's grandfather, Domenico, happened to be in Naples when the fleet was destroyed and remarked in one of his letters:

The English and the Portuguese burned all the ships, frigates and gunboats, of which there were many; they threw the cannon and mortars into the sea, and stripped the arsenal down to the last nail, leaving it unprotected, and they also took away the defences along the shore. What a deplorable sight to see all that thrown away and burnt as it must have cost a fortune.

Sensing that posterity might not look upon this act too kindly, the queen was quick to blame the Portuguese for acting too hastily. She complained to the Austrian emperor on 21 January that 'the Portuguese commander, without waiting, thought it necessary to burn all our fleet and to flee; Nelson had him brought before a court martial'.[23]

All this took place long before the French arrived, and their triumphal entry into Naples was by no means certain. They had reached Capua, the huge fortified camp where the dejected Mack had established his mournful headquarters. There Championnet was forewarned that the Neapolitan government would seek terms to spare Naples the full horrors of war. The French general was therefore prepared when, on 11 January, the Duke of Gesso and the Prince of Migliano arrived proposing an armistice. It was accepted, Capua was handed over to the French, Neapolitan ports were declared neutral, and closed to warships of those powers in conflict with France, and a harsh imposition of 10 million livres tournois[24] was ordered, payable in two instalments. Non-payment would mean that hostilities would resume after three days' notice.

What Neapolitan government there was had signed because they were increasingly terrified by the possibility being left alone to face its own underclass. An increasingly bitter Mack was at Aversa watching as much of his army deserted to the French, whilst the rest begged in neighbouring villages for food, or joined the insurgents, whose ranks were further bloated by men called up by the *banni straordinari* issued on 27 December, so they could take it by force. Mack heard that the mob in Naples was now shouting '*Morte ai Francesi, ai Giacobbini, al Mack, al Pignatelli*'. This was too much for the broken commander and, on 15 January, the general, escorted by 50 dragoons, arrived at Caivano to hand over command to the Duke of Salandra[25] and then went to offer his surrender to the French at Caserta. There, attempting to hand his sword to Championnet, the Austrian was parried by the witty French general's riposte of 'General, keep it; my government forbids me to receive items of English manufacture'.[26]

In Naples the mob was less discerning and had bought swords and muskets off the fleeing soldiery. Then the Nuovo fort by the royal palace was easily stormed by the populace on 15 January, and the Carmine fort, the Uovo fort off Chiaja and Saint Elmo above the city went the same way. Into this combustive atmosphere rode the French commissioners, led by Jacques Philippe Arcambal, to collect the money promised them by the armistice. These brazen emissaries were closely followed by a hostile crowd which attempted to break into the San Carlo theatre and massacre them, but, before they could do so, the French were ushered out of the city.

Pignatelli, understandably overwhelmed and desperate not to become a martyr to misfortune, collected some 500,000 Ducats and took ship with his wife for Palermo on the night of the 15th. He left poor General Spinelli in charge but, in reality, authority, at least in the eyes of the mob, passed to the Prince of Moliterno, one more one-eyed man of the hour. He rode into the city, and declared himself commander of the forces of resistance, appointing Roccaromana as his deputy. However, Moliterno was preparing to double-cross Naples, and engineer a French entry into the city. He called a council of war in Roccaromana's house, where the duke, Captain Gaetano Simeoni, Guglielmo de la Grennelais, Nicola Verdinois and Antonio Sicardi plotted to seize the Saint Elmo fort on behalf of the republicans or 'patriots' as they called themselves. A republican agent, Giuseppe Poerio, slipped down from Caserta and signalled that the French would advance when the city's forts were secure. The patriots captured St Elmo by a ruse on 19 January,[27] the Nuovo and the Uovo forts also being seized. These sanctuaries were soon swollen with those seeking shelter from the coming storm as, outside, the crowd sensed the betrayal and was now busy hunting down Jacobins.

Or those who seemed like they might be Jacobins, or even well-dressed gentlemen. One mob broke into the palace of the Duke della Torre Filomarino, seizing the duke, Ascanio Filomarino, and his brother Clemente. They had been denounced to the mob by their wigmaker, Giuseppe Maimone, for corresponding in French. The result was that the ducal geological and botanic collections were smashed and a priceless collection of manuscripts burnt before the duke shared the same fate. Marinelli noted down in his diary how

> Their house was mercilessly plundered, the walls were stripped bare and the rest of the family only just managed to escape. At around 11 o'clock that evening the duke and his brother were taken to the Mole next to the Porto Salvo where they were shot, 24 carlini in the duke's pocket were stolen, and the two were then burnt.[28]

The shock was tremendous. The cleric Pietroabondio Drusco, along with countless others who had something to lose, was now in fear of his life, writing on 19 January:

> The anarchy has now reached a state of complete violence and the entire city is seemingly in revolt against the Jacobins and is now sacking and pillaging. The plebeians are in any case naturally quite mad, but as they now hold power, then it is quite clear that we have reached the end. No citizen can be sure that his life or his property will survive.[29]

To many it seemed as though only the French could end the chaos. Fortunately, they were on their way. Citing the failure of the Neapolitans to provide the money set out in the terms of the armistice, the French general had set his troops in motion. General Broussier was first to march, but was diverted by the sacking of Benevento's cathedral, from which he liberated 17,000 Ducats of treasure on 19 January, loading it onto 15 wagons. The main body advanced in a more disciplined fashion with Duhesme attacking the Capuan gate, whilst General Kellermann and a handful of Neapolitan exiles were directed towards the Maddalena bridge. Championnet himself was to advance on Capodimonte with his main body of 12,000 men.

Neapolitan resistance was ferocious. Bands of armed citizens, mostly drawn from the lazzaroni, had organised under self-appointed leaders, such as Paggio (a flour merchant), Antonio d'Avella (or Pagliuchella) and Michele Marino, known as Il Pazzo (the mad). They were all angry, for there had clearly been a betrayal. This became obvious when, on 20 January, the 250 patriots in Saint Elmo ran up a tricolour to signal to the French that the fort was in their hands. That evening they were joined by some Neapolitan exiles under Francesco Pignatelli, Colonel Girardon and 350 Frenchmen of the 12th Line. The patriots rejoiced, and swore 'to return to their natural state of liberty, and to live under a democratic government based on liberty and equality'.

The rhetoric was lofty, but the fighting was still bitter as it continued throughout the 21st, 'a day of horror, fear and anxiety' according to Marinelli. The fussy lawyer Carlo De Nicola, hiding in his villa at Antignano, sat listening to the endless rumbling of the artillery. That bombardment was the overture to the final French assault on the capital, and before long their columns began breaking into the city at various points.

On the morning of the 22nd, in combination with the French attack, the patriots made a sortie from Saint Elmo, rushing down towards the palace, whilst a second body of patriots fought their way out of the Uovo fort and then, combined with French detachments, began securing the waterfront. There the Neapolitan republican officer Andrea Mazzitelli, along with 50 French grenadiers of the 97th Line, boarded and captured the frigate the *Cerere*: 'I arrived at the harbour and ordered the drums to beat, and urged the soldiers to board, which we did and we took the frigate without resistance'.

That evening the fighting petered out elsewhere too as the French exerted their control of the key points with only the old Carmine fort holding out, the last bastion of the desperate. Sensing complete victory the patriots were elated. Guglielmo Pépé, an impressionable teenager, noted

> But, more than the others, did the republicans exult and congratulate themselves on the accomplishment of their ardent wishes: they might be seen in the streets embracing each other, even though they were strangers.[30]

As the smoke cleared the new republican flag, sewn together by the monks of the Saint Martin Charterhouse, the Certosini, was soon flying above the bruised and battered city. Reports of victory were trickling back to French headquarters at Aversa. Championnet and his staff had spent the 21 January there, and the French general then slept at the Palazzo della Valle, where Carlo Bourbon had stayed prior to his own victorious entry into Naples in 1734, before riding down into the city to claim his even more stunning victory. One king had fled, and the ghosts of other kings looked on helplessly as Naples was declared a republic.

5

Republic: New Rulers

General Championnet made a triumphal entry into the city that Wednesday morning, trotting gently along behind his green-coated dragoons as the Neapolitan populace made a show of welcoming their liberators. To his left was Giuseppe Poerio, the Jacobin, whilst on his right rode Michele Marino, Il Pazzo, the chief of the lazzaroni. This cavalcade of old and new Naples made its way down the Toledo, the riders shouting 'long live Jesus, Maria, Saint Gennaro and liberty!' to which the people replied, enthusiastically, by chanting back the same words.'[1]

One kingdom less, one republic more but Saint Gennaro was always in attendance and Championnet, sensitive to his sensitive audience, sent a guard of honour to safeguard the cathedral,[2] before turning to address his crowd:

> He harangued them expertly, making use of his expertise in the Italian language, telling them that the republic had not come to conquer them but to deliver them from their oppressors and that he would not hold them responsible for the betrayal and misfortune, for they themselves were victims.[3]

These sweet words and peace were cause for celebration, and, in response, Saint Gennaro gratefully performed his miracle for the masses and the city was illuminated for three nights. Vesuvius added to the glow with some timely pyrotechnics[4] whilst at the Saint Martin Charterhouse patriots and monks danced until morning. Bliss it was that dawn, but cautious bliss for the taverns were told to close early and to ban gambling, and 300 policemen went out to patrol and ensure the *salus populi*. To further the cause of peace, General Dufresse, the French military governor, and a man who had warn a miniature guillotine on his coat lapels during the Terror, declared an amnesty for those handing in stolen weapons, Drusco noting that 'many broken weapons were thrown into the streets and many were returned to the forts. But by no means all of them.'[5]

Championnet worked quickly to restore order, but he also required law. He needed to fill the void left by the flight of the royal family and establish a new government. As he had resolved to establish a sister republic, rather than to treat Naples as a conquest, he turned to key figures from amongst the exiles and from within the city and they gladly stepped forward in the hope of creating their cherished philosophers' republic. Some 20 individuals were selected, all men ready to bind the new regime to the Enlightenment with stout tricoloured thread, and Championnet easily approved the formation of the new government.

Carlo Lauberg, still sporting his French uniform, was to act as president and head of a provisional government balancing powers amongst prolix committees. The central committee, which had four other members (Jean Bassal, Domenico Bisceglia, Ignazio Ciaja and Cesare Paribelli) and Jullien de Paris serving as secretary, was the greatest concentration of power but a further five committees, tasked with legal matters, the police, the military, finances and administration, diluted the sense of direction. Then, confusingly, as it led to an overlap of jurisdiction, the implementation of government policy was placed in the hands of four ministries for war, finance, the interior and justice. With the Neapolitans inexperienced in such matters, it was felt sensible to split such authority between Frenchmen and natives.[6] It was hardly an ideal structure for ruling a nation in a time of turmoil, but this state designed and run by committee was officially proclaimed on Saturday 26 January as the Repubblica Napoletana,[7] and the new government was ceremonially inaugurated in the theatre of the royal palace. To manage the capital a municipal government was also now installed, its members including Giuseppe Serra, Luigi Carafa and that returned exile Andrea Vitaliani, as well as one of the leading lazzaroni, Antonio Avella (Pagliuchella), tasked with controlling the more unruly elements in Neapolitan society.

Championnet, who had done much to prepare the government for the republic, and the republic for government, was undoubtedly relieved to place the burden of running Naples on the slender shoulders of the youngest of France's sister republics. He seemed to genuinely enjoy the inauguration at the palatial theatre and dutifully sat through the harangue by Lauberg, who reminded them of a previous Neapolitan republic and the heroism shown by Masaniello in 1647. Then to the enthusiastic chanting of 'Viva la Repubblica Napoletana, viva la Francia' the tree of liberty, complete with its tricolour flags, was placed within sight of the balcony of the despot's palace.[8] Later that evening Championnet, the man who had acted as midwife to the new republic, was warmly welcomed at the Teatro del Fondo where he watched a performance of Aristodemo by Vincenzo Monti. He met tumultuous applause as he entered the royal box and had a 15-minute standing ovation.[9]

The enthusiasm was understandable, even the mildest men were agitated. Not only had the city avoided a lengthy assault[10] but the anarchy of the last few weeks was being forgotten and many entertained an optimism that the new regime might finally institute good government. Although the republic was born in an act of insubordination, for Championnet had no authority to refashion kingdoms, he had done well to ensure its leaders were drawn from members of the local elite. And to present his masters in Paris with a fait accompli.

Unfortunately for Naples, and for Championnet, the French government was horrified. It had been waging war for supremacy and wealth in recent years, and Championnet seemed satisfied with the paltry returns of gratitude. So it moved quickly to undermine the victorious general, quickly despatching a gang of commissioners to Naples to reserve for their own pockets, and for France if she was lucky, some of the riches now placed at risk by Championnet's idealism. These rapacious bureaucrats, mocked by the army as being *si vils*, a pun on civilians, were responsible for imposing contributions on conquered provinces and the members of the Directory, thinking on their capacious silk purses, and feeling themselves too poor to renounce the rights of conquest, encouraged them to deal harshly with Naples and with Championnet.

So it was that Talleyrand's creature, Guillaume Charles de Faipoult, who had rejoiced in less egalitarian times with the title Chevalier de Maisoncelles, along with Alexandre Méchin and Jean-Louis Marrier-Chanteloup, trotted into Naples. They loudly asserted their claim to collect lucrative levies, rubbing soft hands at the prospect of taking 3% on a punitive contribution of 15 million Ducats, France's fee for ridding the city of the Bourbons. The French officers and soldiers, with pay well in arrears,[11] were aghast and attempted to secure what they could before the three men got wise, Championnet's own aides-de camp confiscating 61 trunks of gold, and their commander sending Colonel Dubreton to secure 'all objects of art found in the museum, the king's residences and those of the émigrés, the property of the king and his family and reserved the right to undertake excavations at Herculaneum and Pompeii.' Championnet used much of this wealth to pay his generals. Faipoult, rising to the challenge, proclaimed his rights to whatever money could be found in the city, sequestered all the royal property for France, and published a notice to this effect in the streets of Naples. Rioting ensued.

Faipoult's proclamation also caused a riot at Championnet's headquarters and the French general, trusting that bayonets trumped the administrators' powers, published his own proclamation declaring that the upstarts would be ejected from Naples. Initially he had considered shooting them but, much to the disappointment of the army, he gave them 24 hours to quit the city and they fled to Rome on 6 February.

This scandalous behaviour had disheartened the provisional government and French squabbling over the spoils of victory had given the lie to much of the impressive rhetoric of the last few weeks. It was a bad beginning and made the difficult task of ruling a city emerging from looting and anarchy so much more problematic. Worse, between Championnet's troops and the commissioners' pockets, and the emptying of the already depleted national treasury by the royal family, the new republic was almost bankrupt before it could address the problems it faced. It was therefore understandable that some of the government's first steps involved getting the national debt consolidated and guaranteed in an attempt to get the bankrupt banks up and running, reduce inflation, and halt the depreciation of paper money.[12]

As it was attempting to put the nation's finances in order, the government also began to approach the thorny problem of how to rationalise the byzantine world of Neapolitan power. Those now in power had dreamt of this moment, but penury, Faipoult and confusion aborted the delights of anticipation. Men of principle, however, don't yield so easily and they held true to their Enlightened ideals whilst sensibly concluding that, although the kingdom had been replaced by a republic overnight, not everything could change so quickly. Bureaucrats, magistrates and justices of the peace were reassured by a decree on 30 January stating that 'all authorities and all magistrates which functioned under the fallen monarchy shall remain in their posts and shall continue to perform their functions as they did in the past'.[13] 'They began to work for the republic as before, but now with less formality, for 'vain and ostentatious' aristocratic titles, or titles accorded to officials such as *magnifico*, were abolished and the 'tu' form of address was to be used in preference.[14] Some of the nobility went further and enthusiastically renounced their titles, the Prince of Montemiletto preferring to be addressed as Antonio Tocco, and there was also a short-lived trend to adopt republican names, especially for those with the now despised name of Ferdinand. Bartolomeo Nardini explained:

No sooner had I recognised these gentlemen, than I saluted them using their accustomed names. 'What,' they snorted, 'didn't you know that I am now called Cassius?'. Another called himself Brutus, a third Timoleon.[15]

Despite the preference for ancient names, the republic was keen to modernise. In those early months it tackled ecclesiastical power, abolishing clerical privilege, and tithes, and instituting civil marriage, but placated the clergy by not legalising divorce. Divorcing the state from feudalism was a more thorny problem. The new government had drafted a detailed proposal by 7 March but was aware that any change would involve removing the state from its twin foundations of the vanity of the priests and the avarice of the nobility. The government hesitated, and, like many governments before and since faced with a complex problem, it opted for an inquiry, in this case run by seven honest citizens. Such procrastination meant that it was only in April 1799 that Albanese's and Abrial's radical proposal for abolishing the medieval system came into force. Work on the constitution also proved difficult. The obvious basis for a Neapolitan constitution was the one adopted by France, tempered by the constitution of the newborn United States. It sensibly called for a senate of 50 members and a council of 100, both overseen by an independent supreme court which would ensure that the constitution was respected, and a tribunal of elders as a final check on despotism. The constitution was finalised that April 1799 and came into effect on 14 May. It proved moderate, sensible and short-lived.

Given the preponderance of lawyers in the new government, it was unsurprising that more progress was made in reforming the legal system. The government showed itself to be progressive and fair, the principle of free and universal justice was declared, and a form of legal aid introduced. Such pernicious maxims as no imprisonment without due process and a ban on torture were introduced, and laws were now to be published in Italian rather than Latin. Public trials replaced secretive procedures and trial by jury, in the English manner, were to be the norm. All this was to take place in a rationalised system of tribunals, which did away with the confusion of competencies and jurisdictions of the old order.

However worthy and wise this new compound of morality and law, the greatly expanded social contract was understandably ignored by a wider populace who experienced little change save novelty, inflation and a dearth of once common-or-garden foodstuffs. The population remained ambiguous when it came to ideas designed to improve their lot, and clearly declined to commit to, or become involved with, the new regime. But some republicans did see the need to enlighten the Neapolitans as to their own true interests in order to, as the poet Eleonora de Fonseca Pimentel put it, transform people into citizens. Attempts to win over, or radicalise the masses, with eager republicans proselytizing in the city squares, earnest ex-clerics preaching the benefits of equality, and opening the patriotic clubs to ordinary citizens, were intensified. Most, however, were to be treated as entertaining sideshows in a city accustomed to pantomime, and so, to bolster their failing efforts, the republicans turned to those established masters of washing brains, the Church, the arts and the media, to republicanise as many ordinary Neapolitans as possible. The Church hierarchy, starting with what was left of San Gennaro himself, willingly collaborated. Bishop Andrea Serrao and Capece Zurlo, Archbishop of Naples, were similarly enthusiastic, and more outspoken. Bishop Rosini of Pozzuoli preached obedience and respect for the new laws and helpfully stressed that liberty and equality were not incompatible to the teachings of the evangelists; Conforti, one of the first ministers of the interior, went further preaching that 'Jesus Christ had commanded that there should be democracy'.

However, such talk didn't really wash with the people, many of whom suspected that these friends of the atheistic French were up to no good and were seeking to abolish carnival or Easter if not religion altogether. So, to drive the message home theatres and puppet shows were also enrolled in the campaign to moralise and promote republican themes. In the Teatro del Fondo, renamed the Teatro Patriottico, and the San Carlo, which inevitably became the Teatro Nazionale, a patriotic flurry of plays, with rather dull plots, and operas, with moralising choruses, was presented. Republicanising the world of print proved more problematic. The abolition of censorship was hailed as an early success until the erotic novel *Teresa Filosofa* was published. It caused consternation in the ruling elite for its depravity, and was denounced for corrupting public morals.[16] Copies were seized and burnt and the ministry of the interior hastily reinstituted the post of censor (*revisore*), to ensure republican virtue triumphed over ingrained vice. Newspapers too were supposed to communicate republican ideals, and sympathetic news, to the populace. First amongst them was the newly-created *Monitore Napoletano*, edited by the forthright Pimentel. The news of the day was also discussed in the new Hall of Public Education, or Sala patriottica, which was opened on 10 February and which subsequently preached to the converted four times a week. The patriotic society soon had 887 members presided over by Vincenzio Russo, the austere doctor and journalist.

All this change made for a rather exhilarating atmosphere within the capital, at least for the middle class. But the situation was fragile, as the revolution was trying to win popular support with esoteric rhetoric whilst the price of bread and salt militated against it. The government struggled to emerge from the tunnel of good intentions in order to address the concerns of Neapolitan citizens and Carlo de Nicola was not alone when he grumbled that 'so many beautiful promises of happiness and liberty, but yet we are more unhappy and enslaved than ever'.

Even within the city the republic, protected by French bayonets, was precarious, the new regime insecure. Outside the gates the situation was much more dire. To expand the republic, overawe its enemies and bring security to its citizens, the new state needed an army. Championnet hoped this would be easy enough:

> The army of the former king has been destroyed and not a single division remains. I have had organised two legions of infantry, each of 3,000 men, a regiment of artillery and two of cavalry. These troops are commanded by the former prince, Rocca Romana [actually Ettore Carafa], an honourable and patriotic man who can be relied upon, as can his officers who, after the flight and treason of their king, see themselves as being absolved from their oath and have sworn a new one to their nation.[17]

These legions were mostly of returned Jacobin exiles, but the deteriorating security situation in the early days of the republic required additional manpower and, unfortunately, the republic's response was a classic example of ideology trumping common sense. The republic rashly disbanded the existing royal army, even though, as Championnet mentioned, many officers thought their oath of loyalty to the crown no longer applied. In its place the idealists declared the establishment, on 6 February, of a National Guard. The spirit of duty and equality even motivated Giovanni Battista Filomarino (the Prince della Rocca) and the Prince of Torella to enlist as common soldiers and some of the clergy also stepped forward: the seminarian Ignazio Falconieri caused a scandal by swapping his vestments for a captain's tunic, whilst Pietro Paola Perrelli, an abbot, went further by donning uniform 'and swearing that he would go to Palermo and pass his sword through the heart of the tyrant'.

Of the 10,000 citizens who enrolled in Naples few wished to venture as far south as Perrelli, most limiting their involvement to very local policing duties. After repeated calls for volunteers, the few men the government could muster for service away from hearth and home formed the Bruzia Legion, under General Schipani, intended for operations in Calabria and later joined by a second legion, the Campana. In Naples a Legione patriottica dei Giovanni Calabresi, or Calabra Legion, was raised, from students or refugees from Calabria. There was also the Tullia Legion, the Volontari delle Società Patriottiche, and, less intimidating, La Speranza della Patria, literally the sons of liberty formed from eight to 16 year-olds to encourage patriotic duty.

Two volunteer cavalry squadrons were also formed after a long debate as to whether cavalry was elitist, and eventually some flashy republican hussars, including Timoleone Bianchi with his hair cut in the fashion of Brutus, served as escorts for the provisional government.

All this was not enough. Disappointed by the number of volunteers, the republic introduced dreaded conscription on 31 March. This necessitated a reorganisation of the army which, in true governmental style, lasted until early May, by which time it was all too late. General Matera did what he could to organise the new cadres and the Sannita (under Antonio Belpulsi), Volturna (under Antonio Pinedo), Salentina (Pietro de Roche) and Lucana (Giosue Ritucci) legions made it onto the muster rolls. Recruits and conscripts were lacking, however, and only a few hundred former army officers and NCOs, with few servicemen present to do any of the actual fighting, eventually took the field.[18]

The local coastal artillery proved more popular and Neapolitans enthusiastically volunteered to man the batteries and fight off any marauding Barbary Corsairs, and the ubiquitous British, whilst still returning home in time for dinner.[19] However, to truly keep such pirates at bay a navy was required. Thanks to the burning of the royal fleet, the Neapolitan Republic could boast a single frigate, a small flotilla of gunboats and a handful of brigs. Admiral Francesco Caracciolo, 'brave as a sailor, brave as a warrior, braver still as a citizen' would later return to Naples to take command of this modest fleet. And modest it was, for even the republic's frigate, the *Cerere*, was never really seaworthy as its captain, Giuseppe De Cosa, explained when Championnet lunched onboard on 24 February.

The day after that convivial lunch Championnet received orders from his superior, Scherer, that he was to proceed to Milan where he would be detained pending a court martial. Faipoult and the *si vil* commissioners had got their revenge and the general now met the unfortunate fate of anyone attempting to come between ministers of government and the potential for enormous personal wealth. Disgraced and humiliated, Championnet was hurried away and, on 28 February, General Macdonald replaced him.[20] Macdonald wrote, on the same day, asking Faipoult and his commissioners, exiled to Rome, to return to Naples.

The Neapolitans were horrified by the hypocrisy of the French and staggered by the payment Faipoult and his ilk were now demanding. Worse, Macdonald, clannish with the Directory, proved no ally, thinking, as he did, that the Neapolitan regime is 'of a kind which is completely vicious, makes a lot of promises, talks a great deal, but never does anything'. Deprived of its most significant guide, the provisional government, lacking the means to impose even their least divisive policies, increasingly began to be driven apart by factionalism. Lauberg, frustrated, left Naples that April and was replaced by Ignazio Ciaja. The resignations of Rotondo,

Fasulo, Caputo and Paribelli followed. Fortunately, an even greater crisis was averted by the timely arrival of Joseph Abrial, who was sent to save the republican government from itself. It was a welcome development, for Abrial, a lawyer with a slight stammer, was a gifted organiser of stability and greatly sympathised with the republic's plight. The provisional government was overhauled, an executive committee of 25, which included such luminaries as the lawyer Mario Pagano and the botanist Dr Domenico Cirillo,[21] ruled alongside a tighter legislative committee of just five. There were hopes that the new order might now start to impose some order on the capital, and a more optimistic Ciaja told his brother 'Abrial, who you know from Turin, has come ... to put an end to the poor organisation which has been damaging the commonweal'.

That commonwealth was something of a fantasy. It was precarious enough in Naples but beyond the city gates a state of anarchy existed where republicanism was failing to take root. The kingdom had collapsed as the Neapolitan army was dissolving the previous December, and stragglers, looters and peasants had swept through many regions in January and February in a carnival of excess. With the king fled, and the young republic emerging from the ruins in Naples, some regions aped the capital, as much in fear of the mob as in favour of republicanism, and declared themselves loyal to the new order. These republicanised enclaves were soon calling for republican or French help as the gangs of the disaffected, who had pillaged their way through January and who were now looking for leadership for larger-scale robberies, began to coalesce into something resembling counter-revolution. As with the insurgency around Rome the mob was being spurred on by priests, landowners and long-standing feuds. In Barletta in January 1799 Camillo Elefante jotted down in his diary that

A terrible revolution has broken out amongst the lower orders, especially those in the countryside around us, all on account of listening to the sermons which have stirred everyone up to take up arms to defend Religion, the State and their farms and to preserve the honour of their families from our French enemies and their Jacobinical followers.

Such forces of reaction, finding it a challenge to find actual revolutionaries, dedicated the early stages of their careers to raiding rival communities or, unembarrassed by the constraints of law, destroyed or looted bourgeois property on the pretext that the owners must be Jacobins. Angelo de Jacobis remembered how the mob came for the gentlemen:

Ah, what a sight to see how the people have gone wild and are breaking and smashing up wooden beams, doors, balconies and burning cloth, mattresses, blankets, crockery, books, documents and anything they could fine in the property of the people of the town, as well as laying waste to the warehouses with oil and grain. They have destroyed so many important legal texts and good-quality furniture all because they belonged to lawyers and gentlemen. What an anarchic mob and one which pretends to stand for the monarchy but really only wants to rob the rich which they then do after calling them Jacobins.[22]

Wanton disorder, and the spectre of a peasant revolt, led to some communities calling out the militia, and then appealing to the only force that represented order, the new republic, for assistance. With a semblance of control imposed on Naples, and rights over property guaranteed, provincial towns understood that the worst of governments is better than none at all, and planted their trees of liberty. Delicate veins of democracy reached out across the bloated carcass of the kingdom, and as winter faded the land teetered between a vanished monarchy and an ethereal republic, between the desire for order and the fear of chaos. To fill the void it was a question of who could organise the fastest and it seemed that republicanism was winning over the towns, whilst the lingering resentments of the old order enforced a reaction in the countryside.

Force made all the difference, however. The province of Abruzzo in the east, tucked under the Papal States, had been the prototype for local revolution. General Duhesme had established Melchiorre Delfico as president of a republican administration at Teramo on 11 December but when the French soldiers moved on to Naples in January, the inurgents swept into the vacuum and Giuseppe Pronio, the leader of some armed bands of royalists, bandits and smugglers hovering around Pescara, organised his mob into an insurgency to make republican life difficult and the civil war in the Abruzzo permanent.[23]

To the west, between Naples and Rome, and along the main road connecting the two, a similar story played out. The passage of troops had led to insurrection, this time led by a miller, the infamous Gaetano Mammone who himself recalled, 'the city of Sora rose up. Sporting the red cockade, and seizing those weapons that had escaped the French sack of the army's magazines, the people, cheering the name of Ferdinando IV, elected Mammone as their leader.' Possibly because of the brutal example Mammone made of anyone who resisted. Pasquale Cayro remembered that

Commandante Muscella and Archdeacon di Gallinaro were taken to Sora and killed there and he [Mammone] placed the head of the former before his house and with the head of the latter he went so far as to drink the blood from it, and other atrocities which would horrify one.[24]

Around Gaeta, a rocky bastion north of Naples, rebels from Itri under the disgraced soldier, Michele Pezza, nicknamed Fra Diavolo on account of him having sung as a boy in the church, made a name for themselves and a fortune for their commander by robbing travellers using the coastal road. Supplies coming into Naples by sea were meagre but at least less prone to such violent risk, especially when the islands of Procida and Ischia went over to the republic. Procida chased out Governor Curtis on 27 January and Antonio Candia planted the tree of liberty on Ischia.

The fruit from that symbolic tree could not feed Naples, however, and the capital was growing hungry as it watched itself surrounded by insurgencies and revolts. So the government persuaded its finest soldier, Ettore Carafa, to break out for Avellino on the strategic road to the Adriatic ports and their warehouses stuffed with necessities. The charismatic former nobleman convinced a squadron of cavalrymen from the garrison at Nola to sport the republican cockade and these, along with a handful of priests, some marksmen raised by his brother, Carlo, and volunteers such as Florestano and Ferdinando Pepe, set off on their modest mission. In order to smooth their way, a vanguard of republican commissaries was sent on ahead to win over the masses caught between two loyalties. One such firebrand arrived in Barletta, in Puglia on the Adriatic coast, on 2 February 1799:

At around 20.00 hours a certain Ruggiero di Mola, who was staying at an inn beyond the city walls, and who seemed unaware of the city's opinion, but was, apparently, a Commissioner of the new republic, was brought in and taken to the city square. He jumped onto the plinth of the Hercules statue and began to preach about liberty and equality and read out, in a loud voice, some texts which were hostile to the monarchy and to our royal majesty. Few people were present to listen, and they drifted away and the man was led off to the house of Giorgio Esperti … they went to the square where they had a mast raised and decked out in yellow, turquoise and red ribbons, erected next to the Hercules statue with a flag flying from its top. Just then the castle fired a few cannon shots and there was much applause and some verses from the Democratic rites were sung by those around the tree.

Events followed a similar course at Trani, as Berarducci noted:

A Civic Guard was raised at Trani and in many other places in the province, to ensure public order. On 1 February, a Friday, it was said that the French commissioners had arrived in Barletta and some thought it would be wise to democratise first. A deputation was sent to find them. It seems that there were two of them, a cleric, named Francesco Ruggiero, and a self-styled French courier who, it was said, used to be a highwayman.

Bari went republican on the afternoon of the 5th February and another 50 Puglian communities joined these important provincial centres in welcoming the new republic, which was fortuitous as Puglia could supply most of the capital's food. But bad news was quick on the heels of good as Trani, a republican hope, soon fell to a counter-revolution, as a diarist relates:

At around nine the police began to order people to take off the tricolour cockade. The disorder became general. The sailors gathered and armed themselves and, with others, ran up to the citadel, got inside, hoisted the royal standard, and pulled down the republican flag, firing a volley as they did so. That was in the fort. The Civic Guard was dispersed, the tree of liberty cut to pieces and arms were distributed so that there were around a thousand armed people who set out hunting for Jacobins, breaking windows and doors, attacking houses, including that of De Felice, which they also fired shots at, and forcing others to put lights in their windows.

At Barletta, a crowd formed threatening to attack the clergy and nobility, some of them confusing Jacobins with those from the San Giacomo quarter[25] but they were beaten off. The whole of Puglia, having initially shown such promise, now teetered on the brink of chaos, as Berarducci noted:

Barletta, has a tree, is democratised and the patriots are in control, the people seem disatisfied.
Trani, the royalists and the people in charge.
Bisceglia, the royalists and the people in charge.
Molfetta, the royalists and the people in charge.
Giovinazzo, indifferent, but threatened by the people of Molfetta.
Bari, has a tree and the people are unhappy, fighting in the hamlets which surround it.
Andria, the royalists and the people in charge.
Corato, has a tree, is poor but indifferent.
Ruvo, indifferent.
Terlizzi, has a tree but the people are discontent.
Bitonto, rumours.

Such a confused picture made it clear that the republic would need to make use of the double-edged sword of French help to impose the republic on the varied provinces of the new republic. Such assistance came in the shape of Duhesme's veterans advancing under their banners of fraternity to liberate Puglia and perhaps even secure possession of Brindisi and distant Taranto, a coup which would enable the French to supply Corfu and even their stranded army under Bonaparte in Egypt. Duhesme therefore set off at a brisk trot, accompanied by some 4,000 men and Carafa's Jacobin volunteers milling around Nola and Avellino, and reached Foggia on 23 February. He then stormed San Severo[26] but was recalled to Naples by the new commander-in-chief, Macdonald, not because of any crime, but because he was a loyal supporter of the now disgraced Championnet. So it was General Broussier who continued the campaign, turning south and reaching Barletta, where he was warmly welcomed, as the diarist Elefante recorded:

> Intermittent rain all day. The French troops arrived, infantry, cavalry, some that were dragoons, artillerymen with artillery pieces, some of which were cannon and some howitzers followed by numerous wagons with drivers in uniforms. The soldiers were generally dressed badly many with long tunics which were dirty and torn, others with greatcoats in different colours or black which allowed them to cover what they had looted. They all had handkerchiefs full of coins or different possessions. The soldiers were lodged in assigned places whilst the officers and NCOs were in different houses, although there were always too many of them for each residence, whilst General Broussier and his suite were in Signor Esperti's house. Looking after general's table was the work of Tommaso Pecorari and Canon Francesco del Vecchio and these were given money for the supplies and other requirements as the table was to be a buffet, available at all hours, and to a large number of people and covered with a large number of different dishes and, for dessert, ice cream.[27]

At least the foot soldiers of atheism and terror were on their best behaviour:

> Very few of the French soldiers go to church as many have abandoned religion altogether or if they have retained it inwardly they don't express it so that they aren't mocked or ridiculed. It is the same with the officers and some of them are right thinking and moral. Few people now visit the San Sepolcri, the women especially stay away in order to avoid trouble from the French who, although they obey their officers in wartime, do not respect anyone else and they greet you looking in your eye, the wondrous results of equality, anarchy and irreligion.

Having digested their ice cream, the French then prepared to attack Andria, after Carafa, whose family domain included much of the surrounding area, had unsuccessfully tried to negotiate a peaceful outcome. On 23 March the French, relying on force of arms to win peace, joined Carafa's men,[28] attacked the Porta Castello, broke into the town, and fought their way through the narrow streets. There was now a massacre, with 685 inhabitants killed, and the town was put to the sack, even the cathedral being plundered.[29]

The story was the same at Trani, the French again storming in and storming off with many valuables, some of which were sold on the open market at Bisceglia:

> The French soldiers came to the town square to sell the loot they had seized from Trani. A coach costing 1500 Ducats was sold for 100. The author bought a coat for 2.4 Ducats.

The French then broke through to assist isolated Bari a week later but there the revolutionary impetus ran out of energy largely because Brindisi, an important port, remained loyal to the king due to a knot of Corsican emigrants. These Corsicans, centred on a group of seven former officers of the Anglo-Corsican Regiment, were led by Colonel Giambattista De Cesari. One of his companions, Casimiro Raimondo Corbara, who had blue eyes and a large nose, was mistaken for the Hereditary Prince and De Cesari cunningly declared himself the Duke of Saxony. Temporarily chased out of Brindisi by the accidental arrival of one of the few French warships to have escaped from Aboukir, the Corsican émigrés and their supporters then rashly marched against Taranto, which had declared itself republican largely because of the influence of the archbishop, Giuseppe Capecelatro. The Corsicans and their army 'of feudal retainers led by gentlemen volunteers' restored royal authority on 9 March. With this important victory, and the French and republicans tied down in what few urban centres they claimed, it was clear that the counter revolution was gaining pace.

This was confirmed when news came that the whole of Calabria had fallen to the resurgent royalist forces.

6

Ruffo: Royalists and Renegades

On 8 February 1799, a small boat approached Pezzo on the toe of Italy. From amongst the confusion of the surf a cardinal stepped ashore, and away he staggered, across the sand and into Calabria. It was a good Friday for there to meet him were a small band of retainers sent by the cardinal's brother to welcome him and his strange entourage ashore. And, indeed, Cardinal Don Fabrizio Ruffo-Baranello companions were an odd mixture. There was the Marchese Filippo Malaspina, a military man; the sycophantic clerk, Domenico Petromasi; three clerics, Lorenzo Sparziani, Domenico Sacchinelli and Annibale Caporossi; and two servants to cook and wash the linen of the men of cloth. Even stranger was that this band formed the nucleus for a crusade and they brought with them a standard of revolt, optimistically embroidered with *In hoc signo vinces*.

Ruffo had disembarked and now launched his reconquest, marking the start of one of the strangest campaigns in European history. Ruffo himself was a strange choice to lead such an adventure. He combined the corruption and innocence of a cleric with the temerity of an Italian bureaucrat, but, despite a life spent in conflict in conclave and corridor, he was largely unversed in the arts of war. His chief talent was administration, and following his return to Naples from reforming the Roman civil service in late 1794, he had dedicated his time to running the San Leucio estate and running after the widow Girolama Lepri. In early 1799, with the royal family cowering in Palermo, and Ruffo in exile with them, he thought to demonstrate his loyalty by rashly volunteering to go over to Calabria and organise resistance to the republic from his family estates around Bagnara and Scilla.

Acton[1] and the royal family were supportive of such an enterprise. Acton secretly hoped that Ruffo's ambition would meet its end in a Calabrian village, whilst the king and queen enthusiastically greeted any initiative to keep the republican hordes as far from Sicily as possible. Ruffo was therefore accorded sweeping powers by the royal council on 25 January, dubbed the royal Alter Ego, elevated to the role of Commissioner General and Vicar General and authorised to act, reward and punish as he saw fit. To encourage him on his way some vague undertakings were made suggesting that the king might follow on with some troops should Ruffo secure a foothold on the foot of Italy.

But the Bourbons were soon telling Ruffo that he would have to build a force from deserters as soon as he landed, the royal family being keen to keep their troops in Sicily as they felt insecure in the alien territory of their island kingdom. Or rather the queen did as the king was happy enough in Palermo, and quickly forgot Naples.[2] Maria Carolina, on the other hand, making much use of Lady Hamilton's shoulder to cry on, detested the island and saw danger everywhere.[3] Plagued by anxiety, she was desperate by February:

> Insurrection is widespread for we unfortunately don't have enough troops to suppress it. ... Messina is ill-disposed and I expect to hear word at any moment that the revolution has started there. Once that place is lost, we will not be able to hold on to Sicily more than eight days.

She felt that only the British could protect her, and once her fears about Messina were shared with Lady Hamilton, it was Nelson, exhausted, despondent and sick, and understandably thinking of leaving all this behind him for a new life in London, who was again prodded into the role of the queen's saviour. The queen and her friend worked on the admiral until he dutifully wrote to General Stuart in Menorca:

> What a State we are in here! without Troops, and the Enemy at the Door: for altho' there are 4,000 Neapolitan regular troops, these are not to be trusted; 13,000 Sicilian Troops are raising, and 26,000 Militia; but I fear, before these are got together, the active French will get possession of Messina, the Key of Sicily. There is a good Citadel, and might be defended for a long time but there is such treachery, that probably it will be given without a shot.[4]

It was indeed hard to be optimistic. Charles Lock, the new consul, noted that 'It is the opinion of Sir William Hamilton and of Lord Nelson that this Island will soon follow the fate of the other Kingdom'. The lack of reliable troops to defend the island was exacerbated by demands on the reduced royal budget. Despite the treasure from Naples, and the establishment of a national lottery to fund defence,[5] it seems the royalists had insufficient money to pay for all demands. The king had rewarded Caracciolo and the crews of the *Sannite* and *Aurora* from his own purse but from 4 February the sailors of the Neapolitan ships were being paid off, effectively leaving the fleet crewless. The result was that the embittered Caracciolo wrote to Acton asking that he and his officers be allowed to return to Naples.[6]

So, having landed, Ruffo initially had to shift for himself with a few deserters or retainers from the estates of his brother, the Duke of Baranello. Fortunately, Calabria was reliably Francophobic and, before long, Ruffo had enough men to move on Gioia Tauro, where his Calabrians sacked the place and made war against bottles and good wine, as Sacchinelli, Ruffo's secretary and admiring chronicler, put it. With the opportunity to cloak such crime in the apparel of royalism and religion, volunteers of all kinds began to flock in. There were bandits under Nicola Gualtieri, nicknamed Panedigrano, and smugglers and released criminals, all intermingled with small groups of regular soldiers, and the cardinal's army was soon a strange assortment of men hastily thrown together by greed, want or hostility to the republican government. Whilst this host would serve under the unifying slogan of the Army of the Holy Faith, Sacchinelli acknowledged that not all of Ruffo's soldiers were true believers:

> In this large body of men there were all kinds of clergy; there were rich landowners, artisans, labourers from the countryside; there were honest men motivated by a fervour to protect their religion, or through attachment to their king and to good order; and, unfortunately, there were murderers and thieves, motivated by a lust for pillage, vendetta and blood.[7]

The republicans, understandably, were even more dismissive of such troops, Gaetano Rodinò, then serving in the National Guard, soon writing that Ruffo's volunteers consisted of:

> The ambitious, robbers, criminals fleeing the arms of justice, dissolute youths, vile deserters who had been dishonoured, quarrelsome and arrogant priests, lecherous and treacherous friars, all flocking to serve beneath the flag of the Holy Faith.[8]

Whilst a few disciplined retainers and a company of gamekeepers elevated themselves above such generalised condemnation it was true that the bulk of the cardinal's recruits consisted of rather wild Calabrian irregulars whose distinguishing features were a white cross on the right side of their hats and a tremendous thirst for plunder. Worse were the convicts and galley slaves whom the British landed on the Calabrian coast, and sent to join Ruffo at Rosarno.[9] Sacchinelli tells us

> The English, in order to reduce the expenses of the Sicilian government, thought to land a large number of prisoners who were in the prisons of Sicily and the other islands on the Calabrian coast, being mistaken in thinking that they might serve the public good by serving in the war. Public order was destroyed and the horrible anarchy which ensued made our heads spin.[10]

As for the deserters who were supposed to seek out employment in Ruffo's ranks, they were a sorry bunch. Petromasi, a voice from Ruffo's ranks, saw some and was not impressed:

> Some of the dispersed soldiers from the army came to join us, they were unarmed, without clothes and not constrained to join but were loyal to the king, although they resembled so many walking ghosts. The 42 men under Perez increased within five days so that three companies of 70 men each were formed. Although they were called soldiers some lacked shoes, others tunics and all were without weapons.[11]

This unorthodox army was obliged to be constantly on the march because inaction endangered the locals and thinned the ranks, and so Ruffo directed his strange mix of commanders to draw up a campaign plan. The former soldier, Pasquale Cayro, who thought the country had gone to the dogs since the times of Charles III, set down his own candid, and dismissive, views on Ruffo's captains:

> They were miserable people, who had gained a living through manual labour, or by transporting things, and who now showed themselves well mounted on good horses, well dressed, with watches and with money, wanting to be seen as gentlemen and making use of the phrase 'of the Holy Faith' whilst staining themselves with sin, so to say, giving out that they were going against the French for religious reasons, although they never attacked them and they were always forced to retreat. [12]

Ruffo's Army of the Holy Faith was, then, a broad church of deserters, freebooters, bandits, priests and dubious soldiers. Fortunately, their first objective, republican Catanzaro, capital of Calabria Ultra and on the east coast of Italy's toe, fell easily enough when Ruffo with 4,000 men and three guns appeared before it in the first week of March. Having thus secured a foothold on the mainland, Ruffo now hoped that the situation was stable enough for the king to fulfil his promise of coming over to lead the Reconquista in person. The queen, more familiar with her faint-hearted husband, sent the cardinal a dose of realism, writing candidly:

> I understand the advantage and effectiveness of having the king come to Calabria, and the possibility to acquire some glory, but it does not depend upon me. Oh how, how I wish I were a man, I would happily come to be alongside your Excellency and would be delighted if I could be of use in your courageous endeavour. But I am only a woman and it is more fitting that I stay at home and pray.[13]

It mattered little for now, the pragmatic cardinal, relying on his own abilities, was learning fast from the testament of bloody war. Cosenza was next to fall, Ruffo writing that 'he hoped the populace had sacked the place along with the attackers, to ensure the nobles and middle class are kept in fear', and then the royalists reached defiant Crotone. This town had a small French garrison,[14] and was ardently republican. Even so, it soon fell, only a handful holding out in the citadel before being forced to surrender. In a sinister prelude of what was to come in Naples, the French received preferential treatment, being sent off to Messina for exchange, whilst the republicans were tried by an extraordinary commission of state under Don Angelo di Fiore. Four of the town's leaders were seized and shot, five were sent to the dungeons or penal islands for life, and 35 others were given sentences of between five and 20 years or sent to the galleys. The king and Acton had, after all, called for punitive measures, Ferdinand telling Ruffo 'for those rebels who fall into your hands, judge them militarily, make examples' and Acton had lyrically called for heads, writing 'a severe but just example is to be made so that we can rein in that spirit of corruption and decay so beloved of the partisans of democracy'.[15]

With much of the province now in royal hands, Ruffo then paused, incorporating a new wave of recruits, including a band under Gennaro Rivelli from Puglia,[16] all of whom had responded to news of his conquest of Calabria, and that he was paying his volunteers a daily wage. Ruffo needed all the men he could get for news came that, at long last, the republican government in Naples had reacted and was marching against him. An expeditionary force led by General Schipani, following in the wake of some 1,500 French troops who had already moved down the coast to Salerno, was fighting its way through insurgents. The French were under garrulous General Sarrazin who, fresh from unsuccessfully assisting one insurgency in Ireland, had come to Naples to put down another. He took the 30th Line and the 19th Chasseurs and prepared to launch an assault on the rebel position at Nocera near Salerno. Before he could do so, a horseman rode out from the Neapolitan lines:

> He came out at the gallop and threw a basket down by our skirmishers, then rode back laughing. They brought the basket over to me. It contained the genitals of a few French stragglers along with this note 'We are ten against one and before the day is done you shall all suffer the fate of these rogues whose private parts we now send you'. There was no need to harangue my soldiers, I merely had to have the basket passed down through the ranks. I forbade any firing but marched with my columns against the heights. I had my cavalry wait on the main road, ready to sabre any fugitives. We overthrew the enemy on first impact and the slaughter was terrible. The cavalry showed no quarter largely because the stragglers who had been mutilated belonged to the 19th Chasseurs.

The insurgents fled with their tails between their legs and Schipani and the French established a gentleman's republic in Salerno under Ferdinando Ruggi and paused to celebrate. The British responded to this republican success with a small expedition that March. Nelson, busy 'making himself ridiculous with Lady Hamilton', according to Admiral Keith, delegated Troubridge to lead a flotilla into the bay of Naples in order to seize Procida and Ischia and cut Naples off from being supplied from the sea. Troubridge obliged, setting sail in the *Culloden*, a name so ominous for rebels, and, with a small Anglo-Portuguese flotilla, and Count Thurn's Neapolitan frigate the *Minerva*,[17] easily taking Ischia. A crowd set fire to the tree of liberty, Troubridge sending two fragments from that forbidden tree to the king at Palermo, whilst the allies moved against Procida. There the republicans under youthful Bernardino Alberini improvised a defence, but, as the Reverend Cooper Willyams makes clear, it was soon over:

> As it was known that many of the inhabitants were desirous of returning their allegiance, Captain Hallowell, accompanied by Mr Rushout,[18] landed on the island of Procida. They were received with enthusiastic joy, and amidst the acclamations of the people, ascended to the castle: the French tree of liberty was cut down, the tri-coloured flag destroyed, and the royal Neapolitan flag hoisted in its stead.[19]

Republican prisoners were now hauled off to the castle off Ischia or held on the British ships, and Troubridge and the Bourbon's avenging agents sent to Palermo for a judge. Nelson anticipated the outcome of Bourbon justice, asking Troubridge to 'send me word some proper heads are taken off; this alone will comfort me'. The court did not disappoint this bloodthirsty wish, sending the infamous Vincenzo Speciale and two colleagues, and by mid-April this trio of inquisitors was trying prisoners *ad modum belli*.[20] Amongst the first to be processed were the priests Nicola Lubrano, Antonio Scialoia and Antonio de Luca. They were found guilty of preaching revolution and were sent to Palermo to be defrocked before any sentence could be passed. Troubridge was furious at the delay, contradicting the judge and demanding that they be hanged at Ischia at once. He wrote

> He talks of it being necessary to have a bishop degrade the priests before he can execute them. I told him to hang them first, and if he did not think the degradation of hanging sufficient I would piss on the damned Jacobin carcass, and recommended him to punish the principal traitors the moment he passed sentence, no mass, no confession but immediate death, hell was the proper place for them.[21]

Troubridge would soon have his carcass, or at least part of it. He received the head of a Jacobin in a basket:

> Your Excellency As a faithful subject of my king Ferdinando (whom God save), I glory in presenting to your Excellency the head of Don Carlo Granozio of Giffoni, who was employed in the administration directed by Ferdinando Ruggi, that infamous commissary. The said Granozio was killed by me in a place called Li Pugi, in the district of Ponte Cagnaro, while he was endeavouring to escape. I beg your Excellency kindly to accept this head, and to consider what I have done as a proof of my attachment to the Crown. I am, with the respect due to you, the faithful subject of the king, Giuseppe Mancuso Vitella.[22]

The British were unperturbed by an alliance with such wholesome allies, and even invited the vulpine Fra Diavolo, that notorious man of blood, to tour the *Culloden* on 26 April. Troubridge was as delighted with the man in person as he had been earlier with tales of his exploits, for he had already enthused to Nelson that he had heard how the insurgent had attacked and killed some women and their escort, adding 'I sincerely hope it is true'.[23]

Meanwhile British support for that other butcher, Sciarpa, around Salerno paid off when his royalists, encouraged by the support of Captain Hood's *Zealous*, managed to provoke an insurrection in the town. There was a merciless slaughter of the new republican administration, in which the eminent 86-year-old Archbishop Sambiase was trampled underfoot, later dying of the shock, before the royal banner once again graced the battlements. Castellammare was also attacked again in late April, the *Minotaur* and *Swiftsure* covering raids on the arsenal and shipyards. In response Admiral Caracciolo, who had assumed command of the republican fleet led his gunboats out to harass the British ships. His expedition was a success and to cap Allied discomfort the French in Naples sent generals Watrin against Salerno and Sarrazin to Castellammare, overpowering their rivals, and capturing many prisoners, including eleven British Marines and Filippo Acton, the youngest brother of Sir John Acton, as well as a British flag and two royal banners.[24]

Troubridge informed Nelson that it had been Caracciolo behind the republican success:

> Caracciolo, I am now satisfied, is a Jacobin. I enclose you one of his letters. He came in the gunboats to Castellamare himself, and spirited up the Jacobins.

The report reached the queen, who branded the Neapolitan 'that great rascal Caracciolo'.

Another blow followed when a republican counter-attack also struck Sorrento, where General Alberto Micheroux, who had been so undistinguished in Abruzzo in 1798, promptly re-embarked his troops on the British ships and departed.[25]

Naples breathed a sigh of relief but the Royal Navy's seizure of Procida had in fact placed an additional strangle-hold on a capital already short of oil, meat and flour. Material shortages were exacerbated by the rumour mill in the city, which captured public attention far more than any government announcement managed to do, De Nicola noting that 'the country is in ferment, the people exult because there may be a change of government and the English ships off Procida are said to be the vanguard of a much bigger fleet' and noted that there were 300 troops of the line and 100 convicts ready to be sent ashore to trigger the counter-revolution. The queen, never idle, exhorted the clergy to 'urge their flock to take up arms against the perfidious French nation and to declare and denounce them as a nation without laws, without faith, and to have them take up arms in defence of holy religion, and His Majesty ....'. Royal partisans within Naples, now liberally provisioned with gold, readied their clandestine networks and prepared for insurrection.

The republican police, perhaps the only government agency with the requisite energy, had kept revolt at bay by noisily arresting suspected schemers.[26] On 9 March General De Gambs, Colonel Baron Abramo de Bock and Major Dillotti were taken into custody. Even so, royalist activity intensified in early April, and the most startling of the plots, the conspiracy centring around the Baccher family, which planned to seize St Elmo and trigger a mass uprising and a massacre of the republicans, caused shock when it was discovered. Secret tokens had been distributed so royalists could recognise their own and one such talisman was presented to Luisa Molina Sanfelice by young Gerardo Baccher, a cavalry lieutenant connected to Moliterno and Roccaromana. She denounced the plot to her family lawyer, Vincenzo Coco, who informed the authorities. Raids were carried out on 5 April and most of the Bacchers were seized and secured in the city's forts.

Republican success in foiling this plot did not kill the sense of foreboding. On 17 April, the diarist De Nicola, noted that doors to a number of houses in Naples had been marked with red, black and white symbols, clandestine instructions as to what was to happen to the inhabitants when the people rose up. The diarist recorded 'they say red will be set on fire, black means to be killed and white means to be plundered'.

Against this background of fear and intrigue, tension was heightened by a change of government. The old structure was overhauled, and the new authority put on the mantle of energy which had hitherto been laid aside. Joseph Abrial, the stammering lawyer, had cleverly concentrated power in a smaller legislative commission of five (Abamonti, Ercole D'Agnese, Albanese, Ciaja and Delfico). This oversaw an executive commission of 25, divided into radicals and moderates, with Abrial, who sympathised with the radicals, reserving the right to select constituent members.[27] There was a flurry of activity, perhaps also because the radicals, especially the Friends of the Law, sent regular delegations, led by the firebrand Rosario Licopoli, to hector the government. The abolition of feudalism was finally declared on 25 April, and ratified on 27 April. The testatico tax was abolished, and taxes on flour went the same way on 9 May. It seemed too little, too late. Soon a revolutionary commission[28] took over the reins of power and the clubs were also radicalising, sending a deputation to lobby the government to demand that private property, starting with that of those who had emigrated or were declared royalists, should be confiscated and nationalised. On 10 May, and in a sure sign of the times, 416 members of the political society took a brave oath for the republic as one of them, Guglielmo Pépé, recalled:

My forebodings did not prevent me from accompanying [Gaetano Coppola] and his brother Nicola Coppola to the sala patriottica which was held in the palace of the ancient Accademia de' Cavalieri, where a pen was handed to me, to inscribe my name on the roll. The title on that roll was the solemn oath of freedom or death.

Freedom or death sounded like a choice, but death was more likely. The loss of Calabria to a cardinal had been a great blow but elsewhere too the tide was turning in favour of the embittered old order. Puglia was next to fall, and to an equally unlikely enemy.

7

Reconquest: The Republic in Peril

A little light rain had made the battlements of Lecce's citadel slippery but the wind was up that April morning and, as the clouds were being swept away, and visibility restored, the sentinels caught sight of five strange sails bearing towards the coast. Soon a little column of riders was seen heading towards the city gates and a Belgian and Russian emissary were ushered into the Adriatic port. They announced that a royal fleet had arrived to restore the crown in Puglia and that Lecce, having withstood the republic, would now be the capital of royalist resistance in the east.

That odd fleet of five ships – two Russian, one Ottoman, one from Tripoli and the Neapolitan *Fortuna* under Captain Staiti – had set off from Corfu on 13 April 1799. Whilst Commander Alexander Andreievich Sorokin was in charge of these ships, and five companies of Russian marines with 10 pieces of artillery, the most important personage on board was, by all accounts, including his own, the suave Chevalier Antonio Micheroux.[1] He was to act as the king's representative in the restoration of royal rule along the Adriatic coast and, after passing the 17 April at Lecce, he wasted no time, sailing up to Brindisi to continue his regal task.

Micheroux had originally been sent to Corfu to persuade Admiral Ushakov[2] to spare some detachments from his combined Russo-Turkish fleet to support the Neapolitan crown in its hour of need. The queen was particularly keen on getting some Ottoman Albanian auxiliaries as she knew of their ferocious reputation and hoped their reluctance to take prisoners would make for a welcome purgative to republicanism:

> I would have them increase the Albanians to 20,000 men and would throw them at the south of France now that transporting them there is easy, saying 'Go my friends, pillage, eat, devastate, ruin and make a

diversion which will hinder and prevent the despatch of reinforcements to Italy, and ruin the home of those vandals'.

Only after Corfu surrendered in early March did Ushakov permit a small expeditionary force to sail for Puglia. Sorokin was therefore despatched with Micheroux and the Russo-Turco-Neapolitan squadron soon set Puglia ablaze with rumour and burning trees of liberty.

It was a fortuitous time for another invasion because a war a little further afield had already sounded the death knell for the republic. On 12 March 1799, a large Austrian army had crossed the border into northern Italy. The Habsburg empire had finally resolved to join the fight against France. On 5 April the Austrians beat General Schérer at Magnano and then, having been joined by the Russians under Marshal Suvorov, the Austro-Russian juggernaut careered into Milan. The French, spread across the peninsula, began to panic as their richest conquests were thrown into jeopardy, and Macdonald, at Naples, was now ordered to bring his troops northwards to stave off further disaster. The republic was being abandoned just as its enemies had wrested Calabria and were wresting Puglia from its weakening grasp.

To bolster republican nerve during the final act of this tragedy, the French left behind garrisons in three of the key Neapolitan fortresses. In Naples Colonel Louis-Joseph Méjan assumed command of St Elmo which dominated the city from the Vomero hill. Méjan was a veteran of French campaigns in Italy and commanded the 27th Light Regiment, which formed the bulk of his garrison of 900 men.[3] This contingent squeezed into the small fort, and when Méjan's superior, Antoine-Alexandre Girardon, promoted on 29 April to general, visited the fort in May he found 'This fort can only accommodate 400 men; the rest of the garrison were camped on the glacis which runs parallel to the ramp that leads down to the city'.

Girardon himself was left in charge of a larger garrison further north at Capua and was also responsible for the fortress of Gaeta.[4] On 7 May Girardon arrived at Capua to review his men.[5] He could see for himself that the castle, town and earthworks around them were in a poor state of defence, but his anxiety was compounded by Macdonald's far from optimistic instructions which told him to beware of his friends as much as his enemies, and which seemed to concentrate on how he should eventually surrender:

Capitulation should not take place until all your supplies have been used up or until a breach has been made which is suitable for assault, but which you should try to vigorously prevent. However, if it proves impossible to come to your assistance within five or six months, although we hope this is not the case, then your capitulation should be honourable: come out with arms and baggage, flags unfurled, with two cannon and, in a separate article, with those patriots who did not save themselves. This article is obligatory.[6]

With the French leaving en masse, the Neapolitan republic nevertheless put on a brave face, telling itself it was independent rather than abandoned. Pimentel was among those who welcomed the challenge, declaring in the *Monitore* that the Neapolitans were now 'a free people, one worthy of the respect and aspirations of all Italy, or harbinger of its despair', but Parthenope had its Cassandras too, Abamonti worrying that a republic was impossible 'without force, without outside assistance, without money, without the provinces'. To distract the fickle populace away from doubt, the republic put on a wave of showy festivities. On Sunday 19 May flags were issued to the National Guard legions and then royalist banners, captured during the British and royalist defeat at Castellammare and Sorrento, were paraded and ceremoniously burnt beneath the tree of liberty. Some royalist prisoners, after enduring the speeches, were also marched through the streets in a torchlight parade, and then fraternally embraced and set free.

Although the festivities masked a certain gloom, there was one ray of hope. News had been received that a French fleet was drawing nearer, but its destination was not yet clear, even to its commander. Admiral Étienne Eustache Bruix had quit Brest and rushed, rather nervously, for the Mediterranean. The British admiralty dutifully warned Lord Keith, floating off Cadiz, and Nelson then ashore at Palermo. Nelson, his hands full with coordinating operations against Malta, the worries of the court, and Lady Hamilton, was alarmed and began to concentrate what ships he had for the defence of Sicily.

The royalists and British certainly feared the possibility of a French naval counter-attack, whilst the republicans were hopeful Bruix might arrive before it was too late. Time was, after all, running out. Ruffo's pilgrimage of hate was gaining strength and appetite, and Micheroux and Sorokin's Russians were easily dismantling the republic's bastions in Puglia. Following the landing at Lecce and Brindisi, the important port of Bari fell to them on 14 May and the Russians then moved against wealthy Barletta which opened its gates on 16 May. There, and in other towns, Micheroux saw how easily liberation could turn into a settling of scores, and wrote, concerned, to Acton:

I understand that the Russian commander is willing to fight against those French and Jacobins who carry arms but will not make use of his forces to assist in the needless and unjust terrorism that many of the so-called royalists have in mind. I wish to separate out that small number of people whose crimes have been documented, or who have been members of the government in Naples or with the French as they democratised the country, or had served the French generals, or had urged the French to bring their troops in, and those are the ones who perhaps deserve to be classed as criminals of state ... Most of these, along with those whose guilt cannot be proven, I shall pardon in the king's name and celebrate a general reconciliation and I think that the [Russian] commodore is of the same mind.[7]

Ruffo was also voicing concerns that harsh punishment for rebels was counterproductive, telling Acton on 3 April that 'if they do not see that they are offered mercy, the rebellious regions will resist all the more'. The prelate issued a pardon for those returning to the royal fold on 17 April, but the more vindictive Acton thought this was premature and shortly afterwards told the cardinal:

His Majesty is setting out some guidelines on how to deal with the rebels and, through their crimes, categorise the feeble, the seditious, the stupid and what measures to adopt against them .... Mercy is certainly proper and natural to the king, as is well known; but the republican government, the noted traitors, and those who served as officials in the infamous rebellion, and who so horribly insulted their sovereigns through deeds and by proclamation, deserve to be classed apart from those who were seduced or obliged to follow.[8]

Despite this, Ruffo still erred towards the generous, extending amnesty to those who had fallen into error through listening to the seditious and disturbing talk of men who were undermining order and public tranquillity, and he again told the court on 30 April that 'our rigour against those who supported the rebellion through necessity leads to desperation'. For now, sacrificing mercy on the altar of obedience, he conceded that a handful of the most notorious republicans probably should be tried but he was soon warning that 'the punishment of so many people would be impossible without leaving an indelible stain of cruelty'. Increasingly pragmatic as resistance stiffened as the Holy Army approached Naples, Ruffo would again warn Palermo that 'the history of France contains many examples of capitulations with rebels' and was tending towards such an arrangement because 'I believe that clemency is preferable to punishment which can't be delivered without justice'.

Ruffo faced a dilemma. Micheroux was preaching to the converted when he emphasised the politic granting of pardons but the cardinal was also aware that the king and queen, cruel in their unpredictability and despotic through their whims, had preferred punishment over pardon. Acton had already asked Ruffo 'to remedy Micheroux's philanthropy which might otherwise allow the most noted rascals to escape'. Then, in early May, Ruffo received the king's guidelines, Ferdinand setting out who it was that he would like to see detained:

> members of the provisional government and executive committee; those on a military commission, or members of the republican police; those in local authorities who had received their commission from the republicans or the French; anyone who participated in any commission to investigate the so-called injustices under my rule or that of my government; officers who had been in my service but who transferred into the republican or French service, indeed it is my wish that such who have taken up arms against my troops or those of my allies shall be shot within 24 hours, without formalities or a trial; landowners who have done the same shall be treated the same way; all those who produced or printed republican newspapers, proclamations or other texts designed to excite my subjects against me. Those who took up positions in the municipality or to elected bodies or who served as such under my previous Vicar General should also be arrested.[9]

This seemed to be quite a sweeping list, but the force of royal argument was undermined by the king's concession that 'These are my wishes for the present, which I charge you to have executed in whatever way you consider feasible, and in whatever places it may be possible to do so'.

The queen was more hardline, and more outspoken about being so, for she had long desired a thorough purge of the kingdom. As early as the first month of her exile she was busy consoling herself with dreams of revenge, telling Gallo:

> At the moment I can only see the Turks and they could come over, some 30 or 50,000 of them, they would destroy everything, but spare those people who have remained loyal to us, and they could, sword in hand, chase out the French and the republicans. The plague is preferable to the continued existence of the republicans and only the Turks would be able to save us and save Italy. I'd prefer it if they destroyed everything, but chased those bandits away rather than see those brigands ruin everything and corrupt those around us.

She repeated the Manichean theme that April:

> I believe we have to get them to declare, and wage, a war to the death, employing all the means available, even their own crimes, in order to crush a monster which has tried to devour and destroy everything, thrones, religions, property, everything. So it will be a general war, war to the death, renouncing, openly, all idea of conquest or compensation, or of dividing and ruling amongst the alliance or sowing mistrust, and weakness. We should have one aim, the destruction of the all-consuming republic and its principles with the firm, clear and guaranteed aim of doing everything to beat the hydra and to destroy it or shut it up in its lair. [10]

However, she was more circumspect, or realistic, when writing to Ruffo and she reined in the four horsemen of her apocalyptic vision to tell the man of cloth 'I don't share your view [about pardoning the rebels], not out of a spirit of vendetta, a feeling unknown to me .... but because the rascals should be ejected from society so as not to corrupt others'. This more moderate position – that the rebels could be expelled from society – was welcomed by Ruffo. He was, after all, dealing with an increasingly complex situation on the ground, and with forces that, he thought, were barely strong enough to take small provincial towns let alone a capital bristling with defensiveness. Given these constraints he was inevitably tempted by mercy as a means to open gates where his flimsy siege train would only fail, and as a way of inducing those entrenched in Naples to end their resistance. His quip to Acton that 'four bombs and a general pardon will finish the business' was only half made in jest. But, for now, Ruffo still held to the official position that there should be punishment for the key sinners, and he craftily criticised Micheroux, who threatened to undermine his own position as Vicar General, for being too dovish, telling Acton:

> Your Excellency knows I am inclined towards clemency, but Micheroux goes too far, granting pardon to anyone, without any distinction ... I could give His Lordship De Cesari and any officer just such a proclamation as the one by Micheroux and this would allow the worst of the criminals a means to escape and these are the ones which should not be pardoned. [11]

When he got the chance to communicate directly with Micheroux a few days later the cardinal admonished his errant disciple for making use of the king's name even if the Russians were for mercy. Ruffo told him that clemency should be used as a tempting bribe, granted to those who surrendered without a fight, whilst those towns that resisted should be 'treated to the rigour of the laws of war, respecting only the common people, condemning to death the rebel leaders, others to imprisonment for life or for some period of time, their goods confiscated only to be restored to the heirs if such should be agreed, but allowing food for the women and children according to their status.'[12]

Micheroux disagreed, but for now he was too heavily involved in planning his own campaign to liberate the Adriatic coast to comment. His ambition had received a considerable boost from the rumours that the French had quit Naples, and that Sorokin had ordered the captain of the frigate the *Schastlivii* (the Lucky), Genrikh Genrikhovich Baillie,[13] to make an expeditionary force of Russian marines, four guns, a handful of Turkish observers and some sailors from the Neapolitan *Fortuna* corvette available for operations inland. Girded by Russian luck and Neapolitan fortune, Micheroux felt confident enough to risk an advance to the important provincial centre of Foggia. It was a risk, for his was still a small force as he confessed to Ruffo:

> In the meantime I shall tell you my secret, which hitherto has gone unsaid for fear that the letter might be intercepted. We are, but I am ashamed to say it. We have a little more than 350 Russians and 70 Neapolitans. We might also include around 100 more sailors who can man the guns.[14]

At least the Russians were veterans, as Micheroux boasted to Acton:

> Feared wherever they appear, loved wherever they remain, they leave behind them a populace in awe of their discipline, their perfection, their gentleness. Precious examples of humanity! Your Excellency should arrange it so that a permanent body of such troops is stationed here so that they may serve as a cadre for our future army.[15]

The jab at Neapolitan discipline was intended, for the organised Russians stood in contrast to some of the other units filling the royalist ranks. Foremost amongst these were Ruffo's difficult-to-domesticate Calabrian irregulars who had followed the holy banners as much for the benefit of their stomachs and purses as for the good of their souls. These Calabrians, as Elefante's diary makes clear, posed as much a danger to their friends as to their enemies:

> Some 150 Calabrian soldiers passed through having caused much disturbance to the country around, causing all kinds of harm

and taking reprisals with the usual excuse that the people were Jacobins or supported the Jacobins. And today they were thieving and plundering and punishing and despoiling even whilst they were calling themselves of the holy faith; well they are an army of the holy faith in name only.

After sending a detachment to liberate Manfredonia, Micheroux's Russians, Puglian volunteer militias and hangers-on set off for Foggia where, on 21 May, a determined body of patriots shut themselves into the Palazzo Doganale and began to destroy any documents that might implicate supporters of the republic. Micheroux granted them their lives if they surrendered, happy that an act of clemency could deliver this regional capital into his hands and glad to inform Ruffo 'for the sake of charity, come quickly. Here there is money, horses, all sorts of good things', and, to prove it, he promptly confiscated 67,500 Ducats in the Dogana Bank.

After refreshing supply wagons and treasure chests at Foggia Micheroux marched on Ariano, calling on Ruffo to speed his march and join forces for a final, united push on Naples.

The bands of the true *sanfedismo* were coming. Ruffo, unversed in the gruelling art of supplying an army, and consequently required to eternally seek out fresh pastures for his saintly marauders, had ventured out of Calabria in late April. He first directed his troops towards the last of the republic's strongholds in the south, Altamura. There, Ruffo's men, supported by bands sent over by the Corsican emigrants, put the town through a most thorough retribution, one in which even the nuns were not spared. For the Army of the Holy Faith was not content to smite just the godless, as a chronicler noted

> No sooner had the victorious army of the Cardinal entered Altamura than the tree of liberty was pulled down, the cross replaced it, and the troops began to kill, set fire, sack and violate women regardless of their condition.

Some 60 citizens were executed as scapegoats including 'the former Jesuit Domenico Scarati and his brothers and the cleric Celio Colonna, whose corpse was exposed for the dogs to eat in the town square. Another, Giovanni Firrao, was killed because his hair was cut short, despite him having already surrendered and having laid down his arms'. Meanwhile, over one hundred carts of loot made their way to the nearby town of Matera, which had long harboured a grudge against Altamura, and 3,000 sheep were whisked off to Gioia.

It took some time for Ruffo to impose order on his men after such a spirited example of patriotic fervour and he remained at blighted Altamura until 24 May. Ruffo appears to have been shocked by the slaughter, and became a convert to the idea that Naples, so much larger, so much more resolute, would be better won by force of words than force of arms. It was with this determination in mind that he led the Army of the Holy Faith, now accompanied by a winding convoy of generously-provisioned wagons, to Melfi[16] in order to join forces with Micheroux around Ariano.

Micheroux badly needed Ruffo's support for the republicans of Naples had woken to the danger posed by a combined royalist army. With the noose clearly drawing closer around the capital the republicans had finally gone on the offensive. And not before time. A frustrated Saverio Salfi, a captain in the National Guard, blamed the republic's leadership for having taken so long, and for having fiddled whilst the republic shrivelled:

> Whilst the Minister of War was drawing maps and plans for campaigns, and so was promoted generalissimo of the republic for his pains, and whilst his aide-de-camp and guides were organised, and whilst they were given gilded lace for their hats and plumes in three colours, we were losing castles and cities, departments and provinces.[17]

When the Minister of War did finally resolve upon a plan, it was the wrong one. The French General Girardon noted wryly from his vantage point at Capua that:

> This general declared that it was his intention to divide his forces into two columns, one of which, 2,200 strong, would conquer Calabria, whilst the other, 2,300 strong and with artillery, would overrun Puglia. I explained the deficiencies of this plan to the Executive Committee, noting that the general had insufficient strength to overrun provinces that were so far away, and that the columns would not be able to communicate either with each other or with Naples. It was clear that the government's authority did not stretch beyond the walls of Naples as all the provinces had rebelled. It was absurd to pretend that they could be conquered with 4,500 undisciplined men.[18]
>
> I suggested that we form a defensive line to protect the capital, its right protected by the sea and a camp at Nocera, the centre at Acera, where another camp would communicate with Capua ... General Manthonè did not share my opinion. He declared that the only way to establish the republic was to march everywhere with six columns, shooting all the royalists as they went.

The republicans went ahead with their foolhardy plan, even though the best of their troops, under Ettore Carafa, were stranded at Pescara on the Adriatic coast and others, under the fickle Roccaromana, had recently deserted to Ruffo.[19] After weeks of inexplicable delay, the republic launched General Federici's cavalry and the 800-strong Campana Legion under Agamennone Spanò on their brief odyssey. Pausing to sack Avellino's cathedral the republicans advanced only to be decimated at Mugnano by a mass of armed peasants. Crushed by those they had sought to free, they fled back to Naples and, a week later, could be found begging for food at the Capuan Gate. Neither the offensive nor the tragedy was over, however. Pasquale Matera's republican Lucana Legion, undeterred by setbacks, uninhibited by experience, joined with the former priest Antonio Belpulsi's Sannita Legion at Nola. This forlorn hope was also destined for a break through to where the republic held state at Pescara but Belpulsi did not get very far, and Matera's troops fared even worse. Ensign Guglielmo Pépé remembered his part in the disaster:

After encamping upon the heights which are close to Monteforte, the general proceeded to push the greater part of his column upon Avellino, leaving only a small body of cavalry, which, such was the scarcity of horses, was not yet mounted, in the direction of Montorio. Supported by the battalion of officers, he proposed an assault upon several hundred insurgents who infested the neighbourhood. On reaching the place where we expected to find them, we discovered they had retreated, leaving no clue to the direction they had taken. Our column then returned towards Avellino. During this counter-march we, the eighth company bringing up the rear, were unexpectedly assaulted in flank and in our rear by a band of peasants armed with carbines. The road through which we were passing was a kind of ravine, overhung on both sides by high ground; from these heights our assailants discharged a brisk volley, killing and wounding many of our men; amongst the wounded was d'Ambrosio, who at a later period of his life acquired the reputation of a most able general. We marched on in the greatest confusion, and Matèra, perceiving all the disadvantages of our situation, assembled us upon the elevated ground in such a manner as to enable our dismounted cavalry to protect our retreat. This was the first day of my being exposed to fire, and it was nearly being the last, for our rear guard was closely pursued by the enemy, who took many of our men prisoners, and, as we afterwards learnt, put them to death in the cruellest manner.[20]

Matera pushed on a little further but soon reconsidered: 'Our general,' noted Pepe, 'perceiving that he had not enough strength to resist the attack of the enemy, directed his march towards Benevento', pausing to sack the town before riding, in high dudgeon, back to Naples on 29 May. A few isolated detachments of dispirited republicans remained at Nola and Marigliano, but the republic's field army had largely dissolved. It had been astronomically costly to go on the disastrous offensive, and failure threw the government into disarray.

Micheroux's men therefore marched unopposed into Ariano on 31 May and the diplomat wrote to the cardinal suggesting now was the time to negotiate the surrender of the republic. He proposed the following conditions: that the dyed-in-the wool criminals should be sent off to Marseille or Toulon with their families and baggage, but with no public property; that the English commodore, Foote, should provide the transport ships with a flag of truce until they reached their destination; that those who supported democracy, or those who committed crimes during that period, could ask for pardon; that those in the National Guard, and troops of the line, particularly officers, could continue to serve under the king; that the French garrison could be induced to surrender and not serve again against the armies of the king for the duration of the war, and also be sent to Toulon.

Ruffo's response to these sensible terms was that he had received 'from the court, instructions which were in accordance with these sentiments and should carry them out, although the time is not opportune.'[21] In fact the court had quite different sentiments. The queen had even set down the names of individuals who deserved to be punished.[22] On 28 April she told her daughter

There are some who have betrayed me, those I counted on. Caracciolo of the navy is one, I rewarded him, and again at Palermo for his honesty;[23] Policastro has been selected to examine the faults committed by the ex-king, of a number of bishops our archbishop, through weakness or stupidity, has published two infamous proclamations; Carlo de Marco, pensioner deserving of the republic, Cantalupo, minister of finances; the soldiers, in short, all of those who have been most rewarded. The Cassano woman and the Popoli woman, who we call their highnesses, go, with hair cut short, into houses offering assistance to the brave soldiers who have fought The Tyrant. What horror! Enrico Sanchez, patriot in the service of the republic, his wife a noted Jacobin who, up until the day we left, kept company, with her children, with me and my children; in short, such outrageous ingratitude crushes my heart and makes life hideous![24]

Ruffo, whose run of good luck might not survive having to actually storm the defiant capital, increasingly now viewed 'forgiving past transgressions' as a better tactic. It might spare the capital the horrors of an assault, and the more he studied his erratic troops, the more he felt he could only recover the kingdom by negotiating a republican exit.[25] Ruffo told Micheroux that he was hoping that the republic would collapse, a possibility given the in-fighting taking place, or that the republicans could flee northwards and escape if he left that inviting road to Rome open. But, to the displeasure of the cardinal, and the joy of Troubridge, Fra Diavolo was rendering such a scheme unlikely by murdering everything that moved between Naples and Rome, behaviour imitated by Gaetano Mammone at Sora and Isola.[26] The French could not force the road open again, Girardon complaining that 'I sent my spy to carry despatches to Rome but a few days later I learnt that he had been caught and hanged.'[27]

So Ruffo met Micheroux and Baillie ('an Irishman who knows no other languages but English and Russian' according to Sacchinelli) at Ascoli, convening a council of war at the Savignano inn to discuss plans for the final battle against the trapped republicans. Micheroux, the inveterate diplomat, and therefore ever the suitor chasing after compromise, pushed for mercy, telling Ruffo that it was important if 'Your Eminence wishes to find a capital rather than a desert'. Micheroux also wrote to Acton, warning the wizened politician of the consequences of a too unforgiving conquest:

> As for the capital, if it should continue to hold out for a long time, or if we are unlucky enough not to be able to take it without causing significant damage, or if beautiful Naples becomes a second Altamura, then it shall be turned into a horrible desert.[28]

Ruffo's Calabrians and Micheroux's Russians and Puglian volunteers finally united on 5 June at Ariano. They were leant a touch of the exotic by the arrival of a group of 84 Ottoman soldiers, commanded by Captain Ahmed, sent up from their ship, the *Manifest of Blessed News* at Otranto, and who raised eyebrows as they swaggered along.[29] The equally showy De Cesari also joined Ruffo for the final kill, his skittish cavalry immediately falling out with Ruffo's Calabrians. Hoping that action would keep his troops united where appeals to obedience were failing, the cardinal now ordered a general advance and on 8 June the incongruous mass, part Catholic Army of the Holy Faith, part Moslem, part Orthodox, united under a banner sewn in gold thread by the queen and her daughters and set off for Naples.

Ruffo informed Micheroux that he expected good news for 'the English fleet with the Prince Royal will come by the 16th at the latest' with Nelson not only bringing much-needed troops but also keeping the Franco-Spanish fleet at bay. The cardinal then quit Avellino on 11 June, and just missing seeing 48-year-old Libero Serafini, republican mayor of Agnone, being strung up from the Puglian Gate, and made for Nola, the flash and dust of his army's approach persuading the republican garrison, just a few men under Francesco Macdonald[30] to run for the capital. The cardinal then sent his main body south towards Somma, at the foot of Vesuvius, establishing contact with the royalists moving up from Salerno. These under Sciarpa and Ludovico Ludovici, Bishop of Policastro, had been brutally purging the Mediterranean coastal ports of republicans and now, encouraged by Ruffo's appearance, and news that Nelson was coming, they surged towards the capital, reaching Torre Annunziata and trapping the republican general Giuseppe Schipani with what remained of his Bruzia Legion.

These swift actions astonished Naples and the royalists soon felt emboldened to make their first stab at taking the city. They probed the fort of Vigliena, commanding the Maddalena bridge over the Sebeto River to the south-east of Naples, and chased General Filippo Wirtz's cavalry back into the much-reduced republic. As the alarm sounded in the capital the vestiges of the Jacobin legions rallied, and a few National Guards showed themselves. These volunteers included Gaetano Rodinò who had been feverish but, upon hearing the alarm 'left the bed in which I had been lying sick, took up my musket and went to Castel Nuovo, the designated place for inhabitants to gather'. He took command of his company as their captain, Alessandro Azzia, was too short-sighted, and readied them to march out in support of beleaguered Wirtz. Admiral Caracciolo also erupted into life, sallying out to help Wirtz by bombarding the royalist detachments inching forward in the shadow of Vesuvius. Meanwhile, women and children were escorted to the Nuovo fort, along with the members of the republican government, whilst a detachment of Calabrian Jacobins secured the smaller Uovo fort. Some of Ruffo's relatives in the city, including the Duke and Duchess di Baranello, were taken as hostages and 39 prisoners, including Filippo Acton, were placed in St Elmo for safekeeping. More were held in the Nuovo fort and it was there that some unfortunates, including the Baccher brothers, were unaccountably executed on 13 June.

Amidst all this republican activity, the French looked down from St Elmo. Méjan sensed defeat was imminent, Girardon noting. 'I received a letter from chef de brigade Méjan who informed me about the paralysis of the Neapolitan government, the lack of confidence it inspired in the patriots, disunity amongst them and how little reliance we could place on them.'

Some in the republic nevertheless hoped that more substantial French assistance, in the form of the fleet under Bruix, might yet turn the tide and save Naples. Bruix had initially hoped to 'sail to Naples, collect the republicans and transport them to an agreed location' and got as far as Genoa before eventually losing heart and turning for Spanish ports. However, as the French admiral sailed along the Italian coast, Nelson was forced to gather up his fleet at Marittimo, quitting Palermo on 20 May.[31] He declared, rather grandly, and altogether in a way sure to reverberate down palatial corridors, that he would defend Sicily to the death: 'I will not pass to the eastward of Palermo, but will there make my stand, and, I believe, should prevent the whole of the F[rench] fleet from destroying us. I will stand or fall with their majesty's and you and Lady Hn; nothing shall swerve me from this determination'.[32]

Troubridge joined Nelson at Marittimo, his line of battle ships, to the delight of the republicans, quitting Procida, leaving behind just Count Thurn's *Minerva*, with the *Zealous* offering more remote support from Salerno. Caracciolo took advantage of this opportunity by launching an attack on the isolated royalist frigate with his flotilla of eight gunboats and six bombards. Fortunately, Captain Edward Foote had been ordered to replace Troubridge and take charge of the blockade of Naples, and he arrived on 22 May, just in time to prevent further damage. Foote had full authority to act in this independent command[33] and was master of all he surveyed: the Swiss and Neapolitan troops on the islands; his own ship, the *Seahorse*; the *Bulldog*; *Perseus*; *Mutine*; *San Leon*; four feluccas and some Neapolitan gunboats. He had darker responsibilities too, writing to Nelson on 2 June that 'Thirteen Jacobins were hanged at Procida yesterday afternoon, and the bearer of this has charge of three condemned priests who are to be degraded at Palermo, and then sent back, to be executed'.[34]

This pleased Nelson who wrote back four days later:

> Your news of the hanging of the thirteen Jacobins gave us great pleasure, and the three Priests, I hope, return in the *Aurora* to dangle on the tree best adapted to their weight of sins.[35]

Having gathered in Troubridge and expecting Duckworth's reinforcements, Nelson sent Jane Austen's brother, Captain Francis Austen of the *Petterel*, to summon Ball and lift the blockade of Malta. But there was still no sign of Bruix and Nelson quit Marittimo on 28 May, returning to Palermo. There Ferdinand took advantage of the admiral's return by requesting that he take an expeditionary force over to Naples to assist Ruffo in capturing the capital. On 6 June Duckworth and the *Foudroyant* arrived, and shortly afterwards the gangly Hereditary Prince and his army of 2,000 soldiers began to be loaded on transports. The *Bellerophon* and *Powerful*, sent over from Lord Keith, who was just then replacing the sick Lord Saint Vincent, also came to Nelson's support just after Nelson had sailed out of Palermo on 13 June. Nelson had a powerful force of 16 ships of the line at his disposal, and was prepared to use it in the service of the Neapolitan royal family.

This was the fleet Ruffo was expecting as he planned how to administer last rites to the Neapolitan republic. The presence of Nelson and his ships, and the prince's soldiers, would be vital for that final battle. But history had other plans.

8

Restoration: Naples Recaptured

It had been centuries since a churchman had ridden at the head of a Neapolitan army. But now, astride a white charger, a cardinal came trotting down through the olive groves leading to the sun-blasted village of Teduccio. Riding through the dust thrown up by his advancing army, and passing a manure heap and a wayside shrine, some overly enthusiastic peasants advanced to greet him brandishing the head of a Jacobin on a pike. Ruffo blanched, but the civilising rites of mass at the church of San Giovanni Battista soon allowed the sacred to erase such profanities. Outside the church, Ruffo dedicated some prayers to Saint Antonio of Padua, his new protector now that Saint Gennaro was tainted by Jacobinism, and presided over the open-air Eucharist. With the bread and wine consumed, and the Holy Army receiving benediction for the final battle between good and evil, the cardinal ordered his men to storm the capital.

Ruffo sent his columns swarming along the coast leading to the Maddalena bridge. They were harassed by republican artillery, and Caracciolo's wasp-like gunboats off Vigliena, before naval support in the guise of Captain Foote of the *Seahorse* came to the cardinal's assistance. Foote pummelled the shore, and managed to force the Granatello fort, close by the ruins of Herculaneum, to surrender. The republican garrison was promptly massacred by the royalists, the fate of their comrades stiffening the resolve of the republicans in the nearby fort at Vigliena. Ruffo therefore opted to merely blockade that position and sent a column of his troops surging down the Via delle Paludi, whilst the main body of the Holy Army marched on the Maddalena bridge where the republicans were frantically massing what was left of their army.

This first assault on the bridge was beaten back by the republic's General Wirtz and the less than majestic retreat of Gaetano Mammone's royalist cutthroats forced Ruffo to deploy some of his reliable reserves to restore order. The cardinal's men tried again and were more successful this time, routing 120 National Guardsmen under Luigi Bozzaotra, before encountering Wirtz's own reserves. It was then that tragedy struck for the republicans. A captain in the 2nd Legion of the National Guard, 20-year-old Giuseppe De Lorenzo, was by the bridge when he saw disaster unfold:

> We found General Wirtz at the head of a small band of the [republican] Calabrian Legion and line infantry, all fighting desperately; there were also some 50 cavalrymen but they were refusing to go forward even though the general was ordering them on with 'cavalry, advance!'. At this point we came up and joined the action in support of these men who, despite fighting with considerable courage, were being pushed back by an enemy superior in numbers. General Wirtz made a bid to encourage his reluctant cavalry by advancing past our defences accompanied by the Marchese di Montrone and the Marchese di Maio, and urging the cavalry to follow him. It was in vain and this act of valour cost him his life. The poor general was hit in his left side by canister fired against the three men and, half dead, he was carried from the field by six gendarmes using their muskets as a stretcher and taken to the Nuovo fort where he died a few hours later.
>
> It was enough to discourage anyone, the cavalry fled and the handful of men from my legion of National Guards, after contesting the ground, found themselves alone and fell back to the square by the cavalry barracks, unable to deter Ruffo's cavalry. These, seeing that our troops would flee, had charged forwards and only the fact that we had two pieces of artillery averted a cruel massacre. The enemy then brought up two large-calibre guns and opened up, to considerable effect, and our gunners cut their traces and fled, as did everyone else, pursued by the swords of the enemy.

At this critical moment Naples was shaken by an explosion. The 150 republican Calabrians at the Vigliena fort had resisted until Francesco Rapini's men broke through the walls late on 13 June. But then, in the confusion of dusk, and in an act of deliberate heroism, the fort's powder magazine was deliberately ignited and the fort blew up, killing defenders and numbers of the assailants. The futile gesture was credited to Antonio Toscani, and it showed Naples that the republic could be majestic though in ruin, and proved that some republicans at least would die rather than surrender.

But it was futile because the royalists were now pursuing victory, and what remained of the republic's defenders were falling back across the Maddalena bridge pursued by Ruffo's jangling confusion of cavalry. Some of the fugitive republicans made towards the safety of the forts, most gaining access to the larger Nuovo fort, with a few dozen running further to the small Uovo on its rocky outcrop and its garrison of defiant students. Others, perhaps hoping to find escape by sea, headed for the arsenal and the port, straining to see whether Caracciolo's gunboats might protect them. A frightened mass ran to the National Palace, which had been partially fortified the week before, whilst some students entrenched themselves in the Incurabili hospital, and a handful of republican troops sought refuge in the San Martino monastery, using refectory tables to construct a makeshift redoubt on the slopes below St Elmo. Down in the city streets Giuseppe De Lorenzo and his comrade, Gennaro Grasso, made for the headquarters of the National Guard at Montoliveto, preferring to try there rather than throw themselves into the Carmine fort which, they calculated, would be the first to be attacked by Ruffo. There was then a merciful pause as Ruffo's men, hesitant to assault the city at night, conserved their energy for the rape of the capital.

It was at first light that Ruffo's Calabrians, clad in nut brown and caramel cloth, and accompanied and outnumbered by an expectant horde of looters, gorged themselves on the exposed city and, as the capital's bells rang out, the city's own vengeful dispossessed emerged to share in any pickings. An echo of the capital's fate made it into Micheroux's first missive to Colonel Méjan at St Elmo demanding the French surrender:

> No longer being able to control the populace, I summon you to surrender as soon as possible and receive a Russian garrison. In which case you will be accorded an honourable capitulation and we shall take pains to ensure that the French garrison be securely transported to any port in France.

A similar message was to be conveyed to the republican garrisons in the Carmine, Nuovo and Uovo forts but in the confusion a verbal summons was deemed sufficient, Micheroux instructing his envoy, Luigi Pousset, to inform the garrisons in the three forts that

> Should you resist, your extermination is guaranteed as you will be attacked from all sides and by all kinds of troops who, and this does not include the Russians, it will be impossible to restrain, as was the case at the Granatello and Vigliena forts. You are advised, therefore, to hope for royal clemency and, without delay, send a deputation to the Vicar General. If not, he will not be responsible for your destruction.

If you do, what you can hope for would be your lives and you would be embarked and transported by ship to France. Such a treaty would be at the discretion of the French in St Elmo and would be an honourable capitulation.[1]

Micheroux's terms were generous but the republicans were reluctant to treat for all the evidence they had seen suggested that Micheroux could not actually guarantee their safety. Their fears soon proved correct. Advancing along the waterfront, the Holy Army had been rattled by some volleys from the Carmine fort. The Turks and some Calabrians surrounded the twin towers and Micheroux sent Pousset to negotiate surrender with its governor Richard Auvet. Auvet, a former officer in the Borgogna Regiment, was Pousset's acquaintance and hopes were high that a peaceful solution could be found. But Micheroux recounts what happened next:

My adjutant was sent there to tell them that they should all expect royal mercy except those who had been sent into exile before the arrival of the French, or those who had spilled the blood of royalists or were guilty of abuse of power during the period of democracy, or those who had seriously offended, through speech, print or writing, the sacred persons of the sovereigns. So he set off but when he reached the Carmine fort he found our irregulars surrounding the fort and these, not understanding the significance of the trumpet and white flag, continued firing their muskets against the castle.

The firing continued and Ruffo issued an order 'to the Neapolitans and the troops of all kinds which are surrounding the Carmine – cease hostilities, or with absolute certainty face execution'. It didn't help. Micheroux continues:

Eventually the crowd was calmed, Commandant Avel [sic] summoned the courage to open the gates; he informed the adjutant that they were ready to surrender, as he had just a few regulars to protect him and his garrison. The irregular troops outside started firing again, and the adjutant became nervous and went to the Maddalena bridge to inform His Eminence [Ruffo] and to have the Russians sent forward. However, whilst this was happening, the irregulars, profiting from the brief armistice, piled a number of fascines against the gate and clambered over the wall, seizing the fort and killing everyone in it, only Commandant Avel, the two sons of the Duke di Gravina and a handful of officers being saved.[2]

This massacre sent a bloody warning to the republicans but it also alarmed the royalists. Ruffo, increasingly distrustful of his fierce flock, had few good men left to impose order and he soon had to send them forwards against the republican garrisons. These were advancing along the Toledo, probing the strength of those taking shelter below the French guns of St Elmo, and skirmishing with those who had sought sanctuary in the San Martino monastery and, in their wake, the mob used the opportunity to sack palaces and houses and strip them bare, with the San Pietro a Majella church and Sansevero chapel also suffering the same fate. The Monteoliveto headquarters of the National Guard was also ransacked[3] and there the fugitive citizen soldier De Lorenzo saw how larceny slipped into slaughter:

> decent people who had been stripped naked by the lazzaroni and disfigured so that they were unrecognisable, and corpses lying here and there, mostly missing at least one limb; ladies, matrons and spinsters of all kinds were stripped naked and paraded before the mob who were told that this belonged to Jacobin families; and heads and limbs were mutilated and positioned at the corners of streets.

The Monte Santo church and complex was also attacked by some of the royalist vanguard aided and abetted by a mass of shrieking inhabitants. The royalist Raffaele Brancati remembers how they took one monastery after another:

> the firing was continuous for four hours, we were targeting the gates and we took three Jacobins alive and killed four in our attack. On the next day we went to attack the Rosariello di Porta Medina monastery, where there were other Jacobins, one of whom jumped and killed himself, whilst another was killed by a Turk.[4]

The streets were full of confusion and mayhem and the morning of the 14th saw the citizens, especially the propertied classes, of Naples completely exposed to vengeance. Ruffo's Holy Army, with some of his less reliable allies, including the '80 cursed Turks', and some of the more thuggish lazzaroni, unbidden but relishing the prospect of violence, were soon making common cause. The ensuing pandemonium in the streets was the first assault on the city, an offensive which took on the character of mass robbery, the prelude to cruel weeks with days of anguish and nights of terror. Salvation could not be expected, all the republican troops were trapped in forts or defensive positions, and hope that the French fleet would come was growing fainter. A few still thought that the one small field army remaining to the republic could march on the capital and fall on Ruffo's disorganised rear. For General Schipani with 1,500 republican troops was swatting at royalist attacks just beyond Portici, and was largely unaware of the disaster that had engulfed the republic. That republic, or what was left of it, now sent off frantic messages by boat, urging Schipani to come at once. Guglielmo Pépé was an officer in Schipani's little army. He recalled how the republicans, unaware of the allied superiority in numbers, bestirred themselves and bravely marched for Naples:

> The battalion of officers formed the vanguard, and about sixty of the most determined men in it occupied the extreme point. I was amongst these. Schipani recognised me, and being himself Calabrian, he smiled upon me with an expression of countenance of great calmness, saying 'the Calabrians always shine in difficult times'.

Pushing into Portici's suburbs his men soon found themselves cornered at the San Ciro church. Pépé describes the ensuing battle:

> The vanguard fought its way into Resina [Ercolano] but at a small distance from the royal palace of Portici we encountered a most determined resistance. Amongst other misfortunes there was a battery so well defended that it stopped our march, which until then had been one of triumph. General Schipani tried to open a passage for us on both sides, but in vain. At three hours before sunset the obstacles acquired greater intensity when a body of Russians followed by about 1000 Calabrians of Panedigrano advanced upon us with fixed bayonets. In this melee, rendered fearful by the obstinacy of our defence and the narrowness of the road, which was close to a fountain, I received a thrust from a bayonet in my right arm, and then a blow from a sword on the temple. I fainted and remained some minutes senseless under a wounded horse, which somehow had fallen upon me. It was not without much difficulty that I succeeded in freeing myself from this immense weight, when I discovered that I had lost my hat. Saturated with blood, I began to follow, as best I might, several of my comrades who were minutely acquainted with the route, and who had taken a small road leading through an archway close to the fountain. We were now about thirty officers armed with muskets, the remainder had either been killed or taken prisoners, indeed, several of the latter had been killed after they had been disarmed.

Micheroux and his Russian allies were shocked by the aftermath of the fighting:

> The Russians are back in Portici. I cannot hide from Your Eminence that they are indignant against our infantry and cavalry which only advanced into battle against the enemy after their defeat. They also bitterly complain that after they took 50 prisoners by promising them their lives, though they were then shot down by the cavalry ordered to escort them. What is more they also complain that our troops robbed even our dead and now say that they do not wish to be attached to such troops and sent on an expedition with them. I too believe that they should not be detached like this, given the impossibility of these two very different nations to work together. Their discontent is above all directed against General De Cesaris whom they say conducted himself very badly on this occasion.[5]

A group of republican survivors under Anton Maria Campana and Pietro Colletta had attempted to avoid this gruesome fate by making for Ponticelli but were soon captured and imprisoned. Pépé was part of this unfortunate group:

> Our small band being hotly pursued, my comrades at length found it necessary to yield. I happened to be in advance with another officer and we pursued our flight. On reaching Ponticelli, however, we were stopped by a body of peasants armed with scythes. After depriving us of our muskets, one of them gave me a blow in the side with the butt end of mine, the violence of which struck me to the ground. When the pain had in some degree subsided and I was bade to stand, we were conducted to La Barra and confined in a damp and unwholesome warehouse, where I found many of the companions with whom I had quitted Resina. We lay upon the ground, which seemed to have been inundated on purpose to increase its natural humidity, and were guarded by peasants who called in their women to behold us, as if we had been a horde of savages, and who vied with their companions in reviling and insulting us.

Schipani with the rest of his defeated army fled for Castellamare but the republicans there, under Giuliano De Fazio, had already surrendered to Captain Foote.[6] Instead of friends, Schipani's fugitives encountered Colonel Tschudi, and Schipani was captured and taken to Procida.[7]

The republicans in the forts now stood alone, and from their battlements they could watch the slaughter, only the pall of smoke from burning houses and funeral pyres occasionally obscuring the fate of those unfortunates who had not made it into the forts. Whatever Acton, over in Palermo, might say about it being 'but natural that the people should take a revenge'[8] the result was limitless slaughter. Dr Marinelli, himself struck down with a fever, was stranded in Nicola Torres' house on the Mercatello (now Piazza Dante), but continued with his diary, noting 'the common people, known as the Santafedisti, hastened to commit every kind of barbarity and cruelty, and that is how it was throughout the nights of Thursday, Friday and Saturday'. The ever-nervous Carlo de Nicola was right to be afraid as he saw a mob gather and smash the streetlights on Toledo before going off to hunt down the gentlemen:

> Now began the horror of the sacking of the city, masses of people began to move against those houses where the most notable Jacobins and patriots lived or hunted them down through the streets wherever they could find them. Close to where I lived they sacked Pagano's house, that of a judge and someone on the military commission, Vincenzo Lupo's and that of Patini, the police secretary. As I write a column is passing by, and the people are cheering 'long live the king'.[9]

Anyone suspected of being a republican, especially those in fashionable clothes, or, in a unique situation where one's hairstyle could save one's life, those with short hair, were subjected to torture or lynching. August von Kotzebue, visiting Naples shortly afterwards, noted:

> The women were the most outrageous; it was sufficient to be pointed out by one of these furies as a Jacobin, to be instantly sacrificed. All who wore cropped hair were devoted victims. False tails were procured; but the deception being perceived, the people ran behind every one they passed, pulled him by the tail, and if it came off, it was all over with the wearer.[10]

He was told about atrocities and about cannibalism:

> everyone still relates with horror that the Lazzaroni roasted men in the streets, and begged money of the passengers to purchase bread to their roast meat. Many of them carried in their pockets fingers, ears, etc, which they had cut off; and when they met a person whom they looked upon as a patriot, they triumphantly exhibited their bloody spoils. They were marching a naked man through the streets and he was bent double clutching his stomach for a demon who stood next to him was, with each step, attempting with his sword to cut off the man's private parts.[11]

In case such accounts might seem exaggerated by memory, or the products of excited republican imagination, confirmation comes from those who were far from being republican apologists. De Nicola, who despised the pseudo-republic, noted down scenes of murder and mayhem, and added 'something too horrible to speak of happened yesterday, but needs to be so that we understand mankind. Two Jacobins were burnt, and a furious mob cut the corpses into pieces and ate them, offering them to others, even to children.' Even the arch-royalist Sacchinelli later asked himself, 'who, in describing such things, can abstain from tears?'

> The rabble rose up and, as the principal Jacobins had taken refuge in the castles, they vented their fury on anyone they deemed to be pro-republican, without regard to the quality of the person or to their sex, massacring, robbing, plundering and burning.[12]

But the mob gloried most in the humiliation and abuse of those noble women who had sympathised with the new order, and many suffered the degradation of being stripped and paraded through the streets so they could be mocked. Petromasi, another ardent royalist, notes how

> there were even a few women belonging to an impious sect who were arrested by the lazzaroni and Calabrians and taken to the prison just draped in a bedsheet to mock the republican representation of liberty, which was of a woman who was half naked.[13]

Such tortured tableaux sometimes ended in death. Princess Caracciolo di Santobono was beaten and mocked for three miles, until the mob grew tired and bludgeoned her to death, leaving her naked body at the doors of the Spirito Santo church.

The atrocities were not works of a moment, they continued for weeks. A British visitor to the city saw blood still being spilt when he visited the city at the end of June:

> The barbarities that were committed on the unhappy patriots, to which I was a daily witness, were most atrocious. One morning I met a crowd of savages carrying a human head on a pole, while a miscreant holding up a severed limb, and sucking on the blood, exclaimed 'Eccolo il sangue d'un Jacobino – date mi a bere!' (here is the blood of a Jacobin, let me drink it). The bodies of many individuals were thus treated, and these horrid outrages encouraged by the junta.

A similar account, probably by Pryse Lockhart Gordon, was published in London's *Morning Star* on 12 August:

> Though no public severities have yet been exercised, it is impossible to conceive the cruelties exercised upon those who had been engaged in the Revolution, by the Calabrians, who are equally distinguished by cruelty and cowardice. I myself have seen the decapitated bodies of Jacobins carried about the streets, and their heads mutilated and suspended on pikes. Nay, I actually beheld a monster with two human heads, the blood of which he was sucking. While the Calabrians alone had the possession of the city, fires were made in the squares, and the bodies roasted publicly; this savage barbarity is even combined with their religious mysteries. I passed into a chapel yesterday in the suburbs, where was exhibited human extremities on an altar, and a large congregation singing Te Deum![14]

Reverend Willyams, serving as chaplain in the British fleet, later landed in Naples and confirmed that similar scenes were continuing throughout that summer:

> Divers atrocious acts of cruelty, and murders attended with circumstances of the most savage nature, were perpetrated in the face of day. One of these, that I witnessed, will be sufficient to relate here in proof of this assertion. An unfortunate gentleman, suspected of being a Jacobin or rebel, was dragged wounded out of the house he had been concealed in, and in an instant was stripped and cut to pieces; his mangled limbs were drawn about the streets, and his head roasted before a fire kindled in them for the purpose. Some of our officers were passing by, and obliged to witness the last scene of horror, of course expressed their concern and disgust at it, to the no small astonishment of the mob.

A republican, Bartolomeo Nardini, who was present in Naples, but probably in one of the castles, describes similar atrocities:

> The royalists rejoiced in prolonging the torments of anyone they seized wearing the uniform of the National Guard or whom they accused of being a patriot. Some, stripped of their clothing were tied to the tails of horses and then stabbed until they were dead. Others had their ears, noses or hands cut off and were then paraded in triumph through crowds shouting insults at them and who then fought for the privilege of washing their hands in their blood.

But the vicarious experiences of British reverends and visitors, or republicans in their crenelated sanctuaries, pale in comparison to those endured by individuals on the receiving end of such vengeance. Giovan Leonardo Marugj, a doctor, reveals in the third person how close he came to being one such victim:

A group of rascals out hunting for Jacobins caught sight of M. lying beneath the orange tree and they cried out together 'Jacobin, Jacobin!' and leapt over the wall, coming at him like hungry wolves. They seized him and stripped him, finding his purse with some money in it. Their first task was to empty it and hand it back. They then started asking questions and M. did his best to answer to lessen their fury. They contemplated tying him up and leading him off to the bridge. M. said he was attached to the king, and that he was a doctor. 'A leading Jacobin' they cried and backed off a little, aiming their muskets and firing. Providence saved him for the muskets failed to go off. They were astonished and again took to asking questions. M. tried to persuade them that he was on their side, saying that he taught science to Acton's nephew, Carlo Acton. One of them said that Acton had betrayed Ferdinand.... One of them came at M. with a knife. M. avoided the blow and fell down and the man was above him, pointing the dagger at his chest when the honest man was saved by heaven for just then a boy, aged about 12, came into the garden, shouted 'what are you doing', then ran off shouting, and the murderers left M. and chased after the boy.

The National Guardsmen Giuseppe De Lorenzo and Gennaro Grasso had fled the fighting at the bridge and then the sack of the Montoliveto monastery. They had thrown away their uniforms, shaved off any whiskers and disguised themselves as monks in order to cross the city and seek shelter with a relative. After various tribulations they found themselves on the Mercatello where they saw that

the tree of liberty had been cut down by the Calabrians and populace, many of whom were busy relieving themselves upon it despite the presence of a great number of women who had been present during the ceremony. Whilst this was going on, a most cruel massacre was taking place which, alas, we were obliged to observe. A large number of victims, designated as Jacobins, were constantly being brought in and these were quickly dispatched close by the tree. The place reverberated with the pleading of these unfortunates who were like cattle being led to the abattoir. They were shot, but the badly aimed shooting only killed some but left many half-dead and others with a limb fractured. The rogues then moved in to finish them off, and then cut off their heads, carrying them in procession, or rolling them across the square as though playing bowls with them.

Gaetano Rodinò, another National Guardsman who had also tried to disguise himself in clerical garb, had also been caught by a patrol on the 15th and arrested. He was attacked as he was being escorted away 'many men and women, of many different kinds, were blocking the street, and flung themselves at us like infernal furies.' It got worse:

> Even after the passage of almost half a century I shall not be able to forget one foul old hag, who got so close to me that I caught the smell of the mouth, and who, with both her hands on her hips, shaking her head after having showering me with words of the most obscene filth, spat on my face with her filthy phlegm. And that sign of great contempt was the signal for an attack and, in the blink of an eye, I had lost my hat and clothes and was on the point of being stripped naked.[15]

He was dragged, barely conscious, to the Granili prison. There he found 'more than a hundred people in an area enough for forty, and all either naked or partially so, and wounded or covered in blood ... I remember Vincenzo Russo, who was naked apart from a simple jacket, and Prosdocimo Rotondo who was more fortunate in that he had a shirt and trousers.' Guglielmo Pépé had a similar experience as he and his companions were also herded towards the city's prisons:

> The greater part of us did not believe in the downfall of Naples; but this illusion was soon dispelled by the mournful spectacle which presented itself to our gaze and which I believe has been rarely equalled. Men and women of every condition were being barbarously dragged along the road, most of them streaming with blood, many half dead, and stripped of every article of apparel, presenting altogether the most deplorable sight that the mind can conceive. The shrieks and baying of that ferocious mob were such that it seemed to be composed, not of human beings, but rather of a horde of wild beasts. They cast stones and every kind of filth at us, threatening to tear us to pieces.

Having run this gauntlet, he too was thrown into the cavernous Granili prison[16] and at least found himself amongst friends:

> Many of them, as I have already stated, were in a state of nakedness; others were disguised in clothes that had been put on to conceal their

real condition and to shelter from the horrible persecutions of the popular fury. Amongst the latter was a young man from Catanzaro by name Gaetano Rodinò. He was attired as a priest but his garments were literally torn to shreds.

Pépé also confirms the presence of many young students from the Ospedale degli'Incurabili along with many of their patients:

The young medical students within the hospital had kept up a brisk fire from the windows upon the Bourbon troops as they passed along the Largo delle Pigne. Thus attacked the latter took the hospital by storm, put a great number of the inmates to death and made the rest prisoners and amongst these were many lunatics taken on suspicion that they were feigning insanity to escape from the hands of their enemies. One of these wretches was the cause of a most disastrous scene which we witnessed. Having struck one of the royal officers on the face the latter called out 'to arms!' and as soon as he was surrounded by his followers he rushed furiously upon the lunatic whom he clove in two by a sabre stroke.

Ruffo had established his headquarters in a villa close by these scenes of suffering but, as the death toll mounted, he felt himself powerless to control the bloodthirsty congregation he had let loose on the city. His tired confession that he was 'depressed that he was unable to find a remedy to put an end to this horrendous anarchy', rings true. Sacchinelli notes how, when a mass of prisoners was brought to Ruffo the cardinal tried to insist that they should be freed, which was reluctantly done, only for them to be attacked and massacred a few seconds later. Ruffo confirms this apocalyptic picture of the massacre of innocents:

They have just brought to me 1,300 Jacobins, whom I cannot place in security, and whom I am keeping at the granaries by the bridge. They have dragged here and shot at least 50 in my presence, without my being able to stop them. They have also wounded at least 200, who were dragged here naked. Seeing that I was horrified by such a sight, they reassured me by saying that those killed were the gang leaders, and that the wounded were enemies of the human race, all notorious individuals. I hope that this may be true, and that comforts me a little.

Micheroux agreed that it was only the more fortunate captives who were hauled off to the prison 'stripped and covered in wounds'. Most were simply assassinated in the streets. De Nicola saw how many were less fortunate and were done quickly to death, noting 'there were many dead scattered in the streets, others were dragged to the bridge and murdered in slaughter and massacre'. Evidence that the area around the bridge was the favoured place of massacre is confirmed by Giuseppe De Lorenzo who, along with his fellow ex-National Guardsman, both still disguised as monks, were taken to Ruffo, their captors swearing that 'if you are found not to be monks, you will be sent to join your companions who have just been sent to the other world'. Escorted by an Albanian armed with a scimitar, De Lorenzo was spat at, insulted and punched but eventually reached Ruffo's headquarters:

We reached the Maddalena bridge. Good God, what misery! They were butchering those who were to be seen by the cardinal in cold blood. Only a few fortunates managed to speak with him. Women, children, spinsters and matrons were stripped, the old, the youth, the young, all who found themselves here met the same fate. Amongst other things I saw a cart which was disposing of the bodies, although most were only half-dead, and it took them and they were immediately thrown into the sea.

The two battered fugitives were shown to the cardinal by a Calabrian officer:

'Eminence, these two prisoners were about to be shot by the mob on the beach, however, I came and prevented the execution and I'm bringing them here because they requested that they be brought before you'. The cardinal turned to us and asked 'well, who are you? Are you really monks?' At this question I readied to make an impassioned response and the cardinal, evidently mistaking me for some desperado, seemed affeared and, to keep me away, punched me with both fists on my chest, exclaiming 'get back, then speak'. I stepped back and, as I did so, his staff surrounded us. 'Speak now,' he said and I permitted myself to address him thus: 'Eminence, we are not monks, it is true. But if Your Eminence permits, I will say that we were both in the Civic Guard and were garrisoning Monteoliveto when the victorious army of His Majesty entered the city this morning. We put down our muskets, and took off our uniforms, in order to return home but, to our shame, we both had short hair. How were we to leave when all those with short hair who had left Monteoliveto ran the gauntlet of a mob intent on killing those with such hair styles? So we dressed as monks and went out, only to be arrested and brought here to be shot at the bridge, where God, who protects the innocent, and who knows what faithful subjects of His Majesty we are, intervened and prevented it'.

The cardinal ordered 'have them sent to the same place as the others', in other words the overcrowded prisons. To make room in those foul places, Ruffo ordered that the inmates now be charged, appointing Saverio Simonetti to administer justice, whilst Gregorio Bisogni and Angelo di Fiore were instructed to organise a commission and start examining the prisoners. Ruffo issued a royal proclamation on 15 June, which railed against the republicans, but was also an attempt to impose some order on the looters, echoing Micheroux's fears of a week ago by declaring that 'anyone wishing to make a desert from this fine land would be displeasing to His Majesty' and that 'any who do not bear arms, or that make no resistance, or do no harm to society, whatever else they might have done in the past, should not be harmed by anyone under the severest penalties including that of the death penalty.' [17]

Whilst distracted by his own miscreants and the all-pervasive chaos, Ruffo's primary concern remained how to cow the French and force the castles to surrender. His plans were confounded when he heard that Nelson had returned to Palermo in order to act against a combined Franco-Spanish fleet under Bruix. This news that Nelson would not be coming, but the French might be, was unsettling for the royalists.[18] Back in Palermo Charles Lock had even heard that Acton had instructed Count Thurn that, because Nelson's expedition had been cancelled, Ruffo should now negotiate a surrender with the rebels:

A few days after the return of the first expedition destined for Naples, the Count of Thurn, commanding the Neapolitan squadron in the bay, received at Procida a dispatch from General Acton informing him of the frustration of the enterprise, in consequence of certain intelligence obtained of the combined fleets being seen off the north end of Sardinia, and as the uncertainty of their intended object, which might be Naples, rendered it imprudent by persevering in their plan to subject the English fleet to the chance of being attacked in the bay by a very superior force, so prudence required that every sacrifice should be made to gain immediate possession of the two castles Nuovo and del Uovo and he authorized him in conjunction with Cardinal Ruffo to treat with the republicans upon any terms for the submission of those garrisons. The Count of Thurn forwarded the original dispatch to his Eminence and a copy of it to Captain Foote of the *Seahorse*.

This may have been palace rumour, but, whatever Lock heard, it was clear enough to Ruffo that he alone must bring the republicans to the negotiating table before the city was destroyed either by the French or by his own supporters. So Ruffo deployed those of his supporters still willing to carry out his orders, and the republican forts now came under fire from the royalist artillery positioned by the waterfront, from Thurn's *Minerva* and from the Carmine fort. The royalists, with Schipani's army scattered, brought up some of their regulars[19] and launched an attack on the harbour, trapping Caracciolo and a body of republicans in the Darsena (the arsenal in the western docks), and sent Panedigrano's men against the makeshift earthworks below the St Elmo fort. This last attack was beaten off with French help.[20] Meanwhile, some other royalist troops under De Filippis were sent against the royal palace, the republicans firing at them from the balconies, whilst a larger body, including the Russians, was sent down the Toledo running the gauntlet of missiles from the balconies and roofs of the palaces lining the street.

On the afternoon of the 15th, as the royalists took up their positions beneath the forts, Pousset and a Russian officer attempted to go up to St Elmo to open negotiations, but they were turned back by the large band of republicans dug-in below the fort's walls. Instead, they went to the Nuovo fort to talk to the fort's commander, General Oronzio Massa, a ci-devant artillery officer raised to general by the republic. Massa correctly observed that 'you are suggesting we surrender without me even having seen your troops' and refused to treat, adding that he was powerless to act in any case as he was subordinate to Colonel Méjan in St Elmo.

The following day, Sunday 16 June, Micheroux sent Pousset back to Massa. The envoy, again accompanied by a Russian officer, made his way up to the Nuovo fort under a white flag. Optimistically he carried with him three copies of a draft surrender and, whilst the rival officers talked, hostilities were postponed for a few hours. Massa conceded that the republicans would like to surrender but stressed that they were subordinate to the French. So Pousset quit the republicans and again prepared to ride up to St Elmo. This time their path was blocked by bands of out-of-control Calabrians shooting wildly, ignoring the cease-fire and even setting fire to a wing of the royal palace. The royal emissaries had to be smuggled out of the fort and a boat brought them to the Maddalena bridge.

That night, before dawn on the 17th, Micheroux, encamped amongst his Russians and his Manfredonian volunteer cavalry outside the Spirito Santo basilica on Via Toledo, again sent Pousset to Massa. Pousset was to apply pressure on the republicans by informing the garrison rather frankly that

any further resistance would be foolhardy, and might cost the garrison their lives for the batteries will soon be established and a breach will soon be made and you are too few to stop the ferocious Neapolitans when they launch their assault and they will slaughter you and anyone they find in the fort or in the royal palace. To prevent such a massacre there is but one solution, to hand over the castle to the combined forces of the king and his allies, and surrender the garrison as prisoners of war or place yourself at the mercy of the king.[21]

The republican situation was indeed unenviable. The realisation that Ruffo was now deploying his entire force against them, forced Massa to concede that only Bruix's fleet could now save them. They would have to play for time and Massa asked for two days to consider the terms, but repeated that they doubted they should be treating with Ruffo directly.[22] The royalists, seeing they could avoid any accusation that they were negotiating with rebels, agreed to the republicans sending a party over to the French colonel to discuss conditions. Méjan was defiant, and declared, brazenly, that he would not agree to a surrender.

As envoys rode from fort to fort, the royalists established more batteries and resumed their firing, this time with rather more success. Ruffo lacked reliable infantry to exploit any damage inflicted on the republic's stone walls and some of the best of those troops were policing the populace and his own band of followers:

> When Tschudi's men return it would be good to have them go up and down the streets, putting an end to the sacking and looting, arresting those persons who are disturbing the peace and committing acts of violence. We will be obliged to do this otherwise the cause of those who favour the monarchy will be hurt and damaged. ... Make sure an interpreter is attached to the Russians, otherwise there might be problems through misunderstandings.[23]

Late on the 17th Ruffo also told Micheroux that the guarding of the batteries should only be performed by regulars:

> I'm sending you a 36-pounder gun, but make sure it is guarded by regular soldiers otherwise we'd be in danger of losing it. In order to round up the irregular troops, it will be necessary to send out patrols of regulars, both infantry and cavalry, and, once they have been brought in, they then need to be guarded so that they do not disperse again.[24]

Even those who stayed with the colours were proving a mixed blessing. As evidence of the poor quality of his army Ruffo added:

Today 60 of our troops advanced from Pizzo Falcone but were then attacked by a sortie from the palace which reduced our soldiers to nervous wrecks.[25]

The republicans and the French were keen to exploit Ruffo's difficulties now that the ceasefire had petered out and, for once, showed themselves capable of some effective coordination. That night they launched a bold sortie. The knot of men below St Elmo, along with what Lieutenant Laugier called '200 veterans under chef de bataillon Derbes' from the French garrison, chased away Panedigrano's men and then, along with a detachment issuing from the republican forts, overran and destroyed a royalist battery of 11 guns along the waterfront. Unfortunately, the republicans then seem to have lost focus and their men went off to loot a café run by a certain Carlo Busto before returning to their original positions. Even so it was quite a setback for Ruffo, and he was unnerved, events reinforcing his sense that perhaps negotiation might prove mightier than the sword. Just then, however, some good news sailed into the harbour.

It wasn't Nelson's missing fleet, which was hoping to meet the combined French and Spanish fleet and was therefore again hovering off Palermo, but Captain Foote's little flotilla was still welcome. It consisted of the *Seahorse*, Commander James Oswald's *Perseus* bomb, Commander William Hoste's *Mutine*, along with the Neapolitan *Sirena*, and it arrived on the afternoon of the 17th.[26] Foote was soon in action. Onofrio Fiani in the Uovo fort recalled that the ships quickly began pummelling the garrison and 'didn't give us a moment of peace' so much so that, at one point, a white flag floated above the pall of blue smoke, only to be quickly pulled down. Those who were for surrender, led by Anguissola, were reprimanded by the more austere Colonel Enrico Michele L'Aurora and he now took over the command.[27]

Foote having positioned his ships to their best advantage sent Oswald ashore with John Rushout, 'a very respectable English gentleman resident at Ischia', the tourist accompanying the commander as his interpreter:

Foote was directed to use every effort and make the best terms to get immediate possession of the castles, and, as he did not understand Italian, he requested me to go at once to Cardinal Ruffo, state the case, and arrange with him whatever was necessary to carry out the object. The hurry was such that the despatches Foote had just received were placed in my hands for perusal, and to serve at once as credentials and instructions for me in my negotiations with the cardinal, to whom I was to apologise for the informality of sending them in such a manner.

An English uniform was procured: thus equipped, I set out, with Captain Oswald, on my mission to the cardinal, who agreed to grant liberal terms.

Oswald and his unusual assistant met Ruffo and all were in agreement that a speedy settlement, so that the capital might be spared an effusion of blood, was in everyone's interests:

The cardinal acquainted Oswald that he had already upon the pressing injunction laid on him by the king's minister,[28] sent a flag of truce to St Elmo with proposals to Méjan, the French commander, for the surrender of the two castles. That Méjan had ridiculed the idea of treating with banditti, and would not hear of any terms for the surrender of places whose defences were hitherto unimpaired, and who had not yet been assailed in a regular manner. The cardinal, however, determined to summon the castles themselves, and entreated Captain Foote by Captain Oswald to summon Castel Uovo as himself would Castel Nuovo.[29]

On the morning of the 18th Oswald was sent into the Uovo fort, offering similar terms to those that Foote had granted the republicans at Castellamare, and protection of the British flag should they surrender.[30] The colonel in charge of the republican garrison, L'Aurora, replied that they 'wished for a republic one and indivisible, and would die for it' and, seeing no tactical advantage in tact, added 'There's your response, now be gone, citizen, quick, quick'.[31] A ruffled Oswald returned to Foote who, angered by the republican's 'very insolent verbal answer', then went to report to Ruffo. Operations must continue, but Foote shared his fears that Ruffo's troops were incapable of, or unwilling to, bring the sieges to a successful conclusion. Ruffo agreed with Foote that his troops were not up to the task,[32] and Matteo Wade, an Irish officer in Neapolitan service, no doubt nodded in agreement, for he was of the opinion that 'a few regular troops would be necessary to influence good order, as those joined with the cardinal seem to have no order, and less discipline.'[33] Privately, Foote also had a poor opinion of Ruffo's military abilities, thinking that 'he kept advancing, without any fixed plan, or project, trusting entirely to the chapter of accidents'. These factors, combined with the likely consequences of introducing vast numbers of irregular troops into the capital, made Foote pessimistic about a quick solution. He had already made his fears known to Nelson on 4 June, presciently writing

Magazines (independent of what the island of Procida may want), field pieces, and all military stores, with a printing press, should be sent here, and not less than two thousand troops, with both civil and military officers to prevent the anarchy that must take place if the royalists of themselves get possession of Naples; an event by no means to be desired, as there is no saying what pillage and disorder would ensue, as few if any of these armed people receive any regular pay, and consequently are obliged to subsist by rapine and plunder, which I fear has given the country people but too much reason to complain of their conduct. With all submission to the better judgement of my superiors, I beg leave to recommend the offering of a free pardon, because, when throwing the dice for kingdoms, personal animosities, jealousies and every trifling object, should be disregarded.[34]

Throughout the rest of the 18th and the night of 18–19 June Foote's boats and the royalist artillery, now directed by British and Russian officers, brought considerable fire to bear against the republican and French positions. One battery fired 54 rounds against the Nuovo fort, 52 hitting their target and opening a breach. De Nicola saw that 'the side of the Nuovo fort towards the Carmine tower, was all in flames'. A party of Calabrians even managed to cross the 40-metre gap between the breach and the nearest houses and temporarily establish themselves by the rubble.

So it was perhaps hardly surprising that at dawn the morning on the 19th a flag of truce was raised at St Elmo and an emissary from the Nuovo fort was ushered in to Micheroux's headquarters, informing him that General Massa wished to be escorted over to St Elmo to discuss terms of surrender with Méjan. The republican general, however, hinted darkly that the republicans 'lacked neither arms, nor provisions nor the means to defend themselves, and indeed they could make use of the most desperate measures'.

With echoes of Vigliena in these words Micheroux felt compelled to comply and so Micheroux, Massa and Baillie rode up to St Elmo to discuss terms. There Méjan set out his conditions, as he later reported:

Negotiations opened, with General Massa, who knew my opinion, wishing to surrender the forts he commanded. He could no longer hold out and hoped to give some weight to proceedings and shared the terms with me, inviting me to mediate in the name of the French Republic. I entered negotiations, drafted a treaty and the council of war approved it. It paid attention to the fate of the Neapolitan patriots and it was agreed and confirmed that they would have the choice of embarking on transports for Toulon or remaining in Naples undisturbed.[35]

It was agreed that the republicans would be escorted to France with a British man-of-war, and Méjan adds that the allies 'proposed that there should be an armistice until the patriots arrived at Toulon'. Both sides confirmed this truce would last for three weeks whilst that voyage took place, with four royalist hostages guaranteeing compliance. Micheroux told Ruffo that the republicans were keen for any agreement to be guaranteed by the allied powers:

> I warn Your Eminence that I think the English are wanted as guarantors of the treaty. I ask then, if this can be done, that it should also be signed in my name and the name of the Russian commander, guaranteed by his sovereign, or, if not, in the name of Your Eminence, myself and the Russian and Ottoman commanders.[36]

Micheroux also relayed Méjan's terms to Ruffo, and sought his thoughts on the degree of leniency that might be allowed:

> It remains now for Your Excellency to let me know whether it is intended, if the capitulation is agreed, that the following terms should be applied, namely a general pardon for all those who have not committed capital offences and secure transfer to France for those who wish to leave, with the possibility of sending their property on afterwards.[37]

Ruffo, who only received Micheroux's comments at 12.00 Italian time, complained that the negotiations were taking too long. No doubt the queen's sentiments were also ringing in his ears:

> Negotiate with St Elmo and its French commander, but no negotiations with our rebel subjects; the king may be clement and pardon them, reducing their punishment through his kindness, but no capitulation, no dealing with those rebel criminals who are in their death throes and who, even if they wished to do harm can't, being caught like mice in a trap. I would, for the good of the state, pardon them, but we shall never negotiate with such vile and contemptuous ruffians.[38]

So Ruffo, seeing that the terms were negotiated between the French and his allies, agreed to Micheroux's conditions, telling him 'the terms should be as proposed for those that are first to surrender themselves, however I am sure it will end to our disadvantage and detriment'. However, the mice in the trap were not done yet, and now stalled for time. Méjan, still thinking Bruix might arrive, craftily added that he could not take full responsibility for a capitulation, and would have to send to General Girardon in Capua to get approval. Ruffo, seeing this was going too far, threatened to call off the cease-fire and launch an assault.

Méjan relented, and the first outline of a generous capitulation with ten articles was circulated. It stipulated that the forts would be surrendered to the troops of the King of the Two Sicilies and to those of his allies; that the troops of the garrison consented to give up the forts when the vessels which will take them to Toulon were ready to depart; that the garrisons would leave with full military honours, and flags flying; that the persons and property of all those comprising the two garrisons would be respected and guaranteed; that those persons, with their families, would be allowed to safely embark on the vessels or to stay in Naples, unhindered; that the conditions of the capitulation would be extended to persons of either sex who have sought shelter in the forts; protection would also apply to any republican prisoners captured by the royalists before the blockade of the forts. In addition, four hostages, Salvatore Spinelli, the Archbishop of Salerno; Micheroux's cousin General Antonio Micheroux; Brigadier Guglielmo Dillon; and Sebastiano de Rosa, Bishop of Avellino, were to be taken from the forts where they were imprisoned and sent to St Elmo until the republicans being evacuated to Toulon arrived there. All the other royalist hostages and prisoners being held in the forts would be set at liberty. One final, but important consideration was that only the commandant at St Elmo had the power to ratify the capitulation with all the above terms only coming into effect upon his approval.

It was far from an immaculate concept, but Ruffo, struggling to contain his Holy Army, approved the articles quickly and surprised Micheroux by not seeking to quibble. Ruffo distanced himself from the agreement but added in the extra safeguard of having his allies guarantee the document, telling Micheroux: 'Your Excellency reached agreement and I am having it approved by the allies, most especially the English ... it being my intention that all the coalesced powers should join in the treaty'. This was simple enough when it came to the Russians and Ottomans, as Baillie and Ahmed Kapudan were in the royalist camp, but there was a pause before an envoy could be sent over to Foote for British acquiescence. Foote, who had been kept in the dark for most of the day, had earlier sent a note demanding to be kept informed of what was happening.[39] Ruffo now replied, telling him that the situation was going well, especially as the number of desertions from the forts had increased:

> a great many began to flee from the two castles, and among them forty Frenchmen at least, besides a great many Italians; and the number of

fugitives will increase more and more under the favour of the night. We have placed some officers round the Castle Nuovo to receive these voluntary prisoners, and to assure them that they shall be forgiven; and this seems to succeed very well; and should those who have not yet fled find the same safe reception and asylum on the water, I do believe that the French, in case of their being disposed to recommence hostilities, would find the two castles empty.[40]

Ruffo added that negotiations were being 'principally carried on in the name of the Russians', with blindfolded envoys passing between the allied and republican positions for much of the day, and that Micheroux would receive Foote's request to see the terms. Shortly after 10 o'clock (Italian time) on the morning of 20 June Foote finally received a draft of the terms and replied that the terms were very favourable to the republicans, as indeed they were.[41] A British observer, who arrived at Naples in July, agreed:

The treaty was no doubt most disgraceful to the King of Naples, as holding forth ample impunity to his rebellious subjects. It stipulated perfect immunity to the persons and properties of those contained in the castles. Permission for those who wished to remain in the country to reside. For those who chose to evacuate it, vessels to be provided at the king's expense to transport them to Toulon. Unlimited time was allowed for the sale of their property, and whatever articles within the castles were claimed by the garrison as personal property, were ceded to them. By this article the plunder of the king's palaces was legalized, and the public sale of his furniture permitted in the Largo di Castello for the benefit of the rebels.

Foote, however, acknowledged that Ruffo had the right to grant whatever terms he saw fit given that the interests of his Sicilian Majesty were 'more particularly in the hands of your Eminence'. He made some slight criticism, saying that the St Elmo garrison would be left in charge of the fort for too long[42] and that any guarantee to the safety of the transports to Toulon reference should be made to 'the dangers of the sea', and sent the draft back provisionally signed and promising to furnish the transports and provide an escort. Ruffo wrote back, reassuringly, but would not revise the articles.

There was, indeed, no time for corrosive doubt for Ruffo had heard, on 21 June, that the French fleet was at sea: 'News about the fleet has come from Palermo, namely that on the 15th the English squadron left and that it was presumed the French were towards Marittimo.'[43] This prompted him to write to Acton to justify his conduct:

> It seems that these considerations may cause us to be merciful towards the rascals locked away in the castles, and to feel pity for the many hostages imprisoned within them. I do not know what the terms will be, but they will be merciful for a thousand reasons, which it would be useless to detail, and which may be imagined from what I have said before.

All that was now required was Méjan's final signature and the capitulation with the rebels could be sealed. Méjan, after sitting with his council of war, and obtaining their consent despite some objections from three of the more radical officers, signed the formal terms. He had made sure the capitulation was set out on paper headed with the motif of the Neapolitan republic, and, with an additional republican flourish, now wrote 'Liberta-Uguaglianza' on top of the document.[44] And he notified his superior, Girardon, that he had reached a favourable agreement:

> The army of Cardinal Ruffo, consisting of the allies of the king of Sicily, and composed of British, Portuguese, Turks, Russians, those from Sicily and those that were newly raised, had entered Naples and the National Guard had offered little resistance. The royal cockade and flag was seen everywhere and the lazzaroni, shouting 'long live the king' broke into the houses of the rich and, pretending they were fighting Jacobinism, robbed, killed and committed the most horrific atrocities. The members of the government, with some 1500 patriots, took shelter in the Nuovo, Uovo and Carmine forts but the latter, under a Neapolitan officer, soon surrendered. The other two forts placed themselves under the protection of the French commandant and he therefore hoped that he would be able to conclude a capitulation to the advantage of the patriots. In actual fact, just such a capitulation was agreed between the officers of the royal army and the commanders selected by the patriots. In brief, the garrison of the forts would come out with the honours of war, would stack their weapons on the glacis and would embark and be taken to Toulon.[45]

The republican Giacinto Sozio overheard Méjan exclaim 'I'll make a good treaty and we'll all go back to Provence'. The republicans too were optimistic, they had what they needed, an honourable surrender, guaranteed by the allies and by the French, and a way out of the mouse trap. Amedeo Ricciardi thought everything was watertight:

on the 15th of June his Eminence Cardinal Ruffo, vicar-general of his Majesty the King of Sicily, published a proclamation to the people, in which he ordered them to respect the bearers of the flag of truce which was about to be sent to the forts to capitulate, so that the articles of the capitulation might be scrupulously carried into effect. As they perceived from this proclamation that the troops blockading the castles were regular troops of his Sicilian Majesty and of his allies, and as the said vicar-general proposed a capitulation which was to be guaranteed by the allied powers — that is to say, by England, Russia, and the Ottoman Porte — the articles of this capitulation were signed on the 21st of June with the ordinary formalities on behalf of Great Britain by Captain Foote, who was then in command of the British fleet in these waters, after they had been approved and countersigned by citizen Mejean [sic], commanding the Fort of St, Elmo, which dominated the Fort of Nuovo. The capitulation provided that the garrisons should surrender the two forts, with arms, provisions, and ammunition, to the army of the King of Sicily and his allies, and should leave them with military honours, laying down their arms on the sea-shore, and that those individuals who did not elect to remain at home should be embarked on cartel ships and taken to Toulon.[46]

It was sad to sign away the end of the 150-day republic, but the republicans drew some consolation from the honourable terms. The royalists were just as content and Micheroux, despite his fears for the life of his cousin, was relieved that the defeat of the republicans would end peacefully:

in order to save the city from even more terrible disasters I had always been inclined to tolerate an agreement with the rebels, without naming them, especially when considering the composition of our troops, the danger posed to so many innocents, the possible destruction of a beautiful capital and the chance that even a small enemy squadron might appear. And I would add that there was a constant stream of messages coming to His Eminence or to me saying that the rebels had dug underground mines … and were constantly threatening to detonate them, and, in addition, that the more desperate elements in the Nuovo fort threatened to blow the powder magazine and that Manthonè, who was less bellicose than the others, posted a permanent sentry in order to frustrate this horrible plan.[47]

Micheroux, calmer with the storm subsiding, had the cardinal and the Russian captain sign the authorised version of the capitulation.

Having done so, a testy Ruffo, worn out on this longest of days, pontificated on the need for haste, telling Micheroux:

> Without knowing the number of those beneath S Elmo, or those who were admitted into St Elmo, but who have now come out, I don't feel I can properly reply to your question. .... I say this with certainty, however, that they wish to delay and waste time. Your Excellency would be wrong to think that I was the cause of any delay, but the problem lies with you not having taken sufficient care of the details.[48]

Micheroux sent the signed document over to Foote that evening adding a note that 'I am at every moment expecting the list of the miserable people who wish to go away; then you will know the number of polacres that will be required'. Foote signed the treaty and sent it back just before midnight, very late on the 22nd. He only noted that, as he was signing along with other Allied powers 'and being little acquainted with the customs, and prerogatives of nations relative to treaties, and signatures', he protested 'against everything that can in any way be contrary to the Rights of His Britannic Majesty, or those of the English Nation.'[49] Thus he covered himself from any criticism that he may have signed under the name of the Turkish and Russian officers, rather than in any other order.

Foote, glad to be of practical use, now busied himself with the details of transporting the prisoners. He had already ordered some transports, and had fitted out the *Bull Dog* to escort them, and on 23 June he requested Thurn to send over some more polaccas, small merchantmen, from Procida. The request reached Procida that same day, and the officials there requested that 41 prisoners, including Francesco Paolo Meli, be included in the Toulon convoy.

A tired Foote then described events to Nelson:

> The enclosed is a copy of the capitulation which was signed yesterday, and I believe an armistice is for the present to take place with the French at St Elmo. I shall direct Captain Drummond of His Majesty's sloop Bull-Dog to take under his protection the Polacres destined to carry the Neapolitan Republicans to Toulon where he is to get a proper receipt for them and then return with the vessels to this bay, considering the sloop he commands as a cartel during her passage to, and from, Toulon.[50]

Micheroux was also burdened with the practicalities of carrying out the articles. On 23 June he watched as the republicans released the bulk of their prisoners, including Cipriano Vitale, a monk who had refused to call himself citizen, called for the spilling of Jacobin blood and had put a French proclamation to 'improper use'. More significantly, the republicans let high-ranking hostages such as Filippo Acton, Carlo de Curtis, Daniele de Gambs and Pasquale Tshudy go and the 12 British sailors who had been captured at Salerno also went free. Events recorded by Amedeo [Amadeus] Ricciardi in his Memoir:

> That which the garrisons promised to do when the capitulation was signed was done and the hostages were sent and the prisoners detained in the forts, whether those we had taken from the British, or the royalists, were set at liberty.[51]

This is confirmed by Ruffo's order of the day before, when he confirmed the release of the British:

> I won't allow the 160 patriots who are our prisoners to enter the Nuovo fort as they could reinforce the garrison so, instead, I have had Count Thurn bring them into the Carmine fort and there treat them with due care. At the same time I beg your Excellency to recollect that there are 10 or 12 Englishmen in the Nuovo fort and that they should be handed over to the English captain.[52]

Then the republicans had the four royalist hostages required under the agreement sent up to St Elmo. That morning Micheroux warned Brigadier Minichini that the four hostages were leaving the Uovo and were to be taken to St Elmo later that day:

> I beg to give you notice that the four hostages in the Uovo fort should be sent to you this morning and you should take them, under escort, in a carriage, so that they might lunch with their wives and from there go to St Elmo.[53]

A few hours later Micheroux promised General Massa that supplies would be made available on the transports and then reassured Méjan that the hostages were coming:

> Yesterday was spent in hastening the preparations for taking the garrisons of the Nuovo and Uovo forts onboard, and these delay in leaving in their distressed condition, so you should not be surprised that we have not sent an envoy to St Elmo, especially as it has been agreed that hostilities have been suspended at all points. As for the hostages who are supposed to be sent to St Elmo I had them brought out of the

Uovo fort; they are with me to enjoy the company of their relatives and, towards evening, they shall be sent to your fort.

Many chose this lull to leave the republican forts and some returned to their homes. Others had their family and property brought over to the forts in preparation for inevitable exile and carriages and wagons were driving back and forth with possessions and nerve-wracked families.[54] As the republicans positively swarmed around the largo a request was sent to the Russians asking them to advance and protect the republicans with pickets by the gates of the two forts.[55] This allowed the republicans from the royal palace and from the earthworks under St Elmo to emerge and fraternise with their comrades from the forts. From a letter sent by Francesco Russo to Micheroux on 24 June it also seems likely that some patriots had already embarked on the transports:

> Be informed that His Eminence the Vicar General of the kingdom wishes that the water, which was cut off from flowing to the fountains at the Royal Palace, the Panatica [military academy], the Santa Lucia quarter, the Uovo fort, the Nuovo fort and the Darsena, might be reconnected, and wishes it to be known to your Excellency that the Jacobins have already started to embark, so that having water available will not provide them with a reason to further postpone their departure.[56]

This is confirmed by a note in De Nicola's diary on 23 June:

> Received reliable information that the patriots from the royal palace embarked during the night.

One of them, a violin teacher, told his informant that 'we are going to play the *Ca Ira* somewhere else, and leave you to this damned city'.

The republican commanders bombarded Ruffo and Micheroux with enquiries as to whether the transports were fitted out and had the necessary supplies onboard for the voyage to Toulon. Ruffo, revealing the frustration peculiar to a man forced into overseeing every little detail, irritably told Micheroux:

> I have ordered that the proclamation which secures the patriots' passage along with their baggage to be published. You might send it to Signor Massa, and even show it to him, but it is public knowledge. Would you confirm the arrival of the hostages in St Elmo, although it isn't necessary to go there, otherwise we'll never be done.

Have Commandant Massa check the food supplies which are on the transports. You see that it is not us which causes delay, but rather they abuse our patience.[57]

Early on the morning of 24 June Captain Foote received a letter from Nelson asking if he could join him at Marittimo as Nelson had no frigates and needed them to track the elusive Bruix. Foote was in no position to assist at this critical moment but mention of the French fleet made him nervous. He worried that he might be trapped between the French ships and the chaotic capital. So it was with repeated apprehension that he kept looking out into the bay. Meanwhile the republicans tended their wounded and arranged their personal effects, but they too also peered out into the bay at the transport ships at anchor, and scrutinised the horizon in hope that Bruix and the French fleet would appear to save them.

Later that morning word was received that 21 sails were indeed off Capri. A fleet was approaching the Neapolitan capital and it boldly sailed in at three that afternoon.

9

Rancour: Nelson's Arrival

To the utter dismay of the republicans the fleet was Nelson's. An earlier attempt to get the admiral to Naples had been aborted in early June. Lady Hamilton had told Nelson that the queen 'begs, entreats, and conjures you, my dear Lord, if it is possible, to arrange matters so as to be able to go to Naples', and he had done so but had turned back with his fleet, the troop transports and the Hereditary Prince when forced to concentrate against the elusive French of Bruix. Had he arrived in the capital he would have been in charge as he carried special royal instructions assigning him sweeping powers:

> All military and political operations shall be coordinated between the Prince Royal and Admiral Lord Nelson. The opinion of the latter shall be decisive, given the respect due to his experience and to the forces at his disposal, and this shall determine what operations are carried out; and also because we are so deeply indebted to him for the zeal and loyalty which he has shown to us on so many occasions. Therefore, should this offensive be launched, the royal forces involved in bringing about the surrender of Naples shall operate with this in mind.

Ruffo, strangely, wasn't mentioned. The instructions, which seem to have been drawn up by the queen and by Acton,[1] did, however, seem to suggest a measure of mercy for the rebels:

> In that military capitulation, however, which shall be agreed with the enemy troops occupying Saint Elmo, terms may be extended to allow for the departure of various rebels, including the leaders, if the public good, or the efficiency of operations, or other important reasons,

make this advisable. Such measures will also be accorded to Capua and Gaeta should the surrender of those places be the result of the course of operations.[2]

Nelson also received a second message from the queen, this time stressing forgiveness:

> I hope that the imposing force by sea, and their being surrounded on all sides, will be sufficient, without shedding blood, to induce them to return to their allegiance, for I would even spare my enemies. For I wish that no blood is spilt, even that of my enemies is precious.[3]

However, this first expedition only got to Marittimo where, following receipt of orders warning him that the Franco-Spanish fleet was at sea, Nelson returned to Palermo on 14 June. Much to the disappointment of everyone in Palermo, he cleared his decks for action by disembarking troops, horses and heir before sailing off in pursuit of poor Bruix.[4]

Whilst he was away on that pursuit the royal family heard on 16 June that Ruffo had broken into Naples,[5] but was meeting resistance. Maria Carolina quickly wrote to Lady Hamilton that

> I heard the happy news that the castles were nearly taken, but that, though pardon had been offered to the scoundrels, they still continued fighting desperately at the palace, a portion of which they have destroyed. Some of them fled, and the people are executing some of the remainder.[6]

Acton informed Sir William on the 17th that

> The king's colours were flying from the Maddalena to St Giacomo, but we do not know as yet whether Castel Nuovo, and that of Uovo are in the hands of the Jacobins are retired in these [sic]. The French in St Elmo seemed quiet and had fired but a few guns.[7]

The next day confirmation came that the republicans and the French were indeed holding out.[8] On 19 June, the queen told her daughter

> Naples is ours, but Saint Elmo is in French hands and the Uovo and Nuovo forts are held by the patriots, despite the proclamations promising pardon. The obstinacy of these wretches is unbelievable, and the damage they have caused incalculable. ... Lord Nelson will do us the honour of hastening there and restoring order by forcing their surrender and making sure they do.

Nelson, who heard from the aptly named *Incendiary* brig that Ruffo was in Naples, did indeed agree to go, later telling his new commander, Lord Keith, that 'I determined to offer myself for the service of Naples'.[9] He again headed to Palermo and as British reinforcements under Admiral Alan Gardner had arrived in the Mediterranean now felt free to tell the royals that he would sail to Naples, restore order, and perhaps curb the cardinal's ego.[10] Acton, resenting Ruffo, was relieved, writing to Hamilton on 20 June that the king 'accepts of the kind offer of Lord Nelson, to present himself before Naples, and procure the intimation for surrendering, to be supported by the English fleet'. Nelson brought his flagship to Palermo on 21 June and conferred with the king, the queen and Acton for just two hours. The queen told him that at least some of the republicans, especially 'unworthy Caracciolo', should not be allowed to escape, the king agreeing that no amnesty should be offered to 'Caracciolo &c'.[11]

The royal couple relied on Nelson to achieve this measure of retribution, and they placed their trust in the British to such an extent that they failed to send the Hereditary Prince or Acton with Nelson. Indeed, only the Hamiltons climbed onboard.[12] Ostensibly the diplomat and his wife were to serve as interpreters, but Sir William would play a more involved role in negotiations, whilst Lady Hamilton was intended to act as the queen's eyes and ears in the capital. With his preferred companions by his side Nelson set sail for Naples, and sufficiently enthused to be oblivious to the old naval adage that it was unlucky to set off on a Friday.

The queen was enthusiastic. Whilst the king was busy shooting woodcock she notified Ruffo that Nelson was on his way, her tone becoming shrill, and more vengeful as victory seemed more imminent. She declared that

> Nelson will summon the castles to surrender, and if they refuse he will force them ... You might treat with St Elmo, which is in French hands, but as for the other two, if they don't surrender immediately and unconditionally when summoned by Admiral Nelson then they should be stormed and treated as they deserve.[13]

On its way to Naples Nelson's fleet came across a Sicilian ship which muddled the situation by telling the admiral that a three-week truce had been signed, as indeed it had with St Elmo. Nelson drafted a note, his Observations ('Opinion delivered before I saw the treaty of armistice, &c., only from reports met at sea') on the morning of the next day stressing that the arrival of the British fleet would alter the situation and render such an armistice, with its infamous terms, meaningless.[14] His thoughts on the fate of the republicans is telling:

> That as to rebels and traitors, no power on earth has a right to stand between their gracious king and them: they must instantly throw themselves on the clemency of their sovereign, for no other terms will be allowed them; nor will the French be allowed even to name them in any capitulation.[15]

Nelson then encountered *La Mutine*, sent over by Foote, and received information from the governor of Procida who corrected Nelson's intelligence and supplied him with the text of the signed capitulation as the British approached Naples. An initial sighting of Nelson's fleet on the gloomy morning of 24 June was confirmed by Thurn on the *Minerva*:

> The English fleet of Admiral Nelson, 24-ships strong, the majority ships of the line, six three-deckers, has been seen and is sailing to anchor off Naples.[16]

Ruffo, who had received the queen's notification of 21 June, told Micheroux of his mixed feelings on hearing the news:

> I hasten to send you the good news that the English fleet is near Naples. I have not seen General Acton's confirmation but there are those who say it is in sight. Instead of rejoicing I am most concerned because I don't see we have sufficient force and perhaps knowing that the court intends to be strict means that they will try and get Nelson not to agree to the treaty, and so make him seem a rather dishonest fellow.[17]

Nelson saluted the royal flags flying at Baja and Pozzuoli as he passed by but was less pleased to see flags of truce flying in the castles and on Foote's *Seahorse*. Rushout captured Nelson's frame of mind at that moment:

> I had been on shore with Captain Drummond, and had left the boat with orders to wait for us until night to take us back, and, on reaching the beach to return, we saw that a fleet had arrived, and were in the utmost distress at the first moment, thinking that it was the French fleet. Our boat was gone, and, having discovered by the signals that were making that it was the English fleet, we took a fisherman's boat and went on

board the admiral's ship, when we found Lord Nelson in a violent passion, which Sir William Hamilton was vainly trying to appease. Lord Nelson told me, 'Tell the people on shore, when you return, that tomorrow I will batter down their city'. I begged to be excused from delivering such a message, and Sir William said 'I hope Lord Nelson will be calmer tomorrow morning, and think differently,' entreating me not to mention what had occurred.

At four that afternoon, Foote, alerted just an hour before that Nelson had arrived, came onboard the flagship, bringing with him a copy of the capitulation. Charles Lock heard that Nelson was still in a vile mood when he met Foote:

Upon the officers of Captain Foote's squadron going onboard the *Foudroyant*, his Lordship with great warmth animadverted to the treaty which had been made, which he reprobated in the strongest terms, as the most dishonourable and said Ruffo had acted without orders, that Captain Foote had exceeded the limits of his authority in signing it, wondered at British officers stamping such a disgrace upon their arms, and swore the treaty should never take effect.[18]

A more phlegmatic Foote related that Nelson informed him that he

was aware I had been placed in an arduous and unpleasant situation; that he gave me all possible credit for zeal, assiduity, and good intentions; but that I had been imposed on by that worthless fellow, Cardinal Ruffo, who was endeavouring to form a party, hostile to the interests of his sovereign.[19]

This seems to have surprised Foote, as it was the first time he had heard the cardinal disparaged, and he replied

I respectfully observed to Lord Nelson, that I had indeed been placed in a most anxious situation; having had more reason, among many disagreeable, and trying circumstances, to expect the enemy's fleet, rather than that under his Lordship's command, in Naples Bay; that I could not be supposed to know, or even imagine, that the cardinal was acting contrary to his sovereign's interests when I saw him retained in his very high and confidential situation; and my instructions directed me to cooperate, to the utmost of my power, with the royalists at whose head Cardinal Ruffo was known to be placed, even before the squadron, under Sir Thomas Troubridge, had sailed from Palermo.[20]

Following this brief exchange of views, and Foote's first vindication of his conduct, Nelson sent a launch to the Maddalena bridge bearing a message for that swelled-up priest, Cardinal Ruffo, written at five that afternoon. It was by Sir William Hamilton, and he, using the word capitulation, wrote:

My Lord Nelson begs me to inform your Eminence that he has received from Captain Foote, commander of the frigate *Seahorse*, a copy of the *capitulation* which your Eminence has judged it expedient to make with the officers in command of the castles of St Elmo, Castello Nuovo, and Castello del Uovo; that he disapproves entirely of these, and that he is quite resolved not to remain neuter with the respectable force which he has the honour to command; that he has detached to meet your Eminence the Captains Troubridge and Ball, commanding his Majesty's vessels *Culloden* and *Alexander*. These captains are fully informed of Lord Nelson's sentiments, and will have the honour to explain them to your Eminence. My Lord hopes that the Cardinal Ruffo will agree with him, and that tomorrow at the break of day he will be able to act in concert with your Eminence. The object of each cannot but be the same; that is to say, to reduce the common enemy, and to make the rebellious subjects of his Sicilian Majesty submit to his clemency.[21]

An hour later, Hamilton wrote to Acton telling him what the state of affairs was and what Nelson intended to do:

Of course the cardinal having now the support of Great Britain, his Sicilian Majesty's faithful ally, cannot be obliged to fulfil the articles he has granted when in a feeble state. In short, the letter Lord Nelson authorised me to write to the cardinal by Captains Troubridge and Ball tells his Eminency that they can be but of one mind – having the force in hand to subdue the common enemy and oblige his Sicilian Majesty's rebellious subjects to submit to the clemency of their gracious sovereign … I feel that if fortunately Lord Nelson had not come here just in time there would have been a page in future history that would have been a dishonour to their Sicilian Majesties and their government which they have by no means deserved.[22]

Nelson explained to Keith[23] that he sent Troubridge and Ball take a copy of his own Observations, although these were clearly superseded by events, and also demanded that a summons be sent to Méjan, giving him two hours to surrender.[24]

Nothing was done, however, to prevent the sacrosanct treaty from being carried out. Indeed, everything carried on as before with the republicans even writing to Micheroux on 24 June informing him that preparations should be made to safeguard their march down to the harbour:

> The position your artillery has taken up by the national palace, and the mob of people which has gathered by the Darsena gate, causes some concern amongst this garrison. I know that your objective is the same as my own, that is to keep the populace respectful, but we must come to an agreement on how to do so and I ask that the gun positioned by the Giant goes to the Panatica whilst that on the Toledo goes back to the Galitta, and that in the strada di Chiaja should be pulled back a little; that at the Darsena gate there should be a large guard of Russians to keep the strada del Molo clear and patrol it and not let anyone enter the Darsena. The prisoners which were taken in various battles between the republican troops and those of the Allies should be treated in the same manner as the garrisons of this fort and that of the Uovo and I would ask you to ensure that they are allowed to embark at the same time. You will remember that the release of the English prisoners should not be regarded as a change of plan but it was a gesture to thank you for your courteous behaviour.[25]

The republicans clearly assumed that the signed treaty was still valid, although the imposing spectacle of the British fleet had made them nervous. Within the city itself the arrival of the British sparked a surge in rumour. Nervy De Nicola noted:

> I have counted 24 vessels large and small this morning; 17 are in the roadstead, seven still some way off. They say that there are, however, 32 and it is rumoured that they have summoned St Elmo to surrender within 24 hours. It is also said that the delay in publishing the capitulation is due to the fact that His Majesty has declined to treat with rebels as one would treat with a hostile power. That might be true, but they had to come to terms in order to spare the city from any damage the desperation of the rebels might have inflicted upon it.[26]

Negotiations continued behind the scenes as the British attempted to get the terms overturned. Ball and Troubridge again met Ruffo on the 25th to repeat Nelson's sentiments. Méjan had rejected their threat of the day before and the British officers brought with them a written warning that he would 'take the consequences.'[27] They also showed the cardinal a

Declaration by Nelson addressed to the republicans in the forts, setting out that he would 'not permit them to embark or quit those places' and that they should 'surrender themselves to His Majesty's royal mercy'.[28] Nelson informed Duckworth:

> As you will believe, the cardinal and myself have begun our career by a complete difference of opinion. He will send the rebels to Toulon, – I say they shall not go. He thinks one house in Naples more to be prized than his sovereign's honour. Troubridge and Ball are gone to the cardinal, for him to read my declaration to the French and rebels, whom he persists in calling patriots – what a prostitution of the word![29]

The British seamen had failed to adequately plumb the depths of Ruffo's resolve to carry out his treaty and were surprised at Ruffo's clear response – the capitulation had been signed by several powers and he would not attempt to undo it, particularly as a British officer, Foote, had added his signature. If this treaty was to be undone, then the status quo-ante would have to apply, and the royalists and the Russians would withdraw to the positions they held before the capitulation and the British alone would have to try to force an unconditional surrender on the desperate defenders. Ruffo had already told Matteo Wade that he would not help Nelson if the capitulation was broken:

> In order to avoid the damages that might happen the citty [sic] by Lord Nelson's firing upon the castello dell'Uovo and the castello Nuovo, still in possession of many Jacobins, upon my arriving here, I applied to Cardinal Ruffo, offering my service in hope he would condescend to grant me a few troops in order to take possession of those castello, but he not only declined it, but absolutely refused that any of His Majesty's subjects should be employed in breaking a treaty authorised with his signature.[30]

When Ball and Troubridge pushed him as to whether he would support an attack on the forts if the treaty were broken the irritated cardinal again made clear his stance replying 'neither with men nor with artillery'. Suave Micheroux, adept at compromise, intervened:

> There was little flexibility in the cardinal's or Troubridge's character, which aggravated their discussion, so I proposed, and it was accepted, that after lunch we would all go together to Lord Nelson's ship.[31]

So the cardinal's retinue, including observant Sacchinelli, were rowed over to Nelson's flagship. A 13-gun salute rang out as they set foot on the holy-stoned deck of the *Foudroyant*. Nelson, with frail Sir William on hand for the diplomatic niceties, and Lady Hamilton, acting as interpreter, stood waiting in the hot sun. Then, in the blessed shade of the cabin, the heated discussion began. Ruffo, anchored firmly to the principle that a capitulation was sacred, and fending off the British calls for him to give way, responded passionately in French and the British, clearly lacking the legal or the moral authority to overrule Ruffo, struggled to persuade. Ruffo's position was simple: the capitulation and the armistice had to be carried out as agreed, both because breaking a treaty would be a blow to public faith and for practical reasons, because it would allow Ruffo to finally tackle the disorder in the city. Foote described the scene:

> Sir William interpreted between Lord Nelson and Cardinal Ruffo, till he was almost exhausted with fatigue. The dispute lasted about two hours, and frequently ran very high; the cardinal, however, proved more than a match for Sir William and his lordship together, in volubility, though far from equal to either in true eloquence. The venerable Sir William, at length vexed and wearied, calmly seated himself and requested his lady, though less loquacious than the generality of her sex, to assist their honourable friend, who continued pacing the cabin with the most determined perseverance in conducting this war of words.[32]

Sacchinelli contradicts Foote, saying Nelson largely kept quiet, allowing Hamilton to hold forth on how a king should not treat with rebels, but Nelson's own account of the meeting, written a few days later to Lord Keith, ran

> I used every argument in my power to convince him that the treaty and armistice was at an end by the arrival of the fleet but an admiral is no match in talking with a cardinal.

Hamilton later informed his nephew, Greville, that things had, indeed, almost got out of hand:

> We had full powers but nothing but my phlegm could have prevented an open rupture on the first meeting between Cardinal Ruffo and Lord Nelson. Lord Nelson is so accustomed to dealings fair and open, that he has no patience when he meets with the contrary, which one must

always expect when one has to deal with Italians, and, perhaps, his Eminency is the very quintessence of Italian finesse.[33]

This odd conclave ended without concessions from Ruffo, and the parties, clearly having achieved nothing save confirmation of their differences, parted. As they did so Nelson tried to wrestle the last word from the meeting by pressing a note into Ruffo's hands which summarised the admiral's opinion that

> Rear-Admiral Lord Nelson, who arrived in the Bay of Naples on the 24th of June, with the British fleet, found a treaty entered into with the rebels; which, he is of opinion, ought not to be carried into execution, without the approbation of his Sicilian Majesty, the Earl of St. Vincent, Lord Keith.[34]

Ruffo was quick to parse that an opinion was not enough to set aside an international treaty, and also saw from this note that Nelson was acting without royal authority (why else would Nelson need to wait for the approbation of the king?). Rather than challenging Nelson directly, he played a subtler card by saying that the representatives of the other Allied powers were signatories and their views should also be taken into account. Ruffo then returned to his casino to confer with Micheroux, the Russian and Turkish signatories.[35] Their opinion was that the capitulation was valid and legal, and they stood by it. Sacchinelli reports their intercession and the resulting protest to Nelson:

> That the treaty of capitulation of the castles of Naples was useful, necessary and honourable to the armies of the King of the Two Sicilies and of his powerful allies the King of Great Britain, the Emperor of all the Russias, and the Sublime Ottoman Porte, seeing that it put to an end, without further bloodshed, the deadly civil and national war, and that it facilitated the expulsion of the common alien enemy from the kingdom. That as it had been formally entered into by the representatives of the aforementioned powers, an abominable outrage would be committed against public faith, if it were not religiously executed, or if it should be violated; and beseeching Nelson to recognise it, they protested their fixed determination to execute it religiously, holding responsible before God and the world, whoever should dare to impede its execution.[36]

Micheroux went back to Nelson's ship to convey the message from the allied powers, and his own concerns that the lives of the hostages, including that of his cousin, were being gambled with, but met intransigence, although a note from Hamilton to Ruffo showed that the Russian complaint had hit a nerve:

> My Lord Nelson begs me to take up my pen again, and to acquaint your Eminence, whom he understands to speak of the Chevalier Micheroux, in the present negotiations of your Eminence for the service of his Sicilian Majesty, that he is quite determined to have nothing to do with anyone, be he who he may, except your eminence, with whom alone he wishes to consult and act. My Lord Nelson also begs me to assure your Eminence, that with respect to the Russian troops, he will always keep in view the honour of his Majesty the Emperor of all the Russias, as well as that of the King his own sovereign.[37]

Sacchinelli sighed 'Nelson and Hamilton were growing more and more obstinate in not recognising the treaty'. Ruffo, aware that there was now a political impasse whilst Naples burned, sent a warning to General Massa and the republicans at the Nuovo fort that, 'although he, and the representatives of the allied powers, held the treaty of capitulation as sacred and inviolable, nevertheless the Rear-Admiral of the English squadron did not wish to recognise it'. He shared Nelson's Declaration with the rebels[38] but suggested that if the garrison wished to follow Article 5, and return home, they could do so by land as sea passage was being barred. In order to protect such individuals, and reduce the number of republicans in the forts, the cardinal proclaimed that anyone doing any harm to or insulting such fugitives would be punishable by firing squad. This was largely rhetoric, Ruffo was aware of the dangers they faced, and already learned that the royalists in Naples were sending some prisoners directly to Procida so they could be executed there[39] rather than be processed by the seemingly lenient cardinal.

Understandably then, fearing Ruffo's message was perhaps a ruse, and with the massacre of the Carmine fort's garrison still haunting them, the bulk of the rebels refused to quit and declared they were sure that all the signatories of the convention would keep their word of honour. Massa made it clear that the republicans had placed their trust in Ruffo and therefore that

> we have given your letter the interpretation it deserves. Standing firm to our duties, we shall religiously observe the articles of the treaty agreed to, persuaded that equal obligations ought to bind all the contracting parties who have solemnly intervened. For the rest, we are not to be surprised or intimidated, and shall resume the hostile attitude if it happens that you try to constrain us.[40]

Massa's next letter, to Micheroux on 25 June, has a hint of nervousness, but a clearly stated wish that the capitulation is enforced and that the garrisons finally be allowed to leave for France:

I warmly remind you that the supplies in our magazines are not to be consumed but have to remain intact under all circumstances. We agreed on a treaty and that which we swore is just about executed. Therefore you must provide everything that is necessary without causing difficulties. The request is a just one and I therefore hope that, without fail, 800 daily rations are provided as per our arrangement. Your naval officers who were supposed to liaise with mine have not come, and the polaccas haven't been inspected and we are very much troubled. I ask you to conclude matters so we can leave as soon as possible.[41]

The republican threat that hostilities would resume, backed up by a barrage of artillery from Méjan, made Ruffo especially nervous. He had not imposed order on the city and had too few troops to do so, reporting to the king that at least 6,000 of his soldiers had fled with their plunder. So Ruffo requested 1,200 British marines and sailors from Nelson. To sweeten the pill he offered to house them in one of his family palaces.

His request was timely because news also arrived that the French at Capua had launched another sortie.[42] This bold move had been quite a success, the assault lasting seven hours and penetrating as far south as Santa Maria Capua Vetere, just five hours 'march from Naples. Ruffo told Hamilton that 'the Jacobins and French from Capua, now reinforced by the desperate refugees from Naples, attacked our soldiers commanded by Gambs, took all their artillery and powder and have killed many men'. The royalists had scattered, losing 120 dead and 300 wounded and Ruffo had had to send his Turks and Albanians northwards to bolster a panicky defence. There was widespread confusion in Naples and consternation when it seemed as though the fighting would break out again.

Under such circumstances Ruffo inevitably stood firm regarding the capitulation, viewing it as the fastest way to restore order and save the hostages in St Elmo.[43] Early on the morning of 26 June Ruffo again repeated to Nelson that if the surrender terms weren't honoured, the British would find themselves alone against the French, the republicans, and the riotous population of Naples. He wrote saying that if Nelson

would not recognise the treaty of capitulation of the castles of Naples, in which among the other signatories, an English officer had solemnly intervened in the name of the King of Great Britain, the whole responsibility would rest on him alone. And that, suspending the execution of the treaty, the cardinal would return the enemy to the state in which they could be found before the treaty was signed, and that he would also withdraw his troops from their most recent positions and would reposition his entire force and leave the English to conquer the enemy by themselves.[44]

Ruffo was within his rights, the laws of war were clear that if the capitulation was rejected then the situation would have to return to how it was before the agreement was made. The castles would then have to be stormed. To underscore this threat, Ruffo reiterated that he would not support Nelson with men or with guns if Nelson persisted in his course of action, and Nelson would have to take all three castles with his 1,200 Marines. 'This frank tone could not have pleased Lord Nelson,' wrote Sacchinelli.[45]

To show he was serious, he had Micheroux prepare to withdraw his men back to their original positions:

> It seems to me that after having withdrawn your outposts Your Excellency can reinforce those posts which you think are most useful in protecting the citizens, and in assisting military operations, so that the citizens of Naples and their houses are not exposed to the fury of the populace. Then, when the patriots advance they must not have their positions further forward than those they held when our envoy was first sent to them. This should not prevent you from guaranteeing the city's safety.[46]

This admonitory manoeuvre sparked panic in the streets of Naples, as Micheroux noted:

> No sooner had the Russians retired from the surroundings of the castle and from the palazzo, as far as the Spirito Santo, than there spread through the city an incredible consternation, so that in a few hours thousands and thousands of persons fled from Naples.

All this had the desired effect on the British, who were visibly shaken by the looming possibility that they might be required to storm the forts and themselves keep order in a Naples slipping ever more fully into the grasp of anarchy. Nelson therefore reassured Ruffo that same day, 26 June, a little later in the morning, by having Hamilton send word that Nelson had resolved not to break the terms of the treaty:

> Lord Nelson begs me to assure your Eminence that he is resolved to do nothing which might break the armistice which your Eminence has granted to the castles of Naples.[47]

Nelson himself sent confirmation that he had read Ruffo's frank message and, rather vaguely, agreed not to break the armistice:

> Sir, I am just honoured with your Eminence's letter, and as his Excellency Sir William Hamilton has wrote you this morning that I will not on any consideration break the armistice entered into by you, I hope your Eminency will be satisfied that I am supporting your ideas. I send once more Captains Troubridge and Ball to arrange with your Eminency everything relative to an attack on St. Elmo. Whenever your army and cannon are ready to proceed against it I will land 1,200 men to go with them under the present armistice. I have only to rejoice that his Britannic Majesty's fleet is here to secure the city of Naples from all attacks by sea.[48]

Troubridge and Ball came to Ruffo that morning and Sacchinelli states that Troubridge confirmed the admiral's change of mind by informing them that Lord Nelson does not oppose the execution of the capitulation, apparently writing out a note which did not quite go so far: 'Captains Troubridge and Ball have authority on the part of Lord Nelson to declare to his eminence that my lord will not oppose the embarkation of the rebels and of the people composing the garrison of the castles Nuovo and Uovo'. Sacchinelli says the officer would not sign it saying that he was only authorised to deal with military affairs and not diplomatic ones.[49] Ruffo confirms the existence of the note, but says that it was by Captain Ball. In any case, he made it clear to Micheroux that the capitulation was to be carried out as planned and that he felt he had received sufficient confirmation from the British:

> I have the letter of guarantee, and that from Sir Hamilton in the name of Admiral Nelson. So Commandant Massa can depart in good spirits; we are incapable of deceiving him and Nelson, whilst before he didn't wish to permit it, has now spoken clearly. Added to this we have what it says at the end of Lord Nelson's letter and the other one written by Captain Ball. You can show the one or the other to Massa and keep them for our records.[50]

Micheroux was reassured by this guarantee and set off with Troubridge and Ball to 'arrange with the republican commanders the execution of the articles stipulated'. Sacchinelli remarked that the cardinal was less sure. Ruffo's suspicion, offspring of his fear that Nelson would prove dishonest in his dealings, led him to sense duplicity:

the cardinal was dubious, suspecting bad faith, but was unwilling to question the two captains and limited himself to ordering Micheroux to accompany the two captains to the forts to liaise with the republican commanders and see to the execution of the agreed articles. A few hours later Micheroux reported to the cardinal that, thanks to God, all had been arranged *by common accord.*[51]

Micheroux confirmed to Acton that the British had provided the necessary guarantees securing the evacuation of the forts, and the sending of the republicans to France; in short, that everyone was unanimous that the capitulation was now to be carried out as agreed:

> I have never been able to understand why, in this situation, Nelson's intentions suddenly changed. I can say that, around 10.00, His Eminence wrote to me that Lord Nelson consented to put the capitulation into effect, and that I would have to bring the Russians back to the abandoned positions. As proof His Eminence urgently sent over the enclosed documents as guarantees to the garrisons but, as they trusted my word of honour, I did not need to make use of the documents.[52]

More confirmation that Nelson had had a change of heart, and was implementing the capitulation, also came from Micheroux's Russian friends:

> Next morning, however, his Lordship sent for Major Bayley [Baillie] the Russian commandant, and after lamenting the indignity put upon the King of Naples by this convention with his republican subjects, added that as it had been ratified by the commanders of all the different powers, it could not now be done away, he therefore requested Major Bayley would superintend the embarkation of the Jacobins on board the polaccas destined for their convoy to Toulon, consonant with the letter of the treaty. That officer in compliance with his directions embarked them all the same day.[53]

This report of what Baillie was told by Nelson probably came to Charles Lock from John Rushout. This English gentleman was at Chiaja when he heard that the capitulation was being put into effect:

> On the following morning some friends were breakfasting with me at Chiaja, when the commander of the Russian forces was announced (his name, I think, was Baillie, and he was the nephew of a Scotsman who commanded the Russian navy). He informed us that Nelson appeared

more calm and quiet, and had directed him to carry out the capitulation according to the terms agreed upon, at which we all rejoiced.

Ruffo was reassured by Nelson's apparent change of heart, and, with confirmation that the capitulation was to be carried out to the letter, now turned to addressing the practicalities. He worked out a plan for the embarkation of the rebels with the two returning captains and, by noon, craft to ferry the republicans to their transports could be seen gathering in the harbour. The situation was improving, Hamilton wrote to Acton in Palermo that

> Your Excellency will have seen from my last letter that the views of the cardinal and Lord Nelson were not at all of accord. At length, after cool reflection, Lord Nelson authorised me to write to his eminence early yesterday morning to assure him that he would do nothing to break the armistice which his eminence had thought fit to conclude with the rebels shut up in the forts Nuovo and Dell'Uovo, and that his lordship was ready to give him every assistance of which the fleet under his command was capable, and which his eminence thought necessary for the good service of his Sicilian majesty. This produced the best effect possible. Naples had been upside down in fear that Lord Nelson would break the armistice. Now all is calm. The cardinal has arranged with captains Troubridge and Ball that the rebels get embarked this evening, while 500 marines will be landed to garrison the two castles.[54]

The cardinal, seeing that the British were willing to actively help in carrying out the terms of the capitulation, put pressure on Micheroux to speed the process. But then Ruffo's wish to end the calvary of waiting, by finishing with the sieges and redeploying his troops to pacify the capital, fell foul of Micheroux's tendency to fairness. So it was an exasperated Ruffo who bluntly told his subordinate:

> As the English now don't oppose the execution of the treaty, no reply to Mr Massa's letter is necessary …. They can embark and do it quickly. They can take whatever skiffs and boats they want and embark because that's what I wish. When he is onboard Mr Massa can seek as many letters of introduction as he wants and I am not obliged to respond to issues which do not concern the execution of the treaty. See to it that only the personal property of the garrisons is loaded, and be quick.

Micheroux, punctilious as ever, evidently reminded Ruffo that not everything was quite ready as not all the supplies were available for the republican departure and that there were concerns as to the status of the republican troops below St Elmo. It drew a rebuke from the cardinal which mixed patronage and irritation in equal measure:

> These affectations on the part of the garrisons are pointless, and I don't understand why you don't immediately carry out the embarkation as I demanded. They cause trouble and the English think it scandalous. Have them embark, I repeat, and at once. Execute the treaty without delay and start them marching down to the harbour to deposit their arms as soon as the first boat can transport them. Ensure that none of the patriots from St Elmo come down until all those from the Nuovo fort have embarked.[55]

The royalists had already announced the evacuation of the forts within the city, 'The public was warned against molesting either the persons or the property of all of those who were about to come out of the castles and other positions, and were warned that anyone abusing them would be shot'. Now Micheroux wrote a final note to Massa making it clear he would protect the republicans as they marched down to the harbour, lay down their weapons, and were ferried over to the transports for departure:

> A party of Russians will be at the Molosiglio and they will protect those patriots who are embarking for the transports throughout the day. All exits from the palace and the fort will be cordoned off by a strong body of Russians and cavalry. Those patriots who are ready to leave will do so by the end of this morning then I'll have those from St Elmo brought down. It is not permitted for firearms to be embarked but naturally officers will retain their swords. Two cannon is fine, Massa.[56]

The British assisted too, disembarking their marines and some armed sailors late in the afternoon of the 26th to assist in escorting the garrisons, including those from the royal palace and a handful from the Darsena, to the polaccas. Whilst the French garrison was to remain in St Elmo many of those republicans sheltering below the fort's guns also agreed to leave.[57] Once the republicans had been disarmed and ferried away, the British were then to take over the Nuovo and Uovo forts., as the *Seahorse's* log recorded: 'A large body of marines went on shore to take possession of castle Uovo and castle Nuovo'. The Hamiltons watched these troops go ashore:

> We were with Lord Nelson in his boat seeing the marines land at the Health Office; the joy of the people was excessive, the British and

Neapolitan colours displayed from many windows, and when we took possession of the castles a *feu de joie* went all over Naples, and at night great illuminations as the former nights. In short, I am now in the greatest hopes that Lord Nelson's coming here will be of infinite service to their Sicilian Majesties.[58]

The Uovo had been the first to open its gates. Brigadier Angiolo Minichini signed an agreement with the commandant, L'Aurora, claiming the fort for the king, securing the magazines and arranging the surrender 'in conformity with the capitulation'. The garrison held a roll call and was asked whether the men wished to embark for Toulon or remain in Naples. Some 34 republicans chose to be go free into Naples and later left the fort under cover of darkness. The other 95, including General François Basset, elected to embark. Onofrio Fiani, one of the garrison, remembered how, exhausted and not having slept for nine days, 'the garrison handed over the fort to the enemy in virtue of the capitulation'.[59] They marched out with some belongings whilst the royalist regiment the Reali Calabresi occupied the little citadel and then the outer walls, and hoisted the royal standard.

At the Nuovo fort, where the garrison was larger,[60] the British and Russians first established a cordon and the British then took charge of the gate facing the royal palace. The Russians did the same at the entrance facing the arsenal. The surrendered republicans marched out of this latter gateway in the early evening, De Nicola later hearing that they 'came out formed up in battle order, with drums beating, and they deposited their weapons before embarking'. They were certainly granted the honours of war by the Russian contingent, and there was a pause as they stacked their weapons on the quay and waited to be ferried over to the transports, although, again in conformity with the capitulation, the officers kept their swords. One of the garrison, Amedeo Ricciardi, recorded the process:

> On their part the garrisons of the Castles of Nuovo and Uovo set the prisoners of state and ten English prisoners at liberty, and placed the troops of his Britannic Majesty in possession of the gate of the royal palace which leads to the Castle of Nuovo, on the other hand the troops of his Majesty the Emperor of All the Russias caused the garrisons to march out with military honours towards the naval arsenal, where they laid down their arms and embarked on the vessels for the purpose of being conveyed to Toulon. By means of these acts the articles of the capitulation, which had been signed by Russia and by England, have been ratified and they received the prisoners and possession of the gate of the castle.[61]

The British secured the evacuated positions, Thomas Strickland's marines taking up residence at the Uovo and Captain Hood assuming command in the Nuovo,[62] and other marines spent two hours ferrying the prisoners from the jetty to the transports. The *Culloden*, for example, 'disembarked 60 privates and 2 officers of marines to take possession of the lower forts, and embarked the Jacobins on board of transports'.[63] Those republicans wishing to remain in Naples were kept in the Nuovo, no doubt expecting to be released soon. But all was not quite what it seemed.

That evening Nelson made a request to Ruffo for prisoners in his hands, asking that Caracciolo and any of the chief republicans be sent to him, as shown by Hamilton's note from the next day 27 June: 'My Lord begs me to add, that if your Eminence judges it expedient to send Caracciolo and the rest of the other rebels to him, according to his proposal yesterday, he will dispose of them'.[64]

The demand, and the fact that the British wanted to have all the republicans in their own hands, might have unsettled Ruffo, but on 27 June, it was a relieved cardinal who began his morning by celebrating a Te Deum at the Carmine Maggiore. He was also no doubt pleased by a fulsome note from Hamilton

Eminence, it is with great pleasure that I receive your Eminence's note. We have all alike worked in the service of his Sicilian Majesty and for the good cause. Personalities have different ways of expressing themselves. Thank God all goes well, and I can assure your Eminence that Lord Nelson congratulates himself on the decision he has arrived at, not to interrupt your Eminence's operations, but to assist you with all his power to put an end to the affair which your Eminence has so well conducted up to the present in the very critical circumstances in which your Eminence found yourself. My Lord and I will be only too happy if we have been able to contribute a little to the service of their Sicilian Majesties and to the tranquillity of your Eminence.[65]

Hamilton, still at sea, and exhausted after days of anxiety, was in his element when conducting such fine diplomacy, but his element was often shadowy and obscure, and he was being disingenuous. That same morning Hamilton had written to his good friend Acton that the rebels were now trapped and he concluded with a prescient note about one of the more infamous captives:

The tree of Abomination is now cutting down [sic] opposite the king's palace, and the red cap will be taken off the giant's head. Captain Troubridge is gone to execute this business, and the rebels on board of the polaccas cannot stir without a passport from Lord Nelson, Caracciolo and 12 of the most infamous rebels are this day to be sent to Lord Nelson. If my opinion is relished they should be sent directly to be tried by the judge at Procida,[66] and such as are condemned be brought back and executed here. Caracciolo will probably be seen hanging at the yardarm of the *Minerva*, Neapolitan frigate, from daybreak to sunset, for such an example is necessary for the future marine service of his Sicilian Majesty, and particularly as Jacobinism had prevailed so much in the Neapolitan marine.[67]

The commander of the republic's marine, Admiral Caracciolo, had escaped Naples in the confusion, quitting the Darsena before the capitulation had been signed. He made his way, with Antonio Chiapparo, to the village of Calvizzano, possibly making use of a safe conduct from the Duchess Bagnara, Ippolita Ruffo. There he was recognised by a family retainer and taken to Scipione della Marra, a creature of Acton and the queen, who sent him to the Granili prison. Nelson, probably informed of the capture by della Marra, requested that Ruffo hand him over, and that request was repeated on 27 June. Ruffo released him to his fate, which, as Hamilton's letter makes clear, had already been decided. Caracciolo was therefore brought over to Nelson's flagship early on 29 June, another letter from Hamilton to Acton recording his arrival:

Such a sight we have seen this morning! Caracciolo with a long beard, pale and half dead, and never looking up, brought bound on board this ship, where he now is with Cassano's son, D. Giulio, Pacifico, and other villainous traitors. I suppose the most guilty will soon be disposed of according to justice. It is shocking to be sure, but I that knew their ingratitude and crimes, felt less than many of the spectators.[68]

Midshipman George Parsons of the *Foudroyant* a young man much given to hyperbole in his old age, was one such horrified spectator:

The veteran admiral, who was placed under my charge, being then signal-mate to Lord Nelson, was brought on the poop strongly guarded by marines. He was a short, thick-set man, of apparent strength, but haggard with misery and want; his clothing in wretched condition, but his countenance denoting stern resolution to endure that misery like a man. He spoke a short sentence to me in pure English, as if perfectly master of the language, and was shortly ushered into our wardroom, where a court was assembled of his own officers, Count Thurn sitting as president.[69]

On 29 June Nelson had indeed directed Thurn to prepare a court of five officers[70] who, although the outcome was known, were to follow the prescribed formalities:

> Whereas Francisco Caracciolo, a Commodore in the service of His Sicilian Majesty, hath been taken, and stands accused of Rebellion against His Lawfull Sovereign and for Firing at His Colours hoisted on Board his Frigate the Minerva, under your command.
>
> You are therefore hereby required and directed to assemble five of the Senior Officers under your command, yourself presiding, and proceed to inquire whether the crimes of which the said Francisco Caracciolo stands charged with can be proved against him and if the charge is proved you are to report to me what punishment he ought to suffer.[71]

Nelson elected to make use of his authority over the Neapolitan navy and, for the purposes of this trial, Thurn was a fortunate choice as president. Not only had he been fired upon by Caracciolo in May, but the two had long resented each other, Caracciolo despising Thurn as a Tuscan interloper. Caracciolo's request that British officers try him had been rejected although, strangely, the scene of the trial was to be the British ship.[72]

The trial began at nine in the morning. It was conducted in Italian. John Rushout was again called in as interpreter:

> I saw Lord Nelson, who told me that the trial had commenced, and that he did not understand Italian himself, neither had he any English officer on board who did, and he wished me to go below and see how the proceedings were going on. I did so immediately, and on entering the wardroom below I found the court martial still sitting: it was composed of Neapolitan officers, the Count of Thurn, who acted as president, and four others of inferior rank and station. The count was known to be the implacable enemy of Caracciolo, and then held the office of admiral, which the Prince Caracciolo had so recently filled. I had been in the room a few minutes only when strangers were ordered to withdraw, upon hearing which, I bowed to De Thurn, the President, to whom I was well known, but the only recognition he vouchsafed was a repetition of the words, 'strangers are ordered to withdraw'.

The trial took place behind closed doors, and was quick. According to Thurn, relishing revenge as judge and prosecutor, Caracciolo did not deny being in breach of Article XIV of the Military Code of 1789 and serving the republic but said that he had been forced into doing so. No mention was made of the fact that he had quit the king's service, which might have been a mitigating factor but Hamilton, writing to Acton as the trial was underway, admitted in his postscript that the judgement, and sentence, was a foregone conclusion:

P.S. — Caracciolos trial is now going on, by officers of his Sicilian Majesty's marine. If condemned, as I suppose, the execution will soon follow. He seems half dead already with fatigue — wanted to be tried by British officers.[73]

Of the judges, Niscemi and Caperozzo were inclined to acquit the admiral, but the other lieutenants found him guilty, and Thurn's casting vote therefore proved decisive: 'After due deliberation, the court martial found the prisoner guilty and condemned him to an ignominious death, and the sentence was presented to Admiral Nelson and he confirmed it'.

Nelson's confirmation, a strangely worded order with its emphasis on *Rebellion* and *Death*, was quickly obtained:

By Horatio Lord Nelson, Knight of the Order of the Bath, Rear Admiral of the Red

Whereas a Board of Naval Officers of His Sicilian Majesty hath been assembled to Try Francisco Caracciolo for Rebellion against His Lawfull Sovereign, and for firing at His Sicilian Majesty's Frigate, La Minerva.

And whereas the said Board of Naval officers have found the charge of Rebellion fully proved against him and have sentenced the said Francisco Caracciolo to suffer Death.

You are hereby required and directed to cause the said Sentence of Death to be carried into execution upon the said Francisco Caracciolo accordingly, by Hanging him at the fore yard arm of His Sicilian Majesty's Frigate *La Minerva* under your command at five of clock this evening, and to cause him to hang there until sun set when you will have his body cut down and thrown into the sea. Given on board the Foudroyant, Naples Bay, 29 June 1799.[74]

and a hurried justification sent on to Acton:

As I have not the time to send your Excellency the whole case against the miserable Caracciolo, I only tell you that he was sentenced this morning, and that he submitted himself to the just sentence of death pronounced upon him. I send your Excellency my confirmation *ad literam*, which was : — I confirm the sentence of death pronounced upon Francesco Caracciolo, and the same will be executed on board his Sicilian Majesty's frigate *La Minerva*, at 5 o'clock to-day.[75]

An attempt to delay the execution, or change the sentence from hanging to shooting,[76] was unsuccessful. Even protests from some of the British officers were dismissed, as Rushout noted:

> The captains and officers of the British fleet, then on board the *Foudroyant*, were speaking strongly and openly against the decision, when Nelson, who had ratified and confirmed the sentence, without which it could not have been carried into effect – the sole government of the country being de facto vested in the commander of the British fleet – became agitated and irritated, and insisted on their putting an end to the conversation and not interfering. Shortly afterwards, whilst several of the officers with myself were pacing the deck, waiting for the dinner hour, Caracciolo was brought up from below, chained and guarded, to be transferred to the *Minerva*, a Neapolitan frigate, where the execution was to take place. On his seeing the officers and myself, to most of whom he was perfectly well known, he threw himself into a supplicating attitude, and, almost kneeling, implored for mercy, and said, 'Misericordia: sono condannato ingiustamente', 'I have not been fairly tried', or words to that effect; but no notice, under the circumstances of the case, could be taken by any officer not in supreme command, and he was hurried away by the officer who had him in charge.

The whole process was over in the time it took to play the Rogue's March and so, at half past one, Caracciolo was placed in a British barge crewed by 30 sailors and brought onboard the *Minerva*. There he was left in the chapel for three hours, before being brought out for execution. Thurn noted 'His Excellency Lord Nelson indicated that the sentence of execution against Francesco Caracciolo should be carried out according to his orders' with 'him being left to hang on the foremast until the setting of the sun, at which time the rope was cut and he fell into the sea'.[77]

So it was that two days after Hamilton had predicted Caracciolo's unpleasant fate, the admiral was hanged, cut down and then, weighted with three double-headed shot tied to his legs, thrown into the Mediterranean. Hamilton for once seemed surprised by the bitterness of Nelson's conduct,[78] uncharacteristically sounding a note of slight regret to Acton. He had already expressed his opinion that the prisoner should have been sent to Procida, and sentenced by Bourbon judges, and now he confessed that the trial and execution had been perfunctory:

My dear Sir, — I have just time to add Caracciolo has been condemned by the majority of the court- martial, and Lord Nelson has ordered him for execution this afternoon at 5 o'clock, at the foremast yard arm of the *Minerva*, and his body thrown into the sea. Thurn represented it was usual to give 24 hours for the care of the soul. Lord Nelson's orders remain the same, although I wished to acquiesce with Thurn's opinion. All is for the best. The other criminals will remain at the mercy of his Sicilian Majesty on board the polaccas — in the midst of our fleet. Lord Nelson's manner of acting must be as his conscience and honour dictate, and I believe his determination will be found best at last.[79]

But he was over his doubts by the following morning, when he wrote:

Caracciolo submitted to his fate with courage, but Count Thurn can best describe his exit. Certainly this quick justice has had a great effect, and gives the people the greater pleasure.[80]

Some suggested that Lady Hamilton rejoiced in the execution, and it is possible she toasted the death of the Neapolitan, as Nelson and the Hamiltons were dining when Caracciolo was executed. However, Maria Carolina, in a letter from Palermo on 2 July, hints at Hamilton's involvement and perhaps even twinge of remorse at the treatment of the republican:

I have received, with infinite gratitude, your obliging letters, three from Saturday [29 June] and one from an earlier date, with your note on the Jacobins that have been arrested and that we have the main scoundrels. I also see that the disgraced and criminal Caracciolo has met a sad end. I understand all that your excellent heart has suffered, which makes me even more grateful.[81]

The queen, and Acton, suffered little[82] and Nelson, too, felt no remorse, later telling the king that he now hoped to deal with the other prisoners in like manner:

The most notorious of the rebels I have in irons on board the fleet, and I hope they will meet the same fate as Caracciolo, who did not attempt to deny the justness of his sentence.[83]

Indeed, by the time the Neapolitan admiral was swinging from the yardarm Nelson had given up all pretence that he was carrying out the capitulation and would allow the other rebels to sail. He had ensnared hundreds of them, defenceless at sea, and would prove deaf as they attempted to deny the justness of his sentence.

10

Retribution: Betrayal of the Republicans

The forts of Naples had been evacuated three days before Caracciolo's body dropped into the sea, and the republicans escorted out and installed on their transports (and unable to move without a passport from Lord Nelson). Nelson had good reason to hope that they would meet the same fate as the Neapolitan admiral, especially as he had engineered matters to that very end. Indeed Nelson, by luring out and trapping the would-be exiles at their most vulnerable, had accomplished far more than the king and queen ever thought possible.

The court had assumed he would arrive before any terms were agreed, and they only received news that Ruffo was finalising a treaty four days after Nelson had left for Naples, as the king noted:

> Received news from Procida which I would rather not have, all is confusion and disorder. Then I received more post with infamous news from Naples, the cardinal having done the exact opposite of what was intended.[1]

Acton noted on the same day that 'Her Majesty however has some accounts of an infamous treaty with the rebels'. And when confirmation came through to Palermo on the 26th that Ruffo's capitulation had actually been signed, there was shock and anger:

> My wife sent me a letter from Procida with even more disgusting news, that the cardinal had signed an infamous capitulation with the rebels.[2]

Acton was also indignant, and wrote to Hamilton that

The cardinal as Vicar General in Calabria, and authorised to act with the same faculties in all the kingdom, when restored and submitted, was commanded to make a separate classification of the criminals. Some were to be judged militarily if found with arms in their hands. Never any capitulation or conditions could be granted to rebels. The king, far from admitting a capitulation with rebels, or any dishonourable articles with the French – and among these dishonourable ones is to be reckoned a truce of 20 days, so much prejudiciable to his majesty's interests – disapproves entirely, and writes to the cardinal that no capitulation is to be made with rebels.[3]

According to Acton the king would write to Ruffo saying he had heard of the arrival of the British fleet and that he 'hopes it is come in time for saving a shameful capitulation against every reason from taking place'. Of course, the fleet had come too late, the treaty had been signed, a fact soon swamped by waves of increasing anger. The royal couple were incensed, Acton saying that they wished to express their 'execration of the news'. The king did indeed write to Ruffo, a broadside, full of incredulity and chastisement, which reached Naples on the 28th:

You write in those letters that an armistice and a capitulation are being negotiated, but you do not state that you yourself are conducting those negotiations. You alone I recognise as being Vicar General, so I fail to understand who might be negotiating on my behalf. You have my instructions which were confirmed very clearly in my last letters and in concise and explicit terms. I understand that a 21-day armistice has been granted to the French in St Elmo and that some ships are being readied to send over to France the patriots, who fought so obstinately against your troops and against the royalists, and those who took shelter in the castles, even the most infamous villains.

I was glad to see the worthy, brave Nelson set sail for Naples, and with whom you will come to an understanding regarding my instructions, so that junior officers, or minor offenders, shall be banished from the kingdom, while the infamous criminals and all the leaders, irrespective of kind, rank and sex shall be put to death.

All I have written to you about the armistice and apparent leniency towards the rebels is to warn you as I cannot believe what is said is true, as I am only too aware of how carefully you have carried out my orders and how you keep in mind honour and the future tranquillity of my kingdom, which can only be achieved if the last seed of this infernal breed is obliterated.[4]

Although this was a warning not to come to terms, it closed with rather belated instructions about what to do should the surrender already have been signed:

> I repeat that I believe that no capitulation treating the rebels as though they were troops of another power is possible, and even if it has been agreed upon, it shall be null and void without my ratification.[5]

On 28 June Lady Hamilton also received a letter, this one dated 25 June and sent by the queen. The queen's blood was up, she had quite forgotten that even the blood of her enemies was sacred, and her instructions make it clear that whatever words she said to Lady Hamilton would transform into deeds by Lord Nelson:

> The rebel patriots must lay down their arms, and surrender at discretion to the pleasure of the king. Then, in my opinion, an example should be made of some of the leaders of the representatives ... The females who have distinguished themselves in the revolution to be treated in the same way, and that without pity. There is no need for a Giunta di Stato; it is not an undecided cause, but a palpable, proved fact. Either these rascals will surrender to the imposing force of the admiral, or the troops and corps must be united, drawn if necessary from abroad; the frightened women and children must be warned to quit, and the two castles to be taken by force, the rules of war being followed with respect to those who are taken with them, and thus terminate a guilty and dangerous resistance. ... Finally, my dear lady, I recommend Lord Nelson to treat Naples as if it were an Irish town in rebellion similarly placed. One must not object to the making France so much stronger by so many thousands of rascals; we shall be all the better. They merit being sent to Africa or the Crimea. It is a charity to send them to France; they deserve to be branded, that others may not be deceived by them. I recommend to you therefore, my dear lady, the greatest firmness, vigour and severity; our future tranquillity and position depend upon it – the faithful people desire it.[6]

Acton also placed his trust in Nelson to save the day, and finally granted him the right to overrule the cardinal, writing 'whatever intimation Lord Nelson shall think proper to make, the cardinal is to abide by it, and every precedent is to be void and without effect.'

Nelson had already acted by the time he received these letters, having emptied the forts through guile a few days earlier.[7] But more was to come.

In addition to this barrage of royal complaint,[8] Acton had also sent a set of letters to Hamilton, received on the 29th and 30th condemning the capitulation and hoping that Ruffo would allow Nelson to overturn it:

> I find by a second note, I believe of the 25th, from my lady (yours was of the 24th), that the cardinal has denied to comply with the just request of Lord Nelson and the only measure for saving the honour of their Sicilian Majesties and their government from the injurious blot, which future history should have laid to the sovereigns of the Two Sicilies for that indignant convention ... If the Cardinal refuses to abide to what Lord Nelson desires for the honour of His Majesty, for the credit, quiet and peace of his faithful subjects, his Majesty begs and desires Lord Nelson to carry on notwithstanding the necessary operation.[9]

To support Nelson's position against the cardinal, Acton sent a suite of instructions. The first was a letter from the king to Ruffo, with a copy to Nelson, telling Ruffo that 'I have read the declaration which he, in the form of observations, had despatched to you, which could not be more wise, reasonable, and adapted to the end, and truly evangelical'. This missive was accompanied by letters from Acton to Ruffo, again sent via Nelson, instructing Ruffo to 'come immediately to Palermo'. This was to be delivered if he did not break the truce immediately, and conform to the court's wishes. If Ruffo made difficulty about that, then Lord Nelson was given the authority to arrest Ruffo and send him to Palermo 'by calling him or procuring him to come on board'. Having kidnapped the cardinal, he would be replaced by Salandra or Gambs.

Acton finished his momentous covering letter with 'All these despatches I send, and shall be at the disposal of Lord Nelson to make use of them as his lordship will think better and convenient for the best service of his Majesty in these tumultuous and critical times'. In the end, Nelson did not need to deliver these letters to Ruffo, and even withheld the king's letter to the cardinal, handing them back to Acton in July. The British, after all, already had the republicans where they needed them. Palermo, of course, had no idea that Nelson had lured the republicans out and thought that should the treaty be broken, Nelson would have to bombard them into surrender. To do so, Acton hoped that Nelson would take charge of military operations 'in concert with our officers the best method for the castles of the rebels, in order that they should be taken instantly'. But Nelson's ploy had delivered the disarmed republicans right into the hands of their executioners. Without a fight.

On 28 June, immediately after receiving the copy of the king's letter, Hamilton wrote, at Lord Nelson's insistence, to Cardinal Ruffo that:

> My Lord Nelson desires me to inform your Eminence, that, in consequence
> of an order which he has just received from his Sicilian Majesty, who
> entirely disapproves of the capitulation made with his rebellious subjects
> in the castles of Uovo and Nuovo, he is about to seize and make sure
> of those who have left them, and are on board the vessels in the port,
> submitting it to the opinion of your Eminence whether it would not be
> advisable to publish at first in Naples the reason of this transaction, and
> at the same time to warn the rebels who have escaped to Naples from
> the said castles, that they must submit to the clemency of his Sicilian
> Majesty within the space of twenty-four hours, under pain of death.[10]

It looked like the British were simply following royal orders, that they
were annulling a treaty on royal command. But if they were, why did they
not then return the rebels to their forts and place them in the position they
were in before the capitulation? And why did they insist on bringing back
and detaining those who had already gone freely into Naples, with Nelson
also sending out a proclamation informing everyone who had held office
during the republic to hand themselves in?[11]

All was now revealed. The British weren't simply following orders, they
had planned it this way. Hamilton quite clearly gave the game away when
he crowed how they had hoodwinked the rebels onto the transports, an
act of treachery 'in our minds necessary', so that all the republicans could
be tried as enemies of state:

> How the cardinal will relish this letter I cannot tell, but I know that
> affairs could not be going on worse for their Majesties' honour than
> they did before *we came to this resolution — in our minds necessary
> for their Majesties' honour* I have reason to believe we have Cirillo
> and all the most guilty on board these polaccas, and the *stroke* was
> quite unexpected, and so will be the arrival of their Majesties and your
> Excellency, should you determine — as we sincerely wish.[12]

To underline to Ruffo that Nelson now held the fate of the republicans on
the transports in his hands the 14 transports were brought under the guns
of the British fleet that same evening.[13] De Nicola, the Neapolitan lawyer,
watched it happen:

> At about 23.00 [Italian time, ie seven in the evening] the English
> squadron changed position, and a short while afterwards three of the
> biggest ships came alongside the Nuovo fort. Saturday 29 [late 28th] –
> the manoeuvre that the English squadron carried out was to get the
> transports with the Jacobins going to Toulon on board under their guns.

They are still there and nobody is allowed out, or on deck. They say the English admiral was furious because the rebels had been allowed to surrender when no quarter should really have been granted to them ...

Captain Saverio Salfi, who had already endured much abuse, lay in one of those floating hulks, kept in the rancid hold that had most recently been used to transport olive oil. Just as cooler air began to blow in from the harbour he was surprised to see a party of red-coated British marines arrive and to hear naval officers shouting out names. He recalled:

> The English officers came aboard the transports and xebecs, seized hold of the members of the executive and legislative commission of the provisional government, the ministers and the generals, and any distinctive or well-known person, and took them with them. We didn't think anything untoward was happening, knowing that the British counted themselves amongst the civilised nations, so we assumed they were to be taken onboard their ships so they could receive better treatment than that available on the transports. So our surprise was great when we learnt that these unfortunates had been thrown, shackled, into the ships' holds.[14]

These high profile prisoners were dragged out and taken onboard Nelson's warships, as the log of the *Foudroyant* confirmed: 'several of the principal rebel officers were brought on board and put in confinement on board different ships of the fleet'. Charles Lock said that captains Hood and Hallowell were told to secure 15 persons to be placed in irons, an unnecessary humiliation but one Nelson could not help boasting about in his next letter to the king:

> The most notorious of the rebels I have in irons on board the fleet, and I hope they will meet the same fate as Caracciolo, who did not attempt to deny the justice of his sentence.[15]

Understandably, the move caused consternation amongst the helpless republicans, men who had, hitherto, thought themselves protected by an international treaty. The good doctor Domenico Cirillo was amongst those to complain of this gross infringement:

> This is the third day since I am in irons without any additional crime, and while my conduct on board this ship has always been

very regular and exact. Therefore, milord, if by your protection and by your orders I could be released from irons I shall take this great favour as the forerunner of that pardon which by your powerful patronage I flatter myself I shall obtain from our merciful king and ministers.[16]

Those shackled on British ships were added to those prisoners who had been brought with Caracciolo from the Granili prison, such as Gaetano Rodinò who was placed in irons on the *Audacious*. A note, in Lady Hamilton's hand,[17] and dated 29 June, listed which prisoners went where: Ignazio Ciaia [Ciaja], Admiral Francesco Carracciolo[18] on the *Foudroyant*;[19] Nicola Pacifico and Vincenzo Troisi on the *Culloden*; Prosdocimo Rotondo and Giuliano Colonna on the *Principe Real*; Emanuele Mastellone and Gennaro Serra on the *Alphonso*; Felice Mastrangelo and Giovanni Letizia on the *Goliath*; Mercurio Muscari on the *San Sebastian*; Francesco Basset and Ercole D'Agnese on the *Northumberland*; Michele Filangieri and General Oronzio Massa on the *Zealous*; Domenico and Antonio Piatti on the *Leviathan*; Gaetano Rodinò and Gaetano de Marco on the *Audacious*; General Gabriele Manthonè and Andrea Mazzitelli on the *Alexander*; Pietro Doria and Giuseppe Abbamonte on the *Powerful*; Raffaele Montemajor and Emmanuel Borgia on the *Majestic*; Giambattista de Simone and Lorenzo Montemajor on the *Swiftsure*; Giuseppe Piatti and Francesco Mario Pagano on the *Minotaur*; Gaetano Simeoni and Giuseppe de Logoteta on the *Vanguard*.

Lady Hamilton's note, for all its faults with Italian orthography, was a near complete list of the key republicans from the government and the military, and it was proudly sent, advertising as it did Nelson's and the Hamiltons' role in trapping these unfortunates, to Palermo. The British were glad to have set the trap which had caught the mice and more continued to be added, for the British were being punctilious about securing all the key prisoners. Salfi, noting Lady Hamilton's role, remarked that 'the English officers, conscientiously fulfilling the duties brought upon them by their dishonourable actions, passed backwards and forwards, day and night, morning and evening, at all times of the day, going from one boat to another, seeking out, arresting and imprisoning victims now destined for the gallows. Lady Hamilton took to sea herself on a number of occasions to point out to officers of her nation individuals required by her worthy friend, the incomparable Carolina.'[20]

The operation was led by the British, and their glee at having decoyed the republicans out and seized them was all too apparent in Sir William correspondence, the elderly gent even going as far as to imagine a suitable fate for the wretches, as he remarked to Acton:

> I think it a good thing that we have all the principal rebels in our power on board the polaccas, whilst the attack of St. Elmo goes on, for we may cut off a head for every ball the French fire on the city of Naples.[21]

The British did not rest there. Nelson's proclamation had gone out calling for those republicans who had opted to leave the forts and return to the city, or indeed those who had never been subject to the capitulation at all, to report to the new authorities. When they did, not a few were then seized for transfer to the Royal Navy. Giuseppe Pignatelli, the municipal president, was amongst the first to fall foul of this ruse. Nicasio Di Mase was also detained and brought over to the transports, suffering the indignity of having to sell his clothes to the ferryman and arriving in his underwear. Even Luisa Molina Sanfelice was found, dressed in peasants' clothes, and dragged back to the city.

These prisoners were first brought to the Uovo fort, where they joined a group of officers Foote had taken prisoner at Castellamare, and who were only in Naples because they had declared their wish to accompany the other republicans to France.[22] There were 18 prisoners incarcerated on 30 June, and the Nuovo fort was then used to house the ever-increasing number. Captain Sam Wood recorded that he held 83, including Michele Ciaja, in that fort on 5 July. From there the important prisoners were ferried out to the warships for safe-keeping and by the middle of July the number of political figures being held on Nelson's warships had grown to 48.

Holding the leaders in irons and keeping the rest on the transports were clearly contrary to the articles set out in the capitulation. They should have sailed for France or been rearmed and returned to their forts. Inevitably, such a breach of honour drew a furious response from the republicans themselves. The day after the key republicans had been seized Ruffo received a letter from Giuseppe Albanese

> All that part of the garrisons which embarked to set sail for Toulon in accordance with the capitulation, finds itself thrown into the greatest consternation. They had expected in good faith that the said capitulation would be executed, although the articles had not been scrupulously observed owing to the confusion of departure. Now that the weather is favourable for sailing, two days have passed and supplies have not yet been taken on board for the whole voyage. And at about 7 o'clock yesterday they witnessed with great sadness a search being made on

board the boats for Generals Manthonè, Massa and Basset, Ercole D'Agnese, president of the executive commission, Domenico Cirillo, president of the legislative commission, and for other individuals, such as Emmanuele Borgia, Piatti, and many others. These were taken on board the vessel of the English commander, where they have been detained all night, nor have they yet returned at six o'clock in the morning. The whole garrison looks to your loyalty for an explanation of this matter and for the execution of the capitulation. Bay of Naples, 29 June.[23]

A similar letter was sent to Micheroux, and another to Captain Baillie, this time with a note that the families who had embarked along with the garrison were now also suffering greatly. Any hopes of exile – such as those of Gaetano Rodinò who had expected that 'we were to be taken to France and I promised that, when we reached Toulon, I would establish a fencing school and with the profits support my companions in exile' – were ebbing away and the republicans, stranded on floating prisons, were reduced to protesting that the capitulation had to be properly executed. A letter from L'Aurora, governor of the Uovo fort, condemns the apparent treachery and oscillates between anger and resignation:

> You had the honour to tell me that 'there might be reasons why the complete execution of the capitulation has been delayed'. I tell you, sir, that there can be no reasons. After so many years of slaughter and of blood being spilt, after having done so much to destroy each other, if, then, the sacred law of surrender is violated, then there will no longer be good faith or trust between Europeans and their ferocity shall surpass that of savages or even cannibals. Any delay or change to the conditions of surrender is a crime.[24]

Shortly afterwards L'Aurora was brought over to the *Zealous* as prisoner and from there sent a plaintive letter to Nelson on the evening of 9 July:

> My Lord, I know you have little time, and you are absorbed for the entire day, but that is why I must remind you again of myself. I was commander of the Uovo fort and the capitulation stated that I, along with the garrison, would be sent to Toulon.[25]

General Massa, also onboard the *Zealous* lamented that 'he had trusted the word of five rulers who could not, he thought, fall short of their word'. But despondency among this shackled elite increased as time wore on, and conditions worsened. They were so bad that the prisoners onboard the *Leviathan* managed to win the sympathy of their captives, the ship's officers, inured to the privations of life at sea, writing a collective letter to Lady Hamilton pleading for intervention:

We, the undersigned officers of His Majesty's ship the *Leviathan*, having sought, but in vain, some means of alleviating the miseries of the unfortunate family of Peatti [Piatti] who are on board here; have at length unanimously assured ourselves that their most effectual deliverance would be obtained if your Ladyship's interference could be procured on their behalf ... We all feel ourselves deeply impressed with the horrid crime of disaffection to one's lawful sovereign and the miseries to one's country that must inevitably ensue; but when we consider the frailty of human nature, how apt mankind are to be misguided, and, above all, the sincere and unfeigned repentance of the Peatti family, of which we have been eyewitnesses, we have flattering hopes that, aided by your Ladyship's benevolence, they will have the good fortune to experience their King's pardon.[26]

If conditions on Nelson's warships were bad, those on the 14 cramped transports were horrific. A list of prisoners on just five of the transports gives 772 names, so there must have been around 2,000 people imprisoned on these rancid hulks. They were of all ages and mixed nationalities and included 15-year-old Luigi Arrighetti from Rome; the Battinelli family with three of their children (aged 10, six and 10 months); Paolo Boos, a Hungarian and Sebastiano Grebber, a German; the friar Saverio Capano; Eleonora Fonseca, the poetess; Giuseppe Grecumbo, a priest from Malta; Giovanni Parisio from Syracuse; and Francesco Maria Iordano, a French émigré and Knight of Malta.

Many were already in a bad way when they arrived onboard. Salfi was robbed of his clothes as he was being transported over to the prison ships whilst Moreno's arrival was greeted with robbery:

yesterday there came a visitor to examine the trunks to see if there were any money there. He threw my linen and clothes and my wife's to the bottom of the filthy hold. This is nothing compared with the loss of my pair of English pistols, which he seized.[27]

Salfi says that conditions were such that 'on numerous occasions we wished for death to put an end to our woes'. He protested to the officers of the *Majestic* delegated to guard his transport:

It was the hottest season, and the heat in Naples was excessive. The ship on which we were being housed was in bad shape and filthy, and had normally been used to transport oil so the smell was overpowering. Many of the patriots were sick on account of the stink and the mistreatment, but were denied doctors and medicine. Our food, supposedly supplied by the king, was scarce and bad. We were being eaten by lice, fleas, bugs, mosquitoes and all kinds of other insects. We slept on sand. The English officer whose duty it was to pay us visits was young and handsome and we thought his body might contain a soul to match. I stopped him one morning and, in pathetic tones, expressed our sufferings; I told him that, whatever our opinions might be, we were humans first, and, trusting in the integrity of the English, we had surrendered to them. In short, I begged him to pity us and our situation. To treat our sick, to grant us better food and a better boat. My prayers, the aspect of death, the sighs of the sick should have moved him to mercy. Vain hope. In a serious and grave tone he told me: 'you will change boats, but only to be taken to the gallows; that's the boat that will suit you best and I wouldn't be surprised if, within the hour, you aren't dragged out and put on it'.[28]

His subsequent complaint that the rotten hardtack was worse than that provided to galley slaves was rebuffed with 'the biscuits are suitable for those who rebelled against God and their king' and Salfi adds that if friends or relatives attempted to bring fresh food over they were chased away by marines with fixed bayonets. Those, he was told, being the orders of Lord Nelson.[29]

We can't be sure if those were indeed Nelson's orders, although he proved himself to have a heart as unfeeling as oak when it came to dealing with the republicans. He could not have been unaware of their plight, for it was well-known that conditions were very bad indeed – De Nicola thinks that 11 prisoners had actually died by the first week of July – and news of conditions in the harbour filtered back as far as Puglia, a diarist noting 'They say that a faint but grim music can be heard [in Naples], that made by the patriots who express their despair out loud as they are being kept on boats as they wait to be transported to Toulon'. The same chronicler noting that 'Giuseppe di Liddo is said to have visited Di Topputi [Domenico Antonio, later exiled for 15 years], who did not look good, on the boats in Naples and said that the king had sent some macaroni and cutlets onboard saying that "this is given to you by the tyrant king".'[30]

As conditions worsened pleas for grace began to pour in, and that summer over 150 addressed to the admiral or Lady Hamilton arrived from the prisoners. Nelson was irritated by such requests, as can be seen from this letter to Lady Hamilton's mother in Palermo:

Our dear Lady is also, I can assure you, perfectly well, but has her time so much taken up with excuses from rebels, Jacobins, and fools, that she is every day most heartily tired. Our conversation is, as often as we are liberated from these teazers, of you and your other friends in the house at Palermo; and I hope we shall very soon return to see you. Till then, recollect that we are restoring happiness to the kingdom of Naples, and doing good to millions.

Amedeo Ricciardi was one such teaser, writing to Nelson on 19 July on behalf of the prisoners in polacca number 14. They were suffering from the intolerable heat[31] and the horrible conditions:

We have now been for 24 days in this roadstead without departing, and deprived of all necessaries of life; indeed, they are only giving us bread and putrid water, and wine mixed with sea water; and they have us to sleep on the ground. Our homes have been completely plundered, and we are in consequence unable to get any help from them. The greater part of our relations have been either massacred or arrested. The deplorable condition we are in has already produced disease, and on board of this polacca there are five sick with epidemic fever, a thing which threatens the lives of all of us. We are convinced that the treatment we are suffering, after having capitulated, and having on our part religiously carried into effect the articles of the capitulation, is entirely unknown to your Excellency and to his Sicilian Majesty, for your sense of honour and his kind heart are both famous. The delay in the execution of the capitulation entitles us to protest, and to appeal to his sense of justice and to yours, in order that a treaty which has been entered into with four of the most civilized powers in Europe, who have always appreciated the inviolability of treaties, may be carried into effect as soon as possible. We hope that by means of your influence with his Sicilian Majesty there may be put into execution the articles of a capitulation which has been signed in the best of faith, and which has been religiously carried out by the garrisons, who implore your protection and the justice of the powers.[32]

Nelson proved indifferent, replying 'I have shown your paper to your gracious king, who must be the best and only judge of the merits and demerits of his subjects'. The protests continued, many betraying confusion as to why they were not being sent to France. A letter from Andrea Ajello written after the events also stresses the point:

I was promoted to the rank of captain in the 3rd battalion of the Legion Salentina. When the republic fell Cardinal Ruffo ordered that I was to be taken on board a polacca. I believed I was going to be taken to

France but instead I was brought back to the land, taken to the Vicaria prison and treated like the most terrible of criminals would be at Gaeta, denied communication with my family, and sufficient food, and this lasted 10 months.[33]

The republicans weren't alone in protesting. Méjan had initially thought that the transports were just being delayed:

It was not certain that the treaty with the patriots would not be executed. They had embarked. We had to believe that the enemy, conscious of public faith, would fulfil its side of the bargain. Nelson's opposition, and his annoyance, would come to an end. No one could imagine that the English would seize, massacre or execute the patriots, only that they were delaying the departure.[34]

But when it became clear that the republicans had been tricked, the French commander called on the allies to remain true to the capitulation, noting that 'we sent a constant stream of complaints to the ministers of the foreign powers'.[35] The Allied representatives also added to the chorus of disapproval. Foote had been sent away to Palermo before the extent of the betrayal became known, but Captain Baillie of the Russian contingent, according to Saverio Salfi, 'protested unsuccessfully against the abuse of the capitulation, but managed to set the famous Cimarosa free'. De Nicola noted in his diary on 17 August that the 'population do not think it right that the capitulation which was signed is not adhered to only because one should not treat with rebels'. He then went on to say that the Russian commander, growing sick of the executions 'announced that either the capitulation must be respected, or that he would retire with his troops, for he could not allow the execution of people who, trusting to his word, had surrendered and capitulated'. A number of British officers also seem to have protested, as Charles Lock, making use of contacts in the fleet, also noted in August:

On the ensuing morning captains Hood and Hallowell were called on board the *Foudroyant* and there received orders from Lord Nelson to get the polaccas under weigh and station one under the stern of each line of battle ship. A list was at the same time given them consisting of the names of 15 persons to be selected from the Jacobins in the polaccas to be put in irons and confined on board line of battle ships named for that purpose. They delayed the execution of this ungrateful order till the arrival of Admiral Duckworth, who they sent to entreat would come instantly on board the *Foudroyant*, in hopes he might prevail upon his lordship to rescind it. Captain Hood in the meantime ventured to suggest to his Lordship, whether it would not be deemed an act of treachery, the having *decoyed* (his own word) them on board the vessels under pretense of fulfilling the convention, by transporting them to Toulon, and then seizing upon their persons? His Lordship affirmed that he acted under the King of Naples's orders, that it was not his doing. Hollowell proposed with great earnestness, in which he was seconded by Hood, to reinstate the Jacobins in the castles and enjoyed with their lives to reduce them by force in 24 hours. His Lordship persisted in fulfilling his orders and when Admiral Duckworth's presence and remonstrance emboldened them to press the matter more home to him, he said 'I see you are all against me, I am determined to adhere to my orders, right or wrong it shall be done. I will be obeyed'. This shut their mouths and they proceeded to the execution of his Lordship's commands.

Prise Lockhart Gordon was also dismayed by Nelson's actions:

The ring-leaders of the rebels, as they were called, were in the men-of-war with sentinels over them; and because the humanity of the captains induced them to relax a little in the execution of this order, by permitting their prisoners to come on deck occasionally to inhale a little fresh air, a general order was circulated to the squadron, commanding more explicit attention to the admiral's orders. Many of our brave officers remonstrated with Lord Nelson for having broken faith with the patriots, and the captains Halowell, Martin, Hood and Troubridge were deputed to express the sentiments of the whole on this extraordinary measure, humbly suggesting the necessity of giving these men, whom they had thus betrayed, back their swords and arms, and of putting them into the possession of their forts as it was found necessary to break the capitulation. To this remonstrance his lordship replied with the utmost sang froid, 'Gentlemen, your duty is to obey, not to advise!', a speech that would tarnish his glories, were they even greater.

Ruffo, whose standing as a churchman and reputation as an officer, and indeed his honour as a gentleman, was most at risk, did not keep silent about this breach of faith. When he saw what Nelson was about, the cardinal had initially sent Micheroux to warn Nelson 'not to tarnish his glory or risk the lives of the four illustrious individuals who, as hostages, acted as surety to the capitulation, and who were being held by the French in St Elmo'.[36]

Then on 28 June, as British officers were hunting down the key republicans on the transports, Ruffo, to his credit, protested directly to the crown:

I beg your Majesty to understand that I was commanded to return order to the country ... regarding the armistice, it was not as it seemed, for we dealt only with St Elmo which granted the surrender of the castles and the removal of the garrisons, which were composed of men of all nations, to France. I hope that your Majesty accepts that my primary object was to recapture the kingdom, which is easier to say than to have the necessary strength to do it. ...

The irregulars constantly fired at the Jacobins and French in St Elmo, and against the palace, and the French, with the help of the people of Santa Lucia, attacked the battery firing against the Uovo fort. The irregulars did not wish to come against them, postponing the demonstration of their valour until the following morning. On such occasions, sire, one cannot dictate the law, but must act according to circumstances, keeping the ultimate goal in mind, namely the recapture of the remainder of the kingdom. Added to these concerns and in a position of weakness I then heard that the help [ie Nelson and the Hereditary Prince] your Majesty was sending had returned to Sicily. I was afraid, and who has not experienced fear, that the French fleet was coming, and that they would destroy everything we had achieved, that the two forts would be in French hands and our batteries rendered useless.

We had few guns, and their munitions were almost exhausted, and the troops lacked muskets although great pains had been taken to supply them with more, the Russians were determined to send in envoys to treat, all this persuaded me to negotiate with the French commandant at St Elmo in order to ensure the deportation of the garrisons of the two castles.

Nelson wished to annul the treaty that had been signed and sealed, and partially carried out, when he arrived. I did not wish to do so and was therefore determined not to allow a breach of faith. A man of my character, sire, and of my profession, and who has just reconquered the kingdom in the name of God and with his assistance, cannot be but true to his word without dishonouring the excellent cause which he represents. That is my excuse. Lord Nelson can do as he pleases, but I convinced him of the truth that if he had told St Elmo to surrender within two hours, and told the castles he opposed the treaty, then the people would have been plunged into terror and the city destroyed, so he allowed the treaty to be executed and agreed to assist with 600 of his men, and this would have resulted in us being able to tackle that which remained to be done. Now it is written that it is desired that they surrender unconditionally by order of your Majesty, and that this order will be carried out.

I cannot consent to the loss of my honour, and fight against anything that requires me to break my word, and hope that this will not be the case. I have nothing else to add. I stand ready to receive my deserved punishment.

I finish my writing now, sire, done in reverence to your Majesty, but I know that my detractors began their work as soon as the situation became decisive, and that I shall be disgraced. I wish to return to being the nullity my detractors wish me to become.[37]

By writing this way he evidently resigned his responsibility over the prisoners in the transports. The court sensed victory, the queen offering Ruffo a branch of rather poisonous olives:

I tell you honestly that I was disappointed by the capitulation with the rebels, for to see the infamous wretches go unpunished and safe caused me pain, especially after the king's clear instructions. I set this down, for I wish to be frank. But now it is all over and all will be explained to you in person, as we hope that now all proceeds of one accord and things gradually take a better turn.

Ruffo knew he had been undermined. His letter to Micheroux of 30 June makes it clear he was no longer in charge:

All goes well regarding the siege of St Elmo, however I'm not sure we will quite manage to finish it yet; as for the rest, I cannot say except that Lord Nelson, to whom the intentions of the king were made clear, has solemnly disapproved of the capitulation.[38]

St Elmo was the one area where Ruffo and Nelson were still obliged to cooperate. The French were warned when, on 28 June, Méjan received Micheroux and an Allied delegation offering new terms:

This morning captains Troubridge and Ball, their interpreter, the Russian commander and myself went to St Elmo. I gave a long speech in which I presented to the commandant and to his council of war all the sound reasons why he might be persuaded to honourably surrender the fort without resorting to vain resistance which, in this crowded capital, might be prejudicial if they renounced the opportunity for a generous surrender. I stressed above all the number of irregular troops we had and their impetuousness, arguing that, should hostilities recommence, it might be impossible for us to restrain them. At this the commandant replied with some grace and moderation, saying that the armistice could be kept in place until Capua fell, which would oblige him to surrender his fort without further resistance. But this did not please the Englishmen and the conference broke up.[39]

Méjan's insistence that General Girardon in Capua, get involved,[40] and various other irritations,[41] left the allies dissatisfied. A way would have to be found to force a capitulation. Rumour, which was stalking the city as much as death that summer, had it that the French would be put to the sword, and that, for every artillery round they fired against the city, the lives of 100 Frenchmen would be forfeit. Perhaps reflecting Hamilton's own threat of 30 June, it was also said that the British would cut the head off one of the prisoners in the transports every time the French opened fire.[42] Or that quarrymen were to be paid 100,000 Ducats to blow the entire fort into the air.[43] Others said that the softer ordnance of bribery was being tried and that Méjan was being offered cash to surrender. Evidence that this was so can be gauged by the volume of the denials, and that the British were openly blaming the Neapolitans for such subterfuge, whilst the Neapolitans pointed fingers at the British. Troubridge got his accusation in quickly, telling Nelson: 'Since finishing my letter, the governor has, through Micheroux [the hostage], sent an offer to surrender for 150,000 Ducats.' Troubridge was probably right, but the scheme was most likely the brainchild of the court as General Gambs[44] had apparently been sent to salve French conscience about surrendering with the medicine of hard cash.[45] It seems as though an offer was indeed made to the French but was rejected, and the money was not paid.[46]

Whatever the rumours, forcing a French capitulation by more belligerent means was the most practical solution and Hamilton, relishing Ruffo's fall from grace, sent a rather barbed message to the cardinal that 'My Lord proposes then, with the approbation of your Eminence, to send the body of marines, about 1,200 men, together with the Russian corps attached to the army of your Eminence, to attack the said castle'.

Artillery was now being dragged forward by lumbering teams of oxen and on the 4th Ruffo, who could spare few men as he needed most of his troops to curb the looters, sent some small parties of Calabrians to clear the last pocket of republicans from the vineyards. They held out from behind a parapet made from tables shouting 'death to the tyrant,

long live liberty!' whilst the royalist irregulars replied with 'death to
the Giacobbe'. The bitter fighting masked the sight of artillery being
positioned for the final assault, as Captain Baillie's report to Admiral
Ushakov makes clear:

> I have the honour to report to Your Excellency that on the 19th of July
> [8 July] the unit under my command besieged the fortress of Saint Elmo·
> positioning itself on the left, and the English attacking from the right
> side. At 3 in the afternoon I sent up the artillery team, with 4 mortars,
> and commenced the battery for 4 guns, each of which weighed 33
> pounds. During the ensuing period I damaged the fort's embrasures and
> my cannon destroyed 4 enemy guns.[47]

The French returned fire to cover a final, desperate sortie by the remaining
republicans on 9 July. It was a gesture overshadowed by a more
momentous development. King Ferdinand and loyal Acton, onboard *La
Sirena*, escorted by the *Seahorse* of Captain Foote,[48] had arrived. The king
had finally left Palermo and had been hovering off Capri since 8 July.
There Cardinal Ruffo had climbed aboard to argue for fulfilment of his
treaty, or even to move His Majesty to mercy. He seems to have given his
frank opinion that 'Nelson, having violated the treaty, had damaged the
dignity of the crown and the reputation of his comrades in arms.'[49] The
king wavered but a glowering Acton,[50] later supported by Hamilton and
Nelson, told him that he should not have treated with rebels and that he
needed to destroy the Jacobin tree from its roots. As resolved as he was
ever likely to be, the king now sailed into Naples' harbour and was saluted
by the fleet and by the artillery on shore. A mass of Neapolitans came
out on boats to greet the monarch, whilst a crowd gathered on the beach
shouting 'Vendetta! Vendetta!' The king, still unsettled, climbed onboard
Nelson's flagship. He put on a brave face

> I have come to end the anarchy, protect the good and secure them for
> the insults and tricks of the wicked rebels. I never wished to negotiate
> with them, having always ruled this out, seeing that their only hope lay
> with them imploring for my mercy.[51]

The king was soon distracted from Ruffo's conscience and 'a strange
and curious letter from Ruffo, asking that he be allowed to resign'[52] by
the excitement of the siege of St Elmo. He was elated when a shot, one
of 1,800 projectiles to strike the fort, hit the French flagpole. But he
was equally excited by the prospect of settling scores with the rebels:
'all the dear Jacobins are next to us and the boats that pass by sing the

Carmagnole ... all the notorious leaders are in our power and tonight I hope to get hold of Vitagliano [Andrea Vitaliani, sheltering in St Elmo]'.

The day of reckoning was not far off, and Baillie noted what happened next

> I opened a breach successfully and continued to widen it. The enemy, who were in bad condition, and seeing that the English had built batteries on the right, raised the white flag and asked to surrender the fortress and capitulate. At 8 in the evening the capitulation was complete, and the auxiliaries of the French were included, and the garrison surrendered as prisoners of war. Losses on our side: dead – 1 officer, 1 private; wounded – 6 privates.[53]

Méjan had indeed wanted the republicans in and around his fort to be covered by his capitulation. The Allies refused, however, and Article 6 of the terms of surrender stipulated that 'when the British grenadiers take possession of the gates all subjects of His Sicilian Majesty shall be handed over to the Allies'. Méjan's council of war had promised 'help, assistance and protection to those who wished to remain with us' and Méjan seems to have only handed over five patriots 'who had remained, not wishing to follow the others who had gone down and joined the bulk going to be transported to France ... the treaty did not apply to those patriots who had defected, who had spurned the monarchy and lost the right to be subjects of the king.'

Lieutenant Laugier says that six Neapolitans were handed over and they were 'worthy of pity' but that Méjan 'had done all he could to have them included in the capitulation' and had saved some by having them wear French uniform. The British then seem to have gone to extraordinary lengths to hunt down these rebels, as Ferdinand informed his wife:

> Despite having promised in the capitulation to hand over any of my subjects, they attempted to hide those Jacobins in St Elmo by dressing them in French uniform. But the brave and honest Troubridge had them examined one by one and seized them and imprisoned them, so we now have Vitagliano [sic], Matera, Michele lo Pazzo, Cenzano's son [Genzano's son, Filippo de Marino] and Costanzo.

The list of republicans captured by Troubridge's thoroughness or handed over by Méjan included Ferdinando Pignatelli (with his wife, Francheschina Renner), Pasquale Matera, Cipriano Gaito, Melchiorre Maffei, and, despite his French uniform, Andrea Vitaliani. Petromasi says these republican prisoners were brought down and placed on the 14 transports so they could await together 'their well-deserved punishment'. The king was soon writing:

> Today had the pleasure of seeing transported onboard all the most notorious ruffians that had been in St Elmo, including Vitagliano who has already been tried and will, without ceremony, be immediately executed, father Belloni and Carlomagno. I saw these men brought aboard the English ships to be secured there.

Antonio D'Avella, or Pagliuchella, was also amongst those seized but he got special treatment and was taken directly to Mondragone, and there tired to a balcony and exposed to the fury of the mob.

But some of the patriots in St Elmo did escape Troubridge's examination. Nicola Neri and Antonio Belpulsi claimed the protection of French rank and remained with the French infantry. Federico del Greco was even incorporated into the ranks of the 27th Light[54] just in time to see the royal flag flying above the fort. At ten o'clock on 12 July he and the French garrison of '700 men, some 30 gunners and a 40-strong detachment of the 7th Light' marched out. Charles Lock, who saw them surrender, told General Graham that

> 1090 French marched out of St Elmo leaving about 40 sick. 80 men with the pox, having lost all marks of virility, were carried down to the water side upon their comrades' shoulder. Méjan, the commandant, affirmed that they had lost 2000 men by that disorder since the army entered Naples.

This bizarre cavalcade of the sick and the dishevelled, the defeated and the hungry, made its way down the street of the seven agonies to the harbour, the men unarmed and in column, the officers leading their horses by the bridle and Méjan in a small coach at the head of the procession. They could not, however, elicit any pity from the population and, as they marched, they were attacked and abused by a mob rejoicing in the 'sweet spectacle of seeing the abject and humbled appearance of its last remaining cruel oppressors'. A British and Russian escort attempting to hold the mob at a safe distance, a French officer gratefully noting how 'the English did all they could to keep the people back as they wanted to shoot us as we boarded the boats, if we had fallen into the hands of the Calabrians we would have been done for'.

They were kept in the harbour for three days, irritating the king by singing republican songs, one including the refrain 'long live the republic, death to kings', and then set sail on nine transports. Whilst there it seems that they did what they could for some of the other prisoners in the harbour. Andrea Valiante, the energetic commissioner of Campobasso, who had formed part of the Nuovo garrison trapped by Nelson, found himself rescued by the French:

> We saw the [French] garrison embark, and they asked that any Frenchmen on the transports be brought to their transports. This was my stroke of fortune for, following your [Championnet's] orders, I had the uniform of a French commissary and I also managed to have my wife and two sons taken onto Méjan's ship.[55]

Méjan, who would be detained on his arrival in France, and his men were shipped to Marseille.[56]

The surrender of the French ended the fighting and instilled some calm on Naples. To celebrate, the city was illuminated. However, this time of rejoicing would soon be replaced by the time for judgement. Even the saints amongst the republicans would not escape. Saint Gennaro, the Jacobin patron, had proved treasonous and was replaced by Antonio of Padua as the city's patron saint and 13 June was made an annual celebration.

The pious had triumphed, and now began their revenge.

11

Revenge: Consequences of Revolt

On 12 July Dr Diomede Marinelli made his way down to the Piazzetta Nilo, there, in the welcome shade of the narrow street, he indulged his favourite pastime of browsing through books. But in liberated Naples, even amiable doctors in search of knowledge ran risks:

> Finding myself in front of the Sant'Angelo a Nilo church, where I had gone to see some books, I heard this firing and a musketball glanced off my thigh without, however, causing injury.

Violence continued too outside of Naples as the last pockets of republicanism fell. Pescara was taken by treachery,[1] and its commander, Ettore Carafa Count Ruvo, was brought to Naples to await his gracious king's mercy.[2] The royalists then prepared to flush the remaining French, and what few patriots they had with them, from Capua where General Girardon was in charge. However, British participation in the final victory was placed in jeopardy when, on 13 July, Nelson received orders from his superior, Lord Keith, to send his ships to Menorca. Nelson turned a blind eye to these orders, and determined to keep his detachment of sailors onshore until the Neapolitan kingdom was pacified. The king was grateful for this needless gesture – there were sufficient troops available to end the campaign without a British presence – and informed the queen:

> About your question as to what Nelson is doing or saying, and on the behaviour of the Hamiltons. For Nelson he is, more than ever, our hero and we are so much indebted to him for, notwithstanding the orders he has received from Lord Keet [sic], to go and immediately cover Minorca, he has sworn that even should Minorca be lost, and that he should lose

his head also, he will not leave and will never abandon us. As for the Hamiltons, his conduct has been that of a senile old fool. Her conduct I couldn't have predicted it, you couldn't even imagine.[3]

He then confirmed what half the fleet already guessed at, that Lady Hamilton's influence over Nelson was in the ascendant:

My lady, to do her justice, has behaved in a way you wouldn't believe; she doesn't deserve to be criticised or reproved, but praised, for she has been so useful in getting what we need from Nelson.

So, to Keith and the Admiralty's chagrin, the British marines and sailors marched off, their rolling gait taking them to Capua to join a small international army braving French guns and mosquitoes. Charles Lock informed his compatriot, General Graham:

Eight hundred of our marines march this evening for Capua, the siege of which is to commence immediately. Capt Trowbridge [sic] and Hollowell returned yesterday from reconnoitering its situation and have determined upon a spot within 150 yards of the works to erect a battery upon. The garrison is said to consist of 1200 French and 600 Neapolitans. I am apprehensive that our men will suffer from the unhealthiness of the place which is in the vicinity of a morass. Five hundred Russians, 400 Portuguese, six hundred Swiss, as many Neapolitan cavalry, a small corps of Albanians and a considerable detachment of those lawless and cowardly Calabrese march likewise.[4]

Nelson had already instructed his subordinate as to what terms General Girardon should be offered, writing on 17 July:

When you send in a summons to the commander of the French troops in Capua, His Sicilian Majesty approves that, on condition the commander immediately gives up Capua and Gaeta, that after laying down their arms, colours, &c, the French garrison shall be permitted to go to France without any restrictions. If this is not complied with, prisoners of war, and as degrading terms as it is in your power to give them – no covered wagons, no protection to rebels – in short, the allies must dictate the terms.[5]

It took a week of intense bombardment before negotiations were opened. Lieutenant Henry Lowcay was sent in to summon Girardon and told him the allies would insist on the same terms granted to St Elmo. Girardon's aide told the Briton that 'the garrison wished to earn the esteem of the republic and were disposed to resist'. 'In that case', replied Lowcay, 'we'll heat things up for you and, when you have had enough, raise a flag and we'll stop, but we can only answer for the [conduct of] British troops'.

A sour Troubridge then informed Nelson that the French were being obstinate:

> The French sent out this morning [27 July], in their usual way, demanding protection for their patriots: I answered – inadmissible; and offered the terms of St Elmo, and to include Gaeta in the capitulation. They desire until tomorrow to hold a council. They offered Gaeta if I would omit the patriots, and promise they should not be molested, and their property secured, which I positively refused.[6]

Indeed, he gave a positive refusal, and a very brusque one. He told the French officer that 'capitulations annoy him and that a ship can no longer defend itself it lowers its flag and it is all over, so he would offer the capitulation accorded to St Elmo and none other'. The king heard that the French had 'wished to have the patriots walk free with their property, but Troubridge told them, as he should, that he would not allow it'.

The French relented and surrendered on 28 July. In conformity with Article 6, all subjects of the king were handed over to the allies. Not all republicans came willingly, and the royalist captain Scipione La Marra went into Capua to help identify those who were attempting to evade royal justice by wearing French or Cisalpine uniform.[7] Hamilton seems to have heard about this vetting of the prisoners, remarking 'Notwithstanding that Brigadier Girardon had given his word of honour that all his Sicilian Majesty's rebellious subjects should be delivered up at Capua, about four score were detected in French uniforms, and secured'.

The next day the French marched out, and were soon being paraded through Naples, as Marinelli observed:

> Before lunch the French from the garrison of Capua, with an English escort, marched down the Strada Foria. Many of the French were practically naked, some barefoot and all disarmed. Even though the French had an English escort, the lazzaroni and Santafedisti insulted them, mocked them and, when they could, mistreated them.

Girardon and his men were met by 'an immense crowd who yelled insults, threw stones and fired a musket at my coach, the officers' belongings were pillaged and some soldiers killed. The massacre would have been horrible had the English escort been less firm, they used their muskets to keep the lazzaroni, amongst whom there were many priests and Neapolitan officers, at bay'.[8]

The captured patriots were also attacked, Marinelli recording

On Tuesday 30 July the state criminals, or so-called Jacobins, that had been in Capua, also passed down the Strada Foria. Gentlemen, priests, bishops and others were abused as they walked, indeed they were badly mistreated by the populace for some time.

The French were taken to the Nuovo fort, the officers selling their horses, and then they embarked for Marseilles, triggering another round of celebrations. The king joined in but remained obstinately onboard Nelson's ship, unwilling to set foot in his capricious kingdom. His majesty eventually tired of the novelty of life on a warship and Nelson accompanied him back to Palermo, the admiral there coming ashore to reside with the Hamiltons.[9]

The king and his loyal retainers would miss the final royalist conquest. The Neapolitan army, bloated with bands of irregulars, advanced from Capua to Rome. On 15 September Captain Louis, on behalf of Troubridge, summoned General Garnier to surrender. He agreed, his garrison and the Jacobin Roman Legion and 250 members of the republican government being included in the honourable surrender. The British and a detachment of Russian marines under Lieutenant-Colonel Skipor and Lieutenant Balabin marched triumphantly into Rome whilst Frà Diavolo and Antonio Caprara, called senza culo [arseless], were sensibly kept outside the opulent city. Camped by the San Giovanni gate they made a terrible noise 'complaining that the promise General Bourcard had made, to be allowed to enter Rome, sack the ghetto and the Jacobin houses, was not being kept'.

Less than a year after the humiliating flight from the eternal city, the Neapolitans were back.[10] It seemed as though the Bourbons' ordeal might be crowned with success as their war drew to a close.

But war, like revolution, is a difficult creature to put back in its cage. And Naples had been mauled by both. Restoring calm would be hard and Nelson was proposing a purge to at least prevent the reappearance of revolution: 'it must take a thorough cleansing, and some little time, to restore tranquillity'. There were many willing to administer the purgative. Marinelli saw that 'the ferocity and fear of the lazzaroni still holds sway'[11] in the streets of Naples and that they were all too eager to quench their thirst for revenge. They had a free hand, the queen having already told

Ruffo that 'I rely on the wisdom of your eminence not to punish anyone who punishes an enemy of the state'. Attention was instead to be directed at punishing the Jacobins.

Ruffo had established a tribunal on 15 June, but it was reconfigured on Nelson's flagship on 21 July, so that the notorious judges Vincenzo Speciale, whose powdered hair was still immaculate despite the grubby work at Procida, Giuseppe Guidobaldi and Felice Damiani took centre stage. De Nicola, no friend of the republic, noted that this new court 'was formed of Sicilians, come as executioners, but ignorant of recent events and of who the authors of the republic had been'. It was this *Giunta del Stato*,[12] newly consecrated at Monteoliveto,[13] which now mete out punishment rather than justice.

Lord Keith had pragmatically told Nelson on 12 July to 'advise those Neapolitans not to be too sanguinary. Cowards are always cruel, and apostates the most violent against their former friends, and too often the least sincere.'[14] This was quite at odds with Nelson's own view, and certainly from that of Speciale and Guidobaldi. At Ettore Carafa's trial, for instance, Guidobaldi set aside any semblance of leniency calling for the republican's hanging, but only after he had been tortured and pincers used upon him, and then demanding that he be cut into pieces, burnt, his ashes scattered to the winds, and his house demolished. Speciale's technique was equally abusive and the royalists happily blindfolded justice that summer to spare her the sight of a royal vendetta.[15]

Numerous victims were already to hand. The prisoners held in irons on Nelson's fleet would be amongst the first to experience injustice. Then the 2,000 republicans on the 14 transports in the harbour, all of whom had thought themselves protected by Ruffo's treaty, but who had been rendered criminal by Nelson's illegal repudiation of the contract, were hauled back into Naples for trial. That process began in early August, as one of their number, Onofrio Fiani, recounts:

> An initial 82 victims were selected from the polaccas and these had been exposed for 40 days to the most insulting mockery of the people. We were manacled like common criminals and, accompanied by the cries of the mob were dragged, on that memorable day of 3 August, to the horrid dungeons of the Castel Nuovo fort. I was amongst those to suffer this horrible fate and shudder to describe the torments endured in that gloomy sepulchre.[16]

They swelled the number there awaiting trial. De Nicola remarked on 12 August that 'there are now 564 state prisoners in the Nuovo fort and 17 have now been sent down to the Coccodrillo dungeon where they'll have bread, some anchovies and water but where they won't even be allowed to shave; amongst these are the Prince della Rocca [Filomarino] and his son, and the two popular leaders Pagliuchella and Michele'.[17]

There were also some 1584 prisoners in the Granili prison on 25 June 1799.[18] Of those 52 were classed as being ringleaders, 218 who had been involved in disturbances and 647 had supported the republic and faced probable banishment. Then there were 31 Frenchmen, one Turk, 14 nobles, 29 women, 132 criminals, 369 escaped galley slaves and 91 patients from the hospitals. The prisoners included Angelo Candarelli, a wigmaker for women; Andrea Carafa, a monk; Antonio Martellucci, a Venetian, soldier in the Macedonian Regiment; Antonio Neiman, a Dane, from the 2nd Foreign Regiment; Carlo Worster, a German; Carlo Carreres, from Spain, commander of the Volturno Legion; Domenico Stiscia, rector of the Incurabili hospital; Francesco Zizzo, a Sicilian painter; Francesco Tordoni, Knight of Malta; Maria Franc, a German widow; and 17 other widows. In addition, Portici contained the broken army of Schipani, and there 166 officers were being detained, along with 835 soldiers.

On 7 September the Prince di Cassaro summarised the situation by estimating that there were 8,000 individuals in the prisons of Naples alone. The number also featured in Hamilton's despatches home:

> There were more than eight thousand persons confined as Jacobins and rebels in the Naples' prisons ten days ago but I understand many have since been removed to Capua and Gaeta, and it is to be hoped that when a sufficient number of examples shall have been made, and the most inveterate and noxious rebels shall have been either shut up or banished from the kingdom, His Sicilian Majesty will grant a general and sincere pardon.

However, Charles Lock noted that, with every day that passed, more and more prisoners were being brought in:

> The severe inquisition instituted on the conduct of every man during the revolution, which occasions the apprehension of hundreds every week, the rigorous imprisonment these undergo, and the small chance of an impartial hearing from a prejudiced tribunal, whose chief object seems that of confiscation for the benefit of the king, but, above all, the infamous and shameless violation of the capitulation of the two castles, which delivered into the king's hands 2,000 of the principal Jacobins – all this system of acting has, I am persuaded, multiplied the number of malcontents beyond calculation.[19]

The courts were pushed to work as quickly as possible. To try the prisoners, normal legal procedures were dropped and a process based on sworn witness statements, or depositions made before magistrates, adopted. The accused could make his or her own deposition but they could not read testimony advanced against them.[20] Evidence wasn't necessary, and rarely available, but, for major crimes, torture, such as the limb-stretching strapada, or hot pincers, was utilised to extract confessions. This streamlined process was designed to 'avoid a rigorous and liturgical inquisition', according to Cassaro, and a panel of five judges, acting as prosecutors with tremendous and sweeping powers, held all the cards. When judges such as Speciale and Guidobaldi presided, the process bore an uncanny resemblance to a show trial.

Given the arbitrary nature of the prosecution, it was inevitable that certain aspects of due process were ignored. Many of those on the transports who had been trapped by Nelson should not, under Neapolitan law, have been tried at all. When they first embarked on the transports on 26 June they had already signed a contract, known as an *obbliganza penes*, an agreement with the state in which they accepted exile. The judges prosecuting Emmanuele Borgia noted that

> On 13 June he, with his whole family, went to the Nuovo fort until it capitulated and then went onboard the transports with them and he signed the agreement not to return to the royal dominions.[21]

Revoking that agreement was a breach of the law. It made no difference. The court took the drastic step of ruling that they could uphold no contractual agreements with rebels. So the trials began. A decree of 7 September established three categories of criminals and the sentences they should receive. Category one included those who had held an important rank, those guilty of *lèse majesté*, or of having caused disorders or published or said anything lacking in respect towards their august sovereigns along with those who had taken up arms against the royal armies or had sought to sustain the former republic, and these would face summary and expedited punishment; category two included those 416 individuals had signed the oath in the Sala patriottica vowing to defend the republic or die ('and so who had, in a manner of speaking, signed their own death warrants', according to the royal command) – these would face exile and confiscation of property; the third category consisted of other transgressors, to be determined, and who faced banishment and loss of property.

This was the theory. In practice the range of crimes for which anyone suspected of Jacobinism could find themselves accused was generously extended to all kinds of real or alleged misdemeanours. Ministers[22] and generals were easy to condemn. The captured foreigners, whether from other parts of Italy or France, or even Brussels (Luigi Dron), Germany (Franco Sherman), Sweden (Federico Schierer who had only arrived in Naples on 11 June), or Bethlehem (Isaac Carus, an Orthodox priest), were easy to expel. But, for the rest, the judges defined crime in the widest possible sense, an approach best summed up by the case of Giuseppe Marseglio from Troia who was being kept in Foggia's prison because 'he is a revolutionary, he has not committed any other crimes'. Arcangelo Santorelli, from Rome, was tried for having attended the 'Sala patriottica every night to see what was happening' and Saverio Chiurazzo, a lowly porter, for going to embrace the tree of liberty each morning. Antonio D'Avella, the 32-year-old son of Pagliuchella, was convicted of having handed out biscuits at the Capuan gate when the tree of liberty went up. Nicola Mazzola was condemned for having cheered the entry of Championnet, for waving his sabre in the air and shouting 'Long live liberty' and for burning the royal portraits. In another case of pure royal vengeance Nicola Ricciardi was condemned to death for having taken up residence in the Caserta palace and stealing some of the furniture. Michele la Greca, who had purchased furniture from La Favorita palace 'to protect it for their majesties' was banished for 20 years for his temerity.

The settling of scores crept also unto the cloisters. Five monks from San Luigi di Palazzo were condemned for having 'denounced a number of monks of the monastery as royalists'. Dionigi Pettito was banished for 20 years for having said the king cannot be 'superior to others as God created him and God created the others too'. The priest Nicola Mitola was arrested because

> During the time of the republic, this priest, Your Excellency, ate meat at home on those days meat was prohibited and to the fascination of many declared that to do so was not forbidden by the doctrines of the Church and he went about, in church and in public, without the collar and cap of a priest.

Verginiano Giacinto was banished for five years for putting aside his clerical garb and wearing a green jacket, as well as co-habiting with Donna Concetta. Another priest, Pasquale Apicella of Foggia, was condemned to banishment for 15 years for 'living illegally with a prostitute' and for having served in the Civic Guard. Gaetano Morgera was executed for introducing women into the monastery and for volunteering to fight for the republic in those cruel first weeks of June.

Antonio Tocco, a lawyer, and Pasquale Assisi, a student, were also condemned to death for having put on republican uniform and for taking part in an expedition which beat the English at Cuma. Montemayor, a naval officer, was executed for having fired against the English from a battery at Baja. Francesco De Angelis, a soldier, was condemned to 20 years in exile, a lesser sentence because 'he is aged less than 18 years of age', as were dozens of other 16 and 17 year-olds, many of them students. Giovanni Varese was singled out for harsh punishment for having helped erect a tree of liberty at the Incurabili hospital. Antonio Amatucci had worn the uniform of the Civic Guard, at the age of 12, and was therefore banished for life. Giuseppe De Lorenzo had merely been denounced by two men, Vincenzo Parente and a certain Aniello, for 'having worn a uniform, mounted a horse, had his hair cut short, worn earrings and worn whiskers'.[23] After sending his uncle to vainly plead on his behalf, he was sentenced to 10 years in exile. The only evidence presented against Salvatore di Mattia accused him of donning republican uniform and also of 'having short hair and a long beard' *alla giacobina*. Vincenzo Cuoco, who 'went around in the time of the French with short hair' and for having being involved, with Luisa Molina Sanfelice, in exposing the Baccher conspiracy, was exiled for 20 years. Francesco Jovine, aged 35, was sentenced to exile for having 'his hair cut short and for having long whiskers'.[24]

Francesca Parazzi, a ballerina, was also arrested for cutting her hair short. The actor Pellegrino Planes was banished for life for having played the part of Timoleone at the theatre, Onorato Balsano for having staged a ballet entitled *The Partenope* at the San Carlo. Giovanni Andreatini was condemned for having composed a cantata praising the French whilst the musician Paisiello was sanctioned for hosting French officers at his own home. The courts also determined that Domenico Cimarosa, who 'had always manifested democratic sentiments in his speech and had published the music of various patriotic hymns and assisted in having the same performed', should be punished. The famous composer, attempting to make amends, wrote a cantata to celebrate Ferdinand's return, but Palermo held no truck with the plasticity of art and sent back that 'His Majesty does not understand how this Cimarosa, who served the republic, and conducted music under the tree of liberty, can write similar compositions recognising His victories'.

In November the royal inquisitors turned on those who had written or published defamatory texts. The playwright and poet Giovanni Gualzetti was condemned to death and hanged for having written, perhaps unwisely, about 'the poor justice system and burdens on subjects' which existed before the revolution. The priest Michelangelo Ciccone was also condemned to death for publishing works which praised the republic whilst Pietro Iodeno was punished for his book 'Thoughts on Republican Ethics'. Marino Guarano was exiled to France for having published a tract on the abolition of feudalism, and declaring that subjects had been relinquished of their oath to serve the king when the monarch fled the kingdom.[25] Gaetano Carcani and two accomplices were sentenced to 20 years in exile for allowing the royal printing press to be used in issuing republican proclamations.

The king encouraged the punishment of all these faults and the queen, always keen to act as judge, also added her own personal, but extensive, list of transgressions:

Cutting the head of statues of the king, stabbing our portraits, or stamping on them; committing horrors; cutting the head off the statue of the King of Spain, father-in-law and esteemed in Europe for his honesty, with a sabre, in public; killing; printing volume after volume of execrable material; dancing half-naked beneath the tree which Madame Cassano and Madame Popoli and their daughters, raised to the republic; carrying earth on their shoulders to build batteries against the tyrants; writings and epithets; old Torella, S. Angela getting the police to garrotte suspected royalists; Policastro writing my biography and researching the crimes of the ex-king, in short, lots of atrocities.[26]

The real atrocities, however, were about to begin, for, with their cursory trials over, the most significant republicans were being brought out for public execution. Traditionally, hanging was for criminals, decapitation for gentlemen,[27] and Matteo Wade, in a fatuous letter to Lady Hamilton, mocked this distinction for rebels: 'The great question is, who is to be hanged, and who is to be beheaded. Few or none dispute that they don't merit death, but then to prolong the moment, each produces his privilege, just as if it was of any consequence whether a man goes to heaven in a coach and six or in a wheelbarrow'.

Following the reading of the death sentence most prisoners were sent to the Carmine fort. There they were given last rites by the white-cloaked clergy of the Confraternity of the Bianchi della Giustizia, and escorted, blindfolded, to their deaths. The king was displeased that these rituals were taking too long, telling Ruffo on 25 August that 'the leaders should be brought out and hanged without ceremony ... The simpler things are the better, quickly, quickly, without keeping the people waiting for hours and growing impatient'.

In Naples the place of execution was generally the Mercato after 20 July, although others were hanged at the Largo delle Pigne or outside the Capuan Gate at a place called the Casanova. A handful of army officers were executed within the Nuovo and Carmine forts, whilst Eleuterio (Peppino) Ruggiero had the unfortunate distinction of being beheaded in the square of Saint Barbara, sent to his death weeping because he had not been allowed to say goodbye to his wife and children. Some 36 executions were carried out on Procida, where generals Spanò and Schipani were killed and where Bernardo Alberini was hanged and his body thrown into the sea; on Ischia; on the Phlegraean islands; at Gaeta; and in some of the other provincial centres.

In Naples Tommaso Paradiso was the hangman, and he was kept busy, receiving 860 Ducats between June 1799 and September 1800.[28] He was often assisted by a *tirapiede*, a young buffoon who was paid three Ducats to cling on to the swinging victim's legs. In Naples, the hanging started even before the final surrender of St Elmo. First to die had been Francesco Caracciolo, then Domenico Perla was strung up on 6 July at the Capuan Gate. He was followed on the 7th by Antonio Tramaglia, executed for having insulted the royal banner, and Giuseppe Cotitta, an assistant at the royal library, married to Domenico Perla's sister. Soon after the king's own bête-noire, Giovanni Andrea Vitaliani, was rushed to death, being tried on 18 July and executed in the uniform of the Civic Guard on 20 July. He was the first to be executed on the infamous Mercato.[29] A jubilant king, who had not forgotten how Vitaliani had plotted like Guy Fawkes to blow his sacred person up, exulted that

> Today sentences were carried out on Vitagliano [sic] in Naples, and Spanò and Schipani on Procida, where, tomorrow, Battistessa will also be executed.

Then the macabre pace increased. In one week, from 22 and 29 October, there were 12 executions (Sforza, Grimaldi, Colace, Morgera, Varanese, Bazzaotra, Federici, Troisi, Cirillo, Ciaja, Pagano and Pigliacelli) and on 28 November alone there were eight executions, including one poet, one doctor and Vincenzo De Fillippis, professor of mathematics. The gallows came down on the night of 7 June 1800, although the last victim in Naples itself was perhaps the most remarkable – the tragic Luisa Molina Sanfelice, beheaded on 11 September 1800.[30]

Ferdinand probably hoped that a speedy execution would not allow the condemned to speak, but he would be disappointed. On the afternoon of 20 August the republican poetess, Eleonora Fonseca Pimentel, drank her morning coffee and then went to the gallows quoting The Aeneid: 'Forsan et haec olim meminisse iuvabit' (A joy it will be one day, perhaps, to remember even this). Felice Mastrangelo called out to the mob 'I die a free man, and I did all I could to make you happy and free!' As he was being taken to be executed Grennelais shouted out 'I recognise many of my friends here: revenge me!' Marinelli heard that Vincenzio Russo 'had called out to the executioner that he had done his duty, and expected the hangman to do his and then shouted 'I die free, and for the republic' as they put the noose around his neck'. His confessor, Gioacchino Puoti, had marked him down as 'unrepentant' in the confraternity's records as he preferred to 'drink to the health of clandestine republicans' rather than to confess his sins, and De Nicola says he shouted 'take that piece of trickery away' when offered the crucifix. More poignant was the fate of Giuseppe Riario Sforza, who had a ring containing a lock of his wife's hair, and handed it to the confessor, declaring that she was the only one he loved. Manthonè told his confessor 'Console me, but do not undermine my loyalty' before stepping out to die. Others were as defiant, the Marchese di Genzano embracing the executioner, whilst Francesco Federici was executed in the Nuovo fort and 'died gallantly, doing all he could to decline the help of the executioner, and telling the soldiers guarding him to be loyal to the king'. Giuliano Colonna did not speak, but laid his head upon the executioner's block whilst Nicola Pacifico 'the Neapolitan poet, more than seventy years old, grey-haired and fat, showed that he knew how to die'.

On 20 August, another elderly gentleman, the frail Michele Natale, bishop of Vico Equenese, was executed, the hangman pushing on his shoulders to quicken his death and declaring, to the roar of the crowd, that he had never ridden a bishop before. Giuseppe Logoteta, who needed an ear trumpet he was so deaf, was hanged in November. Gennaro Arcucci, in his seventies and a man who had 'worked for nine years to bring liberty to his country', was hanged on 18 March 1800. Marinelli heard that the youths weren't being spared either: 'they say one of those executed yesterday [7 December] was too young and went to the gallows whimpering and wailing' and recorded that another juvenile

> Raffaele Iossa, son of the caretaker of the courts, held fast to the hangman, saying that he did not want to die, and whimpering like an animal. He was executed for having fired a cannon at the Capuan Gate.

Vincenzo Belloni broke down on the scaffold, making a confession of guilt and crying out 'my sins have been great and the sentence apt, so I deserve to go to my death.'[31] Genzano Filippo Marino, aged 22, and the only son of a grandee of Spain, was beheaded in August but elicited such sympathy amongst the crowd after they saw him 'crying and protesting that he was not guilty', and pleading for his life and embracing the confessor that 'it was the first time that the crowd did not shout 'Long live the king!" De Nicola notes that people were still regretting the execution that October, the verdict on the streets being that the king, had he been in Naples, would have pardoned the boy. The people did not know, however, that the king had crowed about Genzano's capture at St Elmo and was glad to see him die.

Others were worthy of as much pity, often because of their physical state. D'Agnese was taken to his death in a chair, as he had collapsed and De Marini was dragged to the scaffold by his feet. The blindfolded Pagano met a horrible fate, the confessors' registry of deaths noting 'no stockings, beard two fingers long, bare head, badly dressed, suffered in death'. The 'most obstinate republican' and botanist Dr Cirillo, killed on the same day, also 'struggled in his death'. Baffi was hanged but the rope snapped and he was strung up a second time. However, by all accounts 29 August was the day which stood out for its horror, the two lazzaroni, Michele Marino and Antonio Avella (Pagliuchella), whose loyalty to the republic was bought by French largesse, were first to hang to the shrieks of the mob. Gaetano De Marco, a fencing teacher, and Nicola Fasulo were next. Then came poor Nicola Fiani, General Manthonè's aide-de-camp, whose execution was horrible enough and its aftermath one of the worst stains in Neapolitan history.[32]

Following the cutting-up and eating of Nicola Fiani, and the parading of various parts of his body around the city, the mild-mannered Confraternity of the Bianchi della Giustizia was moved to complain at such excess:

> Moved by the just concern for the welfare of the souls of the unfortunate, as much as by the wish to educate those of the populace who flock in great numbers, motivated by the useless vanity of curiosity as much as by a fanaticism of false piety which increasing degenerates into ferocity, we ask the government to remedy this situation.

The Confraternity also advised the government to increase the pay of the hangman so that he was not tempted to sell the prisoners' clothes, thus avoiding the sight of naked corpses hanging from the gallows 'to the scandal and disgust of every honest person'.[33] With Fiani's fate very much in mind it chided the authorities

> the deplorable ferocity of the mob being the cause, in the most recent execution, of such things, offensive to common decency, that the Confraternity is obliged to ask the *Giunta di Stato* that the executed are buried at once and that the soldiers, sent to calm the populace, do not leave until the unfortunates have been buried.[34]

The chief of police noted that the incident 'went unpunished because we were in shock at such ferocity'. The general sense of disgust led, on 3 September, to the government sending word to Palermo that they thought executions should take place within the confines of the city's castles. Palermo replied with 'His Majesty does not agree with your suggestion, wishing that the execution of the respective punishments is carried out as in the past and in the established manner'.

The hangings continued in public, as did decapitation. The authorities had bought an axe, or *mannara*, for 18 Ducats and put it to good use. Gennaro Serra, who remarked ironically on the scaffold 'I always wished for their well-being, look how they welcome my death', was amongst the first to suffer. Ferdinando Ruggi, Ettore Carafa, Giuseppe Riario and Giuliano Colonna were similarly executed, the latter being important enough to be mentioned in Hamilton's despatches.[35] Army officers such as Ferdinando[36] and Mario Pignatelli, were also decapitated, and Gaetano Russo was beheaded in the courtyard of the Carmine castle after being stripped of his uniform. The axe was a noble privilege, but not always a coup de grace. Francesco Antonio Grimaldi had tried to escape and had been wounded three times by a cavalryman, and was already 'half dead', but he had his head almost cut in two when the executioner missed his neck. Gianleonardo Palombo had to be finished off with the executioner's knife as did the unfortunate Luisa Molina Sanfelice.[37] A soldier's musket accidently went off[38] and the crowd had panicked as her head was being laid on the block, and this seems to have unnerved the executioner too. The confessors' registry noted it took 'three blows of the axe and then her head had to be removed with a knife'. The diarist De Nicola complained that evening that 'barbarity and vindictiveness have been confirmed by this execution of Molino Sanfelice'.

Accounts of such bloody proceedings seem to have shocked Europe, and amongst those who read the sad reports were those republicans who had been banished or exiled. They might have felt themselves fortunate to have escaped but theirs was a heavy sentence nonetheless.

The queen had initially wanted those expelled from the kingdom to be sent to America 'or, if this is too difficult, or costly, France'. France was indeed easier, and a first group of 22 officers, including Antonio Belpulsi and his French-uniformed suite, left for Toulon on 18 July along with the surrendered French. Then, on 10 August, Matteo Wade wrote 'in this moment 800 of the boys part for Toulon', and Captain Salfi, posing as the simple soldier Francesco Salvo, was one of those boys. They sailed on 12 August and arrived in Marseille on 30 August. Another transport left on 14 December, this time transporting 248 exiles including Angelo Marinelli, brother of the diarist, and Dr Eduardo Sangiovanni who reported:

> In 1799, following the French evacuation of the kingdom, I was imprisoned for having been a French supporter and, after four months in prison, I was put on trial, had my property seized and exiled for life from my native soil. I arrived at Marseille and from there came to Paris.[39]

Giulia Carafa and Giuseppe De Lorenzo were also on that transport. The latter had signed the agreement not to return to Naples on 11 December and had been taken to the Darsena the following day where he and his companions 'for the first and only time were given white bread, macaroni, two sausages, some meat, two apples per person, and, the best part, the wine'. After this last supper they were embarked. De Lorenzo had mixed feelings about leaving his native land:

> I confess that quitting my country, my relatives and friends, for an indeterminate period hurt, and heaven knows how much. But soon, as we came out of the gulf, and Vesuvius slipped out of sight, I sank down to my knees and thanked God for having sent me away from a place where I had suffered so much.

Guglielmo Pepe also left Naples on that melancholic flotilla, enduring the final insults of the Neapolitans he had wanted to liberate:

> One night in the month of December I was conveyed, together with about a hundred of my companions, to the docks, where we were placed in a large room to await the moment of going on board. We were put on board three vessels freighted at the expense of the government and a fourth, a smaller one, provided by the two excellent sisters, the duchesses of Cassana and Popoli, both of whom were exiled after having endured a long imprisonment and many insults from the riotous mob. We were in all from six to seven hundred and including those who preceded us and the others who were to follow the number of the Neapolitan exiles amounted to at least 4,000. A man-of-war conveyed our vessel and just as we were setting sail with a favourable wind an immense body of the people, embarked in boats of every description, came alongside us, inveighing against us in the most ignominious terms, and prophesying that we would perish miserably and never more behold our native land.[40]

An additional convoy left on 21 January 1800 transporting 391 Neapolitan republicans including Gaetano Rodinò.[41] Another 192 were despatched in

March 1800 and some 424 more left on 25 April, with a final shipment of 281 exiles leaving in the summer of 1800. Unknown numbers of prisoners were also sent to Nice and to Genoa, but most refugees arrived either in Toulon or Marseille. This great expulsion of a good proportion of the educated classes lasted a year. Most were young professionals from the capital but incomplete Bourbon records noted that 54 were exiled from Terra di Lavoro; 51 from Salerno; 137 from Puglia; and 91 from Basilicata. And that 46 of the total exiled to France were women.

All the exiles arrived in southern France in terrible condition: 'these officers are dying of hunger and all but naked', wrote General St Hilaire. Fortunately, they found a sympathetic reception in a France now ruled by general, or rather first consul, Bonaparte, and they were provided with as much assistance as a France overwhelmed by the thousands who had fled Italy could afford. Those forced to tread the stranger paths of banishment did what they could to resign themselves to their fate, and eke out a new living. The priest Felicissimo Carabba swapped his cassock for the uniform of a French gendarme. The scientist Giuseppe Benchi settled in Paris as an optician. Antonio Santorelli worked as a bookseller, and married a Frenchwoman. Antonio Zuccarelli, an artist, sought work as a decorator. Francesco Ribera and the priest Antonio Scoppa taught Italian for a living and Ferdinando Ridolfini, who had worked for the republic's ministry of the interior, taught language and literature. Those who proved unsuited to earning their keep were assisted with pensions from the French government. These included Domenico Forges Davanzati, a bishop in his seventies, who arrived in Paris in March 1800, petitioning the government that 'they sacked my house, and confiscated my property, I have lost 12,000 Francs and arrive here in France with just the clothes on my back and a small amount of money'. Princess Chiara Belmonte Pignatelli, another republican poetess, was destitute and awarded 90 Francs a month, whilst Mariangela de Riso, the ex-duchess of Capracotta, received three Francs a day before marrying Antonio Curcio, a military surgeon also in exile. Not everyone was as fortunate. Pietro Napoli Signorelli was a 65-year-old lawyer who lived off handouts in Paris whilst Agostino Pecchia, a headmaster in 1806, pleaded that he was destitute because he 'was the victim of the fury of an evil queen, who, after losing all his property, and an eleven-month imprisonment in the dungeons of St Elmo, yearns after his homeland'. Monsieur Torcia, another impoverished and lonely Italian, was described by the French police as 'a Neapolitan, without family, without means, without influence, is a poor writer, would write for anyone and is an individual not comfortable in society'.[42] A handful, including Dr Michele Attumonelli, supplemented their income by spying.[43]

Some of the exiles were soldiers and they were keen, for financial reasons as much for revenge, to take up arms. One was Antonio Leonardi who later petitioned:

When the political changes occurred in Naples I decided, as much out of principle as out of the need to live, to offer my services to the now disgraced republic. That is why, when royal troops entered the city, I was arrested and after a year chained as a criminal, I was exiled to Marseille. Victim of terrible poverty, and given that I was a serving officer under the republic, I applied to serve in the officers' battalion.[44]

Another was De Lorenzo who later found his unit of fellow exiles reviewed by the First Consul:

He placed his hand on my shoulder and asked where I came from. 'Naples, citizen consul'. He then continued 'I will personally lead you back there to eat macaroni, once we've digested a Roman salad'. 'I hope so, citizen consul'. 'Rest assured,' he replied, 'before long you shall all soon see your homeland'.

Not all the exiles would view Napoleon or the French so favourably, some were sure they were being used and others that only through the exertions of Italians could an authentic Italy be made. A handful looked to others powers, having already been disappointed by the experience of French liberation. Stendhal's friend,[45] Domenico Di Fiore, even became mixed up with a plot masterminded by Moliterno and Antonio Belpulsi to have the English remove the Bourbons from the throne.[46] Even those radical Neapolitan exiles who trusted France often viewed the conservative Bonaparte with unease,[47] a feeling forgotten when Napoleon won his tremendous victory at Marengo in June 1800.

As Napoleon was trouncing the Austrians in northern Italy, thousands were still languishing in prison in Naples. They were the survivors. As early as the autumn of 1799 hundreds of prisoners, including many from the transports Nelson stranded in the harbour, now transferred to foul prisons, were simply starving to death. Incarceration in a Bourbon dungeon was a lingering torment. Giuseppe Carrotta (alias Chiapparella) was sentenced to 20 years as a galley slave. Rosa Garofalo who had hoped the Franco-Spanish fleet would arrive, and also 'spoken indecently and with impudence against the royal personages' was placed in custody in the Vicaria prison for five years. A number of prisoners were sent to the notorious penal islands off the Neapolitan coast, the dreaded sentence

Admiral Nelson by Leonardo Guzzardi, an unusual portrait of how Nelson might have appeared in late 1799. Nelson is wearing several Turkish awards and British medals commemorating his victory over the French at the Battle of the Nile. The admiral's hat boasts a Turkish plume of diamonds and is pushed back so as not to rub the wound on his forehead. This portrait, one of several versions by the same artist, was painted in Palermo around November 1799.

Nelson, a miniature by J. H. Schmidt. This portrait of Nelson is rather more sympathetic and was painted at Dresden in 1800 as Nelson and the Hamiltons were returning to England after finally quitting the kingdom of Naples that summer.

Emma Hamilton, another pastel miniature by Schmidt. Lady Hamilton is in her travelling clothes and sports the Maltese cross, a gift from Paul I of Russia in gratitude for her supplying corn to the starving islanders.

Emma Hamilton as a Bacchante, a portrait by Élisabeth Louise Vigée Le Brun. Emma had recently married Sir William Hamilton and was painted in Naples in early 1792 by the French artist.

Right: Sir William Hamilton had arrived in Naples in 1764 and, for the next 25 years, his time was divided between entertaining British visitors and collecting Ancient artefacts. The French Revolution and the wars that followed placed a new and complex burden on his scholarly shoulders.

Below: King Ferdinand IV of Naples and Queen Maria Carolina. The king had married his Austrian consort, sister to Marie Antoinette, in 1768. His interests were largely restricted to eating and hunting but the queen was an energetic politician, sworn to fight a French revolution that had killed her sister.

Sir John Edward Acton Bt
x at Palermo 1811

Above left and above right: Giovanni
Acton, the Neapolitan statesman,
in his youth (ASKB Collection) and
in later life. Acton was to all intents
and purposes the prime minister
of Naples. Son of Edward Acton, a
Catholic exile in France, he helped
reform the Tuscan navy before being
called to Naples to reform the state.

Left: Cardinal Don Fabrizio
Ruffo-Baranello, or Ruffo for short,
had helped run the Papal bureaucracy
before working for the Neapolitan
royal family as the intendant of San
Leucio. In early 1799 he volunteered
to cross over from Sicily and lead an
army, soon branded the Army of the
Holy Faith, to drive the republicans
from Calabria. After a string of
successes and massacres, his army
entered Naples in June 1799.

FABRIZIO RVFFO

A View of Naples in 1800 by Johann Ziegler. The Uovo fort is on the far left; the Nuovo in the centre by the harbor and the mole; the Saint Elmo fort dominates the city from the heights in the centre; and the Carmine fort can be seen on the right with, just beyond it, the Maddalena bridge.

The Royal Palace in Naples by D'Anna. This painting from 1794 shows the front of the palace with Saint Elmo in the background. The square was subsequently altered by Napoleon's brother-in-law, Joachim Murat, in 1809 and then more significantly, by the returning Bourbons, in the 1840s.

The Uovo fort, or egg fort, was garrisoned by students and Jacobins from Calabria in June 1799. This print after Hackert shows the view from the west of Naples.

The Nuovo, or new, fort was built in the 1280s. Although located in a strategic position, between the royal palace and the harbour, the fort's usefulness was undermined by the proximity of nearby houses. It contained the bulk of the republicans fleeing Ruffo and the vengeful Neapolitan underclass in June 1799.

The white Charterhouse priory, or Certosa, and, behind it, the Saint Elmo fort, named after Saint Erasmo. It was garrisoned by French troops in June 1799. Despite its key position it was a small fort, a French general noting: 'This fort can only accommodate 400 men; the rest of the garrison were camped on the glacis which runs parallel to the ramp that leads down to the city'.

A French army under General Championnet stormed Naples in January 1799, paving the way for the establishment of a Neapolitan republic.

On Saturday 26 January a provisional government was formed to run the new republic. Championnet and various dignitaries, including the new president, Carlo Lauberg, a defrocked priest, ride in procession to mark the occasion.

Above left: Gianfrancesco or Francesco Conforti, the republic's Minister of the Interior, was another former priest convinced that Jesus Christ would have approved of democracy. He surrendered with the republican garrison of the Nuovo fort and was executed by the Bourbons in December 1799.

Above right: Domenico Cirillo, botanist and president of the legislative commission. A friend of the Hamiltons he was, nevertheless, executed by the Bourbons for his role in the republic.

Pasquale Baffi, in charge of the royal library and professor of Greek, he assumed a role in the republican government in early 1799 and was executed following the counter-revolution.

Ferdinando Pignatelli, an officer in the republic's army, was captured when Saint Elmo surrendered to Captain Troubridge. He was handed over to the Bourbons and executed in September 1799.

Francesco Mario Pagano, humanist and author of the republic's constitution, was part of the garrison which surrendered to Ruffo. When Nelson broke the treaty, Pagano was seized, placed on the *Minotaur*, and executed in October 1799.

Ruffo's Holy Army was composed of Calabrian marksmen such as this, with most looking considerably less smart and sporting the image of a crucifix on their round hats to denote the cause for which they fought. (ASKB Collection)

Above left: Captain Edward Foote was signatory to Ruffo's treaty of surrender, a document which allowed the trapped republicans to leave Naples and sail for France. Nelson broke this treaty, sending Foote to Palermo as he did so.

Above right: Captain Thomas Troubridge, Nelson's faithful subordinate, had a more sanguine view of rebels, tirelessly working to hunt them down and have them punished. (ASKB Collection)

Right: Count Giuseppe di Thurn had served in the Tuscan navy before transferring to Naples and becoming a royal envoy and naval captain. Nelson placed him in charge of the tribunal that sentenced the republican admiral, Caracciolo, to death. (ASKB Collection)

Charles Lock came to Naples in the hope of replacing William Hamilton as ambassador. He fell out with the Hamiltons, and with Nelson, and was a sharp critic of Nelson's behaviour in the summer of 1799.

Cardinal Ruffo's army began to enter Naples on 13 June 1799, triggering a massacre of all those suspected of having supported the republic.

St Anthony guides Ruffo's army into Naples, a royalist print from 1799. This saint was made the city's patron saint and 13 June proclaimed a holiday marking liberation from the anarchy of revolution.

With Ruffo's army and the mob purging Naples, the republic was reduced to a handful of forts. The French garrison in Saint Elmo protected a few hundred republicans in makeshift earthworks and in the white Charterhouse and here, in a contemporary painting by Alessandro D'Anna, Ruffo's Calabrians open fire on the French and their republican allies. (British Library, London, UK © British Library Board. All Rights Reserved/Bridgeman Images)

Another view by D'Anna. This shows the forts in royal hands, the transports containing republican prisoners in the harbour and Nelson's *Foudroyant* flying the Neapolitan royal standard. It therefore shows the situation in July or August 1799. (British Library, London, UK © British Library Board. All Rights Reserved/ Bridgeman Images)

On 27 June 1799 Sir William Hamilton would write that 'The tree of Abomination is now cutting down [sic] opposite the king's palace, and the red cap will be taken off the giant's head'. This painting depicts that scene, with Captain Troubridge on the podium as the tree is cut down and republican flags and emblems are torn down from buildings and statues. (Private Collection, Photo © Bonhams, London, UK/Bridgeman Images)

This satirical print entitled *Cognoscenti* is by Gillray and mocks Sir William Hamilton as a short-sighted collector and cuckhold. Nelson is represented as a painting of Mark Antony whilst Lady Hamilton, clutching a bottle of gin, is shown as Cleopatra. Nelson's infatuation with Emma began in Naples and Sir William, who evidently knew of their affair, evidently tolerated it.

worded as *'relegazione in un'isola vita durante'*. In July 1799 Charles Lock had heard that the most isolated dungeons were being prepared:

A tribunal is forming to try and condemn these men so cruelly entrapped. It is expected that many will suffer as there are several leading characters amongst them. The islands of Ventotene and Ponza are talked of for the remainder.

Such places were notorious, even amongst the British. Sir William Hamilton noted how: 'the Prince La Torella and the Duke Riardo, the heads of two of the first families at Naples have been sent for life into a subterranean prison in the island of Marittimo off Sicily, a punishment worse than death'. De Nicola agreed, 'he [Torella] shall be sent to the dungeon of Marittimo, a sentence more horrible than death'. The king was less perturbed, gladly telling the Prince of Cassaro how he could see 'from the top of a hill the islands of Marittimo and Favignana, repose of our dear gentlemen'.

There were lots of gentlemen languishing there. At the end of September 1799 Francesco Piatti, Pietro Patti, Emmanuele Mastellone and Pasquale Salerno were loaded onto the *Archimede* and sent over to the island of Favignana to start a life sentence. They were joined by Giuseppe Poerio who had accompanied Championnet on his triumphal march into Naples nine months before. The islands had the great disadvantage that well-wishers could not assist prisoners and in late December the Giunta in Naples received a supplication from three prisoners in Favignana pleading for food 'as their families are unable to provide them with sustenance'.

Conditions were bad enough in the mainland prisons. Even Troubridge, entirely unsympathetic to the republicans, was moved to comment 'death is a trifle to the prisons'. Disease, despair, poor diet, abusive guards and official indifference added to the torment. Money might alleviate some of the worst tribulations, as Carlo Mauro, captured at Baja and held on Ischia, knew, sending a letter to his wife pleading for cash:

I beg you to send me some money as I am without a penny after being robbed when I came to this prison and the rest spent on various needs, such as when I needed a bed and a fire lit in the room; if you want a jug of water it costs a carline. So I ask you to send some money as soon as possible, otherwise I will have nothing.[48]

Most other prisoners had also been robbed of valuables. Brigadier Minichini, for example, seized '30,000 Ducats in paper money, 3,697 in coin, 12,820 in credit notes, 9,370 in promissory notes, 22 gold watches and nine silver watches' from prisoners held at the Nuovo fort.[49] Onofrio Fiani protested that 'the guards had the temerity to put their hands where delicacy forbids me to mention in search of gold'.

The state was supposed to provide some funds, drawn from confiscated property, to keep prisoners alive but, through corruption or malice, the money seldom materialised. On 16 November, Cassaro noted that the *Giunta dei Generali* had received protests and requests from relatives of those incarcerated asking for sustenance for the prisoners, something which 'they absolutely lacked'. But the abuses continued. On 1 September 1800 36 prisoners in Salerno wrote to the king pleading for better conditions. The prison governor was paying for their sustenance out of his own pocket, in the absence of the requisite state funding. The court responded by ordering the governor to desist, but did not rule on where funds might be found for the prisoners.

On 13 December 1800 the secretary of state noted that in the citadel of Manfredonia there were six prisoners (Ducan, Pistilli, Urbano, Pietro, Canescini and Fonzi) who, having consumed their own supplies, were 'close to starving to death'. In Barletta a list of 22 prisoners, including Fasulo Basilio, an unfortunate Greek merchant, noted that they had been placed in the town's citadel but had not been provided with any rations at all. Those who were lucky enough to receive a state ration found it repulsive. The prisoners in Ventotene complained on 25 October that the food consisted of 'a piece of repulsive bread barely baked and full of straw, a tiny amount of beans, full of insects, and half a carafe of wine, almost always vinegar, or the rest of the time badly tainted'. General Guglielmo Dillon wrote in September 1799 that the prisoners in St Elmo in his care were wasting away:

> About the sustenance, there are few nobles and bourgeois who are being kept incarcerated, and some are in such extreme poverty, and so degraded by their conditions, that they are reputed to be plebs, but they could recover over time so long as the hunger, which does not understand reason, devouring them is addressed.[50]

The trial of hunger was augmented by the cold that winter. On 12 January 1801 Dillon reported

> I find that in the St Elmo fort there are the following [seven] soldiers, all of whom are being held by the state, and all of whom have need of being sent to hospital as they are covered in scabs, and they completely lack any form of clothing, being naked. The administrators in charge of confiscated property need to urgently send clothes and the prisoners need to be sent for treatment.[51]

Men of the cloth were not spared these horrors of imprisonment. The Archbishop of Naples went quietly into internal exile, being kept on Ischia, as did the bishop of Melfi, but the bishops of Capri[52] and Montepeloso were initially imprisoned in the Carmine fort, then moved to the Uovo fort. There they implored that they either be taken to a religious house as they were suffering through being locked in 'a small, narrow and dark room in the Uovo fort with two other people'. Major Matteo Wade confirms this by telling Lady Hamilton 'I have here your friend Monsignore Gambone [sic] and as I am told he has some propriety I have united him in the same prison two miserable fellows that has nothing to eat, and desired them that as soon as Monsignore's dinner arrived that they should partake of it, as surely that is real equality and liberty'.

Punishments were harsh, justice was wanting and mercy was in short supply. Acquittal was rare too, even for those who had been granted safe conduct, or thought they were covered by the usual usages of war. The king and court viewed any promises of mercy or pardon as interference with royal justice, and this proved fatal for those who had trusted the British or the Bourbons. Onofrio Colace had given himself up in Naples following Nelson's proclamation that those doing so could expect the king's clemency. Despite winning the sympathy of the entire city, according to De Nicola, he was tried and executed in October, the courts ruling that no agreements with rebels should be held valid. Pasquale Battistessa, captured at Baja, was detained by Curtis and, despite his claim that he could not be prosecuted as he had surrendered honourably as a prisoner of war to Count Thurn, he was tried at Ischia and hanged on 23 July.[53] Such touching faith in the power of documents was clearly misplaced, and the British were remarkably silent at the time when insistence on a more proper sense of justice was badly needed. A glaring example of such injustice was that of Carlo Mauro, who had been forced to take refuge in Baja, then surrendered to Thurn under another safe conduct but was arrested in any case. At first he thought himself secure, telling his wife:

> I believe that I won't be brought to trial as my case ended with the safe conduct. I rely on you too and they say that Nelson has the ear of His Majesty and so you could go to the English and present your case and, without troubling with a trial, send me away from Naples into exile.

However, the king and his ministers decided otherwise:

> As Count Thurn was not authorised to grant pardon, and as it was forbidden to treat with rebels, following the proclamation issued by the

king and published on Procida on 9 June 1799 ... so, notwithstanding he has been condemned to death.[54]

He was beheaded, as befitting a marchese, on 13 December.

Scipione Marziale, an ensign from Sorrento, later complained to Nelson how he had been acquitted by a court but then promptly rearrested and dragged onto Nelson's transports:

> on the 17th of June, some of the people, more for the sake of plunder than from loyalty to the king, attacked your petitioner in the public street, and after loading him with abuse and insults of every description, dragged him to the bridge of La Maddalena. The petitioner's only hope was (knowing his perfect innocence) that he should be brought before the State Council, which after 17 days of painful confinement occurred, the Council saw him, heard him, declared him innocent, and ordered him to be acquitted. He left the prison, but his satisfaction was of short duration, for another mob of villains under the same pretext of Jacobinism, assaulted him, plundered him and conducted him onboard the *Commandant*, in order that they should thereby deprive him of all means of clearing himself. Their design failed, however, as the certificate of Mr Bock, already presented to your Excellency, verifies all that is recapitulated in this petition, and amongst other things that Marziale not only was not arrested by order of the Council, but on the contrary without any order being issued.[55]

Few of those thus ensnared were privileged, or well-connected enough, to use their influence to have their sentences ameliorated. Only rarely did a petition to the right place meet with success. Surprisingly, Joseph Pignatelli's brother, the Prince of Belmonte, managed to persuade the queen to intervene to save him from the executioner. Diego Pignatelli was condemned to death but Cardinal Francesco Pignatelli involved Pope Pius VII and, on 22 April 1800, the sentence was commuted to life in prison. Domenico Cimarosa was rescued from prison by Baillie and his Russian officers, all happy to free a man who had composed for the court of Catherine the Great.

However, Nelson was particularly unyielding when it came to dealing with teazers asking for mercy. Lady Hamilton, also at the centre of many such requests, played a more ambiguous role.[56] She seems to have intervened to save the life of Michele Filangieri, largely because the Princess di Satriano pleaded for his life, and possibly acted to influence the queen to release close friends.[57] Most controversially, Domenico Cirillo asked for her intervention to save him, writing to her on 3 July 'Milady you are a sensible and a charitable lady'[58] and pleading his case. Cirillo had, as we have seen, written to Nelson, also asking for release from irons. Rather than release him, the British trio seem to have sought to get him to confess to a crime and throw himself upon the king's mercy. He did not, and refused to be treated any differently from his incarcerated colleagues. As Nelson wrote, Cirillo 'might have been saved, but that he chose to play the fool and lie'. This is supported by Maria Carolina's comment when she heard he had been killed: 'Cirillo has been executed, he was insolent unto the last'. Sir William, at least, was sorry, remarking that November:

> The trials of the principal Neapolitan rebels having been carried on without intermission ever since we left the bay of Naples, many of all classes have suffered death, by having been either beheaded or hanged; among the latter we have seen with regret the name of Doctor Domenico Cirillo, one of the first physicians, botanists and naturalists in Europe.

Perhaps it had been hoped that his sentence could have been commuted. In reality this was rare. Only Giuseppe Caracciolo and 15 others managed to have their death sentences commuted to life on the penal island of Favignana. The Bourbon thirst for revenge, combined with the complex legal machine of indifference, meant that most were harshly dealt with. Michelangelo de Novi was sentenced to exile for life on 18 February 1800. This was commuted to life in prison on Favignana but, that May, he was nevertheless exiled and his property confiscated for good measure. Many others had their property confiscated too, which, as Sir William Hamilton noted, caused great hardship for many families that winter:

> The prisons are full and every day fresh prosecutions are begun against every persons of every class suspected to have been more or less concerned in the late rebellion and revolution or against zealous royalists that committed some acts that cannot be legally justified. No kind of provision having been made for the families and dependents of the principal rebels that have been executed or banished, or have absconded, and whose estates and property have been either sequestered or confiscated, there are a great number of people in want of their daily bread.

Despite this atmosphere of blood and chaos, the persecution rumbled on. Ruffo's replacement, poor Cassaro, was moved to write and tell his monarch 'Sire, I tell you frankly that the ordeal won't be over until Your Majesty issues a general pardon because the entire country, with few exceptions, was involved in the recent turbulence, either through illwill, or because they were seduced, either by design or out of fear, or merely because they had to find a way to survive'. He predicted that 'if the situation continues like this for two years then at least 800 will be condemned to death'.

Only events outside Naples, particularly Napoleon's victory at Marengo, would force the Neapolitans to leniency and put the brake on the juggernaut of revenge and retribution. Ironically, the first amnesty to be issued, on 11 January 1800, was for those in the Holy Army who had committed crimes. On 23 April 1800 a pardon was issued for those republicans who had hitherto avoided arrest, but those in prison or sentenced were exempted from royal absolution. Only the peace with France, signed at Florence in March 1801, signalled the return of some humanity, curbing the persecution and even including clauses specifying that property and rights were to be restituted. The man who agreed to French demands for this measure of forgiveness was none other than Chevalier Micheroux.

The crown paid lip service to this agreement and were unwilling to restore property to the affected republicans, settling on delay and official obfuscation as the best deterrent to fairness. Celidea Vinnaccia, the mother of Nicola Fasulo, was still seeking the restoration of her son's rights a year after the amnesty. Indeed, such intransigence ruined many families and intense levels of spitefulness caused pain to many more.[59] Others were let down by the characteristic incompetence of the Bourbon state. When Carlo Russi, from Milan, was sentenced to have his property in the kingdom confiscated, the authorities mistakenly seized that of Carlo Russo from Frattamaggiore. The cleric Vincenzo De Filippis experienced the same trauma, the authorities having confused him with a Calabrian of the same name. When the state came to take the property of Domenico Vincenzo Troisi, they wrongly seized land belonging to the widow of a man of the same name who had died a few years previously. Years of wrangling followed whilst livelihoods were ruined.

Livelihoods were also affected by the Bourbon ban on allowing republicans to hold public office. Despite the treaty with France this was only lifted on 12 January 1803, and until then those who sought to regain employment in government service could only do so with a 'certificate of good conduct during the recent anarchy'. When Giuseppe Renella was suggested as canon for the cathedral at Acerra in the summer of 1800 the government wrote back that the king had determined that, as he had held office under the republic, 'he was to be totally excluded from any benefice or office'. Bishop Gamboni found himself barred from resuming office, despite intervention on his behalf by the pope. The composer Giovanni Paisiello was stripped of his title of maestro and, following a lengthy attempt to ingratiate himself, only managed to find employment again in July 1801. Domenico Chelli, a painter employed at the court since 1782 and at the theatre, and who had continued working at the theatre under the republic, was allowed to return to work there, but was banned from painting in the royal apartments or working on decorations for public festivals.[60]

The stigma of being on the wrong side of history outlived the events of 1799. Andrea Valiante managed to escape to Marseilles with two of his sons, but a third, the 13-year-old Domenico Saverio Valiante, had remained behind at his grandparents'. In February 1801 the local bishop received a plaintive letter which informed him that 'the son of prisoner of state, Andrea Valiante, does not wish to remain in the seminary at Aversa as his fellow students call him a Jacobin'.

All this shows how deeply Naples was scarred. The retribution had been unrestrained and relentless, and many were sent to dangle from trees adapted to the weight of their sins. Whilst few of Nelson's biographers have cared to examine the extent of the Bourbon reaction, Italian historians have been more diligent in researching the butcher's bill. Sacchinelli, writing in the 1830s, estimated that 99 republicans were executed, 222 imprisoned for life, 322 imprisoned and 355 banished. The number executed was later refined to 174, but more recent scholarship sets the toll for the kingdom as 213 executed, 566 banished, 185 sent to penal colonies, 60 foreigners expelled, 31 killed by the mob in prison, 48 tried by Ruffo's judges before 14 June, 37 sent into internal exile and two suicides. Some 2,675 other republicans were tried and sent to prison or into exile for various periods, five for 25 years and 37 for 20 years, for example.[61] The middle class suffered most, lawyers, doctors and officers bearing the brunt and some 18 of those executed in Naples were clergymen.[62] The idealists of the university and academies were also punished for their temerity. Four of those executed were from the Military Academy[63] whilst seven professors from the university would be executed and a further 11 arrested. The professors at the hospital also suffered. One, Francesco Bagno, led a body of students, called the Sacred Battalion, against Ruffo. He was executed as were his students Cristoforo Grossi, Gaspare Pucci and Giovanni Varanese.[64]

At least 25 of the dead ended up buried in a communal pit beneath the Carmine Maggiore. There Ruffo had attended the Te Deum on 27 June and given thanks that Nelson had 'resolved to do nothing which might break the armistice which your Eminence has granted to the castles of Naples'.

12

Rewards: Loyalty Repaid

The scope and intensity of royal violence did begin to disgust some of those who had enabled it to come to pass. Lord Keith had hoped to counsel Nelson against the cruelty of Neapolitan revenge, unsuccessfully as it turned out, but even the otherwise severe Troubridge was noting on 12 September that

> They must finish soon, or every family here will be interested in making a disturbance. They should make some examples, and pass an act of oblivion, and let all be forgotten. At present there are forty thousand families who have relations confined. If some act of oblivion be not passed, there will be no end of persecution; for the people of the country have no idea of anything but revenge.

De Nicola, a man who had grown more royalist after every republican hour, asked, two weeks after Troubridge's lament, 'when will all this appalling blood-letting come to an end, there is no such example of so many sacrificed victims even in the history of the revolutions. Good Lord, how the king is so badly advised. The *Giunta di Stato* is a *Giunta* of butchers.'

Chevalier Antonio Micheroux, who had foreseen some of the consequences of a vendetta on a national scale, still thought pardon was the best repose for mankind, and cautioned Acton:

> I think that democracy became terribly strong in this kingdom only because of the work of a few individuals and that these led others astray either because they were not firm enough to resist, or too frightened, or too lazy. If it is required that we are severe towards everyone who followed their orders we will have to act more or less rigorously against

10,000 individuals. In which case it would be better to wipe the slate clean and for the government to concentrate on forming the future character and moral basis of the nation and, above all, to seek to get rid of that cowardice which, I repeat, thousands and thousands have been guilty of showing.[1]

It was not to be and although the executions and brutalist trials in Naples created thousands of victims, thousands more were subjected to the cleansing Nelson had thought necessary, so that, by the time of Micheroux's complaint, 10,000 was perhaps an underestimate. Much of this cleansing had taken the form of a wave of disordered revenge during and after the reconquest as an enraged populace sacked homes one day, and hunted down those who had talked of their liberty, their equality, the next.[2] Naples experienced a summer of such disorder, but, in the provinces, the Bourbons were content to see mob justice at work for months in order to chastise those who had betrayed them. At Bella, in Basilicata, Anna Giordano, widow of Soldano de Falco, was beheaded, 'her head, carried around to be mocked, was placed on the bell tower and stayed there some time'. At Tito on 1 May 1799, Sciarpa's men, who had unsuccessfully attacked in April, seized the town of 2600 people and took Francesca De Carolis the wife of Scipione Cafarelli the municipal president, and their son, Giuseppe Cafarelli prisoner. On 27 May, the young Cafarelli was killed trying to escape, his head shown to his mother on a pike. She was then executed as was Pasquale Cafarelli, uncle to Giuseppe. At Lanciano the royalists killed Francesco Carabba and his wife, Scolastica, and dragged their bodies through the streets. A certain Francesco Paolo Orsini was later accused by a royal commission of roasting and eating a portion of Francesco's body. At Sora Mammone seized Jacobins and plunged them into the latrines, exhibiting them to the public on a Sunday. His men are also said to have killed up to 600 locals, with Mammone focusing on killing those who were rich, or who had a pretty wife, daughter or sister. In the Abruzzo, justice was being meted out by the bands of Pronio who had confiscated the republican archive at Pescara and were blackmailing families incriminated in the documents.

But the shrieks of victims across the kingdom was almost drowned out by the braying of the victors congratulating themselves on their victory. Sir William Hamilton, ignorant of the king's opinion that he was 'a senile old fool' would boast with preening triumphalism to his sister that 'I may without vanity say, I have been instrumental in placing their Sicilian Majestys again on their throne of Naples'. To his nephew he crowed 'I finish my career most gloriously, and I am sure my name will ever be remembered in the Two Sicillies'. Lady Hamilton also leered down from the heady heights of vanity, exclaiming 'But what a glory to our Good King, to our Country, to ourselves that we – our brave fleet, our great Nelson – have had the happiness of restoring the king to his throne, to the Neapolitans, their much loved king, and been the instrument of giving a future good and just government to the Neapolitans!'.

Nelson similarly exulted to Admiral Duckworth on 1 August 'you will rejoice with me on the entire liberation of this kingdom from French robbers',[3] and gallantly told Earl Spencer 'Sir William and Lady Hamilton are, to my great comfort, with me; for without them it would have been impossible I could have rendered half the service to his majesty which I have now done; their heads and their hearts are equally great and good'. He then echoes the haughty phrase he'd used to Lady Hamilton's mother ('restoring happiness to the kingdom of Naples, and doing good to millions') to the earl, but soured by a new tone of self justification: 'I have done what I thought right; others may think differently; but it will be my consolation that I have gained a kingdom, seated a faithful ally of his majesty firmly on his throne, and restored happiness to millions'. To another correspondent he remarked that he had been instrumental in 'restoring peace and happiness to mankind'. Vanity was still whispering in his ear when he ascribed to God some of the credit: 'The almighty has in this war blessed my endeavours beyond my most sanguine expectations, and never more than in the entire expulsion of the French thieves from the kingdom of Naples'. Nelson wrote in a similar vein to his wife 'Thank God all goes well in Italy, and the kingdom of Naples is liberated from thieves and murderers. But still, it has so overthrown the fabric of a regular government, that much time and great care are necessary to keep the country quiet'.

Ruffo, although supposedly closer to God, got less credit, perhaps because Acton, Nelson and the Hamiltons loathed him. Nelson, for one, suspected him of treason, writing on 16 August 'the cardinal appears to be working mischief against the king, and in support of the nobles; he must, sooner or later, be removed for his bad conduct'.[4] Acton, for another, was sure of it and hoped to do something about it, or so Count Roger de Damas thought:

It would have seemed natural for the cardinal to be placed at the head of the restored state for, if he was not without faults, neither was he without ability. But he had made himself useful; he had won distinction; Acton, therefore, must needs fear him, and compass his ruin. He led the King to mistrust his first measures, and look upon him as a subject who had turned dangerous. He made the King refuse to ratify the treaties concluded between rebel commandants and the cardinal, and, by dint of covertly undermining His Majesty's gratitude, he brought about Ruffo's removal and disgrace.

Ruffo was made Lord Lieutenant and Captain General of the mainland provinces to distract him, and received estates in Capitanata and Benevento with a revenue of 15,000 Ducats to reward him; then, mercifully, that autumn, he was saved from further intrigue by the death of the pope. The cardinal sought permission to take part in the more civilised chicanery of the conclave at Venice, and thus, avoiding his ruin, followed the compass northwards.

Ruffo's entourage was rewarded too: his secretary, Lorenzo Sparziani, was given a pension of 1,000 Ducats and modest Sacchinelli received 200. On 1 August Micheroux was promoted to colonel, and awarded a pension of 3,000 Ducats a year and was sent off to Florence to act as Neapolitan representative with the armies of Suvorov in northern Italy. The Bourbon world also proved to bad men benign, and some of the controversial commanders of the Holy Army, and the bandits who chose the right side, were also indulged. Scipione La Marra was given property from the estates of dead Jacobins including Dr Cirillo. Filippo Malaspina was made a lieutenant colonel and given a pension of 600 Ducats a year. The Corsican, De Cesaris, was made a baron and a brigadier and given 4,000 Ducats a year. Pronio was elevated to colonel and given an annual pension of 2,000 Ducats. Even Fra Diavolo, his fine clothes scrubbed of blood, got 2,500 Ducats a year whilst Sciarpa was made a baron in May 1800 and given a pension of 3,500 Ducats, receiving the country house of the Prince di Torella at Portici and an estate near Polla.

Nor were the allies forgotten. Captain Baillie of the Russians was granted an annual pension of 1,600 Ducats from the Neapolitans. In January 1800 Troubridge was awarded an annual pension of 3,000 Ducats for life drawn from sums confiscated from the rebels, it going some way to replace the pay docked by a spendthrift admiralty who refused him his naval salary for the time he spent on land besieging fortresses. Captain Ball was paid a single payment of 6,000 Ducats. Hood also received a generous sum and, along with Hallowell and Louis, and General Graham, were made *cavalieri commendatori* of the Royal Order of Merit of Saint Ferdinand. Captain Foote received a snuff box.[5]

Nelson himself was rewarded with land and a title, recompense for his enthusiastic service to the cause. Initially it was thought that an estate at Bisacquino would suit, but then Bronte in Sicily was deemed more worthy as it had 9,500 tenants. Ferdinand wrote on 8 August that 'these lands at Bronte are the most suitable, but the income isn't enough and should be between 6,000 and up to 8,000'. The title conferred would be that of duke 'as in England this rank is better than the others'. On the queen's birthday, five days later, Nelson was awarded the estate and the title[6] and also given the diamond-hilted sword of Carlos III. This latter was a symbolic gift, necessarily so as Nelson had no sword arm, a token of the king's gratitude for having 'supported my steps by the establishment of quiet and order'.

Sir William was also praised, at least to his face, and told his nephew 'I have got a ring I suppose of 1000 £ value'. Lady Hamilton, meanwhile, received two coaches of dresses, a diamond pendant, with a gold chain inscribed with the words eternal gratitude.

The three joined in one – Nelson was even writing to Duckworth 'we of this house' – moved in together at Palermo, and whilst all three basked in the warming glow of victory Nelson and his friends were willingly caught in a net spun by a court needy for continued support. Sir William noted 'without me Lord Nelson would not stay here, and without Lord Nelson their Sicilian Majesties would think themselves undone'. Nelson told Duckworth 'even favourable as affairs look, was I to move although my flag is only in a transport they would be miserable'. His brother captains, however, troubled by the indiscipline of idle crews and rumours of gambling and excess, grew caustic the longer Nelson remained idle. The mildest rebuke came from Admiral Goodall who in November 1799 told his colleague to get back to sea: *'Cupidus voluptatum. cupidior gloriae* [Be eager for pleasure, more eager for glory]. Back in London even his best ally, Spencer, was noting 'his further stay in the Mediterranean cannot, I am sure, contribute either to the public advantage or to his own.'

The curtain mercifully closed on this opera buffa when General Bonaparte, now First Consul, undid all the Allied success of the year before. His decisive victory at Marengo in that summer of 1800 allowed his armies to once again rampage through northern Italy. In one of the near-misses of history his columns almost encountered Nelson and the Hamiltons, who had quit Naples, tired of intrigue, defeated by rumour, weighed down by debt, and who were themselves tramping across Italy to Ancona. Sir William, sensing he was out of favour in Whitehall, and exhausted by life in the Sicilies, had determined to leave for Britain with his wife. Nelson, even though Malta had not surrendered, volunteered to take them. In May 1800 there was a final, romantic tour in Sicily, Nelson and Lady Hamilton visiting the Temple of Zeus and inspecting the siege at Malta,[7] perhaps in the hope that they would watch it surrender from beneath their parasols. Then, the Hamiltons and their pocket admiral quit the kingdom with the queen who was travelling to Vienna to, as the replacement British ambassador, Paget, remarked, take 'two or three daughters with her who will be sold to the best bidder'. This odd entourage first sailed up the coast to Livorno and there Sir John Moore encountered them and snidely confided in his diary:

> Sir Wm. and Lady Hamilton were then attending the Queen in Naples. Lord Nelson was then attending upon Lady Hamilton. He is covered with stars, ribbons, and medals, more like the Prince of an Opera than the Conqueror of the Nile. It is really melancholy to see a brave and good man, who has deserved well of his country, cutting so pitiful a figure.

From Livorno the circus headed across land to Ancona on the Adriatic, coming within a few miles of Napoleon's soldiers as they did so. From Ancona they were escorted by a Russian squadron to Trieste. The jubilant couple, for Sir William 'broken, distressed and harassed', did not show his wizened face very much, enjoyed an enthusiastic reception at Vienna, being lauded by Austria and serenaded by Haydn.[8] The British then left the queen at her place of birth, travelling up through Saxony,[9] where they made a mixed impression at Dresden, before landing at Great Yarmouth on 6 November. Shortly afterwards, Lady Hamilton gave birth to a daughter,[10] and Nelson and the Hamiltons again moved in together, residing in gentility at Merton.[11] Sir William would die in April 1803 but the married admiral's passion for Sir William's wife continued unabated, and not unnoticed. Nelson, frustrated with public gossip, turned excessively protective, defending Emma from a press and society mocking her journey from Duke Street to a duke's bed, but also casting out friends and allies who were less enthusiastic about their relationship.[12] However, particular scorn was directed towards Nelson's innocent wife, as this letter to Emma from April 1804 shows:

> I send you a very impertinent letter from that old cat. I have sent her a very dry answer, and told her, I should send the sweetmeats to you. I always hated the old bitch! But, she was young, and as beautiful as an angel, I am engaged; I am all, soul and body, my Emma's: nor would I change her for all this world could give me.

They did not have much longer together, for Nelson died his heroic death at Trafalgar the following year. Trafalgar, for all that it saved England, doomed the Bourbons of Naples by limiting French ambition to the continent. None of the queen's intrigues could save them and Acton, seeing the writing on the wall, resolved on the desperate measure of leaving for Shropshire.[13] Humiliation came before he left, and he was removed from power following Napoleon's demands in 1804. For the last seven years of his life he would direct his waning energies at keeping his young niece, and new wife, Marianna Acton, happy.[14] The royals meanwhile called in more foreigners to stave off the inevitable, admitting British and Russian troops into the kingdom in late 1805. But Napoleon's continued victories sent these auxiliaries running and the embarrassed Bourbons found themselves abandoned. Napoleon knew a thing or two about vendetta and he rid himself of these faithless and troublesome Bourbons in January 1806. The royal family fled from his invasion on 23 February 1806 taking an exhausted Acton with them and making sure to burn all the *Giunta*'s court records. Napoleon, mistrusting the locals, installed his brother, Joseph, on the vacant throne. The queen would never set foot in Naples again, instead, increasingly dependent on opium, she sulked in her beloved Vienna, dying unhappy in September 1814. Her friend, Lady Hamilton, outlived her by a few months, but, in evident decline since Nelson's death, succumbed in France in January 1815, having been pursued by creditors to Calais.

The king enjoyed Sicily until the Bonapartes were ejected from Naples in 1815. With Napoleon defeated, and the shades of the French revolution exorcised, Ferdinand returned to his capital convinced that the only way forwards was backwards. He soon found that though the old order was victorious it was, paradoxically, impossible. The kingdom was soon a byword for stagnation, hardly a surprise to Galanti who noted, 'when Naples lost her best, she would take decades to even return to what she once was'. A handful of surviving reformers staged a revolt in 1820, and attempted to impose a constitution on a surprised monarchy, but the Bourbons called in the Austrians to purge the kingdom. The dynasty staggered on, its subjects enduring an infamous anachronism, until, 40 years later, the Bourbons were dismissed by a newer generation of revolutionaries sporting red shirts. Garibaldi's coup forced Naples into joining a new, united Italy, and there it remained, at least on paper.

The life of the Neapolitan republic of 1799 was short, and the Bourbons and Nelson conspired to kill it off for ever. But, rather like the body of Admiral Caracciolo rising to the surface of the waves, the republic proved impossible to dispose of. United Italy would make it clear that the republic of Naples was a stepping stone towards its unified, braver world, and made sure that those who died in such a cause would be transformed from criminals into martyrs. So, just 60 years later, those reviled Jacobins who had gone before the jeering mob of Naples to be beheaded like Ettore Carafa, or torn to pieces, like Nicola Fiani, were transformed into heroes in the pantheon of the Risorgimento. History had returned to salvage their reputation. And history, having elevated their deeds, had to ask who was responsible for their deaths.

13

The Controversy

Europe was scandalised by the events at Naples and their bloody aftermath. The sense of outrage was immediately apparent and gathered pace, disobliging the queen of Naples who had hoped that the affair would be soon forgotten, as she remarked to Ruffo:

> Regarding the state criminals, punishment for the leaders, exile for the rest, pardon and amnesty for the majority, and then eternal silence, no more talk of this, nothing in writing, no mention of the past to anyone. The silence of the tomb must smother so much horror and crime, and a new life must begin, one in which vigilance will ensure nothing like this happens again.

Tombs, however, have a tendency to talk to those willing to listen, and the victims of Nelson's actions in overturning the capitulation had much to offer. Nelson would stand accused of annulling the treaty but many went further, alleging that the admiral had pretended to go along with the treaty until exactly that point at which the republicans were defenceless, luring them out to seize them. To compound this crime, he then refused to return the rebels to their forts, as any breach of the terms of surrender required, and simply handed them over to their executioners. That he had seemingly carried out this act of duplicity on his own initiative, rather than being forced into it by royal orders, sealed the prosecution's case.

The first accusers were, inevitably, the Neapolitan republicans, and the French who had acted as guarantors. However, not everyone in the royalist camp was entirely satisfied either; Ruffo had sent in his resignation when he realised he had been outmanoeuvred and his character besmirched. Micheroux and the Allied signatories had vigorously protested Nelson's coup and Captain Foote, although sent away from Naples whilst the treaty was being violated, later protested that his honour had been compromised by Nelson. Some more of Nelson's fellow officers also seem to have remonstrated at the betrayal, as can be seen from Charles Lock's breathless report to his family:

> You will hear with grief of the infraction of the articles convened with the Neapolitan Jacobins and of the stab our English honour has received in being employed to *decoy* these people, who relied upon our faith, into the most deplorable situation. I have no time to enlarge as Sylvester the messenger is going in a few hours, but the sentiment of abhorrence expressed by the whole fleet will, I hope, exonerate the nation from an imputation so disgraceful, and charge it where it should lie, upon the shoulders of one or two.[1]

Lock provided more detail to General Graham at Messina, informing him how Captain Hallowell and Admiral Duckworth had resisted the deceit, and how Captain Hood had used unequivocal language about the affair:

> Captain Hood in the mean time ventured to suggest to his Lordship, whether it would not be deemed an act of treachery, the having *decoyed* (his own word) them on board the vessels under pretence of fulfilling the convention, by transporting them to Toulon, and then seizing upon their persons?

Lock went so far as to say that the entire fleet was in shock:

> It would be folly to disguise as it would be meanness to gloss a fact which as it is notorious to all the world, so is there but one sentiment upon it in the fleet. These men relying upon British honour, had agreed to surrender the castles upon promise of immunity for themselves and properties and were to be transported to Toulon. Cardinal Ruffo and Captain Foote signed the articles. They were first demurred upon and afterwards ratified by the admiral. The men evacuated the castles, embarked on board vessels under the idea of going to Toulon, were made prisoners and their officers thrown into irons. This is the plain fact. ... That a stigma so disgraceful should be affixed to the British nation and for so paltry a consideration by making us the bait and the agents afterwards in this violation of what is most sacred, as it is the bond of society, is very mortifying. I write to you, my dear sir, à coeur ouvert and with a reliance upon your honour. I think it right you should be informed if you are not already of the naked truth of this transaction.[2]

Foote would confirm this sentiment of abhorrence, as would those British civilians, such as Lord Northwick, and Gordon, who witnessed the admiral's moves. But the controversy only really came to public notice when Gordon's complaints filtered back to Charles James Fox, of the loyal opposition, in London. Fox, emerging from retirement, was roused to make the most eloquent condemnation of Nelson's actions in an impassioned speech to parliament on Monday 3 February 1800:

> When the right honourable gentleman speaks of the extraordinary successes of the last campaign, he does not mention the horrors by which some of those successes were accompanied. Naples, for instance, has been, among others, what is called *delivered*; and yet, if I am rightly informed, it has been stained and polluted by murders so ferocious, and by cruelties of every kind so abhorrent, that the heart shudders at the recital. It has been said, not only that the miserable victims of the rage and brutality of the fanatics were savagely murdered, but that, in many instances, their flesh was eaten and devoured by the cannibals who are the advocates and the instruments of social order! Nay, England is not totally exempt from reproach, if the rumours which are circulated be true. I will mention a fact to give ministers the opportunity, if it be false, of wiping away the stain that it must otherwise fix on the British name. It is said that a party of the republican inhabitants of Naples took shelter in the fortress of the Castel de Uova [sic]. They were besieged by a detachment from the royal army, to whom they refused to surrender; but demanded that a British officer should be brought forward, and to him they capitulated. They made terms with him under the sanction of the British name. It was agreed that their persons and property should be safe, and that they should be conveyed to Toulon. They were accordingly put on board a vessel; but before they sailed their property was confiscated, numbers of them taken out, thrown into dungeons, and some of them, I understand, notwithstanding the British guarantee, actually executed.[3]

This damning rhetoric was reported in the *Morning Chronicle*, and the more raucous opposition press.[4] The speech had not named Nelson or the Hamiltons but, when she heard of Fox's intervention, and the hue and cry of the Georgian press, Emma Hamilton, forgetting the admonitions of her favourite book, *The Triumph of Temper*, was incandescent:

> We are more united and comfortable than ever, in spite of the infamous Jacobin papers jealous of Lord Nelson's glory and Sir William's and mine. But we do not mind them. Lord N. is a truly virtuous and great man;

and because we have been fagging, and ruining our health, and sacrificing every comfort in the cause of loyalty, our private characters are to be stabbed in the dark.[5]

Nelson, accustomed to the boundless adulation of the Palermo court, was outraged, railing to his agent Davison that 'Mr Fox having, in the House of Commons, in February, made an accusation against somebody, for what he calls a breach of a Treaty with Rebels, which had been entered into with a British Officer, and having used language unbecoming either the wisdom of a Senator, or the politeness of a gentleman, who ought ever to suppose that His Majesty's Officers would always act with honour and openness in their transactions.'[6]

For the next few years accusations rumbled on but Nelson's death at Trafalgar led to a slew of biographers picking up their pens and being forced to make sense of the events of 1799. One of the first published accounts of Nelson's life, Harrison's from 1806, alerted Captain Foote to Nelson's opinion that the capitulation Foote had signed was infamous, implicitly blaming Foote for putting his name to such a document. Foote, who had kept removed from the controversy out of loyalty to the service, and aversion to the Whig opposition, now felt compelled to defend his conduct. He vainly hoped that a corrected edition of Harrison's work would allow him to present his own defence; it did not and so, with Duckworth's support, he published a bracing vindication of his treaty. It opened with a general point about respecting treaties:

The very name of an English officer, acting for his country, was esteemed sufficient for the security of all that is dear to men! ... But what can wipe off a gross deviation from a solemn engagement, and an engagement too in which advantage was taken of capitulations to place the unfortunate sufferers completely in the power of those who were determined to punish them with rigour?[7]

Foote continued to stress the moral aspect of his actions, and, by extension, those of Ruffo and Micheroux, but he also neatly summarised the case against Nelson's infraction of this unalterable engagement:

A solemn capitulation had been agreed upon, formally signed by the chief commander of the forces of the King of Naples, by the Russian commander and by myself, all duly authorised to sign any capitulation in the absence of superior powers. This was not a treaty of peace subject to ratification, it was not a truce liable to be broken, it was a serious agreement for surrender, upon terms which involved the lives and properties of men, who might have chosen to forfeit those lives and properties, had they not relied principally upon the faith of a British officer. One hour after the signature of the capitulation was sufficient to render it sacred, instead of thirty-six hours, which had by your account elapsed before Lord Nelson's arrival; although nothing had been done in the execution of the terms agreed upon. It was equally binding on all the contracting parties; the truth, however, is that some parts of the agreement had been performed, and actual advantage was afterwards taken of those parts of the capitulation that had been executed, to seize the unhappy men who were those deceived by the sacred pledge of a capitulation into a surrender of everything that can affect a human being in the most critical moments of his existence.[8]

It was an impressive critique of Nelson's actions but it only really gained wider attention in 1813 when Robert Southey's biography of Nelson took Foote's lament and crafted it into a more general condemnation of Nelson's conduct. Southey, with prose shaped by Whig sympathies and the skills of a poet, breathed life into a sense of outrage that Naples was 'a deplorable transaction! A stain upon the memory of Nelson and the honour of England!'

If Albion had not been perfidious, it seemed as though Nelson might have been. Central to the question of whether the admiral was guilty is Ruffo's treaty of capitulation. Had Nelson overturned a valid treaty, or had he only ignored an agreement with no legal basis?

Ruffo, acting as Vicar General, and therefore a representative who had temporarily assumed the powers of the king, was certainly within his rights to treat and sign such a surrender. He was also within his rights to guarantee immunity to those republicans in the forts and defensive positions of Naples who surrendered to him and his coalition. When he first anointed Ruffo Vicar General Ruffo, the king naturally told him to act as he saw fit, and only to pay heed to further royal orders *if* time allowed. The queen was still telling Ruffo in mid-June 1799 that 'I leave it to your Eminence's wisdom to manage everything' and also informed him that the court deferred 'as in all else to your wisdom and sagacity'. In any case it wasn't just Ruffo behind the drawing up and signing of the capitulation; British and Russian officers signed too and their signatures could not simply be overruled. France, stood as guarantor to the treaty and was the only power called upon to ratify the surrender. The king later claimed that he should have been the one to ratify, telling the cardinal:

> I repeat that I believe that no capitulation treating the rebels as though they were troops of another power is possible, and even if it has been agreed upon, it shall be null and void without my ratification.

211

Ruffo and his contemporaries knew, however, that no treaty of surrender negotiated between commanders required such royal approval. Even if it had, Ruffo, as the king's alter ego, was empowered to act in the king's name. He was still authorised to use these wide-ranging powers when the capitulation was signed and he continued to be so for some time after Nelson's arrival on 24 June. This can be seen by Nelson's struggle to persuade, rather than to order, the cardinal to comply with his wish to annul the treaty.[9] Ruffo's authority to make decisions, even faulty decisions, was only questioned later when Nelson received royal authority to arrest Ruffo.

Nelson's initial lack of authority over Ruffo stemmed from him only being sent to interrupt negotiations as Acton's letter of 23 June to Hamilton makes clear: 'if time and a *prolongation* [of negotiations] allows it Lord Nelson will be there, and we hope in him for a relief of what is against His Majesty's dignity and interests'. Had he arrived before the treaty had been signed, then he might have argued the point about Ruffo's authority and his treaty; but he sailed in to find the agreement signed, sealed and ratified. As Ruffo held firm only violating the treaty would allow Nelson to act as the court's enforcer, something the cardinal knew all too well as he told Micheroux: 'perhaps knowing that the court intends to be strict means that they will try and get Nelson not to agree to the treaty, and so make him seem a rather dishonest fellow'.

Those intent on defending Nelson's reputation often make the case that, although Ruffo might have been authorised to sign, by doing so he was breaking specific orders not to negotiate with rebels. This charge of insubordination is one Nelson himself would have spurned, having consciously disobeyed his superiors on a number of occasions, but the truth is that the orders Ruffo had received before signing the capitulation were contradictory. Palermo had had frequent changes of mind as to whether to allow the pardoning of offenders. In April Acton had clearly told Ruffo to punish the rebels 'provided that this measure, to which his Majesty would give general application, should seem to your Eminence to be adapted to the purpose'. True, the king had then set out in early May a list of 'the most notorious criminals and culprits', but, importantly, Ferdinand had ended his missive with a key condition:

These are my wishes for the present, which I charge you to have executed in whatever way you consider feasible, and in whatever places it may be possible to do so. I reserve to myself the right, once I have reconquered Naples, of giving any further orders which may be required owing to the course of events and the receipt of more accurate information.[10]

In addition to that important caveat, the court had, in early June, as the prize of Naples was within sight, modified its own instructions to such an extent that it was prepared to allow the rebel leaders to leave Naples freely. For example, on 12 June, it issued these instructions to the expedition intended for the Hereditary Prince:

> In that military capitulation, however, which shall be agreed with the enemy troops occupying Saint Elmo, terms may be extended to allow for the departure of various rebels, including the leaders, if the public good, or the efficiency of operations, or other important reasons, make this advisable.[11]

That expedition failed, but this clause is a fair indication of where the court stood in terms of what was admissible for rebels, and it neatly presages Ruffo's own agreement with the French. Moreover, the failure of the heir's expedition probably encouraged the court to relax these requirements still further and there were even rumours that, following that debacle, Acton had instructed Thurn to negotiate to get immediate possession of the castles by non-military means.[12]

Whilst these were rumours, the king had certainly indicated that 'any other means beside force' might be employed to ensure that Naples could be 'retaken with as little damage as possible'. This apparent flexibility was underlined when the court merely singled out a handful of rebels who really should not be allowed to depart. For example, when she heard Ruffo was in Naples, the queen told him in a letter he received on 21 June that 'the only one among the guilty scoundrels whom I do not wish to go to France is the unworthy Caracciolo'.[13] A letter from the king expressed consternation that Ruffo was dealing with the rebels but limited itself to hoping that 'Caracciolo and Manthonè' would not be included:

> They say that when the castles surrender all of the rebels within them will be let go, safe and sound, including Caracciolo and Manthonè, etc, and allowed to go to France. I don't believe this but it would be terrible if those furious vipers, especially Caracciolo, were allowed to live ...[14]

In any case, Ruffo had known the court might find treating with rebels distasteful, and so circumvented any potential criticism by making the treaty one between the allied powers and the French.[15] That rendered any accusation that Ruffo was unauthorised to treat, or was breaking orders, immediately invalid, as Micheroux later told Acton 'I was determined never to consent to anything which would have the appearance of a negotiation with rebels, no mention should be made of them in the formal document of surrender, except as regards the garrisons of the forts.'

This involvement of other powers is significant, for if Ruffo was unauthorised to sign, or was guilty of contravening his orders, the same cannot be said about those other signatories, the British and Russians. Captain Foote, as commander of the small squadron in the Bay of Naples, had inherited Troubridge's authority, and Troubridge had been given much leeway, Ferdinand telling Ruffo 'whilst sending Troubridge a copy of the instructions laid before you in this letter, I have left it to his sense of justice for him to adopt such exceptions as he may think fit with respect to the exercise of the prerogative of mercy'. Foote combined this prerogative with his own authority as a Royal Navy officer, consequently, there was no need for him to consult Admiral Keith or Lord Vincent, his commanders in the Mediterranean, let alone Nelson, about matters at Naples. Foote later declared that he was 'as fully authorised to sign such a treaty as Lord Nelson; he was as much under Lord St Vincent as I was under him'.[16] Charles Lock agreed, telling General Graham:

> Captain Foote though fully aware how wounding to the honour of the king such a convention was, yet as in the capacity only of an ally, cooperating with and assisting the efforts of his servants to replace him on the throne, and knowing that this treaty had been made according to the tenor of express orders for that purpose, he thought himself as little justified in refusing his signature, as authorized to have dictated the terms of the capitulation. He therefore affixed his name to it.[17]

If the court, rightly or wrongly, deemed Ruffo's actions invalid, they could not do the same with Foote's authority and the British guarantee. As Foote himself was aware

> In my apprehension, the King of Naples's secret orders to Ruffo has nothing to do with a capitulation sanctioned by a British officer, to which the National Faith was unquestionably pledged. This being the real state of the case, something unjust was certainly done.[18]

Charles Lock made two further points to General Graham which support Foote's position. He thought that the republicans would not have signed a convention at all unless it had received Foote's guarantee, and that Palermo had only honoured a previous capitulation, at Castellammare, because it had been guaranteed by Foote:

These are the chief circumstances of this much to be lamented violation of a sacred treaty, which the Jacobins repeatedly declared during the framing of they would never have entered into with their countrymen, did they not consider the part the English bore in it as a security to the fulfillment of it.

The king, before he left Naples, to give a colour of reason to this step declared that he had ratified the convention made by Captain Foote with the garrison of Castelamare (although there were amongst those people certain individuals particularly obnoxious to him), as having been framed by and under the simple authority of the English *whose name he would not discredit by a disavowal of it.*

The British had provided a guarantee to the republicans before Nelson arrived to dispute the terms, but so too had the Russians. Their commander. Captain Baillie, was of equal rank to Foote, and was similarly vested with an independent command. He also knew that his immediate superior, Sorokin, had encouraged the granting of a 'pardon in the king's name to celebrate a general reconciliation', and that the officer in command of the entire Russian operation, Admiral Ushakov, advocated clemency. Whatever Nelson or the court felt about Ruffo's authority, or Foote's, neither the admiral or Palermo was authorised to interfere with a Russian pledge, and, judging by this letter from Hamilton to Ruffo, Nelson had clearly been warned against any such infraction:

My Lord Nelson also begs me to assure your Eminence, that with respect to the Russian troops, he will always keep in view the honour of his Majesty the Emperor of all the Russias, as well as that of the King his own sovereign.[19]

But Nelson pushed on regardless. In an age when honouring one's word sealed all agreements, that was a significant slight to all those involved, as Ruffo himself put it:

Nelson wished to annul the treaty that had been signed and sealed, and partially carried out, when he arrived. I did not wish to do so and was therefore determined not to allow a breach of faith. A man of my character, sire, and of my profession, and who has just reconquered the kingdom in the name of God and with his assistance, cannot be but true to his word without dishonouring the excellent cause which he represents.[20]

The argument used by those justifying Nelson's conduct insists that he was merely overturning a capitulation signed by unauthorised officers acting against specific orders. This is just as unconvincing as the next argument made in Nelson's defence, namely that he arrived in time to prevent the treaty, or as he often called it, the armistice,[21] from being carried out. Nelson himself advanced this argument, later scrawling in the margin of an account by the republican sympathiser, Helena Maria Williams, that the treaty was 'never executed, and therefore no capitulation'.[22] This is dubious as a legal objection to a signed treaty but the truth is that Nelson clearly arrived after some significant clauses had already been executed.[23]

For example, between the signing of the capitulation and Nelson's arrival the Allied officers began gathering the necessary transports and Drummond of the *Bull-Dog* was assigned the duty of escorting the transports to Toulon. A number of state prisoners in republican hands were released in good faith, including some British prisoners and Acton's youngest brother, Filippo Acton. The republican prisoners from Castellamare, being held off Procida, settled amongst themselves who would go to France in the convoy, and who would go home, and those republicans who had fallen into royalist hands in Naples were brought to the Carmine fort so they could also be added to the transports.

More significantly, on the 22nd and 23rd republicans from within the garrisons of Nuovo, Uovo, St Elmo and the palace were allowed to exit these places and very many, promised safe conduct and assured that they would be pardoned, made their way home, thereby reducing the strength of the republican troops. Those who had determined to go to France arranged with the Giunta di Stato to sign a *obbligo penes acta*, a judicial contract defining the legal status of those who signed as exiles rather than criminals.

On the afternoon of the 23rd, hostages were sent up to St Elmo to act as guarantors of the surrender and the Russians were then allowed to advance and secure defensive positions under the walls of the republican strongholds to prepare for the evacuation of the now depleted garrisons. A proclamation securing 'the patriots' passage along with their baggage' was also issued and parties of officers went onboard the transports to prepare for the arrival of the main body.

So Hamilton was right to say that when Nelson arrived the convention had 'in some measure taken place' and Nelson was wrong in attempting to deny it. Paribelli, one of the republicans caught in the trap, complained that 'the treaty should have been observed, for that part of it which was detrimental to the patriots had already been carried out'. Breaking the treaty would have required these detrimental parts – the reduction in the strength of the garrisons, and the advance of the royalist lines – to be reversed.

Which brings us to a central, yet often overlooked, point. If Ruffo had acted against orders and the treaty was invalid then there was still a clear and legal procedure to follow. The laws governing capitulations were explicit: if at any point after signature a treaty of surrender was annulled then the enemy would have to be replaced 'in the position which they stood previous to the treaty'. Had the treaty been broken when Nelson first arrived then Ruffo would merely have had to 'withdraw his troops from the posts last occupied', which is indeed what he threatened to do.[24] The treaty itself had allowed for such a possibility, with the republicans conserving their supplies so that they could neatly be reinstated in their defensive positions exactly as they were on 21 June.

But Nelson only declared the treaty invalid after the republicans had embarked, so the only legitimate course would have been disembarking the republicans from his fleet and transports, re-arming them and replacing them in their fortified positions. No doubt such an outcome would have been unpalatable for the royalists, especially as it would allow them to defend themselves, even with the risk, as Foote remarked, that 'they might have chosen to sacrifice their existence rather than to have yielded at discretion to those from whom little mercy was to be expected'. However distasteful, the agreed precepts of the laws of conflict were clear: 'the law of nations requires that everything should be restored to the state in which it was at the time of the signature of the capitulation'. In an age which prized honour, any warring parties declaring a treaty or contract void, and then taking advantage of their vulnerable enemy, would be exposed to universal execration. Indeed, this was about much more than honour, for, before the laws of conflict were codified, respecting agreements was one of the few restraints limiting the evils of war. As the philosopher Emer de Vattel phrased it:

What would become of prisoners of war, capitulating garrisons and towns that surrender if the word of an enemy were not to be relied upon? War would degenerate into an unbridled and cruel licentiousness, its evils would be restrained by no bounds and how could we ever bring it to a conclusion, and re-establish peace?[25]

Annulling capitulations did occur as, for example, in 1813, when the French General St Cyr surrendered Dresden but the capitulation was subsequently declared invalid. The Austrians then offered to place the French garrison back in Dresden, but St Cyr declined, preferring a comfortable captivity in Hungary. In the same year Danzig was surrendered by the French to the Russians but the czar subsequently disputed the terms. Again, the garrison was offered alternative conditions, or the right to be restored to the situation when the capitulation was signed. At Naples in 1799 Nelson's subordinates expected that their commander would adhere to this accepted course of action if he insisted on breaking the terms, and Hood and Hallowell urged the admiral 'with great earnestness' to 'reinstate the Jacobins in the castles and enjoyed with their lives to reduce them by force in 24 hours'. In another letter to Graham, Lock emphasizes exactly this time-honoured approach:

> Had the convention to be derogatory to His Sicilian Majesty's honour and more advantageous than the circumstances of the Jacobins entitled them to expect, there was one obvious course, which was to replace affairs in the status quo and to recommence hostilities. The officers charged with the ungrateful service of disarming these unhappy men engaged to reduce them in 24 hours if they might be permitted to reinstate them in their strongholds.[26]

Surprisingly, Nelson's officers were actually in agreement with the court in Palermo. There, Acton, having ordered Ruffo to be overruled, and even arrested, expected that once the capitulation had been cancelled the republicans would once again be masters of their forts. This expectation is revealed by Acton when he informed Hamilton that after the republicans were returned: 'Lord N. shall have all the chiefs of our good people with him he will concert with our officers the best method for the castles of the rebels in order that they should be taken instantly and what may be necessary for a more regular siege to St Elmo.'[27]

The fact that Nelson was obliged and expected to reinstate the rebels in their forts, but did not, is significant. That he simply declared all agreements void whilst holding fast to his prey, says as much about his motives and methods as any testimony culled from his letters ever could.[28] This means, of course, that Nelson deliberately broke the laws of war. The rebels had come out under the expectation that the capitulation was being put into effect. Nelson was the only actor in the drama to suggest that the republicans had surrendered voluntarily, telling Davison in 1800 that they abandoned their positions with the knowledge that they would 'be hanged, or otherwise disposed of, as their sovereign thought proper'.[29] This is quite preposterous, the republicans had been convinced, by Nelson and the royalists, that they were being transported to France. If they had changed their mind, as Nelson suggested, and were now agreeing to an unconditional surrender, why would they embark on the transports rather than simply hand over the fortress keys?[30] Why would the transports have had to be brought under the guns of the British fleet if the surrender had been voluntary? And why would the British have asked Ruffo 'whether it would not be advisable to publish at first in Naples the reason of this transaction' to alert the Neapolitans to the fact that the rebels were being seized, if they had surrendered voluntarily and didn't need seizing? No, Foote was more accurate when he wrote 'the garrisons of Uovo and Nuovo were taken out of those castles under pretence of putting the capitulation I had signed into execution'. Lock agreed, telling Graham 'The men evacuated the castles, embarked on board vessels under the idea of going to Toulon, were made prisoners and their officers thrown into irons'.

The republicans had certainly read Nelson's initial warning that he would not permit the capitulation or grant them the right to 'embark or quit those places', but this was clearly contradicted when on the 26th they were given permission to *quit the castles* and *embark* and saw British marines assisting in the operation. In addition to the evidence of their own eyes, they heard guarantees from Ruffo and Micheroux, and Troubridge and Ball, that Nelson had relented and agreed to carry out the capitulation as agreed. So it was that the Uovo fort the garrison handed over possession to the Neapolitan officer Minichini with the express statement that they were doing so 'in conformity with the capitulation'.[31] Captain Baillie was even apparently told by Nelson that as the capitulation 'had been ratified by the commanders of all the different powers, it could not now be done away, he therefore requested Major Bayley [sic] would superintend the embarkation of the Jacobins on board the polaccas destined for their convoy to Toulon, consonant with the letter of the treaty'.[32]

The fact that the garrison of the Nuovo fort received honours of war from the Russians as they evacuated their position confirms this understanding. Ruffo also genuinely thought that Nelson, whose marines had also come ashore, had relented and was also carrying out the convention, telling the king:

> Lord Nelson can do as he pleases, but I convinced him of the truth that had he told St Elmo to surrender within two hours, and told the castles he opposed the treaty, then the people would have been plunged into terror and the city destroyed, so he allowed the treaty to be executed and agreed to assist with 600 of his men, and this would allow us to be able to tackle that which remains to be done.

All parties, royalist and republican, seem to have been surprised that Nelson's objections to the treaty had been dropped and that the British were helping to carry out the capitulation as agreed. And everyone was surprised that the transports did not then set sail. Or, at least, everyone except Nelson and Hamilton. For this is the final piece of the puzzle.

Had they, without reference to the court, actually planned this piece of trickery – using the pretense of the fulfilment of the treaty as a bait to lure the rebels out, only to seize them when they were trapped on transports?

Breaking a treaty is bad enough, but conspiring to do so as part of a pre-meditated plan is an even graver accusation. Ruffo, who had already suspected foul play, thought Nelson capable of such a trick; indeed he had only sought guarantees in order to diminish such a possibility. When he saw the republicans were being kept in the harbour, he was, therefore, the first to accuse Nelson of treachery, as can be seen from a note by Hamilton citing an early attempt by Nelson to justify his conduct:

> Lord Nelson assured the cardinal that he did not mean to do any act contrary to his Eminency's treaty, but as that treaty could not be valid until it had been ratified by His Sicilian Majesty, his Lordship's meaning was only to secure his Majesty's rebellious subjects until his Majesty's further pleasure should be known.[33]

This passage, contrary to Hamilton's intent, evidently shows that Nelson had indeed broken the treaty, by not letting the rebels sail. However, just as importantly, Hamilton confirms that the British were indeed trapping the rebellious subjects, or securing them, and doing so without royal approval. So any securing of the rebels was done on the initiative of the British who ruled the prisoners were not to leave the transports without a passport from Lord Nelson (confirmed by De Nicola's remark that 'nobody is allowed out, or on deck').

If there was no royal approval, then the initiative came from Nelson. And if the initiative for breaking the treaty came from Nelson, then why not the ruse which saw, as Captain Hood put it, the republicans being '*decoyed* ... on board the vessels under pretence of fulfilling the convention'. Ruffo could not, of course, charge the British with such a plan, but then he was not close to Nelson's thinking or the discussion amongst British officers. Nor did he have access to Hamilton's correspondence, where the formulation of such a ruse is darkly hinted at. The scheme probably gestated when Ruffo was proving obstinately faithful to his treaty, and was born when the British failed to overrule him with force of argument. At that point Hamilton and Nelson clearly needed an alternative way of getting their hands on the rebels. Promising everyone that the capitulation was being fulfilled, whilst secretly waiting until the republicans were at their most vulnerable in order to announce that they would be handed over to royal justice, was just such an alternative. One spelled out in Hamilton's letter to Acton on 27 June, the morning after the rebels had come out:

However, *upon cool reflection*, Lord Nelson authorised me to write to his Eminency early yesterday morning and assure him that he would not do anything that could break the armistice which his Eminency had thought proper to make with the rebels in the castles ... we shall now act perfectly in concert with the cardinal, though we think the same we did at first as to the treaty his Eminency made before our arrival. *If one cannot do exactly as one could wish, one must do the next best thing* and that is what Lord Nelson is doing and I hope the result will be approved by their Sicilian Majesties.[34]

Exactly as one could wish can only mean convincing Ruffo to break his treaty, and 'the next best thing' can only refer to the securing of the republicans on the transports. Hamilton's hope that the *result* of doing the next best thing would be approved also reveals that the initiative for the ruse lay with Nelson and Hamilton, rather than with the court. This is more blatantly stated in a subsequent note from Hamilton to Acton:

Lord Nelson, finding that his Sicilian Majesty totally disapproved of what Cardinal Ruffo had done contrary to his instructions in respect to the rebels in the castles, and those rebels being still on board of 12 or 14 polaccas and it being in time to remedy that evil, *thought himself sufficiently authorised to seize* all those polaccas and anchor them amidst of the squadron, and there they will remain at His Majesty's disposition.[35]

Hamilton says Nelson *thought* himself authorised to seize the republicans, rather than allowing them to sail or returning them to their forts, a clear indication that it had been on Nelson's initiative. But he was clearly abetted by Hamilton as can be seen in a subsequent boast by Hamilton that he had been involved in the decision:

How the cardinal will relish this letter I cannot tell, but I know that affairs could not be going on worse for their Majesties' honour than they did before *we* came to this resolution — in *our* minds necessary for their Majesties' honour. I have reason to believe we have Cirillo and all the most guilty on board these polaccas, *and the stroke was quite unexpected*, and so will be the arrival of their Majesties and your Excellency, should you determine — as we sincerely wish. At this season it will be a party of pleasure ...[36]

When Hamilton says 'we came to this resolution' it again indicates an independent decision taken before royal instructions were sent, an idea repeated by the statement 'in our minds necessary for their Majesty's honour'. This phrasing also hints that other minds might take issue with securing the rebels and, therefore, that Nelson and Hamilton were aware that they could be seen as doing wrong. Such defensiveness might be suggestive of a guilty conscience, something confirmed by Nelson coincidentally ordering Foote away to Palermo on 28 June, as though expecting he would protest at the infringement of his treaty.

All this suggests that there was wrongdoing. A conspiracy in which Nelson, the man of action, implemented the ruse, and Hamilton, the exhausted courtier, gave it the veneer of diplomacy. But if one had abetted the other it had been Nelson and Nelson alone who took on the full responsibility for its success by deploying his resources – his ships, his men, even his reputation and rank – to ensnare the republicans.

Hamilton's confessions hint that the British knew they were transgressing, but clearly thought they were doing something necessary – something unpleasant, where the ends justified the means. Some of Nelson's other actions, however, colour the episode rather differently, and he proved himself far from being reluctant to transgress against rebels. For Nelson did not limit himself to detaining the republicans, or to minutely searching through the boats in order to apprehend a list of 'ringleaders'. Had he done that, then his actions could charitably be interpreted as being forced upon him by the court. But Nelson and the Hamiltons deliberately sought to hunt down as many of the surrendered republicans as possible, widening their net to catch those from the Nuovo fort who had elected not to go onto the transports and making a determined attempt to have any republicans who had already quit the forts handed over, rather than to remain, undisturbed, in their homes. He even extended the hunt to those republicans who had never been in the forts, not only bringing in Caracciolo and 12 others not covered by Ruffo's convention, but also ordering that any republicans 'within five miles of the city' be given '48 hours to give themselves up or be considered as being still in rebellion and enemies of his Sicilian Majesty'.[37] As Hamilton put it on the 28th 'and that such of his Majesty's rebel subjects, who by the Cardinal's treaty might escape with impunity, might not do so, Lord Nelson published at Naples a printed proclamation'. These are not the actions of a man acting against his conscience but rather circumstantial evidence that Nelson would do whatever was necessary in order to punish as many rebels as possible. Indeed, British officers were clearly conducting a wider, more systematic campaign than that waged against the rights of the republicans on the transports. On Procida[38] they had already been actively processing captured republicans, and had hanged as many of them as they could. By May Nelson's most loyal subordinate, Troubridge, was telling the admiral

'His Majesty will, I hope, the moment he regains Naples, make some great examples of his villainous nobles'.[39] Then, when St Elmo and Capua surrendered that July, it was again Troubridge, presumably following Nelson's orders, who insisted that the patriots were not to be covered by the surrender and who made determined efforts to sort through the French prisoners to ensure that there were no republicans hidden in the ranks.[40]

All these actions betray an active and energetic pursuit of a vendetta designed to please the Neapolitan royal family. Nelson was evidently more than willing to act as the court's avenger, whatever the cost to law, humanity or his reputation. If the results of such behaviour are clear, the motives for Nelson acting so ruthlessly against republican enemies are more open to conjecture. Some detractors point to the subordination of Nelson's will to that of the queen's protégée, Emma Hamilton, and others to his hatred for republicanism. Emma certainly had an influence over Nelson and sought to persuade him to do the queen's bidding when it came to revenge. It is also true that Nelson's atavistic loathing for Jacobinism, and professional horror of rebellion or mutiny, was stronger than that of many of his peers fighting for kings and country.[41] But the two strands, uniquely, come together at Naples in the first half of 1799. There Nelson, assisted by loyal Troubridge, seems to have pursued a personal grudge, whereas most British officers, equally involved in protecting an ally and upholding a monarchy, took the pragmatic view that the rebellion was an internal Neapolitan affair.[42]

For Nelson it was personal because he had readily adopted a Manichean belief in the sacred cause of Ferdinand and Maria Carolina and was in thrall to the idea of smiting their enemies. The idea of crusading to protect the king and queen against Jacobin hordes was an idea nurtured by Lady Hamilton, but Nelson had himself taken it to an extreme as early as 12 March when he informed a surprised Acton that 'I only wish to die in the cause'. By May, as the counter-revolution looked to be succeeding, such chivalry become still more florid, the admiral writing 'lay me at the feet of their Majesties; tell me how best I can serve them!'. Then, after the reconquest of Naples was over he made perhaps the most incisive comment of all, declaring 'I feel myself above every consideration but that of serving faithfully'.[43]

One of those considerations beneath the admiral was legality. Nelson's penchant for sweeping aside whatever stood between him and what he reasoned to be victory earned him eulogies in battle. But those methods deployed against laws and agreements were a very different matter. Joseph Conrad recognised this uncompromising trait in Nelson, writing 'I do not think that Nelson at Aboukir or Trafalgar was not the same man as in the Bay of Naples. This seems to me self-evident.'[44] Nor was the Bay of Naples a unique case of the admiral destroying treaties, he had, after all, broken the treaty of surrender at Livorno in December 1798, and that merely to get possession of French and republican ships in the harbour.[45] His justification for ignoring that agreement was 'I act, from the circumstance of the moment, as I feel it may be most advantageous for the honour of the cause which I serve, taking all responsibility on myself'.[46] It was, then, not so strange that he would do the same at Naples or, indeed, afterwards. Less than a year after that signal act of wrongdoing he was resolving to break an agreement regarding those French troops in Egypt who had signed a convention allowing them to be returned to France:

> In my present situation in the King's fleet, I have only to obey; had I been, as before, in the command, I should have gone one short and direct road to avert this great evil – viz, to have sent a letter to the French, and the Great Vizir, in Egypt, that I would not, on any consideration, permit a single Frenchman to leave Egypt; and I would do it at the risk of even creating a coldness, for a moment, with the Turks. Of two evils, choose the least; and nothing can be so horrid as permitting that horde of thieves to return to Europe.[47]

For Nelson, breaking the treaty in Naples would count as being the lesser evil, allowing the rebels to sail the greater sin. Capturing them, in order to punish them, was most advantageous for the honour of the cause he was serving. And Nelson had been long been an advocate of punishment, sometimes more so than the royals he was serving. He had relentlessly campaigned for the hanging or disposing of the Neapolitan rebels throughout the entire duration of the war against the republic. In June, for example, the admiral had told Foote that 'Your news of the hanging of the thirteen Jacobins gave us great pleasure, and the three Priests, I hope, return in the *Aurora* to dangle on the tree best adapted to their weight of sins.'[48] On 30 June he had told Ferdinand: 'The most notorious of the rebels I have in irons on board the fleet and *I hope* they will meet the same fate as Caracciolo, who did not attempt to deny the justice of his sentence.'[49] On 23 August Nelson was complaining to Duckworth that 'the nobles are caballing against the power of the king, and as yet, *none of them are hanged*'. His comment on an account of proceedings by Helena Maria Williams declared that 'Miss Williams has, in my opinion, completely proved, that the persons she has named *deserved death* from the monarchy; they failed, and got hanged for their pains'. Given this fervent wish to punish, Nelson's lack of respect for Ruffo's treaty is hardly surprising.

previous errors. He was wrong to say that neither the cardinal nor Captain Foote had the power to treat, they both did, and was also mistaken that the paper they signed was not acted upon – it had been ratified and partially carried out before Nelson arrived. The most erroneous statement, however, is that the republicans surrendered to Nelson and hoped for clemency from their sovereign. They clearly did not, they had negotiated a treaty with Ruffo which specifically protected them from having to trust the judgement of their sovereign and came out on the understanding it was to be executed.

Luring out the republicans, ensnaring them and then violating the treaty which protected them, is, of course a stain on Nelson's reputation. Not then intervening to plead for clemency, but intentionally calling for the harshest punishment, compounds the accusation. For Nelson could so easily have kept his honour intact, and the restoration of the monarchy, and cleansing of the state, could have been achieved in a more merciful way either by letting the republicans sail, or by brokering a new capitulation. Nelson would have done better to imitate that other son of a clergyman, Captain Foote, who, although aware that the king, along with his immediate superiors, viewed the rebels as outlaws, had offered a protective guarantee to the garrison of Castellamare to prevent bloodshed. The republicans surrendering to him there had requested that:

> The whole of the garrison and crews of the flotilla have to request you will allow them to march out of the fort .... Leaving it to their option to go where they think proper; and relying on British generosity they trust you will receive such of them on board your ship as think proper to avail themselves of the protection of the British flag. [54]

Foote granted these terms to spare the effusion of blood, and justified this granting of such generous and favourable terms to the rebel garrisons with the following:

> When endeavouring to recover a kingdom, relieve it from anarchy, and the dominion of foreigners, violent measures, and personal animosities should be avoided; and as their Sicilian Majesties were pleased to think I had rendered them some service I begged, as a personal favour, that the capitulation which I had made with these garrisons might be regarded as sacred. [55]

Had Nelson pressured the Bourbon court for clemency, rather than enabled their revenge, it is likely that Palermo would have complied. He could have been magnanimous, like the Russian Field Marshal, Suvorov, who, as Micheroux noted, refused to become an agent of vendetta:

> We say we have sins to expiate, crimes to punish, all of which seems strange talk to Suvorov and the Austrians who have not touched the hair on the head of a single Jacobin in the whole of Italy ... the Marshal simply would not understand a different argument. He, whose victories might cost 50,000 lives, employs only kindness to those who are before him but who do not have weapons in their hands.[56]

Which shows that even in an age of revolution, an arbiter of nations could choose to wage war by restraining revenge. Nelson, in contrast, called for the heads of rebels at Naples, and deliberately extended the conflict to include anyone who had opposed the Bourbon regime. Such championing of Bourbon whims placed hundreds caught without weapons into the hands of their tormentors.

Caracciolo, too, was defenceless, and he became perhaps the most dramatic case of how Nelson forfeited his good name in the enthusiastic pursuit of a royal, and royalist, vendetta. The unnecessary severity of Caracciolo's treatment and execution became the other controversy that dogged Nelson's reputation and bedevilled his Victorian partisans. One critic, Sir James Macintosh, had found the betrayal of the republican garrisons shocking but reserved real his incredulity for the treatment of the Neapolitan admiral:

> I read over the passages which respects them [the republicans] three or four times, in hopes of discovering a vindication; but, alas! it is impossible. The breach of faith to the garrisons of the two castles is too certain and too atrocious. The execution of Caraccioli [sic] is an act which I forbear to characterise. The writers admit that, at this execution, was present that ferocious woman who lowered the illustrious name of an English matron to the level of a Parisian fish woman, and who made our chosen hero an instrument in deeds of cruelty and dishonour.[57]

Here again is that sense of premeditated revenge. Caracciolo's sentence and punishment had clearly been agreed before the trial began with Hamilton noting on 27 June, two days before, that 'Caracciolo will probably be seen hanging at the yardarm of the *Minerva*, Neapolitan frigate, from daybreak to sunset, for such an example is necessary for the future marine service of his Sicilian Majesty.'

Nelson felt himself authorised to act unilaterally against a republican who had been the one notorious rebel repeatedly named by the court. Hamilton, however, sensitive to the blame which might attach itself to the British name, had tried to argue for a trial by a Neapolitan judge on Procida, but he was overruled by an impatient Nelson. Hamilton dropped the matter, merely noting that 'Lord Nelsons manner of acting must be as his conscience and honour dictate'. Lord Nelson's manner of acting was to convene a court martial of five trustworthy Neapolitan officers to try Caracciolo on a British ship. Again Nelson could have avoided becoming involved by refusing to prosecute a foreign officer. Six months before, in January, when a scapegoat was needed for the burning of the Neapolitan fleet, he had refused to act against Commodore Campbell, a Portuguese commander, and had stated 'was Commodore Campbell an English officer, I should instantly order him to be tried by a court-martial for the positive breach of my orders to the Marquis de Niza. I am sorry it cannot be done by me to an auxiliary squadron.' There was no such reprieve for Caracciolo.[58]

Unsurprisingly, given the outcome had already been established, Caracciolo's trial of 29 June quickly led to a guilty verdict. The officer presiding, Count Thurn was, as well as being a rival of Caracciolo's, was also the officer Caracciolo had fired at off Procida. Thurn was also quite clearly more than a naval officer, being at the king's entourage in Rome in December 1798 and when the royal family was evacuated from Naples later that month. He was a royal confidant, an insider. And he cast the presiding vote.

The trial itself was makeshift, only paying lip-service to the demands of due process. Acton would call it speedy, Hamilton called it quick. There was no time to call witnesses, very little evidence was presented, and no appeal was considered. The execution was also rushed. The prisoner was sent to hang, rather than being shot like an officer, and to hang that same afternoon. Both Thurn and Hamilton protested that it was customary to grant the prisoner 24 hours for reflection, but this, too, was denied.

It is unclear why Nelson took personal responsibility for the process and haste of execution, and in the degrading manner of Caracciolo's death. Acton had wanted death, it is true, writing: 'I flatter myself that the scoundrel Caracciolo and his adherents will have received a proper reward before his Majesty's arrival.' But this was written the day after Caracciolo's execution.

Lord Nelson's manner of acting was again hasty and vindictive. He seemed to be aware of the court's feelings, and no doubt reminded of them by Lady Hamilton channelling the queen's vengeance, and hurried to do what he thought might best please them. But he was pre-empting their whims, trapping the rebels on the transports rather than returning them to their forts, as Palermo expected, [59] and brazenly hanging Caracciolo before even the court had time to rule on where and how he should die.

This attitude adds to the circumstantial evidence that Nelson was prepared to do wrong in tricking and seizing the rebels. But Nelson's ill-considered enthusiasm for so dishonourable a cause exposed him to public criticism of his conduct, albeit it tempered by the hero's fame, and, ultimately, he was reduced to deploying that ultimate argument, that virtue of the vicious, that the ends justify the means:

> I have done what I thought right; others may think differently; but it will be my consolation that I have gained a kingdom, seated a faithful ally of his majesty firmly on his throne, and restored happiness to millions.

Others have, indeed, thought differently, but Nelson chose to sweep promises aside merely to indulge the caprice of England's unprincipled and repulsive allies. Of course, the entirety of the crime cannot be shouldered by Nelson alone, the hangman too must take some of the blame. As too must Sir William Hamilton, for whom duplicity was becoming an adjunct of policy, and his artful Emma, who acted as the queen's agent in all matters pertaining to settling scores. But if Nelson and Sir William were conspirators in luring the republicans out of the forts and onto the boats, it was clearly Nelson who enabled the entire enterprise, Nelson who ordered his men and his fleet to carry it out and Nelson who used his authority and rank to override every objection from every side.[60] All this was done whatever the cost might be to his own honour and reputation. That Nelson blindly took these risks, and committed these grave faults, solely to impress Lady Hamilton is unproven. That he did so for the Bourbons of Naples is ridiculous, for they were the least-deserving recipients of the sacrifice of Nelson's good name.

Indeed, Nelson had sinned against the norms of civilised conduct for no higher purpose than to restore the odious Ferdinand and calculating Maria Carolina. Ironically, this sacrifice only brought them a fleeting respite, and could not keep them on their throne; after five further years of mismanagement, injustice, intrigue and vendetta, they once again fled into exile to Sicily. The kingdom that had been gained at the cost of so much honour was gone in an instant. This probably mattered little to a Nelson blinded by the zeal of saving His Majesty's honour, but his deplorable transaction has troubled the conscience of his supporters ever since.

As for history, it too should have a conscience. Few emerge particularly well from this episode of Neapolitan history. The French proved greedy, the Neapolitan patriots adept at bickering, whilst the British and royalists showed themselves cruel and treacherous. Whilst the cruelty was criminal, it could only take place because of that more deplorable stain, treachery.

The events at Naples in the summer of 1799 show Nelson in his poorest light, as the willing tool of an odious and perfidious court. G K Chesterton was surely right when he alluded to the one-eyed admiral and his reactionary tendencies by writing 'Nelson turned his blindest eye, on Naples and on liberty'. It is perhaps true that the admiral cared little for Neapolitans and still less for the principles of liberty. Nelson held in higher esteem his reputation and his honour.

Unfortunately, at Naples, he forfeited both.

Annex: The Capitulation

The queen's annotated text of the Capitulation Ruffo accorded to the rebels in the forts of Naples (B.M. Add. MS. 30999, f. 84). Received by the Hamiltons on 29 June 1799. The text is on the left, the queen's marginal comments are on the right.

Article 1. — The castles Nuovo and Uovo shall be delivered up to the commanders of the troops of his Majesty the King of the Two Sicilies, and of those of his allies, the King of England, the Emperor of All the Russias, and the Ottoman Porte, with all military stores, provisions, artillery and munitions of every kind now in the magazines, of which an inventory shall be made by commissaries on both sides, after the present capitulation is signed.	To capitulate with one's weak rebel subjects, who were without hope of succour either by sea (or by land)! With persons who, after the clemency displayed to them by their king and father (promising to pardon them), fought desperately, and now only come to terms through fear! I find it to disgraceful to treat with rebels! They should either have been attacked in full force, or else left alone until a more favourable opportunity.
Article 2. — The troops composing the garrisons shall keep possession of the forts until the vessels, mentioned below, destined to transport those who wish to be taken to Toulon, are ready to sail.	This is a real insult for the rebels address their sovereign on equal terms, and with an air of being his superior.
Article 3. — The garrisons shall have the honours of war, and will march out with arms and baggage, drums beating, colours flying, matches lighted, and each with two pieces of artillery and they shall lay down their arms on the beach.	This is so infamous and absurd that I can barely come to speak of it, honour for the standard of rebellion. This is so absurd that I cannot tell how they ever came to conceive of it, much less to sign it.

Article 4. — The persons and property, both movable and immovable, of all the individuals composing the two garrisons shall be respected and guaranteed.	This means that the traitors shall not suffer even a slight punishment or loss for such a grave crime.
Article 5. — All these individuals shall have the liberty of embarking on board the cartels, which shall be prepared for the purpose of taking them to Toulon, or to remain at Naples without being molested together with their families.	This article makes one ask oneself why troops were sent, if the felons are allowed to remain and depart without being molested. This will encourage them to do it all again, but with more thorough preparation, and will stimulate the evilly disposed persons in Sicily to do likewise, since there is nothing to lose and much to gain.
Article 6. — The conditions contained in the present capitulation extend to every person of both sexes now in the castles.	The fact that the two sexes are deliberately mentioned proves that there are criminals of both sexes. The clause shows this.
Article 7. — The same conditions shall apply in respect to all the republican troops taken prisoner by the troops of his Majesty the King of the Two Sicilies in the different divers battles which took place before the siege of the castles.	The same principle of full liberty and security for felonious rebels is continued, in order that they may return with better success to their evil doing.
Article 8. —The Archbishop of Salerno, Micheroux, Dillon and the Bishop of Avellino, detained in the castles, shall be delivered to the commandant of the castle of St Elmo, where they shall remain as hostages until word of the arrival of the individuals sent to Toulon shall be ascertained.	What an absurdity to hand over hostages, as though we were the conquered! The fact that the traitors depend on a handful of Frenchmen, and wait for their orders, renders Naples a vile French garrison which the British squadron should therefore proceed to bring them to obedience, as it would with Toulon, Brest, or Rochefort.
Article 9. — All the other hostages and state prisoners, confined in the two forts, shall be set at liberty immediately after the present capitulation is signed.	I would have no one released — all should be made to win their liberty with arms in their hands, for their honour and for the good of the kingdom and the city.

Article 10. — None of the articles of the said capitulation shall be put into execution until after they shall have been approved by the commandant of the castle of St Elmo.	This is the epitome of disgrace and cowardice. They do not ask for the approval of their own sovereign to whose orders and instructions their action is diametrically opposed, but they demand the approval of a small number of Frenchmen. This shows the villainy of the rebels, and the treachery or ignorance of those who signed it.

Queen's note: This is such an infamous treaty that if by some miracle of Providence something does not take place which will break and destroy it, I shall count myself as lost and dishonoured, and I believe that at the risk of perishing from malaria, fatigue, or from a rebel bullet, the king and the prince by his side, should immediately arm the provinces, march against the rebel city, and die beneath its ruins if they resist, rather than remain vile slaves of the French wretches and their infamous followers, the rebels. That is how I feel; this infamous capitulation (if it takes place) grieves me a great deal more than the loss of the kingdom, and will have a far worse consequences.

Bibliography

Archives Nationales de France (ANF): Basse Leonore
Archives of the Russian Fleet (ЦГАВМФ): Fond 192 (Ushakov in command of the Black Sea Fleet).
Archivio di Stato di Napoli (ASN):
  Archivio Ruffo di Bagnara, 114.
  Ministero degli affari esteri, 4138, 4259, 4298, 4332, 4591, 5292.
  Archivio Borbone, 42, 43 (letters from Ferdinand to Maria Carolina), 99 (Maria Carolina's correspondence).
Archivio Storico Diocesano di Napoli (ASDN).
British Library (BL):
  Additional MSS 30999 (Rushout's recollections), 34902, 34909, 34911, 34912, 34913, 34915, 34944, 34945, 34946, 34989, 34991 (Nelson's comments on Williams' book), 36873 (Foote's correspondence), 37077, 42069, 42071.
  Egerton MS 1614 (Nelson's letters to Lady Hamilton), 1615–1619, 1620, 1622, 1623, 2640 (ff 153–165 is Acton's correspondence from December 1798).
National Maritime Museum:
  Phillipps-Croker (CRK 1-22, Lady Hamilton's correspondence is 19–22).
  Girdlestone Collection (GIR3 and GIR3/A on Naples).
Somerset Heritage Centre: DD/DU 234. Duckworth Papers.
University of Manchester: Rylands Collection.
US Naval Academy: Christian A. Zabriskie Collection.

Acton, Harold, *The Bourbons of Naples: 1734–1825.* London, 1957.
Albanese, Camillo, *Cronache di una rivoluzione.* Milan, 1998.
Alessi, Giorgia, *Giustizia e polizia. Il controllo di una capitale. Napoli 1779–1803.* Naples, 1992.
Anon, *Filiazioni de' Rei di Stato condannati dalla Suprema Giunta di Stato e da'Visitatori Generali, in vita, e a tempo ad essere asportati da'Reali Dominj.* Naples, 1800.
Badham, Francis Pritchett, Admiral Baillie, in *Scottish Review,* 36, 1900.

Badham, Francis Pritchett, Nelson and the Neapolitan Republicans, in *The English Historical Review*, 13, 1898.

Badham, Francis Pritchett, *Nelson at Naples: A Journal for June 10–30 1799*. London, 1900.

Badham, Francis Pritchett, Nelson and Ruffo: A Discussion of the Events of 26 June 1799. *Revue napoléonienne*, IV, 1903.

Barra, Francesco, *Michele Pezza detto Fra' Diavolo. Vita, avventure e morte di un guerrigliero dell'800 e sue memorie inedite*. Cava dei Tirreni, 2000.

Battaglini, Mario, *Atti, leggi proclami ed altre carte della Repubblica napoletana 1798–1799*. Chiravalle, 1983, 4 volumes.

Battaglini, Mario, *Il Monitore Napoletano 1799*. Naples, 1974.

Battaglini, Mario, *La repubblica napoletana : Diari, memorie, racconti*. Naples, 2000.

Beltrani, Giovambattista, Un manoscritto inedito di Onofrio Fiani da Torremaggiore su i fatti del 1799 in Napoli, in *Archivio Storico per le Province Napoletane* (ASPN), 1896.

Beraducci , *see* Bisceglia.

Bertaux, E, Documenti inediti dell'Archivio di guerra francese – I lazzari – Il miracolo di S. Gennaro – Méjan, in *Archivio Storico per le Province Napoletane* (ASPN), 1899.

Bisceglia, Vitangelo, *Cronache dei fatti del 1799 di Gian Carlo Berarducci e Vitangelo Bisceglia*. Bari, 1900.

Bocquet, Louis, *Mémoire historique de tous les événements politiques et militaires qui ont eu lieu dans Naples, depuis le départ de l'armée française, jusqu'à l'époque de la reddition du fort St Elme*. Marseilles, 1800.

Caldora, Umberto, *Diario segreto di Ferdinando IV di Borbone*. Naples, 1965.

Castelcicala, Prince, *Pisma Kniaz Castelcicala s Graf S. R. Vorontsov*. St Petersburg, n.d.

Chastellux, Comte de, *Relation du voyage de Mesdames, Tantes du Roi*. Paris, 1816.

Cimbalo, Antonio, *Itinerario di tutto ciò che è avvenuto nella spedizione dell'Em. mo sig. D. Fabrizio Card. Ruffo*. Naples, 1799.

Coleman, Terry, *The Nelson Touch*. London, 2002.

Conforti, Luigi, *Napoli nel 1799: critica e documenti inediti*. Naples, 1889.

Coppa-Zuccari, Luigi, *L'invasione francese negli Abruzzi, 1798–1810*. L'Aquila, 1926–1928.

Cortese, Nino, *Memorie di un generale della Repubblica e dell'Impero. Francesco Pignatelli principe di Strongoli*. Bari, 1927, 2 volumes.

Critelli, M P, Napoletana o Partenopea? Note storiche in margine a una denominazione, in *Rassegna storica del Risorgimento*, 79, 1992, p. 23–34.

Critelli Maria Pia, Segarini Georges, Une source inédit de l'histoire de la Révolution romaine: les registres du commandant Girardon. L'insorgenza du Latium méridional et la Campagne du Circeo in *Mélanges de l'Ecole française de Rome. Italie et Méditerranée*. 1992. See Girardon for later operations.

Croce, Benedetto, Esuli napoletani in Francia in conseguenza dei casi del 1799 (Dalle carte della Polizia francese) in *Archivio storico per le provincie napoletane* (ASPN), 1932.

Bibliography

Croce, Benedetto, Il Regno di Napoli dal luglio 1799 al marzo 1806, in *Archivio storico per le provincie napoletane* (ASPN), 1932.

Croce, Benedetto, *La riconquista del Regno di Napoli nel 1799. Lettere del cardinal Ruffo, del re, della regina e del ministro Acton.* Bari, 1943.

Croce, Benedetto, *La rivoluzione napoletana del 1799. Biografie, racconti, ricerche.* Bari, 1968.

Croce, Benedetto, L'emigrazione Napoletana a Parigi nel 1802, in *Archivio storico per le provincie napoletane* (ASPN), 1906.

Croce, Benedetto, Relazioni dei Patrioti Napoletani col Direttorio e col Consolato e l'idea dell'Unità Italiana, in *Archivio storico per le provincie napoletane* (ASPN), 1902.

Croce, Benedetto, *Studi storici sulla Rivoluzione napoletana del 1799*, 2nd ed. Rome, 1897.

Cuoco (or Coco), Vincenzo, *Saggio storico sulla Rivoluzione di Napoli del 1799.* Milan, 1801.

Czisnik, Marianne, *Admiral Nelson: Image and Icon.* Thesis, University of Edinburgh, 2003.

D'Ayala, Mariano, *Vite degli Italiani benemeriti della libertà e della patria uccisi dal Carnefice.* Rome, 1883.

De Lorenzo, Giuseppe, *Memorie*, edited by Paola Russo, Naples, 1999.

De Nicola, Carlo, *Diario napoletano (1798–1825).* Naples, 1906, 3 volumes. Originally published in the *Archivio Storico per le Province Napoletane* (ASPN) in 1902.

Dorat-Cubières, Michel de, *Citoyen français, a Jean Acton.* Paris, 1790.

Douglas, Norman, Blind Guides, in *English Review*, 14, 1913.

Drusco, Pietrabondio, *Anarchia popolare di Napoli dal 21 dicembre 1798 al 23 gennajo 1799. Manoscritto inedito dell'abate Pietrabondio Drusco ed i monitori repubblicani dal 1799.* Naples, 1884.

Dupaty, C.M.J.B. Mercier, *Lettres sur l'Italie en 1785.* Volume II. Paris, 1788.

Durante, Vincenzo, *Diario storico delle operazioni di guerra, intraprese nelle due provincie di Lecce e Bari, contro i nemici dello Stato e del Trono, dai due Offiziali Anglo-Corsi D. Gio. Francesco Boccheciampe e D. G. Battista De Cesari.* Naples, 1800.

Elefante, Camillo, *Giornale dal 1799. Di tutto ciò che accade in questa Fedelissima, Ed Illustrissima Città di Barletta, tanto riguardo il tempo, che alli fatti, Governi, ed altro, facendosi l'Autore l'istessa protesta, che nel Tomo antecedente.* Volume II. Barletta, n.d.

Fleury, William-Aimable-Emile-Adrien, *Soldats ambassadeurs sous le Directoire, an IV-an VIII.* Paris, 1906.

Foote, Edward James, *Captain Foote's vindication of his conduct, when captain of H.M.S. Seahorse, and senior officer in the Bay of Naples in the summer of 1799.* London, 1810.

Fortunato, Giustino, *I giustiziati di Napoli del 1799.* Rome, 1882.

Fortunato, Giustino, *I napoletani del 1799.* Florence, 1884.

Fraser, Flora, *Beloved Emma: The Life of Emma, Lady Hamilton.* London, 1986.

Gagnière, A, *La reine Marie Caroline de Naples. D'Après des documents nouveaux,* Paris, 1886.

Galanti, Giuseppe Maria, *Breve descrizione della città di Napoli e del suo contorno*. Naples, 1792.

Giglioli, Constance, *Naples in 1799: an Account of the Revolution and the Rise and Fall of the Parthanopean Republic*. London, 1903.

Girardon, Antoine, *Precis des Opérations du général Girardon*, edited by Georges Segantini and Maria Pia Critelli and published as *Le patriotisme et le courage : la repubblica napoletana del 1799 nei manoscritti del generale di brigata Antoine Girardon*. Naples, 2000.

Goethe, J. W von, *Italian Journey*. London, 1816.

Gordon, Pryse Lockhart, *Personal memoirs: or, Reminiscences of men and manners at home and abroad, during the last half century. With occasional sketches of the author's life*. London, 1830.

Gridel, M E., *Cahiers de vieux soldats de la Révolution et de l'Empire* (Chatton and Leclère). Paris, 1902.

Gutteridge, H C, *Nelson and the Neapolitan Jacobins. Documents relating to the suppression of the Jacobin Revolution at Naples, June, 1799*. London, 1903, (Navy Records Society, 25).

Hamilton, Sir William, *The Hamilton Letters: The Naples Dispatches of William Hamilton* (edited by J Davis and G Capuano). London, 2008.

Helfert, Joseph Alexander, Freiherr von, *Fabrizio Ruffo: Revolution und Gegenrevolution von Neapel*. Vienna, 1882.

Helfert, Joseph Alexander, Freiherr von, Horatio Nelson im Juni 1799, in *Historisches Jahrbuch*, I, 1880, p. 55–76,

Hueffer, Hermann, La fin de la république napolitaine. *Revue historique*, 83 and 84, 1876.

Imbert de Saint-Amand, Arthur-Léon, *La jeunesse de la reine Marie-Amélie*. Paris, 1891.

Jeaffreson, John Cordy, *Lady Hamilton and Lord Nelson: an Historical Biography based on letters and other documents in the Morrison collection*. London, 1897.

Knight, Carlo, Gli Imbarcati Del 1799 in *Accademia di Archeologia*, 67, 1998, pp. 469–515.

Knight, Carlo, La contabilità privata di Sir William Hamilton, in *Archivio storico per le provincie napoletane* (ASPN), 24, 1996.

Knight, Carlo, Sir William Hamilton e il mancato rispetto, da parte di Lord Nelson, della 'Capitolazione' del 1799, in *Atti della Accademia Pontaniana*, 67, 1999, pp. 373–397.

Knight, Cornelia, *Autobiography of Miss Cornelia Knight, lady companion to the Princess Charlotte of Wales, with extracts from her journals and anecdote books*. London, 1861.

Kossman, Robby, *Lord Nelson und Herzog Franz Caracciolo*. Hamburg, 1895.

Kotzebue, August von, *Souvenirs d'un voyage en Livonie, à Rome et à Naples*. Volume III. Paris, 1806.

Lahure, Louis-Joseph. *Souvenirs de la vie militaire du lieutenant-général Bon L.-J. Lahure*. Paris, 1895.

Laugier, Capitaine Jérôme-Roland, *Les cahiers du Capitaine Jérôme-Roland Laugier du 27ème Régiment d'Infanterie légère*. Aix, 1893.

Lemmi, Francesco, Nelson a Napoli nel giugno 1799, in *Archivio Storico per le Province Napoletane* (ASPN), 58, 1929.

Bibliography

Lemmi, Francesco, *Nelson e Caracciolo e la repubblica napoletana (1799)*. Florence, 1898.

Lomonaco, Francesco, *Rapporto al cittadino Carnot*. Milan, 1802.

Macdonald, Jacques Etienne Joseph Alexandre, *Souvenirs du Maréchal Macdonald, duc de Tarente*. Paris, 1892.

Mahan, Alfred Thayer, The Neapolitan Republicans and Nelson's Accusers, in *The English Historical Review*, 14, 1899.

Mahan, Alfred Thayer, Nelson at Naples, in *The English Historical Review*, 15, 1900.

Maresca, Benedetto, Gli avvenimenti di Napoli dal 13 giugno al 12 luglio 1799. Compendio dei fatti accaduti in Napoli dall'arrivo délie truppe di S. M. e dei suoi alleati sino alla resa di Sant'Elmo, narrati dal Cavalière Antonio Micheroux, in *Archivio storico per le provincie napoletane* (ASPN), 24, 1899.

Maresca, Benedetto, *Il cavaliere Antonio Michevoux nella rivoluzione napoletana dell'anno: studio critico*. Naples, 1895.

Maresca, Benedetto, Il cav. Antonio Michevoux nella rivoluzione napoletana dell'anno 1799, in *Archivio Storico per le Province Napoletane* (ASPN), 1893–1894.

Maresca, Benedetto, Compendio del Diario del cav. Micheroux, in *Archivio Storico per le Province Napoletane* (ASPN), 1899.

Maresca, Benedetto, Memoria degli avvenimenti di Napoli nell'anno 1799 scritta da Amedeo Ricciardi, in *Archivio Storico per le Province Napoletane* (ASPN), 1888.

Maresca, Benedetto, Racconti storici di Gaetano Rodinò ad Aristide suo figlio, in *Archivio Storico per le Province Napoletane* (ASPN), 1881, p. 266–269.

Maria Carolina, Queen, *Correspondance Inédite De Marie-Caroline, Reine De Naples et de Sicile, avec Le Marquis De Gallo*. Paris, 1911.

Marinelli, Diomede, *I giornali di Diomede Marinelli*. Naples, 1901.

Méjan, Louis Joseph, *Reponse du citoyen Mejan chef de la vingt-septième Demi-Brigade d'Infanterie legere, commandant du Fort Saint-Elme à Naples a l'ecrit intitulé Memoire historique de tous les Evenemens politiques et militaires qui ont eu lieu*. Marseilles, 1800.

Montigny, Charles Claude de, *Mémoires historiques de Mesdames Adélaide et Victoire de France*. Paris, 1802.

Morkva, Valeriy, Russia's Policy on Rapprochement with the Ottoman Empire in the Era of the French Revolution and Napoleonic Wars, 1792–1806. Thesis, Bilkent University, 2010.

Morrison, Alfred, *The Collection of Autograph Letters and Historical Documents Formed by Alfred Morrison*. London, 1893.

Nardini, Bartolomeo, *Mémoires pour servir à l'histoire des dernières révolutions de Naples, ou détail des événements qui ont précédé ou suivi l'entrée des Français dans cette ville, recuillés par Bartolomeo Nardini témoin oculaire*. Paris, 1806.

Nelson, Dispatches, *see* Nicolas, Harris.

Nicolas, Harris Nicholas, *The Dispatches and Letters of Vice Admiral Lord Viscount Nelson*. London, 1844, vol. II 1795–1797; vol. III January 1798 – August 1799; vol. IV September 1799 – December 1801.

Paget, Augustus, *The Paget Papers: Diplomatic and Other Correspondence of the Right Honourable Sir Arthur Paget*. Volume I. London, 1896.

Palumbo, Raffaele, *Carteggio di Maria Carolina con Lady Emma Hamilton*. Sala Bolognese, 1906.

Parsons, George Samuel, *Nelsonian Reminiscences: leaves from Memory's Log*. London, 1905.

Pepe, Guglielmo, *Memorie del generale Guglielmo Pepe intorno alla sua vita e ai recenti casi d'Italia scritte da lui medesimo*. Paris, 1847, 2 volumes.

Perella, Alfonso. *L'anno 1799 nella provincia di Campobasso*. Caserta, 1900.

Petromasi, Domenico, *Alla riconquista del Regno. La marcia del Cardinale Ruffo dalle Calabrie a Napoli*. Naples, 1801.

Pettigrew, Thomas Joseph, *Memoirs of the Life of Vice-Admiral Lord Viscount Nelson*. London, 1849.

Rao Anna Maria, Conspiration et Constitution : Andrea Vitaliani et la République napolitaine de 1799, in: *Annales historiques de la Révolution française*, 313, 1998, pp. 545–573.

Rao, Anna Maria, Esercito e società a Napoli nelle riforme del secondo Settecento, in *Rivista italiana di studi napoleonici*, 25, 1988, p. 93–159.

Rao, Anna Maria, *Esuli: l'emigrazione politica italiana in Francia (1792–1802)*, Napoli, Guida, 1992.

Rao, Anna Maria, L'ordinamento e l'attività giudiziaria della Repubblica Napoletana del 1799, in *Archivio Storico per le Province Napoletane* (ASPN), 1973.

Rao, Anna Maria (ed), *Napoli 1799 fra storia e storiografia*. Naples, 2002.

Ricciardelli, Pasquale, *Nicola Fiani di Torremaggiore e la Rivoluzione napoletana del 1799*. Sessacapriola, 1961.

Rodino, G, Racconti storici ad Aristide suo figlio, in *Archivio Storico per le Province Napoletane* (ASPN), 1881.

Ronga, Nello, *Il 1799 in terra di lavoro: une ricerca sui comuni dell'area aversana e sui realisti napoletani*. Naples, 2000.

Rose, George, *The Diaries of the Right Honourable George Rose*. London, 1860.

Russo, Saverio, *La Capitanata nel 1799*. Foggia, 2000.

Sacchinelli, Domenico, *Memorie storiche sulla vita del cardinale Fabrizio Ruffo*, Napoli, 1836. Sansone, A, *Gli avvenimenti del 1799 nelle Due Sicilie*. Palermo, 1901.

Sarrazin, General Jean, *Mémoires du Général Sarrazin, ecrit par lui-meme*. Brussels, 1848.

Sermoneta, Vittoria Colonna Caetani di, *The Locks of Norbury*. London, 1940.

Sickel, Walter, *Emma lady Hamilton from new and original sources and documents, together with an appendix of notes and new letters*. London, 1905.

Stassano, Antonio. *Memorie storiche del Regno (1799–1821)*. Venosa, 1994.

Thiébault, Paul Charles, *Mémoires du baron Thiébault publiées sous les auspices de sa fille M.lle Claire Thiébault d'après le manuscrit original*. Paris, 1894.

Ulloa, Pietro C, *Intorno alla Storia del reame di Napoli di Pietro Colletta. Annotamenti*. Naples, 1877.

Traversier, Mélanie, 'Transformer la plèbe en people'. Théâtre et musique à Naples en 1799, de la proclamation de la République napolitaine à la Première Restauration, in *Annales historiques de la Révolution française* [online].

Bibliography

Trench, Melesina Chenevix St. George, *Journal kept during a visit to Germany in 1799, 1800*. London, 1861.

Volpicella, Luigi, L'anarchia popolare in Napoli nel gennaio 1799 raccontata da Domenico Puccini, in *Archivio Storico per le Province Napoletane* (ASPN), 35, 1910, p.485–500.

Williams, Helen Maria, *Sketches of the State of Manners and Opinions in the French Republic Towards the Close of the Eighteenth Century*. London, 1801.

Willyams, Cooper, *A Voyage up the Mediterranean in His Majesty's Ship* The Swiftsure. London, 1802.

Wraxall, Sir Nathaniel William, *Historical memoirs of his own time*. Volume I. London, 1836.

Endnotes

Overture

1 Anonymous chronicler, *Cronista di San Paolo*, in Fortunato, p. 27. It was the custom to leave the bodies of criminals not born in Naples hanging for an extra day.
2 ASPN 1896, p. 403.

1 Rulers and Ruled: Naples and the Neapolitans

1 Ferdinand's other older brother, Charles (born in 1748), was heir apparent to the Spanish throne, succeeding only in 1788, but he moved to Spain in 1759.
2 Ferdinand was just as unflattering, confiding that 'she sleeps like someone who has been murdered and sweats like a pig' (Wraxall, p. 250).
3 Acton. p. 141.
4 Wraxall, p. 233.
5 The French largely agreed. On 24 May 1783 the French representative at Naples, Dominique Vivant Denon wrote 'He is no doubt an excellent prince. One could not wish for a better nature, jovial spirits or aptitude for those things which please him. But, with such a poor education, the king's generosity is, one might say, a disaster – and that is what this king is' (Imbert de Saint-Amand, p. 33).
6 Sir William Hamilton would later remember 'When I had the honour to be here 28 years ago with the king and queen of Naples (who used then to shoot also) I remember the party, consisting of 18 guns, killed in this forest, in one day, 2400 head of fallow deer, and of which the queen killed upwards of 60.'
7 Wraxall, p. 234.
8 Kotzebue, III, p. 118. Her authoritarian tendencies were on show again when, in late 1799, she lamented that 'nothing is more terrible than to govern people at a time when each tailor thinks he can pass judgement on the government'.
9 Francesco was commonly acknowledged as being hopeless. Even the king noted, on 22 June 1798, that 'Francesco was at table but talked of nothing

else but his dogs and he described the exact genealogical tree of each one of them'.

10 Imbert de Saint-Amand, p. 55. She repeated this assertion in 1791: 'Only six years ago the king of Naples was unheard of or was regarded as a viceroy sent from Spain and one of her dependencies, but now would play a great role with glory and honour. I swear that's most satisfying and prestigious'.

11 Tuscany enjoyed some astonishing reforms. It was the first state to abolish the death penalty on 30 November 1786. This inspired a lawyer from Flanders to call for its abolition in France in May 1791. He was Maximilien Robespierre.

12 Acton was born on 3 June 1736 and was the eldest son of Dr Edward Acton (1709-1781), an English Catholic who had been employed in France and settled at Besançon.

13 Acton was named by the Chevalier de Cussy as one of the queen's lovers. This imaginative writer also went on to claim that, according to his friend, the Prince de Partana, Maria Carolina was normally chaste but when she was pregnant 'gave herself up to all kinds of pleasures of the senses and to all sorts of libertine exploits, with men as well as with women'. Similar allegations were made by the British who administered Sicily when the queen was there from 1803 – they joked that the queen's numerous lovers were organised into a unit called Queen Mary's Rifle Corps.

14 *Revue des question historiques*, 86, 1904, p. 432.

15 Baronet of Aldenham in 1791.

16 Acton contracted William Bolts, in 1785 to establish the Royal Asiatic Society of Naples and to sail to China and California on a ship christened the *Ferdinand*. Discussions led to a charter for the Royal Society of the Indies of Naples was drawn up. Nothing came of the plan, Bolts would die in a Parisian poorhouse in 1808.

17 Acton lured Giuseppe di Thurn und Taxis-Valsassina and others from Tuscan service to serve in the new navy.

18 He was made Minister Plenipotentiary in 1768 but technically was never an ambassador.

19 The principal residence was at Pizzofalcone, the Palazzo Sessa, costing 804 Ducats a year. Then there was the casino, or country house, at Caserta, the Villa Angelica at Portici and, later, the three-roomed Villa Emma at Posillipo.

20 In April 1794 he told Charles Greville, the avid collector of minerals, 'Mrs North, the Bishop of Winchester's wife, has made an immense collection in your way – cristals, gems and minerals – whether good or bad I know not; she is sending them home, keep your eye on them, for I don't believe she will return home alive, although in no immediate danger at this moment'. Henrietta Maria North died in 1796.

21 Rylands collection, HAM1/4/4/3. Hamilton added that Catherine 'was a perfect Christian, and 7 years in this corrupt country made not the least impression on her morals or sentiments'.

22 The power of electricity to stimulate misbehaving limbs and organs was a fashionable fad at the time. Strangely, Dr Graham's treatment was echoed

years later when Sir William Hamilton wrote in April 1800 that Nelson was receiving electric shocks to restore the sight of his bad eye: 'The eye that was totally blind has been, however, by Electricity recovered sufficiently to distinguish objects, and hopes may be entertained of His Lordship recovering that eye.'

23 The inscription placed above Dr Graham's celestial bed.

24 Hamilton was right, even his peers made fun of the old man and his comely wife. In December 1799 the Earl of Dalkieth told Paget, Hamilton's replacement, that: 'I think you had better supply his place in the full sense of the Word; and occupy Lady Hamilton too, a place you are certainly much better fitted to fill than the old Knight'.

25 NMM, LBK/6.

26 Fraser, p. 91. Letter dated 14 June 1786.

27 Goethe, p. 199, letter of 16 March 1787. All this was confirmed by Sir Gilbert Elliot in 1797 who admired her attitudes and noted that Sir William added 'and besides all this she makes my apple pies'.

28 Lady Holland, p. 242, writing in 1793.

29 Lady Holland, p. 243.

30 Sermoneta, p. 165.

31 Josiah Nisbet, Nelson's rather uncouth stepson who developed into a source of anxiety and disappointment for Nelson.

32 Despatches, I, p. 326.

33 Letter dated 30 September 1798, Despatches, III, p. 138. Moral posturing did not sit well with the fact that Nelson, although married to the long-suffering Lady Frances Nelson, started an affair with Adelaide Coreglia, or Correglia, from Livorno, in 1794, which would last until early 1797. It is not clear whether she was a fiddler or poet, but she was certainly an opera singer.

34 The Marquis de Sade was a witness to this festival whilst he was at Naples in early 1776. The description found its way into his grotesque novel *L'Histoire de Juliette*. An episode in that novel took place 'in the palace of the king of Naples, on a balcony overlooking one of the city squares; there Juliette and her partner Clairvil, who is also her mentor in crime and in debauchery, are invited to watch the cuccagna by King Ferdinand and his wife Charlotte, each as libertine as the other'.

35 There were some 670 Jesuits expelled. The Crown also seized Jesuit lands and buildings, plus, in Puglia alone, 500 cows, 24 horses and seven mules.

36 Dupaty, p. 225.

37 Estates of those who died without heirs passed to the crown, so this number was on the rise.

38 In 1763 and 1764 some 200,000 people were estimated to have died from hunger or disease. The state proved itself powerless to intervene against a monopoly of grain merchants granted extensive and lucrative powers by the state and the nobility. The disaster underlined how precarious Naples was, how ineffective its government, how clumsy its economy.

39 The San Carlo theatre was built and opened in 1737, and it quickly established itself as Italy's leading opera house.

40 The Illuminati also made inroads in southern Italy especially as their founder, Friedrich Münter, using the pseudonym Syrianus, was a regular visitor to Naples.

41 The king, not to be outdone, formed his own secretive society in 1787, the Neapolitan Noble Society of Diana the Huntress. Only dedicated huntsmen could join, following royal invitation, and it included Luigi Serra and 'Sir Hamilton'.

2 Revolutions:.Naples in the 1790s

1 Dorat-Cubières, p. 26.

2 Morrison I, p. 167. The queen agreed, telling Gallo 'we are tranquil here. Rebellion, revolution, trouble of whatever import, we hope to be able to avoid all of that'.

3 This was the famous Francesco Caracciolo, born in 1752. He was a naval officer of some renown and had volunteered to serve onboard the British ship the *Marlborough* in 1779 during the American Revolution.

4 These new Italian clients, which included the Cisalpine and Ligurian republics, were termed sister republics, but rather resembled obedient daughters.

5 Borel was not happy with his work, writing on 7 April that 'I have to go to the patriotic club with L'Aurora tomorrow, and will probably catch a cold after singing republican songs at the top of my voice'. Cited in Rao (1998). p. 555. Hamilton's listing of dangerous republican terrorists is in Egerton, 2640.

6 The youths were sent to Sicily to serve as private soldiers. The Neapolitan foreign minister justified the arrests using the law of 8 March 1798, which banned foreign fashions, a law which was, one presumes, selectively enforced.

7 Despite the secrecy, the French official newspaper, Le Moniteur, rather bizarrely mentioned Egypt as a destination. This was published on 1 April, so could have been an early attempt at disinformation.

8 Later, the king confided to his diary 'At 1.30 saw the new Cisalpine minister, worthy of being hanged'.

9 Knight. p. 109. The event was also recorded by the Neapolitan Admiral Caracciolo: 'At two on the 3rd an English naval brig sent by Admiral Nelson from the Badia di Requez at the mouth of the Nile came in and anchored.' ASPN, 1932, p. 71.

10 Nelson, Dispatches, III, p. 71.

11 The Neapolitan letter was a plea sent in the hope of stirring a reluctant Austria to war against the French. Austria was most reluctant, as Naples knew full well and in June Ferdinand had already whined 'God forgive the emperor for his laziness, it will be our ruin'.

12 Dispatches, III, p. 130. At this stage it seems that Lady Hamilton wanted to see Nelson's wife as a friend. She would tell Nelson that 'I told Her Majesty we only wanted Lady Nelson to be the female tria juncta in uno for we all love you and yet all three differently and yet all equally'.

13 Nelson again rather unkindly telling his wife 'I hope some day to have the pleasure of introducing you to Lady Hamilton, she is an honour to her sex. Her kindness, with Sir William's, to me, is more than I can express: I am in their house, and I may tell you, it required all the kindness of my friends to set me up.'

14 Like many old men Hamilton was repeating himself having used the phrase in letters written on 28 October 1796 and 4 August and 8 September 1798. Now, however, the animosity was clearly directed at Gallo. On 29 August Nelson joined in, calling Gallo 'a wretch who minds nothing but fine clothes, his snuff-box, and ring; this is the best I can say of him'. In another letter, dated 29 September, to Earl Spencer, Nelson wrote 'This Marquis of Gallo I detest ... He admires his ribbon, ring, and snuff-box so much, that an excellent petit-maitre was spoiled when he was made a minister'. This is interesting because Nelson is clearly imitating Lady Hamilton for she had described Gallo to Nelson on 30 June as 'a frivolous, ignorant, self-conceited coxcomb that thinks of nothing but his fine, embroidered coat, ring, and snuff-box' (NMM, CRK20/55).

3 Rome: War and Defeat in 1798

1 It was a brutal civil war. The republican Inspector Franchi was, according to Girardon, 'burned alive with the tree of liberty and just about all of his family were massacred with the exception of the very young children and these Bisleti had pardoned but only after they were to be operated on in such a way as to extinguish the family forever'. Girardon visited the mutilated children to confirm the truth of the report.

2 Portugal had tried to obtain the ever-busy Mack but, in 1797, had to make do with the disgraced Prince Christian August of Waldeck, who died before he could do any lasting damage.

3 On 12 December 1798 a diarist in Barletta noted 'This evening around 200 Montenegrins, who will be in the Camiciotti, arrived destined for the camp'.

4 Recruits joined for eight years in the infantry and artillery, 12 for the cavalry and a mere six for the foreign regiments. Personnel had to be aged between 16 and 35, and be no shorter than 1 metre 55 centimetres.

5 The selected were called bussolati, as the names were chosen from an urn or bussola.

6 Militi, Manuela. *Il costo della Repubblica 'sorella' per gli ebrei di Roma.* p. 94.

7 In an ironic twist punishment for murder could be commuted to service in the army, a practice only outlawed in September 1800. In 1798 Gaetano Rodinò, who was guilty of lesser crimes, elected to serve in the Sannio Regiment at Gaeta rather than to be imprisoned.

8 Austria had entered a defensive alliance with Naples in July 1798, only promising to assist if Naples was attacked.

9 Dated 13 October. Nelson's bold urging was clearly a gamble, especially as a few weeks later he would write 'Naples is just embarked on a new war: the event, God only knows; but without the assistance of the Emperor, which is not yet given, this country cannot resist the powers of France'.

10 Maria Teresa, the queen's daughter, and wife of the Austrian emperor, made it clear 'I can only tell you that despite the most sincere attachment to you, and to my father, and the interest he has in seeing your state kept from ruin, he is the father and sovereign of his subjects and must look after them ... we cannot send you troops'.

11 Despatches, III, p. 141. Nelson, alluding to his visit of 1793, also declared that 'the anxiety which you and Sir William Hamilton have always had for the happiness of their Sicilian majesties, was also planted in me five years past'. The postscript also perhaps best sums up Nelson's support for the Hamiltons and their royal friends, to which he remained true throughout this period: 'Your ladyship will, I beg, receive this letter as a preparative for Sir William Hamilton, to whom I am writing, with all respect, the firm and unalterable opinion of a British admiral, anxious to approve himself a faithful servant to his sovereign by doing everything in his power for the happiness and security of their Sicilian majesties and their kingdoms'.

12 A letter to his superior on 4 October concludes with news of a different campaign 'I am writing opposite Lady Hamilton, therefore you will not be surprised at the glorious jumble of this letter. Were your lordship in my place, I much doubt if you could write so well; our hearts and our hands must be all in a flutter. Naples is a dangerous place, and we must keep clear of it.'

13 *Revue d'histoire diplomatique*, 1888, p. 523.

14 Marquis Pinto-Guedes de Nizza Reale had a four-ship squadron off Malta since September. It consisted of *Principe Real*, *Rainha de Portugal* (Captain Stone), *San Sebastian* (Captain Mitchell) and *Alfonco Albuquerque* (Captain Campbell).

15 Sichel, p. 237.

16 This ship was wrecked off the Scilly Islands on 10 December. Hamilton was enraged, writing on 22 March that 'My philosophy has been put to the trial by the loss of the *Colossus*, you give me but little hopes, but I have heard that the body insolvent of Admiral Shuldham has been saved from the wreck ... damn his body it can be of no use to the worms, but my Collection wou'd have given information to the most learned.' Molyneux Shuldham's corpse had been collected in Lisbon and was being transported for burial.

17 On 25 October Nelson offered the French garrison transportation to France and added 'I will take care that the lives of all those Maltese who have joined you shall be spared'. However, if the offer was rejected, then 'much less will I intercede for the lives or forgiveness of those who have betrayed their country'.

18 The queen had sent a letter to Emma Hamilton, hinting that British subsidies were vital. This plea for money is almost instantly converted into a letter from Nelson to the Duke of Clarence. The admiral remarked that 'the king, queen, generals Acton and Mack, have all assured me, and I am convinced, that this country cannot, under its present difficulties, carry on the war without pecuniary assistance from us.' Sir William informed the court that *there would be money* if they continued to 'pursue vigorous measures'. However, this was a lie. Downing Street had already told Hamilton he should tell the court 'in the most decided though friendly matter' that money was out of the question. In March 1799 Hamilton was chastised by his masters in London, who reiterated 'when the war was renewed by the King of Naples, it was under an express declaration, as stated to you in my No. 6 abovementioned, that no such aid could be afforded by His Majesty.'

19 Maria Carolina, I. p. 540 , 20 November

20 Critelli, p. 446. Report dated 25 November 1798. Louis-Joseph Lahure also noted that 'each time when the Neapolitan generals marched against positions occupied by French troops they were proceeded by an officer who would declare that the King of Naples was not at war with the French Republic'.

21 The queen wrote to her daughter 'God willing you will help us, as our fate is in the hands of your husband and if he delays we will be lost, so in the name of God let him not delay, or we shall be lost'. The Austrians remained impassive.

22 These troops left Naples on the 22nd and reached the neutral port on 28 November. Nelson and Naselli sent a summons into the port setting out the terms for surrender, which followed soon after. Nelson, who hoped to seize shipping in the harbour, declared himself ready to ignore the terms of the capitulation he had put his name to, writing 'I thought my object was to get possession on any terms, and that I should be ready to take all or any part of the odium of breaking them for the advantage of His Highness the Great Duke [of Tuscany] and the King of Naples'. Naselli was reluctant to break the agreement. Nelson remarked 'the General prudently, and certainly safely, waits the orders of his court, taking no responsibility on himself; I act from the circumstance of the moment, as I feel it may be most advantageous for the honour of the cause which I serve, taking all responsibility on myself.' (Morrison, II, p. 29).

23 Caldora, p. 385.

24 ASPN, 2009, p. 260.

25 On 28 November the Neapolitans threatened to execute one French prisoner for each shot from the fort. Burkhardt told Valterre, that 'French soldiers currently in hospital in Rome shall be kept as hostages and for each cannon shot from the castle, one shall be put to death in reprisal.'

26 Joseph Xavier Charles Raphaël Philippe Bénit (1767-1802) had fled the French revolution to serve in the Russian army. There he had an argument with Prince Schterbatov, who hit him with his cane, and soon after moved to Naples. In 1802 he again came across Schterbatov at Teplitz in Bohemia and the 67-year-old Russian killed him in a duel. He was rumoured to have been the Queen of Naples' lover, Hamilton writing in 1797 'I have reason to believe that such an impression took place lately in the heart of the queen of Naples; for she showed for some time passed a remarkable attention to the Prince of Saxe ... he is a young man of a very good figure and does not want talents'.

27 Nelson wrote to Duckworth on 6 December, declaring 'my situation in this country has had, doubtless, one rose, but it has been plucked from a bed of thorns'.

28 Letter sold by Christies, Lot 327/Sale 5621, 26 June 1996, London.

29 Caldora, p. 401. The king's secret diary is peppered with asterisks to denote lovemaking.

4 Rebellion: Anarchy in the Capital

1 The Hereditary Prince, Castelcicala, Manuel y Ariola, Belmonte and Pignatelli were also present.

2 Nelson had returned to Naples on 5 December and was again living with the Hamiltons. Nelson told his wife: 'I live as Sir William's son in the house'.

3 Montigny, III, p.68.

4 Egerton MS 2640, ff. 153-154.

5 Helfert, Ruffo, p. 513. She also stated that Nelson would save them from a second Varenne, an allusion to when her sister, Marie Antoinette, was captured whilst trying to flee France.

6 Nelson told St Vincent that 'the whole correspondence relative to this important business was carried on with the greatest address by Lady Hamilton and the queen, who being constantly in the habits of correspondence, no one could suspect'.

7 The Neapolitan admiral Caracciolo was back in Naples on 4 December. The *Archimede, Aurora* and *Fortuna* arrived on 8 December and Nelson asked Niza to supply some Portuguese sailors to strengthen the Neapolitan crews. On 16 December the *Tancredi, S. Gioacchino* and *Sibilla* also sailed in.

8 Ball was possibly more dubious than Troubridge would have been. Troubridge, the London baker's son, was a stern disciplinarian, mistrustful of his crews. He once famously remarked 'whenever I see a fellow look as if he was thinking, I say that's mutiny'.

9 Nelson repeats the queen's 'all is corrupt', another example of how close he was to the queen and Lady Hamilton's point of view. On 7 January he admitted that 'I speak as the queen tells me'.

10 Gaetano Lotti, an eyewitness to the events, noted wryly that '800 barrels were loaded aboard the English ships of Lord Nelson who, two months before, had been proclaimed, with much rejoicing, our liberator'.

11 Egerton MS 2640, ff. 159-160.

12 Caldora, p. 408.

13 Nardini, p. 19.

14 Marinelli, p. 398. A few days later he wrote that the victim was 'a courier of the court who was taking a letter from Acton to Nelson'.

15 Later Pryse Lockhart Gordon met Lady Hamilton at Palermo and noted 'she rehearsed in a subdued tone a melange of Lancashire and Italian, detailing the catalogue of her miseries, her hopes, and her fears, with lamentations about the dear queen, the loss of her own charming palazzo and its precious contents, which had fallen into the hands of the vile republicans. But here we offered some consolation, by assuring her ladyship that every article of the ambassador's property had been safely embarked in an English transport, and would be despatched in a few days'. It was true, however, that Sabatino, left behind in Naples, had sold off as much as he could (including 300 bottles of Port wine and Sherry, sold to a 'Mr Varden') but told his master, Hamilton, on 14 January that: 'I wanted to place onboard the four-seater coach, but it was not possible as the frigate was too small and could not take such a thing. But I did what I could to save the best of the things, although it was impossible to secure the carriages as nobody wished to look after them through fear of the French' (British Museum, Add 42069, 184, cited by Knight, ASPN, 1996, p. 207-208).

16 Gaetano Lotti calls this the 'scala segreta del caraco'.

17 Helfert, Ruffo, p.384.

18 The queen hadn't wanted them to come to Sicily as she later told Gallo 'If they had caused problems and wished to stay with us, and come here, I had resolved not to make it easy for them.' Galló himself had set off for Austria, sailing from Manfredonia on Captain Luigi Ciuffredi's ship just before the Mesdames arrived.

19 ASPN 2003, p. 278. Lady Hamilton was certainly hostile to the visitors, writing 'But we remained 2 days in the bay to treat with the Neapolitans – but, alas, with such vile traitors what can you do?'.

20 ASPN, 1932, p. 76.

21 Even before the operation was carried out she had told Gallo 'The sailors were fleeing. They could not be prevented from doing so for gold. Forteguerri came to say that he knew that they wanted to kill him. So four ships, five frigates, 10 galleys, 12 corvettes, brigantines, 90 gunboats, mortar ketches were consigned to the flames and they couldn't, on account of the sailors who all shouted 'Long live the king!' whilst they fled, couldn't be saved – the fruits of so much effort, so much money! Niza was the one who stayed behind to complete the operation.' The king's more economic version was that it was determined to 'to leave the Portuguese to bring along as many boats as possible and to burn the rest'.

22 Nelson's letter of the same day to Captain Hope was specific: 'you will prepare the frigate and corvettes for burning ... taking care they are burnt before you sail'. On 28 December he would tell his superior, Lord St Vincent, that 'it was my duty not to leave the chance of any ships of war falling into the hands of the French, therefore every preparation was made for burning them before I sailed; but the reasons given me by their Sicilian Majesties, induced me not to burn them till the last moment'.

23 Nelson's position is odd. Nelson did indeed lambast Niza on 11 January for having burnt the ships, possibly prompted by the fact that 'the king has complained to me'. He told Campbell 'I am sorry to tell you that I entirely disapprove of your destroying the ships of his Sicilian majesty'. However, on 2 January he had told Earl Spencer that 'Niza is prepared to burn the ships when the French get a little nearer', and Hamilton had already noted 'Lord Nelson could not consistently with the common cause allow of such a considerable naval force being left to the chance of falling into the hands of the enemy, and consequently that it would be absolutely necessary to burn such of the ships as could not immediately sail'. In the event Nelson informed Acton that he could not try Campbell because Campbell was serving in an auxiliary squadron.

24 Some 2.5 million Ducats.

25 Poor Salandra informed Pignatelli that 'General Mack has left. Those troops who were sent to Naples have been disarmed. The rest of the army has been reduced to 2,500 men of dubious intent. Food is lacking, as is forage. There is no money to give to the soldiers.' (*Revue historique de la Revolution Française*, 1912, p. 115.)

26 Mack was sent off to Briançon as a prisoner of war. He was later allowed to escape by the French who thought he might be more beneficial to the republic in the Austrian army.

27 They advanced, whereupon Luigi Brandi, the chief of the lazzaroni, remarked 'I don't like the look of these toffs, we should cut their heads off'. But he allowed them in and was persuaded shortly afterwards to go and collect food supplies. The patriots seized control of the fort in his absence.

28 Marinelli, p. 33. The perpetrators were tracked down in 1799 and executed on 6 May at the scene of the crime. These included Giuseppe Maimone, the wigmaker, Gioacchino Lubrano, for having fired the first shot and Salvatore Capuano for burning the bodies.

29 Drusco, p.23.

30 Pépé, p. 44.

5 Republic: New Rulers

1 Maresca (1889), p. 50.

2 Led by Thiebault, who made his way through the crowd, later recording 'I shouted, as loud as I could 'Long live San Gennaro!', even though he had been dead 1492 years, and threw a handful of coins towards the most menacing looking characters.'

3 Lahure, p. 206.

4 In Rome, news of the fall of Naples was confirmed on 28 January. That evening a farce, entitled 'Ferdinand, conqueror of Rome' was put on at the Argentina theatre.

5 Drusco, p.38-9.

6 On 18 April the ministers were G. Manthoné, Macedonio, V. De Filippis and G. Pigliacelli. The salary of the ministers was set at 5,000 Ducats a year, whilst the editors working on finalising the republic's proclamations received a measly 800. Twas ever thus.

7 Nelson used Vesuviana out of contempt as did Maria Carolina, in an acerbic letter to Gallo on 9 February. No contemporary Italian or French document used the term the Parthenopian Republic.

8 The giant statue of Jove, in front of the palace, got a red cap on 18 February.

9 A more boisterous crowd watched the opera Nicaboro on 27 January. De Nicola's diary entry from the next day reads 'yesterday, at the Teatro di S. Carlo there was a lot of agitation and they shouted 'long live liberty, death to the tyrant' and they also included the names of other people who were hated by the nation, including Acton, Castelcicala and others.' Over at the Teatro dei Fiorentini it was said that on the 29th the theatre's prima ballerina danced half naked before an astonished crowd. De Nicola, reeling from all the rumours, was dubious, noting 'I don't believe it, for the maxim of the government is 'virtue and liberty' and not libertinage'.

10 The diarist De Nicola noted 'without a doubt Naples was most fortunate to have been taken by a French army led by this general as he was averse to violence, most averse to spilling blood, humane and noble. An officer told me that had Bonaparte met with such resistance, then the city would have been burnt, ruined and plundered.'

11 Some senior officers were able to avoid inconveniences by having the municipality pay for their upkeep. General Bonamy stayed at the La Crocelle Inn and charged the bill of 2,949 Ducats, 13.54 of which was for ice cream, to the city of Naples.

12 The paper money was 56% its nominal value on 11 February and 60% on 28 February.

13 This led to the rather unusual situation of a judge such as Ippolito Porcinari, a man who had tried Jacobin conspirators in 1794, now working to impose revolutionary justice.

14 In Barletta Camillo Elefante's diary noted that a new sense of equality reigned at church: 'people were to be allowed into church wearing everyday clothes and could sit where they pleased, and this was done so as not to prefer the aristocracy and as a mark of equality.'

15 The Marchese di Montrone did change his name to Timoleone dei Bianchi.

16 It was written by Pier Nicola Annonj using the pseudonym Niniolo Antrianocipe. He had already shocked readers by publishing a pamphlet on liberty and equality for the monks of Naples.

17 Lahure, p. 336.

18 The names of the officers reflect the international origins of the Neapolitan army, with Luigi Inchoff, Giovanni Macklin, Michele Huber and Giuseppe Foster acting as captains.

19 Martinengo stated that 'in the last two years the Barbary Corsairs have seized more than 225 Neapolitan merchant ships'. On 8 February Nelson instructed his captains to view shipping from Naples 'as a good and lawful prize'.

20 Scherer was quite explicit about what Macdonald should do with his power: 'seize all of the wealth of the kingdom, and thereby assure that the French Republic is conserved. Feed and pay the troops. Give what help you can to the provisional government, make friends amongst them, but do not trust them.'

21 Cirillo was a doctor and botanist, and was fluent in English, Dr Burney noting that he spoke English better than any Italian he knew, and 'as such had been the physician to much of the English community ... his politics were reformist, his education enlightened'.

22 Coppa-Zuccari. Volume III, p. 61.

23 Pronio was born around Vasto in 1760 and had started his career in the Church. André Vieusseux described him as 'a stout, square-built man, with a sunburnt countenance, looking something between a country priest and a farmer'. Success did not make him universally popular even amongst his allies. Pasquale Cayro, who was a royalist, noted that Pronio was a 'villain, thief, murderer, issued from the galleys'. Pronio was one of the more humane insurgents but, confusingly, he was given the nickname 'Gran Diavolo', which has become confused with that more brutal insurgent 'Fra Diavolo'. ·

24 ASPN, 2009, p. 276.

25 This was not a unique case, there are other examples of the mob chanting death to the giacomini rather than to the giacobini.

26 An inhabitant recalled that the French were 'drunk with wine and exhausted from their sins and crimes'. The republican volunteers from Foggia were particularly keen on sacking the town which generated bad feeling between the two towns which rumbled on over the summer.

27 The next day he went into further detail about French gastronomic habits: 'The French 64th Regiment of Line infantry arrived and was billeted in

different houses as were the officers and NCOs and these wanted coffee, with milk, at one o'clock or had a breakfast at half past one consisting of a large number of eggs and mozzarella, bread and wine. At noon they had a lunch of some six dishes as well as lots of eggs and drinks in abundance and for supper they had the local wine or rosolio, although some had coffee, and they were allowed to take back with them what they wanted. They consume a lot of wine and also put it in the soup at supper time which they then drank after having eaten the bread. Some wanted to take full bottles back with them so they could drink it in the night if they woke up and then they could fall back to sleep'.

28 'Carafa's mounted Legion, so-called as the former Count of Ruvo and Duke of Andria is now their colonel, wear the uniform of the French-Neapolitan Republic with cropped hair and moustaches'.

29 Elefante noted 'It was horrendous to behold a French soldier with the richly embroidered cloth of gold taken from the Holy Virgin Mary of Mount Carmel church. He was sheltering from the rain with it and trying to sell it.'

6 Ruffo: Royalists and Renegades

1 The relationship between Acton and Ruffo was sour. Ruffo alleged that Acton was a traitor and would write to the king in March 1799 that 'the proximity of the General compromises the security of Your Majesty, and that of the royal family'. Nelson aligned with Acton, telling Troubridge on 25 April 'In respect to the cardinal, he is a swelled-up priest'.

2 According to the queen 'He goes to the theatre upon an evening, or a masked ball, and is happy; I admire him, he thinks as much about Naples as he does the Hottentots'.

3 The queen was horrified when 140 blind French invalids, swept up on Sicilian shores on the return leg from Egypt, landed at Augusta. Most were massacred, Charles Lock reporting that 'the rage of the populace went so far as to roast and eat their livers'. This event took place in January 1799, and Nelson's comment on the event, written to Captain Louis, does him little credit: 'At Augusta, 140 French arrived from Alexandria; 82 were killed by the people on the 20th, the rest were saved by a Neapolitan frigate (what a fool!)'.

4 Despatches, III, p. 267. The letter was dated 16 February and was contemporaneous to the queen's complaint. The gouty General Charles Stuart arrived at Messina in early March 1799 and placed 1000 English troops in the citadel.

5 The lottery was introduced on 26 January 1799. The winning numbers in the first draw were 35, 2, 34, 48, 71.

6 Caracciolo and some 571 other officers and ratings seem to have left Messina for the capital before 15 February. The queen was incensed, and felt betrayed: 'We are in danger of losing our navy which wishes to go to Naples with Caracciolo. All the officers request that they be allowed to go to Naples and we'd have ships without officers and without crews, and then be easy prey for the French'.

7 Sacchinelli, p. 95.

8 ASPN, 1881, p. 304.

9 Artillery sent by Troubridge was also landed at Policastro, and was commanded by a volunteer, Captain William Darley. He was involved in operations around Salerno in May, as Reverend Willyams noted: 'Captain Darly [sic] of the marines, who had landed here [Salerno] from the *Zealous*, being well acquainted with the Italian language, volunteered to penetrate into the country to join Cardinal Ruffo.'

10 Sacchinelli, p. 141.

11 Petromasi, p. 5. Another chronicler, Antonio Stassano of Eboli, noted that, as well as deserters, criminals were joining the ranks, 'only in order to obtain a certificate of service so that they would be amnestied for their crimes'.

12 ASPN, 2009, p. 279.

13 Croce (1943), Maria Carolina to Ruffo, 21 March.

14 The 39 Frenchmen were convalescents returning from Alexandria in Egypt when they were run aground in Calabria.

15 The king commented 'I regret that you were too gentle towards the rebels, especially those who had formerly been in my service'.

16 Gennaro Rivelli soon achieved a certain notoriety for brandishing the head of a Jacobin woman, along with a foetus cut from her body, before a Calabrian crowd.

17 Nelson was not impressed by either the Portuguese or Neapolitan ships, writing at the end of November that 'the Portuguese squadron are totally useless' and then on 7 January that 'I have nominally a great force but anybody is heartily welcome to the Neapolitan and Portuguese ships'. Christies, sale 26 June 1996.

18 John Rushout, later 2nd Baron Northwick, who had been in Italy for most of the 1790s.

19 Willyams, p. 182.

20 Speciale was sent from Palermo with instructions from Nelson and Hamilton, and acted under Troubridge, the king had merely appointed him. The king hoped the judges would be severe, telling Ruffo that *Mazzi e panelle fanu i figli belli*, literally 'the rod and bread make for good sons'. Ruffo thought the appointment 'impolitic' and likely to make Naples resist even more ardently.

21 Troubridge told Lady Hamilton 'I have given the old Judge all the wholesome advice I am master of, and tomorrow he means to begin'. The prisoners were sent to be degraded by the Bishop of Cefalu, and then returned to Procida for execution on 15 June. They were hanged and 'the crowd watched in profound silence but eventually they began to shout 'long live the king' and seemed satisfied to see them justly punished'.

22 Nelson remarked: 'our friend Troubridge had a present made him the other day, of the head of a Jacobin; and makes an apology to me, the weather being very hot, for not sending it here.'

23 BL Add. MSS 34490.

24 Filippo Acton (1739-1820), a lieutenant colonel in Neapolitan service, was taken to Naples and held in St Elmo.

25 The Allies suffered a further setback when Colonel Jauch, who had been sent up with Oswald of the *Perseus* to gain control of Neapolitan territory in Tuscany at Orbitello and on Elba, also failed. Oswald's complaints

at Jauch's cowardice infuriated Nelson. However, Nelson's response is disconcerting: 'the king must instantly order his trial and if guilty of cowardice or treachery he must be shot and degraded in the most infamous manner, what a villain, good for to see shot flying and not taking the post of honour entrusted to him by his gracious master. If an example is not made of this wretch for he has not one inch of a man about him, the king will never be well served for who does not like to live if dishonour is no disgrace, excuse my feelings but I cannot bear such gracious monarchs should be so ill-served. .... Lay me at the feet of their majesties, tell me how I can best serve them, only disgrace this Hog and my life is at their disposal ....'. (Zabriskie Collection.)

26 It was hardly the Terror. On 14 May a man who was disseminating counter-revolutionary propaganda was placed under house arrest. As punishment a member of the revolutionary society went to visit him and lecture him on his civic duties.

27 In the course of the life of the republic the council would have 25 sessions. Pagano presided over eight sessions, Cirillo over the rest.

28 Led by Rocco Lentini, Giuseppe Renti, Timoleone Bianchi, Francesco Rossi and Gabriele Manthonè.

7 Reconquest: The Republic in Peril

1 Micheroux, whose family was Walloon in origin, was born in Naples in 1755. He was a cadet in the Hainault Regiment in 1771 and owed much of his advancement to being a freemason.

2 A man who seems to have provoked Nelson's ire. When he heard a Russian ship had visited Ball Nelson told his subordinate 'I hate the Russians, and if she came from their admiral at Corfu, he is a blackguard'. In September he would write 'The Russian Admiral has a polished outside, but the bear is close to the skin'. An odd attitude from a man who had considered volunteering for the Russian fleet in April 1790. Nelson, however, was convinced the Russians wanted to take Constantinople and the Greek islands, as well as Malta, which, Nelson hoped, might be 'restored' to Naples.

3 The 27th Light (1st and 3rd battalions) had 854 men and there were some French and Italian gunners, 17 sappers and five men from the 11th Cavalry.

4 Gaeta had lost its Polish garrison and now had 1,300 men of the 7th and 8th Light under the colonel of the former, Joseph-Jacques Berger.

5 Just over 1,000 men of the 64th Line, 830 men of the 2nd Cisalpine Regiment, 250 sappers and artillerymen and 76 cavalry from the 11th Cavalry. He was also responsible for 800 sick and 120 'Turkish' prisoners being held in the fort. Strange as it seems these were probably the gardeners from the palace at Caserta, for the king used captured North Africans as labourers.

6 Girardon, p. 38.

7 Maresca (1895), p. 83.

8 The queen also thought it worth telling Ruffo that the king meant to be merciful, but her caustic tone belied the seeming reasonableness of her argument: 'The king could and should, as a Christian, and father, forgive his horrible, wretched and ungrateful subjects; but he should not enter into a

treaty or armistice out of seeming afraid.' Which, of course, suggests that he might be willing to enter into a treaty from a position of strength.

9 Sachinelli, p. 156-161.

10 A message she repeated to Gallo that May: 'I beg you that there should be no truce, or pardon or treaty with those wretches. They have to be punished.'

11 He was more charitable in a letter to Troubridge, telling the British officer that 'the clemency shown by Micheroux has had a great effect and should be imitated at Naples, except in the case of the very worst offenders.'

12 Maresca (1895), p. 124. Acton told Ruffo 'Micheroux is not authorised to forgive wrongdoers, nor to publish pardons'. Which implies that Ruffo was.

13 Henry Baillie, sweetly rendered as Don Gregorio Bayley in Italian records, was a Scot born in 1756 and who entered Russian service in 1783. Robert Lyall met Baillie at Sevastopol in 1818 and found him 'a plain, open man who had many of the characteristics of the seafaring profession'. Baillie was in bad health and surrounded by an astonishing number of cats.

14 Micheroux (Ministero degli affari esteri, 4138) puts the force at '330 soldiers, 120 sailors and 20 Russian artillerymen, and 30 of His Majesty's naval soldiers'. Russian sources have Baillie's expeditionary force as consisting of 8 officers, 21 NCOs, 27 grenadiers, 318 marines, 7 drummers, and, for this campaign conducted by gentlemen, two barbers and a servant. He also had 156 Russian sailors, 36 artillerymen and 6 guns and 31 Neapolitans from the *Fortuna* corvette. The infantry were drawn from Lieutenant-Colonel Skipor's battalion, some of the 45 officers and 2,056 marines assigned to Ushakov's squadron.

15 Ministero degli affari esteri, 4138, letter dated 6 June.

16 It was here that Ruffo received two Ottoman emissaries. They dined with the cardinal and were offered wine, which, according to Sacchinelli, the Turks took, saying 'defend Christians, drink wine'.

17 Battaglini (2000), II, p. 49.

18 'Their army has 4,500 infantry, three companies of volunteer hussars, an artillery unit, all without discipline and badly organised. There is a large but very ignorant general staff at the head of which sits the Minister of War, Manthone, whom the government had promoted to the rank of commander in chief.'

19 After his key role in the fall of the monarchy, this veteran had spent the first months of the republic surrounded by a coterie of beautiful women at the casino of Chiatamone. He then reluctantly raised a small republican cavalry regiment, deserting with it in April 1799.

20 Pepe, p. 74. Girardon's account of the episode was 'The Neapolitan general, Manthone, sent 1,200 men, and two howitzers, against Marigliano to there form the vanguard of the column which was to march on Puglia. When these soldiers arrived they set about pillaging and the inhabitants rose up against them. The soldiers fled, abandoning their artillery and weapons so that they could keep the items they had stolen, and fled back to the capital.'

21 Maresca (1895), p. 152.

22 Had not Maria Carolina written on 5 April that 'no mercy should be shown to those who have rebelled against God and myself'.

23 The queen later hardened her attitude towards the Neapolitan seaman, telling Ruffo 'the conduct of that ungrateful wretch horrifies me'. She also accused Caracciolo of having issued a proclamation in which the king was called 'the most vile tyrant'.

24 Helfert (1882), p. 567. Nelson was also inclined towards vengeance, telling the Duke of Clarence on 10 May that 'The Jacobins must now shift for themselves, and I hope they will be severely punished, in person by their king, as they already have been, in pocket, by their Allies'.

25 When the war was over De Nicola made a note in his diary of a letter Ruffo is alleged to have sent to Acton, the cardinal writing that pardon would open doors and that 'with this system, general, with prudence, good conduct, humanity and religion, I have reconquered the kingdom and arrived before Naples where I was welcomed and respected. I did what nobody else would have dreamed of doing'.

26 Bloodthirsty Mammone would be arrested in 1802, his royal masters fearing that he was becoming too powerful in his fief.

27 Girardon could hardly expect any help from the French in Rome. General Garnier didn't have the manpower and by June he was attempting to bribe his Roman National Guard into the field by offering them 'a bonus of 6 ecus and a pair of boots and a shirt'.

28 Ministero degli affari esteri, 4138, letter dated 6 June.

29 At Bisceglia a diarist noted 'Our women are not at all afraid of the Turks, some of them even saying that once they have chased the French from the kingdom they will come back here and sleep with them'. They passed through again at the end of July: 'Two mounted Turks arrived at the entrance to the city one with a white cloth on his head and his shoulders and he was carrying a red silk banner with a white crescent in the middle and a silver crescent by the pole. Following them came around 20 disorganised Turkish troops, badly clothed and in different styles. Behind the commander came a coach containing another officer, an interpreter and members of the municipality. The men did not want to eat meat which had been set before them, but had a salad of lettuce, cucumber and onions. After eating this they went to bathe in the sea and some women came to wash their shirts and to see and to flirt with these circumcised men. But the men finished and only said thank you to the women and that is all they got.'

30 Francesco Macdonald was the son of Giuseppe Macdonald de Klor Renald (Clan Ranald), and Maria Luigia Molloy, and was born in Pescara in 1776. He was later reputed to be the lover of Caroline Bonaparte, supposedly marrying her in 1830. She herself had been queen of Naples when wife of Joachim Murat, who ruled Naples from 1808 to 1815.

31 Nelson left Palermo writing to Lady Hamilton that 'to tell you how dreary and uncomfortable the *Vanguard* appears is only telling you what it is to go from the pleasantest society to a solitary cell'. A needy Sir William told him 'I can assure you that neither Emma nor I knew how much we loved you

until this separation, and we are convinced that your Lordship feels the same as we do'.

32 Morrison II, p. 47. He also changed his will on 25 May, gifting two snuffboxes to Lady Hamilton and a ring to Sir William. It might not all have been chivalric bombast; on 28 May he was complaining about his shattered carcass.

33 Troubridge passed on Nelson's instructions and confirmed Foote as taking charge of the blockade of Naples, governor general of the islands and commanding officer of the troops there.

34 Foote, p. 56.

35 Foote, p. 61. The 'us' isn't made clear but the end of the letter closes with 'with every kind wish from all of this house' makes it clear that he, at the very least, meant the Hamiltons. The thirteen Jacobins hanged on 1 June included a pharmacist and two farm labourers.

8 *Restoration: Naples Recaptured*

1 ASPN, 1928, p. 254. Micheroux, in his report to Acton, quoted later, says that he told the republicans that some categories of transgressors would not be allowed to go.

2 ASPN 1899, p. 452. Petromasi claims that the Calabrians burnt down the fort's gate and broke in, killing the garrison.

3 Pasquale Cayro, a royalist, was told that 'a general of artillery who was around 90 years old, and was no longer capable of military service, had taken shelter in the Monteoliveto monastery and was living in an apartment with the abbot of those monks, when the Calabrians, along with the lazzeroni who called themselves royalists, broke in and sacked everything, even going as far as to seize the armchair where the old man used to rest.' ASPN, 2009, p. 237. Giuseppe De Lorenzo, who was there, recalled that 'a mass of inhabitants, brigands, women, urchins and armed men' descended on the monastery to loot it. They were led by the man who used to make his wigs.

4 Ronga, p. 139.

5 ASPN 1928, p. 252, 14 June 1799. The Russians, consisting of 100 marines, 30 sailors and two guns, were under the command of Lieutenant Alexander. They lost three dead and eight wounded. Sergeant Roman Linev distinguished himself in the battle for which he was promoted to lieutenant by the czar.

6 Captain Foote also accepted Rovigliano's surrender and informed Nelson that 'to prevent the effusion of blood I was induced to grant rather more favourable terms to the garrison of Castellammare; at sun set yesterday [the 15th] evening this important fortress, and gun-boats, were delivered up to Captain Oswald ... the prisoners are in number about three hundred.' The surrender terms stated that the prisoners would be treated as prisoners of war, coming onto British vessels to receive protection, with Foote interceding on their behalf with the king, or alternatively, they could 'go where they think proper'.

7 He would be executed, along with General Spano, at Ischia in July 1799.

8 Egerton 2640, 23 June.

9 De Nicola was fortunate in that his building billeted a small group of regular troops commanded by 'an Englishman calling himself His Highness Cesar', ie the Corsican De Cesaris.

10 This tugging of pigtails to see if they were genuine was widespread as the republican Vito Treroteli from Grumo recounted: 'the Calabrians pulled on one's queue to see if one had a Jacobin hairstyle; a friend of mine had attached mine so strongly with pins that it withstood being tugged numerous times by the Calabrians.'

11 Kotzebue, III, page 132, which includes the anecdote about the naked man, omitted from the English version *Travels through Italy*. Cannibalism did take place in Naples in 1799. There was a belief that by eating the body of someone who had died a violent death then he would be in no position to visit you as a malignant spirit.

12 Sacchinelli, p. 219.

13 Petromasi, p. 69. The poor woman mentioned here was probably Laurence Prota.

14 Writing in 1802 Joseph Forsyth commented 'A gentleman, whom I knew at Naples, had unguardedly entered a street where a circle of such cannibals stood revelling round a fire. He wished to retreat; but he was afraid of appearing afraid. He, therefore, advanced towards the crowd, who instantly seized and threatened him with the fate of a rebel. In vain did he protest his loyalty to the king and cardinal. 'You must prove it,' said they; 'here, take this broiled slice of a Jacobin's haunch and eat it before us.' He shuddered at the idea and hesitated for a moment, till one of the monsters forced it into his mouth, and thus created a perpetual loathing of all animal food.'

15 Lorenzo had a similar experience: 'I will omit, for the sake of not disturbing my readers, all the insults heaped upon us by the populace, suffice it to say that, by the time we reached our destination, I was half-dead and blinded from all the slapping, hitting and punching, much of it encouraged by our guards.' He also confirms that the prisoners being held in the prisons were naked and quite often wounded: 'There we found a number of unfortunates in the same condition, although we were a little more fortunate than they as they had been stripped naked and had been brought here, thus, in procession, and, what is worse, many of them were wounded, some mortally, and, within an hour, two of them had died.'

16 His description of the place was 'The vast halls adjoining the public granary and destined to contain corn intended for the consumption of the city were converted into prisons. The utter want of every kind of cleanliness, the husks of the different grains which were scattered about the place, the insects which abounded there, and the immense number of persons who were crowded together in it, rendered it an extremely unhealthy abode. In the hall where I was there were upwards of three hundred prisoners, who had no other resting place than the bare ground.'

17 De Nicola noted 'notwithstanding the proclamations prohibiting arrests and looting, the people, united with the Calabrians, continue to seize people and plunder everything'.

18 Nor would the Russians be supplying troops in time. The 12,000 originally destined 'to liberate the territories of His Sicilian Majesty from the French yoke, and then restore order and tranquillity', as Paul I put it (Ministero degli affari esteri, 4138), had been diverted into assisting Suvorov in northern Italy.

19 Ruffo seems to have had only 200 Albanians, 700 Calabrian regulars, 700 under La Marra, 400 under Tschudy, 800 fusiliers and 450 cavalry that could be termed reliable, along with Micheroux's Russians. Acton told Hamilton on the 19 June that Ruffo had '32,000 men, 15 of which are under organisation as troops', a gross exaggeration.

20 Cesare della Valle, who had quit the National Guard and was hiding in Monte di Dio recalled 'The patriots had established a position on the Certosa, which was being protected by the French garrison in Saint Elmo, and they swept the street with grapeshot so that nobody could come out of their houses'.

21 Maresca (1895), p.183. Micheroux told Pousset 'if they ask what hope there is, tell them they may save themselves and embark for France on transports, leaving in good time and putting an end to their woe'.

22 That same day Ruffo had informed Micheroux that 'I learnt from a report by the officer commanding the artillery battery directed against the Uovo fort that the commandant of the fort would treat with Count Thurn but not with me, on account of me being a clergyman'.

23 ASPN 1928, p. 257-258. Ruffo to Micheroux, 17 June 1799.

24 ASPN 1928, p. 257. Ruffo to Micheroux, 17 June 1799.

25 ASPN 1928, p. 256. A message from 17 June 1799.

26 Foote had sent Captain John Harward's *San Leon* brig to Palermo with the Castellammare capitulation. He sent a xebec to Procida to escort the prisoners of war he had taken at Castellammare. Humanely, he told David Morgan of the Marines to ensure that 'you will not only treat the persons committed to your charge kindly and civilly, but you will do your utmost to prevent their being insulted in any way whatever'.

27 Enrico Michele L'Aurora was a Roman Jacobin who had 'imbibed the maxims of Robespierre' and volunteered to form an Italian Legion for France during the Terror. Once this failed to materialise, he founded the Emulators of Brutus, and attempted to create a utopian republic in the Duchy of Castro, before insurgents chased him out in November 1798. He took part in organising the Neapolitan National Guard, and was made commandant of the fort in May 1799. Interestingly, L'Aurora had, in 1797, sworn to kill Napoleon for having betrayed the ideals of the French Revolution.

28 This is the message Charles Lock mentioned, in which Acton ordered Ruffo to come to terms at any price.

29 NLS MS.3599, ff.50-53, 22nd August.

30 Foote's note (Foote, p. 112) runs 'Being grieved at the misfortunes which naturally afflict a nation immersed in all the horrors of civil war, and earnestly wishing to restore peace and tranquillity to your unhappy country, I am willing, previous to having recourse to arms, to observe to you, that your situation is truly dangerous, and to offer you an asylum under the flag of my sovereign.'

31 The defiance was more surprising because the garrison was so small. One of them Onofrio Fiani, who had his arm broken in the siege, recalled 'The Uovo fort was defended by 130 youths, all educated in letters but never having learned siegecraft or the art of military defence. We did not sleep for nine days, we ate little and badly, and worked desperately.'

32 'I have sent 200 of the foreign troops, and now send 500 more of our fusiliers to Chiaja; but the fright has been great, and they go reluctantly. They must be placed in the houses, where they will make a better stand, than when uncovered and unsheltered.' (Foote, p. 145).

33 BL Add 34912, letter to Hamilton dated June 1797 [sic].

34 Foote, p. 58. Foote added in the same letter 'If St Elmo cannot be bought, it will be advisable to blow it, and its vile tenants, into the air, more especially if foreign force is not immediately expected'. This is the first suggestion that the French might be bribed into surrendering.

35 Méjan, p. 27.

36 ASPN 1928, p. 264.

37 ASPN 1928, p. 264.

38 Croce, p. 216. These were the queen's opinions, which, despite being forthright and emphatic, did not carry the weight of a legal command.

39 Ruffo told Micheroux 'I have just now received the letter from the English Vice Admiral which Your Excellency enclosed with your letter'.

40 Foote, page 152. Note the promise that should the republicans be assured that they will be forgiven then they would come out of the forts.

41 Some in the Neapolitan camp were horrified, Count Thurn writing to Acton on 21 June that 'the conditions for the capitulation of the forts in the city are not very advantageous, especially as the castle of St Elmo is not to be included therein.' But he did add 'we are most eagerly expecting the evacuation of these castles', which shows that the royalists were ready to abide by the terms. It was Thurn who sent a copy of the capitulation to Acton the next day, saying that it was fear of the arrival of the French fleet which persuaded them to agree.

42 Regarding St Elmo he stated that the 'fortress cannot, with propriety, be attacked until advice is received of the arrival of the republicans at Toulon' (Foote p. 160).

43 ASPN 1928, p. 267.

44 Méjan was sympathetic to the cause of the Neapolitan republic, writing to Foote hat 'I am quite amused, sir, with the political existence which you wish to give to that phantom of a monarch, whom you call Sicilian Majesty; he will, before long, experience the treatment which a monster, who has only existed to render mankind unhappy, merits, like all other tyrants of his description' (Foote, p. 132).

45 Girardon replied 'I am delighted that you obtained terms for the patriots. What became of the government? If you feel you can no longer hold out, evacuate to Capua after spiking your guns'.

46 Gutteridge, p. 322.

47 ASPN, 1899, p. 458. Indeed at the Uovo fort Onofrio Fiani heard that 'The majority of the garrison resolved to set fire to the powder magazine, and follow the example of Vigliena, but this was prevented by the vigilance of the commander, and by the advantageous terms of the capitulation then being offered and which would spare us from becoming the victims of a vendetta.' ASPN, 1896, p. 403.

48 ASPN 1928, p. 273. 22 June 1799. The republicans under St Elmo were in a bad situation, De Nicola noting that 'those outside St Elmo lacked any

provisions to sustain themselves and St Elmo wouldn't give them anything as, naturally, the French only think of themselves'.

49 Foote, p. 103. As Foote explained: 'I was at that time acting as the immediate representative of my king, whose dignity with foreign states I had no right to infringe'. Foote justified his signature with 'I signed this capitulation lest, on a reverse of fortune, or the arrival of the enemy's fleet, it might have been asserted, that my refusal was the cause of such misfortunes as might occur, and because I considered that the Cardinal was acquainted with the will and intention of his Sovereign; and that the Count de Thurn had told me that the Chevalier de Micheroux was authorised to act in a diplomatic character.'

50 Foote, p. 82, 23 June.

51 ASPN, 1888, p. 72. The British were the 12 marines taken from the *Zealous*. Captain Saverio Salfi in the Nuovo fort calls them 'the English prisoners in our hands'.

52 ASPN, 1928, p. 270. Regarding prisoners in royal care, the cardinal noted 'they will be well treated and I will issue orders accordingly forthwith, for we have a duty to humanity which I concede should be applied to all.'

53 ASPN, 1928. p. 273.

54 ASPN 1928, p. 273.

55 Micheroux wrote 'The preparations for the departure of the rebels were finally brought to a conclusion and on the morning of the 23rd they themselves requested that the Russian troops occupy and secure the entrances to the fortress and the palace'. ASPN, 1899, p. 459.

56 ASPN 1928, p. 274

57 Ruffo to Micheroux, ASPN 1928, p. 274.

9 Rancour: Nelson's Arrival

1 The king had told his wife on 7 June that 'you have much more talent and sense than me, you know how to deal with them and to ensure that matters turn out properly and most worthily for our cause'.

2 This was clause 6, clause 10 noted 'the acts of mercy concerning the notorious offenders, and any pardoning of the same, are reserved to the king *excepting those set down in the articles of capitulation*'.

3 Pettigrew, I, p. 229. Letter to Nelson, dated 11 June, signed Charlotte.

4 At that point Nelson was desirous of battle, writing to Lady Hamilton that 'I long to be at the French fleet as much as ever a Miss longed for a husband'. Then adding 'to the queen you will, I'm sure, say everything which is proper. Answer for my attachment, and that I will fight in defence of her crown and dominions whenever the proper time arrives, and that the damned French shall not get to Sicily with their fleet but through my heart's blood.'

5 The king's diary entry read 'Returned home before midnight, where I received the good news that the royalist vanguard was already in Naples and that the Carmine fort had fallen to them.' The queen's note to Gallo on the next day confirmed this: 'I have the consolation of informing you that, apart from the castles, Naples is in the hands of its legitimate sovereign.'

6 Pettigrew, I, p. 229. Letter dated 18 June.

7 Egerton MS, ff. 259-60.

8 Helfert (1882), p. 578. Acton told Sir William that 'Naples is in our hands excepting St Elmo, with the French in it. Castel Nuovo and Dell'Uovo in the hands of the felons. In those two places consists at present the Neapolitan republic.'

9 Hamilton told Nelson 'you may decide your own way; for we are under no kind of engagement'.

10 Nelson told Lady Hamilton on 19 June that 'I should ... go to Naples, that their majesties my settle matters there, and take off (if necessary, the head of) the cardinal'. It is an early indication that Acton and the queen, and the Hamiltons and Nelson, saw Ruffo as an enemy. Acton told Hamilton that 'I hope my dear Sir that all our hopes in a few days will be blessed with success by the excellent and brave Lord Nelson's operation: which will, I flatter, put an end to the business without any cross meddling of the cardinal'.

11 The queen had expressed herself to Emma Hamilton that 'we rely on your arrival with the squadron, and on the firmness of the admiral'.

12 Charles Lock informed his father on 30 June that 'Sir Wm and Lady Hamilton embarked with great secrecy for Naples about 10 days ago, in the *Foudroyant* which came singly for them off the harbour with Ld. Nelson on board. I underwent a severe mortification in not being invited to accompany Sir William or receiving any intimation of their designs.'

13 Maresca (1895), p. 203.

14 This was later 'read and explained, and rejected by the cardinal'.

15 Despatches, III, p. 385. On 25 June Nelson sent Captain Hoste to cruise off Gaeta and instructed him 'you are not to subscribe to any terms with rebels, but unconditional submission to their sovereign'.

16 ASPN, 1928, p. 275. Micheroux wrote the next day (Ministero degli affari esteri, 4138) that 'I must not forget to mention that yesterday Nelson's fleet arrived in this harbour, it is 18 ships strong, of which six are three-deckers.'

17 ASPN, 1928, p. 274.

18 NLS MS.3599, ff.50-53, 22 August.

19 Foote, p. 21-22.

20 Foote, p. 23.

21 Rose, p. 236. My emphasis.

22 Gutteridge, p. 208. This admits that a capitulation was in place, and that Hamilton though that annulling it, merely because Ruffo had been reinforced, was perfectly right.

23 A letter which was initially begun to Lord St Vincent, then sick and departing for Britain. Nelson told Keith: 'I sent Captains Troubridge and Ball instantly to the Cardinal, Vicar-general, to represent to his Eminence my opinion of the infamous terms entered into with the rebels, and also two papers, which I enclose. His Eminence said he would send no papers, that if I pleased I might break the armistice, for that he was tired of his situation.'

24 Méjan's own account recorded 'I received two summonses, one in English, by Admiral Nelson, the other signed by the ministers of Naples. Both required the fort of St Elmo to surrender within two hours'.

25 ASPN 1928, p. 275.

26 By way of confirmation of such republican desperation he noted down rumours that a mine had been placed under the royal palace and the forts.

27 Girardon at Capua recorded that, on 29 June, 'a spy, a child aged 15, sent from Naples, brought a letter from Méjan, commandant of the St Elmo fort, announcing that the British had arrived at Naples and that Admiral Nelson had summoned him to surrender the place'.

28 This Declaration reached Palermo on 27 June. Ferdinand wrote to Ruffo: 'I have heard, with inexpressible consolation, of the arrival, after dinner, of my frigate from Naples and also of the happy arrival there of the very noble and faithful admiral, Lord Nelson. I have read the declaration which he, in the form of observations, has despatched to you, which could not be more wise, reasonable and adapted to the end, and really saintly. I do not doubt that you immediately conformed to it, and acted on consequence on his advice'. Ruffo, of course, had already signed a capitulation, and was bound by it.

29 Despatches, III, p. 387. Dated 25 June.

30 BL Add 34912, letter to Hamilton dated June 1797 [sic].

31 ASPN, 1899, p. 459.

32 Foote, p. 74.

33 Gutteridge, p. 318-9. Letter to Greville, 14 July. Lady Hamilton kept Palermo informed, Acton noting 'Lady Hamilton wrote to the queen wherein Lord Nelson's intentions are mentioned'.

34 The names of the two senior British commanders occur in Foote's version of the text. Foote, in his *Vindication*, notes the treaty was already partly executed, despite Nelson's opinion of it, and that nobody wrote to ask Nelson's two superiors about it.

35 Captain Foote's intervention was not sought. Foote was sent to Palermo early on 28 June, as per the secret order by Nelson:'You are hereby directed to proceed in His Majesty's ship *Seahorse*, under your command, with all expedition to Palermo, and there wait the orders of their Sicilian Majesties, who may, in all probability, embark on board for this place.' When Foote brought the king into the bay of Naples Nelson once again sent the captain away with the *Thalia*.

36 Sacchinelli p. 251.

37 Rose, p. 236. Letter dated 25 June 1799.

38 As Micheroux noted: 'On the morning of the 25th captains Trowbridge and Ball came to me to demand that I send the ultimatum to St Elmo along with the other in the same vein in the name of Lord Nelson. At that meeting they also requested that I write to the commandant, enclosing the ultimatum. This was done, according to their wishes'.

39 The king, as soon as he heard about Ruffo's capitulation with the rebels had written to Governor Curtis saying it did not apply to prisoners in Procida. Speciale and Curtis were doing a fine job executing republicans. On 2 July it was the turn of Giuseppe Coppola who was hanged 'after a public confession of his misdeeds'.

40 Sacchinelli, p. 252.

41 ASPN 1928, p. 276. The talk of supplies is important. Should the capitulation be broken, then the situation would have to return to how it was before the agreement. So the republicans conserved their supplies, and received material from the royalists. Ruffo thought Micheroux was being too generous in what was allowed: 'as for us supplying forage for the horses, that's insolence as that's warlike material and goes too far, next they will be asking for gunpowder and bullets with which to kill us'.

42 An earlier attack on 23 June had seen the French destroy the Neapolitan Re regiment, the colonel saving himself by riding off in his shirt tails. Girardon noted how 'The flag was captured and our troops returned to camp, each soldier who had managed to seize an item of the colonel's clothing carrying it back on their bayonets'.

43 On the 25ᵗʰ the republicans had apparently threatened to ask Méjan to hang the hostages, starting with the bishops, then Micheroux's cousin, and then Dillon. The threat was because the transports weren't sailing, despite the good weather, and the patriots therefore suspected 'some act of violation' against the treaty.

44 Sacchinelli, p. 254.

45 That the rejection of a capitulation would lead to the reinstatement of the garrisons in the situation they were in before the treaty was signed was self-evident at the time. The Sardinian ambassador in Palermo, Cavaliere Balbo, writing on 26 June, noted that, 'Cardinal Ruffo granted a capitulation to the castles of Naples and to the country's Jacobins but the king and Nelson rejected it. They will have to take them by storm.'

46 ASPN 1928, p. 277. 26 June 1799.

47 Gutteridge, p. 232

48 Gutteridge, p. 233. 'Supporting your ideas' is an admission that the capitulation could now be carried out.

49 The note appears in Sacchinelli's memoirs as a facsimile, but historians have contested its authenticity even though Troubridge's name is, for once in a contemporary report, correctly spelled. Ruffo, however, clearly says that he received such a note from Captain Ball and Micheroux seems to have sent copies to Acton ('the enclosed documents as guarantees to the garrisons'), now unfortunately missing from the archives. On the 26ᵗʰ the captains were authorised to treat on 'all matters and things relative to the said siege of St Elmo, and all other things necessary for the good of His Majesty's service'.

50 ASPN, 1928, p. 278. Ruffo mentions 'what it says at the end of Nelson's letter'. This must be a letter missing from the archives, as Nelson does not discuss the capitulation at the end of any of his recent letters to Ruffo. The letter of guarantee also seems to be missing.

51 Sacchinelli, p. 256. Gutteridge also presents a translation of this text, but unaccountably misses out the last sentence.

52 Micheroux was accompanied by Troubridge and Ball when he gave his word of honour. The documents are missing from the archives.

53 NLS MS.3599, ff.50-53, letter from Lock to General Graham, 22 August 1799.

54 Gutteridge, p. 249. There is some controversy about the date of this letter. As Hamilton says 'yesterday morning' it looks as though it should be dated 27 June but the rebels were embarked on the evening of the 26th.

55 ASPN 1928, p. 278.

56 ASPN 1928, p. 279. The last enigmatic phrase refers to the fact that article 3 of the capitulation allowed the garrisons to march out with drums beating, flags flying and preceded by two pieces of artillery. De Nicola confirmed the cordon 'Russian troops are encamped at Santa Lucia a Mare [just south of the palace] and a cordon has been drawn from the heights of San Nicola Tolentino to the palace'.

57 Not all of them, a small body elected to remain in the San Martino Charterhouse.

58 Gutteridge, p. 251

59 ASPN, 1896, p. 401.

60 Ruffo told the king that 'The persecution of the Jacobins and non-Jacobins in the city was daily increasing the number of defenders in the castles and beneath St Elmo, and although we heard there were only 500 in the Nuovo fort, there were actually 800.' However, many of these had already escaped by the time of embarkation.

61 Gutteridge, 323.

62 The handover triggered some disorder, Vincenzo Minichini complaining that the Neapolitan artillery were in imminent danger of having their possessions pillaged by the British.

63 As Troubridge reported 'Agreeable to your lordship's orders, I landed with the English and Portuguese marines of the fleet on the 27 June [ie 26 June, the 27th is the nautical date], and, after embarking the garrisons of the castles Ovo and Nuovo, composed of French and rebels, I put a garrison in each'. Badham (1903), p. 55.

64 Gutteridge, p. 253.

65 Gutteridge, p. 252.

66 News of British actions on Procida even made it to Puglia. Gian Carlo Berarducci noted that 'They say that the English have executed large numbers of the patriots that were embarked for Toulon on the island of Procida or in the waters around the island'.

67 Gutteridge, p. 251.

68 Gutteridge, p. 277. Lady Hamilton, apparently told John Rushout that 'Well Mr--, we have most important news for you. The arch-traitor, Caracciolo, is taken. He was found concealed in a ditch, and now is onboard this vessel awaiting his trial, which Lord Nelson has appointed to take place at one o'clock today.'

69 Parsons, p. 4. Thurn was the commander of the only Neapolitan ship in those waters; the *La Sirena*, under Captain Diego Naselli, had only recently left for Palermo.

70 Thurn presided. Senior lieutenants Giambattista del Corat and Diodato Micheroux, and the more junior Giuseppe Niscemi and Andrea Caperozzo, were the other officers. Lieutenant Emanuele Lettieri, Thurn's aide-de-camp, acted as secretary..

71 BL Add MS 34912 f.135, dated 29 June, copy of original by J Tyson.

72 This stands in contrast to January 1799. In January Nelson, who had wanted to punish Campbell for burning the Neapolitan fleet, had told Acton 'was Commodore Campbell an English officer, I should instantly order him to be tried by a court-martial for the positive breach of my orders to the Marquis de Niza. I am sorry it cannot be done by me to an auxiliary squadron'. Nelson could similarly have declined involvement in the sentencing of the Neapolitan commodore.

73 Gutteridge, p. 277.

74 BL Add MS 34912 f.135, dated 29 June, copy of order signed by J. Tyson.

75 Gutteridge, p. 279. Nelson did not tell Acton about leaving Caracciolo's body on display for five hours, or having him buried at sea.

76 Lieutenant Parkinson, who was guarding Caracciolo, took his request that he be shot to Nelson. Nelson told Parkinson to attend to his duty.

77 BL Add 34944 f. 262, noted dated 29 June 1799.

78 And eerily reminiscent of Nelson's desire to have General Jauch punished in May.

79 Gutteridge, p. 279. The mention of conscience reflects a comment made by Nelson himself when he broke the convention before Livorno in December 1798. He declared 'I act, from the circumstance of the moment, as I feel it may be most advantageous for the honour of the cause which I serve, taking all responsibility on myself'.

80 Gutteridge, p. 287. Acton agreed 'Caracciolo did certainly deserve his fate; I think that the speedy execution will have done a proper and useful effect on the people'.

81 Palumbo, p. 215. The note is the list of republicans on Nelson's ships sent by the *Balloon* brig. The queen added 'I hope that things with the cardinal settle down, but I predict a few storms'.

82 Acton noted 'I flatter myself that the scoundrel Caracciolo and his adherents will have received a proper reward before his Majesty's arrival'.

83 Zabriskie Collection, Letter to Ferdinand, 30 June 1799. Local legend would have it that Caracciolo would attempt to deny the justice of his sentence by rising up from the depths, resurfacing in time to terrify the newly-returned king. As a tale of macabre revenge it is hard to beat but difficult to believe. Strangely, however, despite his dead body being weighted down with shot, Caracciolo's body was recovered and is now entombed in the Madonna della Catena church. He was as difficult to dispose of in death as he had been in life.

10 Retribution: Betrayal of the Republicans

1 The king's diary entry for 25 June, although the court had been prepared to treat with the French and countenance the departure of the rebels as recently as 12 June.

2 Not from Charles Lock who had this to say 'The Jacobin forces which are in the castles del Carmine, del Uovo and Castel Nuovo, with the remainder in an entrenched camp, have surrendered on conditions and are to be transported to Toulon. A very wise measure, though on the point of being rejected by the royalty party, as it effectively sweeps the kingdom of the disaffected who, when banished and their property alienated, may be considered virtually dead.'

3 Egerton MS, f. 269.

4 Hamilton, p. 231-2.

5 This is clearly the king's wish, but he had no legal grounds to stand on and carrying out this threat would have necessitated the garrisons returning to their forts and a resumption of hostilities.

6 Pettigrew, p. 235. Dated 25 June 1799.

7 Later, the queen would write to Lady Hamilton that 'I beg you to interpret and have interpreted to his lordship that my silence is only because it is impossible for me to express the depth of my gratitude for the heroic firmness that Lord Nelson showed at the dangerous moment.' Palumbo, p. 210.

8 The queen's views on the capitulation arrived on the 29 June, when she sent her annotated copy (see the annex).

9 Gutteridge, p. 256. Acton to Hamilton, 27 June.

10 Rose, pp. 238-9. Nelson's proclamation, published on 29 June, added that those 'within five miles of the city had 48 hours to give themselves up or be considered as being still in rebellion and enemies of his Sicilian Majesty'.

11 In a subsequent letter to Acton Hamilton noted that this proclamation was designed to ensnare those rebels who had avoided being caught in the British trap: 'should any very notorious rebel appear, Lord Nelson would confine him on board one of his ships as he has done by Manthone, Cirillo and many more from the polaccas, that have been the principals'. Acton would reply expressing his hope that 'we shall have in the king's forces [power] all those who triumphantly are still walking the streets in Naples, and may do further mischief'.

12 Gutteridge, p. 271. 28 June 1799. Acton's answer (Egerton 2640) on 30 June was: 'I have seen with the highest consolation what Lord Nelson has done with the rebels, and that no military honours were allowed for these scoundrels, the polacres remain as you tell me to His Majesty's disposition upon which the resolution is to be made as soon as possible.'

13 The intention to secure the transports was clear from much earlier on that day when a signal was given for all barges to be 'manned and armed'.

14 Battaglini (2000), II, p. 70.

15 Zabriskie Collection, Nelson to Ferdinand, 30 June 1799.

16 BL Add 34912, written from the *San Sebastian* on 15 July 1799.

17 The list, now in the Girdlestone Collection, was probably a copy of the one sent to the queen on the Portuguese ship the *Balloon*, under Captain Wilsh, and which the queen had described as 'your note on the Jacobins that have been arrested' and her gratitude that 'we have the main scoundrels'. Correspondence between the queen and Lady Hamilton was frequent 'I send her every night a messenger to Palermo, with all the news and letters, and *she gives me the orders* the same'. There are other lists of prisoners at the NMM. At the foot of a list of prisoners in a naval officer's hand, dated 3 July, the name of Dr Cirillo and the two Pignatellis has been added in LadyHamilton's handwriting (NMM GIR/3/A).

18 Tried and executed that afternoon.

19 On 13 July, after the king had arrived and was again on Nelson's flagship, the monarch told his wife: 'The leaders are being held in the holds of the ships,

and on our ship too, I don't know how they were selected, but we have Ciaja who is sometimes allowed to exercise on deck, and I have spoken to him'.

20 Battaglini (2000), II, p. 71.

21 Gutteridge, p. 277. 30 June. This odd assertion is confirmed by the lawyer De Nicola who noted in his diary on 29 June that 'the English admiral has threatened to cut off the prisoners' heads if St Elmo resists and harms the city'.

22 Foote had been scrupulous in adhering to the convention with the republicans from Castellammare and Rovigliano. Some were allowed to return home, including Eugenio Palumbo and Gabriele Pica who 'retired to their home in Naples, but they had scarcely reached it when they were surrounded by a group of Lazzari who robbed them of their clothes and ornaments and took them to the Granili del Ponte where they were thrust among the other prisoners, and reduced to a state of misery, exciting compassion even there.' The bulk of the prisoners, enjoying the guarantee of British protection, were in boats off Procida and on 26 June they were asked whether there were any amongst them who wished to go to Toulon, as Foote's expectation was that all the prisoners could be sent to France together. A view not shared by Acton who wrote to Hamilton 'if Captain Foote has kept his declaration, then these prisoners might come to Sicily, when they shall be ordered to Africa till further orders'. Hamilton passed this news on to Foote changing it to 'they shall be ordered to Ustica till further orders'. Acton had personally promised Foote that 'on my account the most obnoxious should only be confined during the then very unsettled state of the Neapolitan dominions'. However, all of them do indeed seem to have been arrested and tried, for the king noted that 'those from Castellammare and the castles are incarcerated, to the number of 4,000'. These were then also processed and tried as can be seen from the fate of the officers, and from a passage in one of Lock's letters to Graham, when he noted 'A memorial arrived here three days ago forwarded by Mr Compton and supported by an excellent letter from that worthy person begging the fulfilment of his majesty's gracious intentions pronounced in favour of the garrison of Castellammare, previous to his departure from Naples, as the tribunal was proceeding to try them for having been in arms against their sovereign. Whether this act of treachery will be given remains yet to be known'.

23 Sacchinelli, p. 262.

24 ASPN 1928, p, 280.

25 L'Aurora then had an interview with Nelson. His account, which can't be verified, runs: 'We had a heated argument, which ended by me saying that he had swindled me and that by violating the terms he, and his nation, would be eternally disgraced, that posterity would look upon his name with horror and loathing. Nelson, irritated, sent me to a dungeon, and I was kept locked up, shackled by hand and foot, half naked and suffering all manner of privations. I was in that state until the battle of Marengo, and was then sent to the penal island of Santo Stefano and released at the peace after 23 months of captivity.' [Ronga, p. 366.]

26 Morrison II, p. 56. The *Leviathan* was Duckworth's ship and the letter was signed by seven lieutenants (Peacocke, Church, Gregory, Kelly, Morrell,

Broeskman and Cottrell), a master (Holbrook) and a surgeon (Anderson). Lady Hamilton probably conveyed the request to Palermo but there was no royal pardon. The Piatti family was severely punished. Domenico and Antonio, held on the ship with Andreana, Elisabetta and Giovanni Battista, were executed on 20 August. Pietro Piatti was exiled. The family had its family jewels confiscated too, with Vincenzo Ballerini being rewarded 300 Ducats in January 1800 for revealing the hiding place.

27 BL, Add. MSS 34945.

28 Battaglini (2000), II, p. 72.

29 A second officer behaved more decently, and Salfi asked him whether the capitulation was to be carried out and received an enigmatic reply: 'your country is too rich, that is why Nelson acts as the hangman for your tyrant, and we his henchmen'.

30 This appears to be the case as following the final defeat of the republic the king sent a meal of 'macaroni, meat and other food to the Jacobins being held on the English ships, and had them informed that this came to them from the tyrant'.

31 Lady Hamilton had written to Greville on 19 July that 'we sit down to write in this heat and onboard you may guess what we suffer'.

32 Gutteridge, p. 324. That this *memoria* was sent is confirmed by Saverio Salfi who noted 'the Neapolitan patriots sent a *memoria* to Lord Nelson in which they deplored their situation, reminded him of the trust they placed in him, the honour of the English nation, and protested that the capitulation was solemn and sacred, and signed by the representatives of four kings and guaranteed by an agent of the French Republic.'

33 ASPN, 1932, p. 380.

34 Méjan, p. 41.

35 According to his superior's account, Méjan given a novel excuse for it not being implemented in the agreed manner: 'Everyone within the forts embarked and were being kept under the guns of the squadron when the king's commissioners contradicted their own generals, declaring that they would never treat with rebels. Chef de Brigade Méjan summoned the English commander to adhere to the terms of the treaty that he had signed in the name of his government. Later, they put out the explanation that they would only consider the National Guards as constituting the garrison and the government, ministers, deputies, magistrates and all those who held public positions in the name of the republic were seized and would be executed.'

36 Méjan refused to kill them saying 'executing the hostages would have legitimised the actions of Nelson'.

37 Battaglini (1983), II, pp. 628-32. Letter to Ferdinand, 28 June 1799.

38 ASPN, 1928, p. 280.

39 ASPN, 1899, p.461.

40 On 29 June Girardon in Capua wrote to his superior, Macdonald, saying that the French were holding firm, but that the republic had dissolved: 'The counterrevolution took place at Naples on the 12th of this month and, since then, I have been blockaded. The patriots surrendered to Nelson and the representatives of the king of Sicily, with the commandant of St Elmo acting

as intermediary. They were allowed to be taken to Toulon, with the English occupying the two forts.'

41 Méjan recorded that 'Captain Troubridge grew angry at the motto 'death to tyrants' which I had as the heading on my paper. He said it was an outrage.'

42 De Nicola noting 'if he [Méjan] thinks of hitting the city, it will be on pain of one French [ie the republicans] prisoner, who are on the English boats to the number of 1,500, killed for every shot fired'. Even in Puglia a chronicler noted that 'it has been learnt that they are preparing to attack Saint Elmo and that they are ready to take it by assault' and adding that the English had told the French general that 'if he fires on the city then they would kill many of their Jacobin prisoners taken from the two forts which had surrendered'.

43 The royal family sent over Angelo di Cosenza, 'who knows all the secret tunnels under St Elmo' but he was captured by corsairs on his way. Troubridge said he would mine the castle and blow the French, and the hostages, to 'Old Nick, and surprise him with a group of nobility and republicans'.

44 Maresca (1895), p. 243. According to Micheroux, 'General Gambs described how he had tried to negotiate offering money, telling me about the initial French offer. I sent this to the English, letting them decide how best to deal with it'.

45 The queen acknowledged that the Neapolitans were prepared to bribe Méjan, telling Lady Hamilton that: 'I swear we shall not pay a sous to Méjan, after such an obstinate resistance it would have been as though we were being cheated so I think that's why the Cisapline General (Micheroux) wanted to share it with Méjan. I hope you will stop such weakness and baseness as the admiral stopped the infamous armistice or capitulation with our rebels.' She later told Lady Hamilton that 'The Micheroux affair is infamous. The 150 thousand Ducats might perhaps once have been distributed, but not handed over after so many setbacks and I think the armistice of four months is infinitely more of a crime ... but I need to know more about this so that I can see who might be to blame and I don't even know if the king permits such things.'

46 Micheroux later testified on behalf of Méjan: 'I can attest that Chef de brigade Méjan commander of the fort of Saint Elmo, after having forced into treating for the surrender of the place, wrote a response worthy of a brave soldier and an honest man. He, with a view to spare the capital the horror of a siege was offered a sum of money to surrender the place, but he honourably rejected such a proposition in the most worthy way.' (ANF, LH/1818/47.) In December 1801 Méjan was petitioning the Ministry of Justice in Paris that 'I am overcome with misfortune, I am ruined. I have lost all, have need of everything and have no support.'

47 ЦГАВМФ, f. 192, d. 3, p. 29.

48 The king was escorted by three small Neapolitan vessels, a Portuguese brig, Foote and 37 merchantmen. Some 1,600 troops, under Bourcard and Giuseppe Acton, also sailed.

49 Ulloa, p. 135.

50 The king's phrase was that Acton was 'in a pestilential mood'. The cardinal remained with the king for three hours.

51 Maresca (1895), p. 229.

52 Most likely the letter of 28 June handed to the king in person the day before. The queen, once she'd read this missive, told Ruffo on 15 July that 'I cannot doubt that you are physically exhausted, neither that you feel disgust'.

53 ЦГАВМФ, f. 192, d. 3, p. 29.

54 He went on to survive and live in Paris, marrying a Ms Beaufort.

55 Perella, p. 522.

56 Championnet, commander of the Army of the Alps, wrote, on 11 August 1799, that: 'I have just been informed, Citizen Minister, of the official news that the 600 troops which had formed the garrison of Naples are in the lazaretto of Marseilles. I do not know of the capitulation by which these troops have been transported to France, but I do know for certain, thanks to a trustworthy letter which I received this morning, that 2,000 patriots included in the surrender were delivered up to the English and the mercy of the monarchy.' The letter almost certainly came from a Lieutenant Bocquet, energetically supported by Cesare Paribelli.

11 Revenge: Consequences of Revolt

1 When Naples fell, the republicans sought terms but, just as the surrender was being agreed, the citadel's magazine blew up, and the royalists rushed in before the word treachery could be pronounced.

2 Ettore Carafa was taken to the Carmine prison in Naples, and there shackled and chained to the wall with an iron collar. His brother, Francesco, wounded in Naples on 13 June, fared little better, being kept in the notorious Coccodrillo, a dungeon in the Nuovo fort which was the width of half a man.

3 Caldora, p. 502.

4 NLS MS.3598, ff.234-237, 19 July.

5 Despatches, III, p. 413.

6 Article 3 of the draft asked that 'the inhabitants of Capua or any others sheltering in the fort shall not be molested on account of any political opinions that they might have held, or for any public office they might have had under the republic'. This clause was not allowed, even though Gaeta was included in the surrender. Captain Louis, who went to tell the commandant at Gaeta was informed by Nelson that 'there is no way of dealing with a Frenchman but to knock him down. To be civil to them is only to be laughed at, when they are enemies.' Nelson added to Darby 'if the fellow is a scoundrel, he must be thrashed'.

7 A number of patriots, including Ignazio Falconieri and Vincenzo Cuoco, had donned Cisalpine uniform in an attempt to prevent themselves falling into Allied hands but they were identified and arrested.

8 He had his pistols stolen by a Calabrian and Count Thurn took his horses and coach. However, he informed the Spanish ambassador at Naples that 'the French troops were insulted and robbed in Naples, I owe my own escape to the kindness of the British officers'.

9 'I am living with Sir William and lady Hamilton, therefore I need not say, in private life, I am happy'.

10 Maria Carolina's latent ambition rose to the occasion, suggesting that the king could now perhaps become the king of Italy.

11 The spirit of vengeance was such that the unfortunately named Vincenzo Giacobino was moved to come before the magistrates pleading that he be allowed to change his name. They agreed, and he adopted his mother's name.

12 A second court, the *Giunta dei Generali*, or military court, was directed by generals Spinelli and De Gambs.

13 It was there that a prisoner, Antonio Velasco, broke free from his guards and jumped from the top floor of the building, inspiring the ending for the opera *Tosca*.

14 Troubridge was also critical but Nelson told him on 13 August 'the Neapolitans must manage their own Jacobins. We have, thank God, done with them'.

15 Speciale ended an argument with the prisoner Pagano with 'this is useless, you are destined to die, the court hates you and the people desire your death.' To which Pagano replied 'I'll die happy if the people have a will which can be imposed on their magistrates.'

16 A more detailed list gives the names of 79 prisoners brought from Nelson's ships for trial in the capital.

17 De Nicola, 12 August.

18 Data from *Rassegna Storica Napoletana*, 1935. Rao analysed the professions of those prisoners in the Granili at the end of June, and found that 16% were clergy, 12% were lawyers, 7% were officers, 16% were soldiers, 9% were artisans and 11% were from the countryside or labourers.

19 Sermoneta, p.179.

20 Hence Carlo Mauro's frantic letter to his wife 'find out at once what I am accused of doing and let me know, and whether there is any evidence in my favour'. He had been accused by five people but hoped that a lawyer, Angelo Cardea, could go to the judges, intervene and prove their statements false.

21 Sansone, p. 329.

22 Not just Jacobins, even the members of the government of Naples who had to hold the city against the French in December 1798 and early 1799 were punished. The Duke of Monteleone was executed, and 19 other office-holders were imprisoned. Giovan Battista De Sterlich was treated just as unfairly, he was imprisoned for having burnt the gunboats off Naples on 8 January 1799.

23 Such statements were common; the spirit of denouncing republicans to the restored authorities was flourishing. Sometimes more personal motives for such actions came to light. In 1800 Gaetano Manfredi was arrested because his wife's maid denounced him as a Jacobin who had threatened to kill his wife for uttering a royalist slogan. Inquiries revealed he had threatened to kill his wife, but for having entertained a royalist captain at home while the husband was absent.

24 Ferdinand's fear of whiskers was pronounced. He took offence at General Borozdin's whiskers when that Russian general arrived in Palermo in late 1799. Charles Lock records a similar story in 1800 'one night he had a Portuguese officer taken out of the pit [of the opera] to be shaved, who broke from his guards, joined a knot of brother officers who happened to be at the opera, and having informed them of the cause of his apprehension, they all

rose towards his majesty, pointed to their whiskers, burst into hoarse laughter and sat down again'.

25 Tragedy struck in 1802 when, on his way back to Naples, the 71-year-old was robbed and killed on the road home.

26 Helfert (1882), p. 583. Giulia Carafa had married Luigi Serra, Duke di Cassano, in 1770. Their son, Gennaro Serra, would be executed in August 1799. The short and delicate Mariantonia Carafa married Carlo di Tocco Cantelmo Stuart, Duke of Popoli and Prince of Montemiletto, in 1779.

27 Rocco Lentini was sentenced to hang but his brother, Giuseppe Lentini, sent a petition imploring 'that the said sentence of hanging be altered to that of beheading for the honour of his family'.

28 Matteo Wade was wrong to say that 'the hangman is, I am told, entitled to no fees; therefore if the fellow does not make his fortune now, I hope he will never meet so favourable an opportunity'. Morrison, II,. p. 62.

29 He hadn't been born in Naples, and tradition dictated that his body be left on display for 24 hours, however, as on the following day a cross was being raised on the market place, to replace the tree of liberty, his unsightly presence was unwelcome and he was cut down on the same day.

30 Executions in the provinces continued and at Matera Oronzio Albanese was executed on 30 December 1800, bringing an end to the wave of terror.

31 The king, through Acton, asked that a copy of this confession be sent to him so it could be verified and published in the *Gazzetta*.

32 He had served in the Garde du Corps, and been arrested in the plots of the 1790s, and released in 1798. Chased out of Puglia by the insurgents in February 1799, he had fought in Naples in June 1799 and escaped to the Uovo fort. There, along with his brother, Onofrio, he was embarked on the transports in the harbour and then brought back to await trial. Onofrio would be sent into exile. A third brother, Giambattista, had been killed in a royalist riot in February 1799.

33 Carlo Pedicini of the confraternity had written noting that many prisoners had been reduced to a state of nudity before execution, causing considerable disquiet.

34 Letter of complaint in ASDN, Registri della Compagnia dei Bianchi della Giustizia, 1799/1800.

35 'There have been many executions of the lower class but few of the nobility have suffered death. The Count Ruvo Duke of Andria one of the most guilty has however been hanged at Naples and a son of the Prince Stigliano [Colonna] and another of the Duke Cassano Serra have been beheaded'. This was coincidentally almost an exact retelling of the queen's lament to Ruffo that 'The boys are punished whilst those who made laws, like that rascal Bruno, stroll freely around Naples'.

36 Ferdinando Pignatelli had taken shelter in the St Elmo fort and had written to Ruffo on 21 June asking that he might buy his passage away from Naples on a Genoese ship. He was caught up in the surrender, and kept prisoner on the transports, along with his wife, Francheschina Renner. He was executed in September, she gave birth to his son in April 1800. Ferdinando's brother, Francesco, commander in the Roman Republic's legion in 1798, had left

Naples in May and escaped punishment. The youngest brother, Vincenzo, aged 22, was exiled.

37　Luisa Molina Sanfelice was initially kept in prison with other female republican prisoners, Francesca Buonocore (later exiled herself) and Maria Pizzoli, and she was being given last rights in the chapel of the Carmine fort when she declared she might be pregnant. She gained a reprieve from execution as tests were made. On 11 July 1800 the court ordered Cassaro to send her to Palermo, she arrived on 3 August, further tests were carried out, and she was found not to be pregnant and fit for execution.

38　On 16 November 1800 the soldier was sentenced to 15 years of forced labour.

39　ASPN, 1932, pp. 355-6.

40　De Lorenzo provides further details of the convoy: 'Our expedition was composed of two Neapolitan merchantmen and a Ragusan, escorted, as far as Roman waters, by a Neapolitan corvette. The first two contained the entire garrison of Capua, taken as prisoners of war, and those condemned to exile, whilst the Ragusan carried the daughter of the Duke di Cassano and the brother of the Duke Riario [Luigi Riario] who were also going into exile but who had chartered their own ship.'

41　In case he ever came back Rodino's features, along with all his colleagues, were described in a list of exiles published in 1800. He was 'of the city of Catanzaro, son of Cesare, aged 24. Height five foot 4 inches, hair and eyebrows blond, straight forehead, olive eyes, wide nose, oblong face, straight beard.' It wasn't much to go on.

42　Torcia was working on his Martirologio of Neapolitans who died during the revolution even though he was 74 years old.

43　The French police warned Napoleon 'Amongst the large number of Neapolitans who sided with France there were a considerable number of individuals of the kind who trouble society, such as thieves, vagabonds and people who had committed all kinds of crimes, as well as a number of spies, and these were placed amongst the illustrious group of French allies and, mixed up amongst them, were deported to France.'

44　ASPN, 1932, p. 380.

45　He appears in the *Red and the Black* as Count Altamira.

46　Moliterno lived with Dorinda Ausler, variously called Newman or Rogers. She was Irish, or 'a native of London', who travelled as an American, and used the codename Pispinette. In September 1802 the two got as far as Calais in an attempt to reach London and open negotiations with the British, before being apprehended. They managed to flee to Hamburg, and set up home calling themselves Sarconi.

47　A feeling shared by many French republicans, the genuine radicals took to calling their new leader Napoleon Bon-à-pendre (good for hanging) because he had betrayed the republic.

48　Croce (1968), p. 48.

49　Most of the loot was deposited in the Banco di San Giacomo to be used for the expenses of the Giunta. A gold watch was later returned to Raimondo di Gennaro, but others were sold off cheaply to raise funds.

50　Ronga, p. 108.

51 Sansone, p. cxxlii.
52 Morrison, II, p. 68. The white-haired bishop of Capri was Nicola Saverio Gamboni (1776-1807), who was later sent into exile.
53 The hanging was bungled, Speciale sent orders to have the victim's throat cut.
54 Sansone, p. 275.
55 Morrison, II, p. 60. The *Commandant* would seem to be one of the 14 transports.
56 Count Roger de Damas thought that Hamilton did not respond to such requests with mercy: 'She was a far more relentless judge than a moody, violent sailor would have been. Her point of view seemed to be 'If one listens to them all, not a man will be hanged!' and she coolly and light-heartedly selected the victims.'
57 It was William Compton who intervened with Lady Hamilton on behalf of the princess.
58 NWD/6/M403 Nelson Ward Collection.
59 The Bourbon authorities could be petty to an intense degree and Michele Manlio, for example, forced into exile and his property confiscated, found that when the property was returned, following amnesty, the state had deducted two Ducats and 73 grani for administrative expenses.
60 Traversier, p. 335.
61 The social composition of the condemned is also revealing. A sample of 1920 condemned criminals 121 were described as artisans, 14 peasants, 338 lawyers, 159 doctors, 148 landowners and 102 merchants. Of the noted Jacobins in Aversa, an affluent little town near Capua, some 83 men were active in propagating republicanism. Of these 25% were clergy, 19% were in the legal profession, 16% were officers, 13% were commoners or artisans and the rest being made up of those from the professional or propertied class. An additional two were women. Of the 83 men, four would be executed, 26 exiled and 32 imprisoned.
62 Natale, Bishop of Vico; Francesco Conforti; the seminarian Ignazio Falconieri, a teacher of Greek from the Nola seminary who had caused a scandal by donning National Guard uniform; Marcello Scotti; Antonio Scialoia; Niccola Lubrano; Antonio de Luca; Gaetano Morgera; Francesco Guardati; Nicola de Meo; Severo Caputo; Orazio Pacifico; Vincenzo Troyse; Nicola Palumbo; Michelangelo Ciccone; Vincenzo Belloni; Antonio Moscatelli; and Francescano Zoccolante.
63 Pasquale Baffi, Clino Roselli, Francesco Saverio Granata, and Pietro Lossa.
64 Students were also exiled. Of a sample of 132 refugees, 112 were aged less than 35. Four were students of the Incurabili aged between 17 and 19.

12 Rewards: Loyalty Repaid

1 Maresca (1895), p. 232.
2 Joseph Forsyth, will all the contempt a gentleman could muster, could see that the mob was destroying its own interests: 'Intent on the piddling game of cheating only for their own day, they let the great chance lately go by, and left a few immortal patriots to stake their all for posterity, and to lose it'.
3 Somerset, DD/DU 234.

4 To Lord Minto he was more direct, writing on 20 August that 'for the sake of the civilised world let us again work together, and as the best acts of our lives, manage to hang Thugut, Cardinal Ruffo and Manfredini'.

5 'I can assure you, Sir, that it affords me infinite pleasure to convey to you this distinguished mark of his Sicilian Majesty's approbation. The dispatch expresses for most important services when left with the command in the Bay of Naples, when Lord Nelson was obliged to order Commodore Troubridge to join him and for taking Castellammare.' Dated 14 September 1799. Foote, p. 95.

6 Nelson adopted Nelson & Bronte as his title. The use of Bronte had some unintended consequences when Patrick Brunty, an Irish cleric, changed his name to Bronte out of admiration for the admiral. He added an accent to assist the linguistically-challenged English, opting for Brontë. He was to be father of the Brontë sisters.

7 Nelson and Lady Hamilton were certainly romantically involved since February 1800, with the 12th later being celebrated as an anniversary, and the relationship was intensifying up to and during the cruise to Malta. The voyage was followed by sexually charged correspondence and, nine months later, the birth of a daughter.

8 Lord Fitzharris, who thought Lady Hamilton 'the most coarse, ill-mannered, disagreeable woman' said that Emma neglected Haydn in favour of the Faro table.

9 Lavalette, a French envoy, noted how 'Lady Hamilton is an enormous woman whose braying laughter recalls her origins and those places were she received her initial education'. Trench noted in her Journal, 'The Electress will not receive Lady Hamilton on account of her former dissolute life. ... Lord Nelson, understanding the Elector did not wish to see her, said to Mr. Elliot, 'Sir, if there is any difficulty of that sort, Lady Hamilton will knock the Elector down, and me, I'll knock him down too'.' She also noted 'Lady Hamilton, who declared she was passionately fond of champagne, took such a portion of it as astonished me. Lord Nelson was not behind-hand, called more vociferously than usual for songs in his own praise, and after many bumpers proposed the Queen of Naples, adding, "She is my Queen ; she is Queen to the backbone".'

10 Horatia Nelson (Horatia Nelson Thompson] was born on 29/30 January 1801.

11 Where they lived with Mrs Cadogan, Nelson's favourite Sicilian valet, Gaetano Spedillo, and the rather more exotic Fatima Emma Charlotte Nelson Hamilton, a Nubian, sometimes known as Quasheba, whom Nelson had rescued off Egypt and presented to Emma as a maid.

12 Poor Cornelia Knight, who had written odes in praise of the Hero of the Nile, was being dismissed with 'what a bitch that Miss Knight is' by October 1801.

13 Nelson's verdict on the court, given on 20 May 1804, was: 'The histories of the queen are beyond whatever I heard from Sir William. Prince Leopold's establishment is all French. The queen's favourite, Lieutenant Colonel St Clair, was a subaltern; La Tour, the captain in the navy, and another! However, I never touch on these matters; for, I care not how she amuses herself. It will be the upset of Acton; or, rather, he will not, I am told, stay. The king is angry with her; his love is long gone by.'

14 He had married her in February 1800 when she was just 13, and had sought and received a Papal dispensation to do so.

13 *The Controversy*

1 Sermoneta, p. 170, 13 July 1799. Written the day after Lock joined the fleet at Naples. The word decoy echoes the language of Captain Hood.

2 NLS MS.3598, ff.234-237, 19 July.

3 In 1803 Fox would write that his brother Henry 'who has been all through Italy, confirms all the accounts of the abominable conduct at Naples, on the part of the King of Naples'.

4 Gordon was friends with the editor of the *Morning Chronicle*, Mr Perry 'I had the happiness of making his acquaintance early in life, and of living in intimate habits of friendship with him for a period of forty-two years. ... Supported by such friends, and having the good wishes of Mr Fox and his party, the *Chronicle*, under its new direction, could not fail to succeed'. It is likely that the *Chronicle*'s accounts of the atrocities in Naples came from Gordon, John Rushout and perhaps also Charles Lock.

5 Sichel, p. 320, 29 February 1800.

6 Despatches, III, 510, 9 May 1800.

7 Foote, p. 17.

8 Foote, p. 48.

9 This is recognition of Ruffo's authority, but, equally, it shows that Nelson and Hamilton patently lacked the authority to overrule Ruffo themselves. The original plan had been to send the Hereditary Prince, as the king noted: 'to profit from Nelson's offer we should, if we don't send troops, at least have Francesco and Acton embark so that when they reach Naples they can make themselves useful by arranging everything with the cardinal.' For unknown reasons, the pair remained in Palermo when Nelson sailed for Naples on 21 June.

10 Croce (1943), p. 198. Letter to Ruffo, 1 May 1799.

11 Rose, p. 236.

12 NLS MS.3599, ff.50-53, 22 August. The order is missing but Thurn, once the capitulation was agreed, told Acton that 'we are most eagerly expecting the evacuation of those castles'. These are not the words of someone who had been ordered not to carry out a capitulation until the king's ratification.

13 Croce (1943), p. 221. Letter to Ruffo, 19 June 1799.

14 Croce (1943), p. 223. Letter to Ruffo, 20 June 1799.

15 On 21 June he told Acton that 'It seems that the rebels in the Uovo and Nuovo forts are close to surrendering to the Russians and Micheroux ...'. On 28 June he told the king 'the Russians were determined to send in envoys to treat, all this persuaded me to negotiate with the French commandant at St Elmo in order to ensure the deportation of the garrisons of the two castles'.

16 Foote, p. 77.

17 NLS MS.3599, ff.50-53, 22 August. The express orders Lock refers to are those apparently sent from Acton to Thurn telling Ruffo to come to grant any terms in order to get possession of Naples.

18 Foote, p. 60.

19 Rose, p. 237, 25 June 1799.

20 Battaglini (1983), II, pp. 628-32. Letter to Ferdinand, 28 June 1799.

21 There was no real confusion. On 27 June Acton in Palermo was quite clear about what Ruffo had agreed when he spoke about arresting Ruffo if 'he persists to refuse to break the truce and infamous capitulation'.

22 Despatches, II, p. 495.

23 Why else would Acton inform Hamilton that 'every precedent is to be void' when informing him that Palermo was against implementing the capitulation?

24 This is probably the point at which Nelson and Hamilton reflected that getting the republicans out of the castles and then seizing them pending royal justification would be easier than attempting to storm the castles with their marines alone.

25 Vattel, *The Law of Nations* (1760), Book III, p. 552.

26 NLS MS.3598, ff.234-237, 19 July.

27 Egerton 2640, 28 June.

28 No subsequent attempt was made by Nelson, or by the diplomat Hamilton, to suggest the rebels be restored to their forts or for them to broker a new capitulation. Had Nelson or Hamilton been compelled to act as they had done by royal command it stands to reason that they might have complained or queried the legality of such a move. That they did not shows that it is far more probable that the ruse was one of their own invention, especially when one considers the court's subsequent gratitude.

29 Despatches, III, p. 510. Letter to Davison, 9 May 1800.

30 It is also true that Nelson's opinion 'that the treaty entered into with the rebels … ought not to be carried into execution' was also rendered worthless by embarking the rebels.

31 Gutteridge, p. 240. Minichini's *verbale*, 26 June.

32 As per Charles Lock; Baillie was hardly likely to have misunderstood for, although he was a Russian officer, he was a native Scotsman.

33 Gutteridge, p. 312. Letter to Grenville, 14 July 1799.

34 Gutteridge, p. 251. The draft read '*one must make the best of a bad bargain*', rather than 'one must do the next best thing', which makes Hamilton's intention clearer.

35 Gutteridge, p. 270. My emphasis. Palermo seemed surprised by the news, further indication that they weren't behind the ruse. Acton replied to Hamilton: 'the polacres remain as you tell me to His Majesty's disposition upon which *the resolution is to be made as soon as possible.*' These are hardly the words of a man who had planned to seize the rebels.

36 Gutteridge, p. 270-1. My emphasis. The letter is clear that Nelson and Hamilton are behind the unexpected stroke, or coup, rather than following orders from Palermo. See also p.314 where Hamilton boasts that he and Nelson 'contrived to keep everything going on decently by supporting the king's vicar-general' and so prevented 'his Eminency from doing any essential mischief'.

37 Those who did give themselves up were promised mercy. But the promise was not kept. Onofrio Colace appealed that he had voluntarily given himself up

but he was executed in October 1799, and others were seized and imprisoned and exiled despite written promises of safe conduct.

38 It is important to note that as soon as the court heard that the republicans in Naples might be evacuated, they wrote to Procida to make it clear that nobody there would be covered by Ruffo's agreements: 'Regarding the pardon granted and the proclamations newly issued by Cardinal Ruffo, vicar general of the kingdom of Naples, we wish to confirm the course of action to be taken against prisoners of state. You previously received instructions and you are to carry these out exactly in conformity to existing orders, and continue with the trials as rigorously as possible and will not deviate from these instructions until you receive new orders from his Majesty.' Letter dated 25 June 1799, the Prince di Cassaro to Speciale. Sansone, p. 80.

39 Adding 'I have two or three to settle with, if we get in'.

40 In marked contrast to the surrender of Rome in September 1799. There 250 members of the republican government and Jacobin supporters were embarked for France. De Nicola remarked 'there was a general pardon ... how I wish to God our king had settled affairs in such a way'.

41 Which makes it even stranger that the real deceit was practised not only against Jacobins, but against the word of the pillars of the establishment: a Calabrian cardinal, a Russian emperor and a Turkish sultan.

42 Keith even told Nelson that the royal family should negotiate with the rebels, telling Nelson 'do not let these good people carry their heads too high. Let them return on any terms that are tolerable.'

43 On 18 November Nelson even went as far as to tell Acton that 'I am placed in such a situation – a subject of one king by birth, and, as far as is consistent with my allegiance to that king, a voluntary subject of his Sicilian Majesty – that if any man attempted to separate my two kings, by all that is sacred, I should consider even putting that man to death as a meritorious act.'

44 Conrad was writing to Norman Douglas about his article 'Blind Guides' in April 1913 (Collected letters, V, p. 204-5).

45 His account noted: 'I thought my object was to get possession on any terms. And that I should be ready to take all or part of the odium of breaking them for the advantage of His Royal Highness the Great Duke [of Tuscany] and the King of Naples.'

46 Despatches, III, p. 183.

47 Despatches, III, p. 214. 30 March 1800. Significantly this threat to a treaty was contained in a letter to Sir William Hamilton.

48 Foote, p. 61.

49 Gutteridge, p. 287.

50 Despatches, III, 392. A letter dated 27 June, and therefore penned when Nelson was clear it was a treaty and after the rebels evacuated their forts, but not sent until 29 June or thereafter. Here he says his approbation, rather than that of the king or queen. In May 1800 he confessed that 'the whole affairs of the Kingdom of Naples were, at the time alluded to absolutely placed in my hands'.

51 Although the witness testimony begins to fall apart for Hamilton clearly calls it a treaty, whilst Nelson labels it a truce.

52 Despatches, III, p. 406. Letter to Earl Spencer, 13 July 1799. Nelson had instructed Hamilton to write to Ruffo on 28 June to tell him they were seizing the rebels who were on the transports, so he clearly knew that they hadn't surrendered but were expecting to sail.

53 Letter to Alexander Stephens, 10 February 1803. Nelson also added 'I must beg leave to warn you to be careful how you mention the characters of such excellent sovereigns as the king and queen of Naples.'

54 In his letter to Davison Nelson alludes to Foote's actions when writing 'the terms granted by Captain Foote, of the *Seahorse*, at Castellammare, were all strictly complied with; *the rebels having surrendered before my arrival*. There has been nothing promised by a British officer that his Sicilian Majesty has not complied with even in disobedience to his orders to the cardinal'. One should note that the republicans in Naples had *also* surrendered before Nelson's arrival, as well as the false statement about the promises of British officers.

55 Foote, p. 27.

56 ASPN 1928, p. 282. Letter of 28 August 1799. Admiral Ushakov followed a similar policy in the Ionian Islands. Shown a list of local collaborators on Cephalonia, he pocketed it and did no more about it.

57 *Memoirs of the Life of Sir James Mackintosh*, p. 139.

58 In May 1799 when General Jauch was denounced for cowardice, Nelson called for an example to be made. Troubridge counselled not getting involved, telling Nelson 'as he is in the service of another sovereign, I submit to your Lordship if we had not better leave them to themselves'. Regarding Caracciolo, Hamilton suggested a similar approach, but Nelson ignored him.

59 Even the queen thought they might end up being harmless, telling Ruffo: 'they must be taken to America, or should this be too difficult or expensive, to any place in France ... these men will not increase the fighting strength of France, for they have neither courage nor energy'.

60 There are indications in the correspondence between Acton and Hamilton that the ruse was also Nelson's idea: from 'one must do the next best thing and that is what Lord Nelson is doing' to 'I have seen with the highest consolation what Lord Nelson has done with the rebels'.

Index

Abbamonte, Giuseppe 161
Abrial, Joseph 67, 71, 85
Acton, Carlo 112
Acton, Filippo 84, 99, 128, 216, 254
Acton, Giuseppe 271
Acton, John Francis Edward 22, 23,
  33–7, 39, 43, 46, 49, 52, 53, 54, 55,
  57, 77, 79, 81, 84, 89, 90, 91, 92,
  93, 98, 109, 112, 116, 125, 131,
  132, 133, 134, 136, 145, 146, 149,
  150, 152–8, 162, 172, 200, 202,
  205, 206, 212, 213, 216, 218, 220,
  221, 223, 229, 243, 247, 249, 250,
  251, 253, 256, 257, 258, 260, 261,
  263, 264, 265, 267, 268, 269, 271,
  274, 277, 278, 279, 280, 281
Acton, Marianna 206
Ahmed, Captain 98, 123
Albanese, Giuseppe 67, 85, 162
Albanese, Oronzio 274
Alberini, Bernardo 82, 186
Alberto, Prince 58
Amatucci, Angelo 184
Amelia, Princess 36, 58
Andreatini, Giovanni 184
Angelis, Francesco de 184
Antoinette, Princess 58
Apicella, Pasquale 183
Arcambal, Jacques Philippe 60
Arcucci, Gennaro 187
Arezzo, General 44
Arrighetti, Luigi 164

Arriola, Giovanni Battista Manuel y
  45, 48, 53, 248
Ascoli, Duke of 51, 98
Assisi, Pasquale 184
Attumonelli, Michele 191
Ausler, Dorinda 275
Austen, Captain Francis 100
Austen, Jane 100
Auvet, Richard 105
Avella, Antonio (Pagliuchella) 61, 64,
  174, 181, 183, 188
Avella, Antonio 183
Baccher, Gerardo 85, 99
Baffi, Pasquale 188, 276
Bagno, Francesco 199
Baillie, Captain Genrikh Genrikhovich
  93, 98, 121, 123, 145, 163, 167,
  172, 173, 196, 203, 215, 219, 256,
  279
Ball, Captain Alexander 46, 53, 100,
  136, 137, 138, 144, 146, 170, 203,
  219, 249, 255, 263, 264, 265
Basilio, Fasulo 194
Bassal, Jean 64
Basset, François (Francesco) 148, 161,
  163
Battistessa, Pasquale 186, 195
Belloni, Vincenzo 174, 187 276
Belmonte, Prince 54, 55, 196, 248
Belpulsi, Antonio 70, 96, 174, 189,
  192
Benchi, Giuseppe 191

Contents

Berarducci, Gian Carlo   44, 73, 74, 266

Berthier, General   39

Bianchi, Timoleone   70, 252, 255

Bisceglia, Domenico   64

Bisogni, Gregorio   116

Bock, Abramo de   85, 196

Bocquet, Lieutenant   272

Bolts, William   243

Bonamy, General   251

Bonaparte, Napoleon, Corsican adventurer   38, 40, 41, 42, 44, 48, 75, 191, 192, 198, 204, 205, 206

Boos, Paolo   164

Borel, Jean-François   39, 245

Borgia, Emmanuel   161, 163, 182

Borozdin, General   273

Bourbon, Adélaïde   52

Bourbon, Charles   18

Bourbon, Felipe   18

Bourbon, Victoire   52

Brancati, Raffaele   106

Bristol, Lord   26, 39

Brontë family   277

Bruix, Admiral   89, 100, 101, 116, 118, 122, 130, 131, 132

Broussier, General   61, 75

Buonarroti, excitable revolutionary   35

Burkhardt, General   49, 248

Busto, Carlo   119

Byres, James   25

Cacault, Ambassador François   22

Cadogan, Mrs   24, 277

Cafarelli family   201

Campana, Anton Maria   108

Campbell, Donald   59, 229, 247, 250, 267

Candarelli, Angelo   181

Candia, Antonio   73

Capano, Saverio   164

Capecelatro, Giuseppe   76

Capel, Thomas   41

Caperozzo, Andrea   152, 266

Caporossi, Annibale   77

Caracciolo, Domenico   35

Caracciolo, Admiral Francesco   54, 58, 70, 79, 84, 97, 99, 100, 102, 104, 117, 133, 149–55, 160, 161, 186, 206, 213, 222, 224, 228, 229, 230, 245, 249, 253, 257, 266, 267, 281

Carafa, Andrea   181

Carafa, Ettore   69, 73, 75, 76, 96, 176, 180, 189, 206, 253, 272

Carafa, Giulia   190, 274

Carafa, Luigi   64

Carcani, Gaetano   184

Carlo, Prince   21

Carlo Emanuele IV, King   45

Carreres, Carlo   181

Carrotta, Giuseppe   192

Carus, Isaac   181

Cassano, Princess   97, 150, 185, 274 (see also Giulia Carafa)

Cassaro, Prince di   181, 182, 193, 194, 197, 275, 280

Castelcicala, Prince of   55, 248, 251

Cayro, Pasquale   72, 80, 252, 258

Cesari, Giambattista De   76, 92, 98, 108, 203, 258

Championnet, General Jean Etienne   48, 49, 51, 52, 59–66, 69, 70. 75, 175, 183, 193, 272

Chastellux, Count of   46

Chiurazzo, Saverio   183

Ciaja, Ignazio   64, 70, 71, 85, 161, 186, 269

Ciaja, Michele   162

Cimarosa, Domenico   167, 184, 196

Chiapparo, Antonio   150

Ciccone, Michelangelo   184

Cirillo, Dr Domenico   29, 71, 159, 160, 163, 186, 188, 196, 197, 203, 221, 252, 255, 268

Clark, James   23, 55

Coco (or Cuoco), Vincenzo   85, 184, 272

Colace, Onofrio   195, 280

Colleoni, Giovanni Estore Martinengo   40, 57, 252

Colletta, Pietro   108

Colonna, Celio   94

Colonna, Giuliano   161, 187, 189, 274

Concetta, Dona   183

Conforti, Francesco   68, 276

Conrad, Joseph   223

Corbara, Casimiro   76

Cotitta, Giuseppe   186

Cubières-Palmézeaux, Michel de   35

Curtis, Governor   73, 128, 195, 264

D'Agnese, Ercole   85, 161, 163, 188

Damas, Roger de   202, 276

Damiani, Felice   180

Darley, Captain William 254
Davanzati, Domenico 191
Delfico, Melchiorre 72, 85
Denon, Ambassador Dominique Vivant 21, 22, 242
Deo, Emanuele de 38
Dentice, Father Eustachio 15
Dillon, Brigadier Guglielmo 123, 194, 233, 265
Dillotti, Major 85
Doria, Pietro 161
Dron, Luigi 183
Drummond, Captain 127, 134, 216
Drusco, Pietroabondio 61, 64
Dubreton, Colonel 65
Duckworth, Admiral John 100, 101, 138, 167, 168, 202, 204, 208, 210, 224, 248, 269
Dufresse, General 63
Duhesme, General 61, 72, 75
Elefante, Camillo 71, 75, 93, 252, 253
Faipoult, Guillaume Charles de 65, 66, 70
Falconieri, Ignazio 69, 272, 276
Fazio, Giuliano de 108
Federici, General Francesco 38, 96, 186, 187
Ferdinand IV, King of Naples 18, 19, 20, 21, 22, 30, 35, 36, 38, 40, 42, 45, 47, 49, 50, 52. 58, 66, 72, 81, 83, 91, 101, 112, 172, 173, 184, 186, 203, 206, 212, 214, 223, 224, 230, 242, 244, 245, 251, 264, 267, 273
Ferdinand, Archduke 36
Ferreri, Alessandro 54
Fetherstonhaugh, Sir Harry 24
Fiani, Nicola 15–16, 188, 206
Fiani, Onofrio 16, 119, 148, 180, 194, 260, 261
Filangieri, Gaetano 32
Filangieri, Michele 161, 196
Filangeri, General 22
Fillippis, Vincenzo de 186
Filomarino, Giovanni Battista 69, 181
Fiore, Angelo di 81, 116, 192
Firrao, Giovanni 94
Fonseca Pimentel, Eleonora 67, 164, 186
Foote, Captain Edward 97, 100, 102, 108, 116, 119, 120, 121, 123, 124,

126, 127, 130, 134, 135, 136, 138, 139, 162, 167, 172, 203, 207–11, 214, 215, 217, 219, 222, 224, 225, 226, 227, 258, 260, 261, 262, 264, 269, 271, 281
Forsyth, Joseph 259, 276
Forteguerri, Admiral Bartolomeo 52, 53, 57, 59, 250
Fox, Charles James 209
Fra Diavolo 73, 83, 98, 179, 203, 252
Franc, Maria 181
Francesco, Hereditary Prince 21, 36, 50, 242, 278
Francis II, Emperor 45
Freemantle, Thomas Francis 26
Gaito, Cipriano 173
Galanti, Giuseppe Maria 32, 206
Galiani, Vincenzo 38
Gallo, Marquis of 23, 42, 43, 45, 46, 52, 56, 91, 245, 246, 250, 251, 256, 262
Gambs, General De 85, 127, 142, 158, 171, 271, 273
Garnier, General 179, 257
Garofalo, Rosa 192
George III 23
Gesso, Duke of 59
Giacinto, Verginiano 183
Giordano, Anna 201
Giordano, Annibale, maths genius 31, 37, 38
Girardon, General Antoine-Alexandre 48, 62, 88, 95, 98, 99, 123, 125, 171, 176, 177, 178, 246, 256, 257, 261, 264, 265, 270
Goethe, Johann Wolfgang von, excitable German poet 25
Goodall, Admiral 204
Gordon, Pryse Lockhart 111, 168, 209, 249, 278
Graham, General Thomas 174, 177, 203, 208, 214, 218, 219, 269
Grasso, Gennaro 104, 112
Grebber, Sebastiano 164
Greco, Federico del 174
Grecumbo, Giuseppe 164
Grennelais, Guglielmo de la 60, 187
Grenville, Lord 225
Greville, Charles, dour bachelor 24, 25, 139, 243, 270
Grimaldi, Francesco 189

Gualtieri, Nicola, known as
  Panedigrano 78, 107, 117, 119
Gualzetti, Giovanni 184
Guarano, Marino 184
Guellichini, Captain 59
Guidobaldi, Giuseppe 180, 182
Gusler, Sebastian 16
Hallowell, Captain Benjamin 82, 160,
  167, 168, 177, 203, 208, 218
Hamilton, Lady Catherine 23, 243
Hamilton, Lady Emma 13, 24–7, 38,
  40, 41, 43, 46, 50, 52, 53, 56, 57,
  78, 82, 89, 131, 132, 133, 139, 147,
  154, 157, 161, 164, 165, 177, 185,
  196, 201, 202, 204, 205, 206, 209,
  223, 230, 245, 246, 247, 249, 250,
  254, 257, 258, 262, 263, 264, 268,
  270, 271, 272, 276, 277
Hamilton, Sir William 13, 14, 19,
  20, 23, 24, 25, 27, 30, 36, 38, 39,
  41, 42, 43, 47, 52, 53, 55, 78, 133,
  135, 136, 139, 141, 142, 143, 144,
  146, 147, 149, 150, 152, 153, 155,
  158, 159, 171, 172, 177, 178, 181,
  193, 195, 197, 201, 202, 204, 205,
  216, 218–22, 225, 226, 228, 229,
  230, 242, 243, 244, 245, 246, 247,
  248, 249, 250, 254, 260, 263, 266,
  268, 269, 272, 278, 279, 280, 281
Hart, Emma see Hamilton, Lady
  Emma.
Harward, John 260
Hood, Captain Samuel 84, 148, 160,
  167, 168, 203, 208, 218, 220, 278
Hope, Captain George Johnstone 53,
  55
Hoste, William 41, 55, 119, 263
Iodeno, Pietro 184
Iordano, Francesco Maria 164
Jauch, Colonel 254, 255
Joseph II, Emperor of Austria 19
Jovine, Francesco 184
Keith, Lord 82, 89, 101, 133, 136,
  139, 140, 176, 177, 180, 200, 214,
  225, 263, 280
Kellermann, General 61
Kelly, Charlotte, procuress 24
Knight, Cornelia 40, 277
Kotzebue, August von 109, 259
L'Aurora, Colonel Enrico Michele
  119, 120, 148, 163, 245, 260, 269
Latouche Treville, Admiral 37

Lauberg, Carlo 33, 37, 39, 64, 70
Lentini, Rocco 37, 255, 274
Leonardi, Antonio 191
Leopold, Grand Duke 22
Leopold II, Emperor 36
Leopoldo, Prince 55, 58, 277
Lepri, Girolama 77
Letizia, Giovanni 161
Liddo, Giuseppe di 165
Linev, Roman 258
Lock, Charles 26, 78, 116, 135, 145,
  160, 167, 174, 177, 181, 193, 208,
  214, 218, 219, 253, 260, 263, 265,
  267, 269, 273, 278, 279
Logoteta, Giuseppe de 161, 187
Lorenzo, Giuseppe de 103, 104, 106,
  112, 115, 184, 190, 192, 258, 259,
  275
Lotti, Gaetano 249
Lowcay, Henry 177, 178
Louis, Captain 179, 203, 253, 272
Louis XVI, King of France 33, 37
Lubrano, Nicola 83
Luca, Antonio de 83
Ludovici, Ludovico 99
Macdonald, Francesco 99, 257
Macdonald, General 43, 70, 75, 88,
  252, 270
Macintosh, Sir James 228
Mack von Leiberich, General Karl
  44–50, 53, 57, 59, 60, 246, 247,
  250
Maffei, Melchiorre 173
Maimone, Giuseppe 61, 251
Maio, Marchese di 103
Malaspina, Filippo 77, 203
Mammone, Gaetano 72, 98, 102,
  201, 257
Manthonè, General 95, 126, 161,
  163, 187, 188, 213, 251, 255, 256,
  268
Marco, Gaetano de 161, 188
Maria Carolina, Queen of Naples 18,
  19, 20, 25, 33, 35, 36, 38, 40, 44,
  56, 58, 59, 78, 132, 154, 197, 223,
  230, 232, 243, 251, 257, 273
Maria Clementina, Archduchess 36
Maria Johanna, Archduchess 18
Maria Josepha, Archduchess: 18
Maria Louisa Amelia, Princess 36, 58
Maria Teresa, Empress of Austria 18,
  20

Maria Theresa, wife of Emperor Francis 36, 246
Marie Antoinette, Queen of France 18, 33, 35, 36, 38, 249
Marinelli, Diomede 16, 39, 55, 61, 62, 109, 176, 178, 179, 187, 190
Marino, Genzano Filippo 187
Marino, Michele (Il Pazzo) 61, 63, 173, 188
Marra, Scipione della 150, 178, 203, 260
Marrier-Chanteloup, Jean-Louis 65
Marseglio, Giuseppe 183
Martellucci, Antonio 181
Marugj, Leonardo 112
Marziale, Scipione 196
Masaniello, famous rebel 64
Massa, General Oronzio 117, 118, 121, 128, 129, 130, 141, 142, 144, 146, 147, 161, 163
Mastellone, Emanuele 161, 193
Mastrangelo, Felice 161, 186
Matèra, General 70, 96, 97, 173
Mauro, Carlo 193, 195, 273
Mazzitelli, Andrea 62, 161
Mazzola, Nicola 183
Méchin, Alexandre 65
Méjan, Colonel Louis-Joseph 88, 99, 104, 117, 118, 120, 121, 122, 123, 125, 128, 136, 137, 142, 167, 170, 171, 173, 174, 175, 261, 263, 264, 265, 270, 271
Meli, Francesco Paolo 127
Metternich, Klemens von 17
Micheroux, General Alberto 49, 50, 84, 233
Micheroux, Chevalier Antonio 87, 88, 89, 91–5, 97, 98, 99, 104, 105, 108, 114, 116, 117, 118, 121, 122, 123, 124, 126–9, 134, 137, 138, 140, 141, 142, 143, 144, 145, 146, 147, 163, 168, 170, 171, 198, 200, 201, 203, 207, 210, 212, 213, 219, 228, 255, 256, 258, 260, 261, 262, 263, 264, 265, 271, 278
Micheroux, Diodato 266
Migliano, Prince of 59
Minichini, Brigadier Angiolo 128, 148, 193, 219, 266, 279
Mitchell, Captain 247
Mitola, Nicola 183
Moliterno, Prince of 60, 85, 192, 275

Montemajor, Lorenzo 161
Montemajor, Raffaele 161
Montemiletto, Prince of 66, 274
Monti, Vincenzo 65
Montrone, Marchese di 103, 252
Morgan, David 260
Morgera, Gaetano 183
Muscari, Mercurio 161
Nardini, Bartolomeo 66, 111
Naselli, Diego 266
Naselli, General 49, 248
Natale, Michele 187, 276
Neiman, Antonio 181
Nelson, Admiral Horatio 13, 14, 16, 26, 27, 34, 38, 40, 41, 42, 43, 45, 46, 47, 49, 50, 52, 53, 54, 55, 56, 57, 58, 59, 78, 82, 83, 84, 89, 99, 100, 101, 116, 120, 127, 130–172, 175, 176–82, 192, 195, 196, 197, 199–231, 244, 245, 246, 247, 248, 249, 250, 251, 252, 253, 254, 255, 257, 258, 262, 263, 264, 265, 266, 267, 268, 269, 270, 272, 273, 276, 277, 278, 279, 280, 281
Nicola, Carlo De 62, 68, 84, 85, 86, 109, 110, 114, 121, 129, 137, 148, 159, 165, 167, 180, 187, 188, 189, 193, 195, 200, 220, 251, 257, 258, 259, 261, 266, 269, 271, 280
Nisbet, Josiah 244
Niscemi, Giuseppe 152, 266
Niza, Marquis de, Portuguese Admiral 59, 229, 249, 250, 267
North, Alexander, talented son 4
North, Evgenia, tolerant wife 4
Northwick, Baron see Rushout, John.
Oswald, James 119, 120, 254, 258
Pacifico, Nicola 161, 187, 276
Pagano Francesco Mario 32, 71, 109, 161, 186, 188, 255, 273
Paget, Arthur 20, 204, 244
Paisiello, Giovanni, gifted composer 36, 184, 198
Palombo, Gianleonardo 189
Paradiso, Tommaso, executioner 15, 186
Parazzi, Francesca 184
Parente, Vincenzo 184
Paribelli, Cesare 64, 71, 216, 272
Paris, Jullien de 64
Parisio, Giovanni 164
Parsons, Midshipman George 150

Contents

Paul I, Czar   45, 259
Pépe, Guglielmo   62, 73, 86, 96, 97,
   107, 108, 113, 114, 190
Perla, Domenico   186
Perrelli, Pietro Paola   69
Pettito, Dionigi   183
Petromasi, Domenico   77, 80, 110,
   173, 258
Piatti family   164, 270
Piatti, Antonio   161, 163, 270
Piatti, Domenico   270
Piatti, Francesco   193
Piatti, Giuseppe   161
Piatti, Pietro   193, 270
Pignatelli, Princess Chiara Belmonte
   191
Pignatelli, Diego   196
Pignatelli, Ferdinando   173, 189, 274
Pignatelli, Francesco (Strongoli)   50,
   62
Pignatelli, Francesco (Laino)   54, 55,
   58, 60, 248, 250
Pignatelli, Giuseppe (Joseph)   162, 196
Pignatelli, Mario   189
Pinedo, Antonio   70
Planes, Pellegrino   184
Poerio, Giuseppe   60, 63, 193
Policastro   184
Popoli, Princess (Mariantonia Carafa)
   97, 185, 190
Porcelli, Giuseppe   35
Pousset, Luigi   104, 105, 117, 260
Pronio, Giuseppe   72, 201, 203, 252
Puccini, Domenico   59
Puoti, Gioacchino   187
Quasheba   277
Renella, Giuseppe   198
Renner, Francheschina   173, 274
Renzis, Leopoldo de   50
Riario, Giuseppe   189
Ricciardi, Amedeo   126, 128, 148,
   166
Ricciardi, Nicola   183
Riso, Mariangela de   191
Ritucci, Giosue   70
Rivelli, Gennaro   81, 254
Robespierre, Maximilien   37, 243, 260
Rocca, Prince della   see Filomarino.
Roccaromana, Duke of   60, 85, 96
Roche, Pietro de   70
Rodinò, Gaetano   50, 79, 99, 113,
   114, 161, 163, 190, 246, 275

Rosa, Sebastiano de   123
Rotondo, Prosdocimo   70, 113, 161
Ruffo, Cardinal Don Fabrizio   13,
   77–81, 90, 91–9, 101, 102–7,
   114–6, 118, 119, 120, 122–9,
   131–44, 146, 149, 150, 155, 156,
   158, 159, 162, 166, 168–72, 180,
   185, 197, 199, 202, 203, 207, 208,
   211–15, 217–22, 224, 226, 227,
   232, 253, 254, 255, 256, 257, 260,
   261, 263, 264, 265, 266, 272, 274,
   277, 278, 279, 280, 281
Ruffo, Ippolita   150
Ruggi, Ferdinando   82, 83, 189
Ruggiero, Eleuterio   186
Rushout, John   82, 119, 134, 145,
   151, 153, 209, 254, 266, 278
Russi, Carlo   198
Russo, Gaetano   189
Russo, Vincenzo   68, 113, 187
Sabatino, Vincenzo   55, 249
Sacchinelli, Domenico   77, 79, 80, 98,
   110, 114, 139, 140, 141, 143, 144,
   199, 203, 256, 265
Sade, Marquis de   244
Salandra, Duke of   60, 158, 250
Salerno, Pasquale   193
Salfi, Saverio   39, 95, 160, 161, 164,
   165, 167, 189, 262, 270
Sambiase, Archbishop   84
San Nicandro, Prince of   18
Sanchez, Enrico   97
Sanfelice, Luisa Molina   85, 162, 184,
   186, 189, 275
Sangiovanni, Eduardo   190
Santobono, Princess Caracciolo di
   110
Santorelli, Antonio   191
Santorelli, Arcangelo   183
Sarrazin, General   82, 84
Saxe, Chevalier de   50, 248
Scarati, Domenico   94
Schérer, General   70, 88, 252
Scialoia, Antonio   83
Serafini, Libero   99
Serra, Gennaro   161, 189, 274
Serra, Giuseppe   64
Serrao, Andrea   68
Schierer, Federico   181
Schipani, General Giuseppe   69, 81,
   82, 99, 107, 108, 117, 181, 186
Sforza, Giuseppe Riario   186, 187

Sherman, Franco 181
Sicardi, Antonio 60
Signorelli, Pietro 191
Simeoni, Captain Gaetano 60, 161
Simone, Giambattista de 161
Simonetti, Saverio 116
Soderini, Gasparo 28
Sorokin, Alexander Andreievich 87, 88, 89, 93, 215
Southey, Robert 13, 211
Sozio, Giacinto 125
Spanò, Agamennone 96, 186, 258
Sparziani, Lorenzo 77, 203
Speciale, Vincenzo, judge 83, 180, 182, 254, 264, 273, 276, 280
Spencer, Earl 47, 202, 204, 246, 250, 281
Spinelli, General 60, 273
St Vincent, Earl 27, 43, 45, 101, 140, 214, 249, 250, 263
Staiti, Captain 87
Stiscia, Domenico 181
Stone, Captain 247
Strongoli, Prince, see Pignatelli, Francesco.
Stuart, General Sir Charles 51, 78, 253
Suvorov, Marshal 88, 203, 228, 259
Tanucci, Bernardo 18, 22, 33
Thurn, Count Giuseppe di 54, 55, 82, 100, 116, 117, 127, 128, 134, 150–4, 195, 213, 229, 243, 260, 261, 262, 266, 272, 278
Tocco, Antonio 184
Topputi, Domenico di 165
Torcia, Monsieur 191
Tordoni, Francesco 181
Tosca 273
Torella, Prince of 69, 185, 193, 203

Torelli, Giuseppe 39
Torre Filomarino, Duke della 61
Toscani, Antonio 103
Tramaglia, Antonio 186
Troisi, Vincenzo 161, 186, 198
Troubridge, Captain Thomas 82, 83, 84, 98, 100, 135–8, 144, 146, 149, 168, 170, 171, 173, 174, 178, 179, 193, 200, 203, 214, 219, 222, 223, 249, 253, 254, 256, 258, 263, 265, 266, 271, 273, 277, 281
Tschudi (or Tschudy), Colonel 108, 118, 128, 260
Ushakov, Admiral Fedor Fedorovich 45, 87, 88, 172, 215, 256, 281
Valiante, Andrea 175, 199
Valle, Cesare della 260
Valterre, Francois 49, 248
Vattel, Emer de 217
Velasco, Antonio 273
Verdinois, Nicola 60
Vinnaccia, Celidea 198
Vitale, Cipriano 127
Vitaliani, Andrea 37, 38, 39, 64, 173, 186
Vitaliani Vincenzo 38
Vitella, Giuseppe Mancuso 83
Wade, Matteo 120, 138, 185, 189, 195, 274
Williams, Helena Maria 216, 224
Willyams, Cooper 82, 111, 254
Wirtz, General Filippo 99, 102, 103
Wood, Captain Sam 162
Worster, Carlo 181
Wraxall, Nathaniel 19, 20
Zizzo, Francesco 181
Zuccarelli, Antonio 191
Zurlo, Capece 68